Implicit Religion
in
Contemporary
Society

Edward I. Bailey

KOK PHAROS PUBLISHING HOUSE
DEUTSCHER STUDIEN VERLAG

CIP-GEGEVENS KONINKLIJKE BIBLIOTHEEK, DEN HAAG

©1997, Kok Pharos Publishing House
P.O. Box 5016, 8260 GA Kampen, The Netherlands
Deutscher Studien Verlag – Weinheim/Germany
Cover design by Atelier Warminskyi/Dik Hendriks
ISBN KOK 90 390 0581 8
ISBN DSV 3 89271 694 3
NUGI 631/619

Contents

Implicit Religion
in
Contemporary
Society

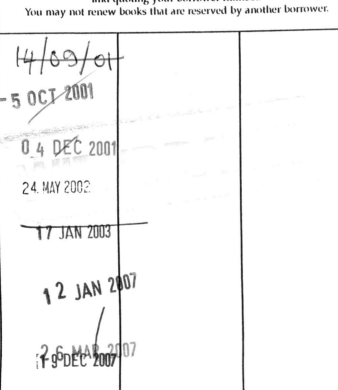

10. J.A. van der Ven, Entwurf einer empirischen Theologie, Kampen / Weinheim, 1990.

11. B.J. Groen, Ter genezing van ziel en lichaam. De viering van het oliesel in de Grieks-orthodoxe kerk, Kampen / Weinheim 1990.

12. C.A.M. Hermans, Wie werdet Ihr die Gleichnisse verstehen? Kampen / Weinheim, 1990.

13. J.A. van der Ven & H.-G. Ziebertz (Hrsg.), Paradigmenentwicklung in der Praktischen Theologie, Kampen / Weinheim, 1993.

14. J. Siemerink, Voorgaan in de liturgie. Vorming van vrijwilligers, Kampen / Weinheim, 1993.

15. H.G. Heimbrock, Gottesdienst: Spielraum des Lebens. Sozial- und kulturwissenschaftliche Analysen zum Ritual in praktisch-theologischem Interesse, Kampen / Weinheim, 1993.

16. R. Jeurissen, Peace and Religion. An Empirical-Theological Study of the Motivational Effects of Religious Peace Attitudes on Peace Action, Kampen / Weinheim, 1993.

17. H.-G. Ziebertz, Sexualpädagogik in gesellschaftlichem Kontext. Kampen / Weinheim, 1993.

18. Fred van Iersel & Marijke Spanjersberg, Vrede leren in de kerk, Kampen / Weinheim, 1993.

19. Frank Kwakman & Jan van Oers, Het geloof in de katholieke basisschool, Kampen / Weinheim, 1993.

20. B. Biemans & J.A. van der Ven, Religie in fragmenten. Een onderzoek onder studenten, Kampen / Weinheim, 1994.

21. E. Henau & R.J. Schreiter (eds.), Religious Socialisation, Kampen / Weinheim, 1995.

22. J.A. van der Ven & H.-G. Ziebertz (Hrsg.), Religiöser Pluralismus & Interreligiöses Lernen, Kampen / Weinheim, 1994.

23. J.A. van der Ven & Eric Vossen, Suffering: Why For God's Sake?, Kampen / Weinheim, 1995.

24. Hendrik J.C. Pieterse (ed.), Desmond Tutu's Message; A Qualitative Analysis, Kampen / Weinheim, 1995.

25. Kl. Sonnberger, Die Leitung der Pfarrgemeinde, Kampen / Weinheim, 1996.

26. B. Schwaiger & Th.W. Köhler, Wer studiert heute Theologie? Kampen / Weinheim, 1996

27. M. Viau, The New Practical Theology (in preparation)

Herausgegeben von
H.F. Rupp, A.H.M. Scheer, J.A. van der Ven, H.-G. Ziebertz.

Acknowledgements

The desire to express one's gratitude, for anything that is of merit in the work that follows, is tempered by the difficulty of knowing where to begin, or end...

For the germ of the idea which follows, I am grateful to the Revd Roland Walls, the former Dean of Chapel of Corpus Christi College, Cambridge; and to Sri M M Thomas, formerly Assistant Director of the Christian Institute for the Study of Religion and Society, Bangalore (and chairman of the World Council of Churches' Central Committee); and to (the late) Dr James L Henderson, formerly Lecturer in International Relations at the London Institute of Education. For the invitation to develop that idea I am grateful to (the late) Revd F B Welbourn, formerly Senior Lecturer in Religious Studies at the University of Bristol.

For various kinds of assistance and encouragement along the way, I would like to express my gratitude to the (late) Revd and Worshipful E Garth Moore, Professor John Roach, my brother Noel S Bailey, Bishop Peter Walker, the Revd Professor David Martin, Professor Eileen Barker, Professor Ninian Smart, Mr Kenneth Adams, the Revd Dr Raymond Foster, Mr Donald Munro, Professor Alistair Kee, Mr J R Henderson, Bishop John Tinsley, Professor Michael Pye, Mr Michael McCrum, the Revd Mark Pryce, Professor Phillip Hammond, Mr Graham Howes, Dr John Hull, Canon Thorley Roe, Professor Robert Bellah, Canon David Isitt, the Venerable Anthony Balmforth, Dr David Hay, Dr Grahame Miles, Dr Ian Hamnett, Canon Roger Clifton, my nephew Cal Bailey, Mr Neil Croucher, (the late) Professor Paul Chalfant, Professors Christine and Noel and Ursula King, Professor Don Wiebe, Revd Dr W H Swatos Jr, Dr Malcolm Ruel, Professor Arnaldo Nesti, Professor Meerten ter Borg, Revd Dr Roger Grainger, Professor Anders Thyssen, Professor Guy Ménard, Revd Dr Peter Jupp, Professor Jon Davies, Dr John Polkinghorne, Mr Ian Munro, members of Trinity College, Bristol, and of the Department of Theology and Religious Studies in the University of Bristol... and (not least) to Professor Wilhelm Dupré; and to so many others, particularly those with whom I have lived and worked in the parish, those whom I served in the pub, and those whom I interviewed; and indeed all who, over the years, have shown interest in this approach, not least by joining in the Denton Conferences, Religious Education courses, and Winterbourne Study Days.

Above all, however, I wish to and must thank (not least for their patience) those who by their practical assistance have made possible the development of the Network for the Study of Implicit Religion, such as Mrs Churchman, Mrs Lawes, Mrs Lomas, Mrs Greatrex, Miss Jefferies, and Mrs Diane Rix (for typing numerous drafts of this, and much else); and my clerical and lay colleagues in the parish of Winterbourne, and the staff of Denton Hall, Yorkshire; and my family – Joanna, and Charlotte, Christopher and Catherine.

1967–97   Edward Bailey

Chapter 1

WHAT MIGHT IMPLICIT RELIGION BE?

1.1 By Way of Definition

1.1.1 Of religion

The definition of religion is notoriously difficult. The attempt is also profoundly worthwhile: provocative, and instructive. It may be seen as part of the modern endeavour to define Man, or human being; or as a parallel to the medieval endeavour to define the soul, or to earlier endeavours to define divinity. Although an anthology of attempted definitions would be enlightening and stimulating, this is not the place for it. Some reflections may, however, be offered upon the search.

The hellenistic origin, and monotheistic spread, of the concept of religion has been traced by Wilfred Cantwell Smith (1964). A C Bouquet (1954) demonstrates the preference of the founders of both Buddhism and Christianity for the concept of "the Way". Unfortunately a Toynbeean history of its usage in different civilisations is still lacking, let alone a global collection of near-parallels. However, it is reasonable to suppose that the phenomenon was conceptualised in the context of, and propagated in the wake of, the Roman Empire.

It might, therefore, be instructive to discover the meaning of its Latin form, *religio*. It is also daunting (or comforting), however, to discover that not only St Augustine (354 - 430), but even Lactantius (c.240 – c.320) and Cicero (104 – 43 B.C.E.), acknowledged that the meaning of the word was a matter of debate. None disputed its "connecting" and "binding" quality (as in *ligament*). But interpretations differed as to whether the reference was to the binding of people, or to the binding together of a people and its gods; or to the ritual or to the moral rules, by which either grouping was bound together.

Such etymological speculation, whether or not it is supported by philological *minutiae*, at least encourages analysis. The reference of the concept is subject to continual change, and may even be reversed (cp Lord Chancellor Thurlow, quoted in Chapter 1.1.4 below). So these distinctions may not have been drawn, or possible, let alone in these dichotomous forms, "originally". And, even had the phenomenon itself remained constant, such prototypical descriptions or analyses need not necessarily be taken as determinative, final, or infallible.

Buried in Hastings (1918), but deserving resurrection, is a general article on Religion by Stanley Cook. He suggested that religion was "not so much different from the rest of life, as life at its most intense." Not surprisingly, therefore, he suggested that the definitional problem may be insuperable, since "our understanding of the nature of religion may depend upon our understanding of the nature of life."

In keeping with this suggestion, is the intuition whereby the teacher in this field introduces each scholar's thought by outlining his biography (eg J Waardenburg, 1973). Readers may well wonder whether, in view of their apparent experience, religion could ever have meant much more to (say) Freud or Durkheim or Frazer, than patriarchal morality or societal identity or ethical gentility. Likewise, if students know the denominational origin or loyalty or destination of (say) Robert Bellah or Mary Douglas or Evans-Pritchard, they may feel they can more surely grasp the drift of their thinking.

Thus, just as recent decades have seen growing awareness of the significance of the history of History, and of the sociology of Sociology, so beginnings are now being made (eg E J Sharpe, 1975; F Whaling, 1984-5) of a historical and social-scientific account of the Historical and Social-scientific study of Religion.

If, for instance, we place Cantwell Smith and Stanley Cook in their respective *Sitzimleben*, the former is of Presbyterian origin, worked in a missionary context in (what was then, West) Pakistan, taught the history of religions in Toronto, and has pioneered scholarly, inter-faith dialogue at Harvard. The latter, by way of contrast, belonged to the Church of England, spent most of his adult life within a single college, and taught Biblical and other ancient oriental languages, in the University of Cambridge, England.

Thus there is an "elective affinity" between their personal experience, context, and experienced audience, and their understanding, definition and description of religion. Cantwell Smith's confessed ontology of God and the self, is echoed in his analytical distinction between tradition and faith, and refers to historical civilisations; Stanley Cook's preferred emphasis on the unity of religion and life, is echoed in his provocative speculation regarding foetal influences, and refers to small-scale society, wherever found. Speaking in terms of ideal-types, the first is typically (or, rather, characteristically) describing a kind of religion which is a conscious, or self-conscious, *relationship*, within life; while the second is describing a kind of religion which is a conscious, or unconscious, *dimension*, of life. The first tends to lead to talk in terms of the holy; the second in terms of the sacred (cp Chapter 6.3).

The definitional difficulty, however, is not simply due to the inner differences between the observers. It is also due to the outer differences between the nature of religion in different contexts. As F J Streng (1969; *et al.*, 1973) has said, there are different *ways* of "being religious". The different formulae scholars use as titles of their studies of religion, arise out of the nature of the material itself, not simply the personalities through which it is being presented (or the progress made in analysis of the phenomenon). Different religions have different essences - and different *kinds* of essence.

Marrying the insights of Cook and Streng, we might say that there are as many ways of being religious, as there are of being human. However, two (or three) main *types* of religious experience can be identified, in line with the two (or three) types of social, psychic, and human experience that are broadly acknowledged. If only two, then they are: a sense of a (the) sacred, in small-scale society, and an encounter with a (the) holy, in historical societies. What the third - their equivalent in contemporary society - might be, is of course the object of the present search.

These two acknowledged kinds of phenomena are not mutually exclusive, either empirically, or even as ideal-types. For a relational religion (an encounter with a holy) which does not also impinge upon the rest of life, would, both usually (cf. Chapter 3.3) and normally, be seen as a hobby, not as a religion; while a dimensional religion (a sense of a sacred) that was incapable of being expressed in any specific manner ("made no difference", to any thing, in life), by actor or observer, would cease to be a dimension. The relational is the dimensional, focussed and brought to a more personalised point, which in turn enhances the potentiality for conscious relationship.

From these reflections, one observation, and one question, follow. The observation is that, in view of the diversity of the phenomena that are recognised as religious, among scholars and by "common" sense, the criterion of religiosity must be primarily subjective (which is neither the same as arbitrary, nor the same as judgemental). The specifically religious attitude finds expression in, and is found by deduction from, the varied combinations of rituals, beliefs, and community; but its religious character depends upon their intention, meaning, or spirit. This by no means precludes their study, or understanding. It simply makes such consideration an art, as well as a science (if that contrast still be allowed).

The question is this. If the human quality of dimensional religion in small-scale universes can be summarised as a *sense of the sacred*; and if the human quality of relational religion in historical civilisations can be summarised as *encountering the holy*; what form (if any) does religious experience typically take in contemporary society or culture? It is with that question that these studies are concerned.

1.1.2   Of secular

The phenomenon, or group of phenomena, to which "secular" refers, has been keenly debated in the closing half-century of this second millenium (D A Martin, 1978; H J Singh, 1967). The discussion may be seen as a contemporary, mirror-like, form of the older debate regarding the meaning of the concept of religion (cp G Kehrer & H Bert, in F Whaling (ed), 1985: 149-177). However, in this case there has been little discussion of the empirical etymology or reference of the Latin original (*saeculum*: the age). This is a pity. For, in the abstract, its meaning is clear, simple and consistent, despite the variation in its content. It always means the opposite – of whatever "religious" means.

So, to describe the parish clergy today as "secular" would be considered paradoxical, and taken as either jocular or judgemental (whether meant critically, or appreciatively). Yet "secular" was first used (in a religious rather than economic context), to describe those who, though in holy orders, were not bound by the (originally, Benedictine) Rule of Life. Subsequently, it was used to describe the nationalisation (or privatisation) of what had hitherto been under monastic or ecclesiastical control, such as property or education (D Knowles, 1979 vol III, W O Chadwick, 1975).

The transition between these two uses came about due to the equation of religion with Church, rather than with monastic Rule, following the "monasticisation" of the Western Church (G Tellenbach, 1940; D Knowles, 1979; W Ullman, 1953), and the development of other institutions. Thus "laicisation" and "secularisation" remain problematic terms in some European languages, politics, and theologies: their meaning depends upon their motive and the response to it (M Weber, 1930).

More recently, "secular" has been used to refer to the opposite of what Schleiermacher referred to, in his "Lectures in Defence of Religion, to its Cultured Despisers" (1799). There was an "elective affinity" between the development of such an outlook in the nineteenth century, and the need of "the new clerisy" (S T Coleridge, 1830) for "a place in the sun". The contrast was now with Christianity as Ideal, rather than as Rule or Church. Albeit linked, the three uses are distinct, and different.

Ideological secularism can still be found, pitting itself against a dualistic religiousness that once appeared to think itself nearly omnipotent, regarding the supernatural, and omniscient, regarding the mundane. However, with the increasing pluralism of both Church and society in the west, the "secular" has increasingly come to mean little more than the ordinary, the everyday, the non-ultimate, and un-absolutist. Its epitome and model is the deliberately self-limiting scope of the questions, and the provisional quality of the answers, which characterise the "scientific" *method* (n.b.). Indeed, as a cultural characteristic, or as a spiritual discipline, "limited" (or "self-limiting") might serve as a contemporary synonym for *secular*, referring alike to a secularity which is seen as sacramental ("Who sweeps a room as for thy laws Makes that and the action fine"), and one that is agnostic.

To define the secular simply as the opposite of the religious, may seem a chicken-and-egg solution. It will only disappoint, however, those who look to semantics (or etymology), not only for evidence of cultural history, but for an instant and final phenomenal analysis. Nevertheless, the lack of a substantive opposite to "religion", in popular or scholarly discourse, may be phenomenally, as well as phenomenologically, significant.

"Religion" does have an opposite, in "irreligion" or "secular*ism*". This is, however, a relatively rarefied usage. Not all learning takes place in educational institutions; not all who teach or learn in them are concerned with their theory or administration. The same principle applies to buying, selling, eating, healing, acting, and other facets of human life. Religion is undoubtedly a major industry, and almost universal pursuit; yet, for most, it is a means to an end (M Weber, 1965), rather than an end in itself. So "irreligion" and "secularism" can only be seen as contraries of "religion", by those for whom religion is primarily an organised institution or a self-conscious ideology.

In Britain, if not elsewhere, few people would describe themselves as religious, in this ideological and institutional sense. Consequently, the number of anti-religious activists, or professed secularists, is even more miniscule. For they are a minority of a minority: they both reify religion, and evaluate it negatively. The majority, however, would see themselves as religious, in some other sense, which they would consider equally important, and at least as valuable (cp Chapter 3.3.9).

Should they come across some secularist literature, such people would be as wary of its negative passion, as they would be of an *alternative* (organised - and organising) religion; but they would agree with most of what it stood *for* (including its criticisms of organised religion, where the facts still fitted). In that sense, they could rightly be described as "secular", although not secular*ist*. They would accept that label, and yet also continue to see themselves as religious. Their own feelings of disjunction, or suggested disjunctions, might not be resolved; they would, however, be largely ignored. For contradictions, and incomprehension, are a perennial experience (A Greeley, 1973; J Huxley, 1964). One of the classic functions of religion is the resolution of such antinomies. Indeed, the actual content of religiousness usually legitimates much of what others call secular (H Cox, 1965).

For the term 'secular' is not their own: it is not in general use. Not only is there no substantive opposite to "religion": even the adjectival form is limited to (a portion of) the intelligentsia. Certainly, there are contingent historical reasons why "religion" has received pride of place, ontologically and morally, in this culture. Yet the apparently widespread and continuing failure to apprehend *secularity* as a self-authenticating dimension of reality, could have a wider significance. Both religion and the secular are means to ends, even in contemporary society; but the former continues to provide the frame for living secularly. It may also provide the categories for understanding both that secularity, and the philosophy of secularism itself.

1.1.3   Of the Boundary between the religious and the secular

The meaning of "secular" has just been defined, empirically and structurally, as "the opposite of religious". Just as the relationship between them is direct, though inverse, so the meaning of "secular" is simple, although fluctuating. It changes constantly, but consistently. The meaning of religion has also been described, if not defined, as similarly changing: not arbitrarily, but in accordance with the distinguishing characteristics of the phenomena to which it refers, and of the associated individual or cultural interpretations of these phenomena.

Development of the insights achieved by the separate concentration upon religion and the secular may perhaps be furthered by this conjunction of them. For not only does the secular appear to possess a secondary quality: religion itself appears incomplete, when it is without relevance to that which is not religious. This would seem to be a structural, rather than cultural, characteristic. Should it ever appear to be absent, then both the religious and the irreligious are united in pointing out the omission. They may disagree as to the nature of the relationship between the religious and the social (which is "first cause", and which is the dependent variable), but both stress the necessity of a link, if the religious is itself to qualify as religious.

The overwhelming character of this connection is portrayed by the use of the model of the sacred and the profane (E Durkheim, 1915). It also stresses the phenomenological primacy of the phenomenally most positive. It finds its sociological expression in the power of institutions, such as the monastic and the sacramental (the Last Supper, the Crucifixion), and its cultural expression in the ever-increasing use of religious categories (myth, ritual, communion, charisma, missionary, soul, for instance; cp E I Bailey, 1990: 209-210) as metaphors or interpretations of the more "intense" (cp S A Cook, 1918) or "extreme" phenomena of human life, in politics for instance.

In the ideal-typical small-scale society, it is said, the whole of human experience falls within the category either of the sacred or of the profane (M Douglas, 1970). In historical societies this is ideal in the other sense, rather than typical (J Thrower, 1980). In contemporary society, however, room has to be found for a middle ground between the sacred and the profane. For most of life is neither specially sacred, nor positively profane (anti-sacred), but simply - ordinary. It is the prevalence of this third reality that has led to the development of another ideal-type, which sees contemporary society as (totally) secular.

The sacred-profane model allows due weight to be given both to the sacred, and to the tension between it and the profane. It would also allow due weight to be given to the profane, and to the dependence of each pole, not simply upon its opposite, but upon the whole of the remainder of experience. Its application to contemporary society, however, requires that the dichotomy be made a trichotomy; or, rather, that the dialectic be made into a trialectic, the dualogue into a trialogue.

In considering contemporary society, refinement is also required of the distinction between the *sacred* and the *religious* (H Becker, 1950, P E Hammond, 1985: 3-5). The former tends to be used by anthropologists, describing small-scale societies; the latter, by sociologists, describing historical societies. In accordance with the nature of the data, the former begins with the experience, the latter with the institutional. The recognition that these two key-concepts are not to be treated synonymously, and that each is appropriate in its own context, raises the possibility of either of them (or both of them) being distinguishable in contemporary society and/or of the suitability of a third key-concept.

This hypothesis led to the present studies. Initially (in 1968) it was conceptualised (E I Bailey, 1969) in terms of the possibility of a "secular religion", which might, for instance, be expressed through both secularism, and organised religion, but which would be wider than both, and be present in most of life for most people. Subsequently (in 1969) it was re-phrased as "implicit religion" (E I Bailey, 1976) in order to avoid either obfuscation, or confusion with irreligion (C Campbell, 1971).

This term is also not without its difficulties. Thus, the evidence may be highly articulate, and the actor may even acknowledge its religious character. Some other possible terms are listed in the following sections of this chapter. Other suggestions have included "inherent religion" (although that may suggest a doctrinaire universalism), or "innate religion". However, "implicit religion" has proved reasonably satisfactory, as a working rubric (cp Chapter 6). So, it must now be defined - so far as that is possible to do, on a general basis, in advance of each separate, empirical study.

1.1.4 Of implicit religion

The definition of "implicit religion" may be thought to be dependent upon the definition of "religion". It could, for instance, emphasise interiority; and might also suggest a judgemental attitude towards religion itself. The expression does not, however, intend either of these. As already indicated, it was anticipated that ("explicit") religion *could* be a vehicle of "implicit religion". So, if there is a link between the two definitions, it is rather in the other direction: "religion" means whatever *is* "implicit religion". If the implicit is the more real, its description as "religion" is inclusive, not exclusive; empirical, not evaluative.

One of the purposes of a definition is to provide alternative words that can be substituted for the term under discussion. Single-word definitions therefore meet this test best. A single-word definition of "implicit religion", would be *commitment*. (Whether this would also be a satisfactory definition of religion in general, or at least of religion in contemporary society, will not be pursued here.)

Such a synonym highlights the way in which the concept combines scholarly consistency and popular comprehension, by concentrating upon human attitude, rather than the forms of its expression. These cannot be divorced: legislation educates morality, and rituals reach parts of the psyche that verbal symbols cannot touch. Nevertheless, culture is at least as various, and ambiguous, as personality. Roman citizens of the early Empire may have seen religion in terms of public ceremonies; Lord Chancellor Thurlow may have expressed his approbation of it in public life, at the same time as complaining to "Mr Wesley" about his attempt to make it "interfere with private [*sic*] life"; but today, and not for the first time, religion is interpreted first and foremost in terms of spirituality, albeit both individual and social, and seldom in terms of politics. "Commitment" pinpoints that interiority - while politics shows the variety of ways in which it can be *expressed*.

Another function of definitions is clarification. This can be achieved by the inter-section of two concepts. "Implicit religion" may therefore be defined, without much loss of brevity, in terms of *integrating foci* (cp "nodes" of meaning, in R Robertson & C Campbell, 1972).

This paraphrase suggests the value of the concept in overcoming the tendency of the various divisions within human experience (essential in themselves as heuristic distinctions) to become dichotomies which hinder the overall understanding of human being. Thus there is a tendency to divorce the natural from the social environment; the individual from society; the chosen from the cultural; the conscious from the unconscious; the subjective from the objective; the rational from emotional; the ethical from the ontological; the transcendent from the immanent (P L Berger, 1971b); the divine from the human; the the supernatural from the natural (J Oman, 1931).

"Commitment" being ambiguously singular or plural, "integrating foci" similarly makes plain that any body (singular or plural: an individual, social, societal or corporate body) may have more than one focus of commitment. Indeed, a life which expressed a single religion, without conflict, contradiction or remainder, would be totally integrated (and, perhaps, potentially, totally integrating). This definition therefore overcomes the assumption (sometimes apparent in cultures that are influenced by monotheistic traditions - despite their own scriptures), that it is empirically *possible* (as well as desirable) to have a single religion.

If a slightly longer alternative be allowed, then implicit religion would be described as *intensive concerns, with extensive effects* (cp. F B Welbourn, 1960). This dual measure of commitment prevents its confusion with momentary (even if repeated) passions, that are not otherwise influential; or with general predilections, that are not themselves of serious import.

As it happens, the first of these definitions, *commitment*, is described as the concept or content underlying the forty Themes that are found in the Interviews (Chapter 3.3); the second of these definitions, *integrating foci*, is the term used to describe the seven carriers of implicit religion observed in the single arena of the public house (Chapter 4.3); and the third of these definitions, *intensive concerns with extensive effects*, is the expression used to organise the analysis of the life of the residential parish (Chapter 5.3). Unconsciously, each of these three suggested paraphrases must have subsequently been sensed as more appropriate in the different contexts; but each of them could in fact have been used in all three of the reported studies (cp Chapter 3.4; and, in effect, 5.1).

The provision of three definitions, rather than one, may signify, not so much the vagueness of the concept, or the ineffability of the suggested reality, as the meaningfulness of its apprehension. Indeed, as was aptly said by a distinguished student of religion (Alistair Kee), the term is "apparently broad, but in fact very precise". To suggest that anything may be implicitly-religious, by no means suggests that everything is (implicitly or otherwise) religious; any more than the anthropological commonplace about there being no limit to what *can* be sacred, suggests that in any context *every* thing *is* sacred.

A similar point has been made (by U Bianchi, 1975), tongue-in-cheek yet seriously, regarding the study of religion: "We can not know, in advance of our study, what it is that we are going to study". Such uncertainty is not peculiar to religion, however. Engineers have been heard to say, "We cannot say what the problem is, until we have solved it". It is similarly impossible to predict the precise character, vehicle, media, issues or patterns, that will form the substance of politics, or the arts, or education, or work, even in our own culture, even in the next generation. What can be said is that the form will never be arbitrary, even when its "choice" appears to the actors to be determined, by individuals or by their circumstances.

Such "inconvenience" seems to be the "price" of retaining the human dimension in humane studies. They must include intentionality, conscious or unconscious. The study of (implicit and explicit) religion may thus be a model and type-case for understanding what being human can mean.

1.2   Associated Concepts and Studies

1.2.1   Historical

In the 1970's, over fifty specific terms pointing in the direction of something of the nature of implicit religion were listed, along with some of their sources (E I Bailey, 1976, vol. III: 189, n. 2). During the 1980's, a second such list could probably have been compiled, as the collection of bibliographical resources has grown to some four thousand items. However, as with etymology, so with bibliography (eg E I Bailey, 1990a), nothing is thereby "proved" (in the naive sense, of eliminating the possibility of contradiction).

Yet the list is significant. The number of such "pointers", in the form of specific terms or of general *schema*, the diversity of their original contexts, and the authority accorded to many of their originators, strengthens the conviction that the concept refers to a reality, and that it is significant. This is particularly important when (like some Loch Ness monster) it lacks detailed evidence, official recognition, general categorisation, or agreed title. Their multiplicity and variety also increase the likelihood of arousing, in others, the memory of a similar apprehension.

Selective mention of such pointers may help to contextualise the concept, and suggest issues for further discussion. The choice will reflect personal debts, and cannot help reflecting personal limitations (whose rectification will be appreciated); but (as with the empirical studies, reported in subsequent chapters), some one must start some where.

Their arrangement will likewise be somewhat arbitrary. Its four sections, however, reflect an attempt to gradually "home in" on the target. They begin with the historical, and then proceed to more recent studies from the point of view of man as a socio-cultural being. They move on to studies from a religio-cultural angle, which are instructive from the present standpoint. They conclude, in the third section of this chapter, with a number of studies, or (more often) pleas for studies, of areas which are associated with (or with a part of) what is here meant by implicit religion, although they do not themselves use that term.

So we may start with Plutarch (fl. 66 CE), the classical Greek historico-geographer:

> In wandering over the earth you can find cities without walls, without science, without rulers, without palaces, without treasures, without money, without gymnasium or theatre, but a city without temples to the gods, without prayer, without oaths and prophecy, such a city no mortal has yet and will never see.

The passage has sometimes been quoted as evidence of the universality of religion (eg A Moreno, 1974). The validity (as opposed to longevity) of any such view is, of course, no more a necessary function of antiquity, than it would be of modernity (as distinct from development). Plutarch, however, lists examples of the more formal, institutionalised expressions of religion, associated with historical societies: gods, prayer, oaths, prophecy. Indeed, he specifically says he is talking about "cities". He is, therefore, positing the urbanity rather than the ubiquity of religion. So, the civic necessity of religious institutions is linked with, but is not to be equated with, the universality of religious experience.

Plutarch's silence regarding religion outside the city is also significant; for religion, as he understood it, did not exist in the countryside. For Hellenistic Romans, a country dweller (*pagus*) was likewise presumed to be "pagan", unless he had taken deliberate steps to enrol in a religion (as in Baptism). Rural religiosity could not be put in the same category as urban: it was mere *superstitio*.

The geographer's suggestion that religion is an urban universal finds support in the history of the "world religions". Thus, M Weber 1965: ch. VI says East Asian religions, and post-exilic Judaism, and Christianity up to the seventh century, all regarded the peasantry as "godless". E C Parrinder, 1968a: ch I, likewise says the invading Aryans regarded the indigenous Indian people as "irreligious". Moslem traders and Christian missionaries in Buganda similarly thought that those without their form of *dini* (literally: [sacred] reading) were without religion altogether (cp R Firth, 1967a: 475-480, and 1967b: 366-7). Swahili lacked terms for religion, as for music, because neither of them had been divided from its context (in life, or in dance), and thus become separately institutionalised.

For the world religions, especially in their more dynamic expressions, have tended to be urban phenomena: epistles were written from towns to towns, theologies came from universities, evangelism accompanied self-conscious traditions, fundamentalisms develop their traditions by trying to define them. At their most characteristic, indeed, they encapsulated and communicated the cultures of (would-be) world *civil*-isations, and regarded country-people as "godless", because lacking (their) God. They have never been sure how to distinguish the specifically religious from the general way of life in the small-scale societies which they have encountered, and have tried to absorb – but which have continued in their midst. Indeed, students who have been trained within urban cultural traditions have had difficulty in evolving any generic name for the fledgeling religious institutions of such small-scale societies.

The historical association of religion with civic life contradicts the modern assumption (D A Martin, 1967; E R Wickham, 1957), expressed in secularisation theory, that the city is the graveyard of religion. The contrast is explicable by the change in the character of the city. The "political nation" of Plato's *Republic* excluded all slaves, and all females, as well as the young and the uneducated. Thus the "visible" population hardly exceeded the few hundred of today's legislative assembly, or the few thousand of the modern civil or ecclesiastical parish. Indeed, until the Industrial Revolution, and well beyond, most urban populations were relatively both small, and, except as a mob, corporately invisible; and most city settlements were composed of tightly-knit units (E Jones, 1966), included social open spaces (C W J Alexander et al., 1977), and had a radius which left all within easy walking-distance of open countryside.

The continued description, both of such towns and of modern conurbations, as "cities", obscures a division between them which is as deep and as significant as that between the first townsmen and the peasantry (or that between the first settlers and the earlier hunters and gatherers). A similar confusion is caused by the continuing use of "religion", in its earlier sense. As with (mechanised) "manu-facture", the term can be extended, to include functional equivalents; for instance, by the (temporary?) addition of "implicit". However, the conspicuous survival of older forms of religion, tends to maintain a restriction on the use of religion, which the hidden character of the genuinely hand-made was unable to impose in the case of "manufacturing". For it could be that, just as there is continuity of some sort between the original "hand-made" and the post-modern "hand-made", so there is a kind of continuity between the old small-scale religious traditions, and the new, do-it-Yourself (implicit or explicit) expressions of religiosity.

1.2.2   Folkloristic

"World" religions, in alliance with "High" Cultures, and "Advanced" Technologies, have tended to see small-scale societies as characterised by fetishism and taboo, witchcraft and sorcery, superstition and magic. As "the centre falls apart" on the one side, however, so the "other" begins to be regarded with more respect. Characteristics are considered phenomenologically, labelled less judgementally, and found to have parallels nearer home. Just as religion in small-scale society cannot be exactly divided into its parts, or distinguished from other institutions, so studies of these parallels point towards, without necessarily naming, a form of religion that is largely implicit.

The folkloristic tradition, in practice and in theory, typifies this process of reinstating continuities, such as those between the rural and the urban (cp J Seabrook, 1967); the small-scale society and the large (A Smith, 1969); the non-literate and the literate (J Goody & I Watts, 1962-3); informal training and social education; the childish and the adult (D Heller, 1986); the child-like and the mature, the small tradition and the great tradition (S A Cook,1918: Part III, paragraph 27), and even between the most developed traditions (the Buddha as St Joasaph in Christianity, or Jesus as a prophet in Islam); the

local and the cosmopolitan (M Young & P Willmott, 1962); the antique and
the contemporary (eg K Cragg, 1965:163); the popular and the official (E J
Hobshawn, 1969:115); the non-rational and the profound; micro and macro;
symbol and reality (cp Chapter 1.3.4).

Iona and Peter Opie represent several of these continuities:

> If a present-day school-child was wafted back to any previous century he would
> probably find himself more at home in the games being played than with any other
> social custom (1969:7).

> The folklorist and the anthropologist can, without travelling a mile from his door
> examine a thriving unself-conscious culture (the word "culture" is used deliberately)
> which is as unnoticed by the sophisticated world, and quite as little affected by it,
> as is the culture of some dwindling aboriginal tribe (1959:1).

E Durkheim, indeed, had already said (1947:51) that "those phenomena
which constitute the matter of folklore [in] general ... are the débris of passed
[sic] religions, inorganised survivals; but there are some which have been formed
under the influence of local causes."

At the very least, such folkloristic studies concern the *Sitzimleben* of whatever might be called religious. Thus H Webster (1942: chapter XI) saw the
rules of etiquette, politeness, court ceremonial, euphemisms, sanitary customs,
and beliefs about bad luck, as possible survivals of taboo; but said, "There is
nothing specifically religious or ethical in the conception of taboo; it seems to
be just as much outside religion and outside morality as notions of 'unluckiness'
among ourselves".

C Kluckhohn (1967: Part II, chapter 2) took another aspect of this continuity:

> The almost universal distribution of certain elements gives probability to Clements'
> intimation (in F E Clements, 1932) that a complex of certain witchcraft beliefs [eg
> "the near-universality of exuviae and of intrusive objects (and sucking)"] was part of
> a generalised Palaeolithic culture which, in some sense, forms the ultimate human
> basis of all cultures.

In this connection, M A Murray (1921) went so far as to "... suggest that the
cult of the fairy or primitive race survived until less than three hundred years
ago, and that the people who practised it were known as witches"; while G
C Baroja (1961) reproduces accounts from direct witnesses of (non-revivalist)
witchcraft in Spain in the 1930s.

D A Martin (1973: 84), indeed, has suggested that "a common substratum
of European folklore, which remains alive to the present day", was "overlain
by three partial Christianisations" (cp J Gretton, 1969: 695 regarding Denmark): the "Catholic, the Puritan and the Evangelical" (cp H A R Gibb, 1947:
chapter II, regarding the "cult of the Prophet", as the extent of Islamisation),
"supplemented by elements of 'civic religion', particularly in the sixteenth and

eighteenth centuries" (cp P Walcot, 1970, regarding the Greek peasantry, ancient and modern, and J McLeish, 1969, regarding the Welsh and the Mendips peasantry about 1800). E Benz (1952) marries Martin's opinion to Kluckhohn's time-scale when he suggests that "thirty generations of Christianity [or, one might say, of any other named tradition] cannot eliminate one hundred and eighty thousand earlier generations" (cp F Heer, 1966).

Thus H-J Schoeps (1966: chapter VI) declares his own division of religions into the "extinct" and the "living" to be "superficial", since the "extinct" ones are still living influences. He compares the influence of Etruscan religion to that of the Etruscan language upon Latin (and, we might add, the influence of Icelandic spiritism upon contemporary Icelandic religion, both Lutheran and Roman Catholic). Indeed, M P Nilsson (1925: 133) considers Zeus to have been the *only* god in ancient Greek religion to have been certainly imported by the invading Aryans. Similar suggestions have been made (eg N J Hein, 1965) with regard to the Aryans' capitulation to, rather than conquest of, Indian religion.

"Superstition", upon whatever definition, says M P Nilsson (1948: 162) does not die; it "merely bides its time [cp R F Gray, 1963, regarding witchcraft in Tanganyika], and spreads abroad again when the mental atmosphere changes". Reference can also be made to M Eliade, 1969: 4, regarding "cosmic religion" in Europe and "cosmic sacrality" in Judaism; and to J V Taylor, 1958: chapter X, and F B Welbourn, 1965: chapter IX, regarding the resurgence of traditional religion in Buganda, specifically in 1953; and E G Parrinder, 1968a: chapter I, regarding the re-emergence (following the Rig-Vedas) of reincarnation, in the Upanishads, and of Krsna and Kali.

Attention may now be briefly divided between various aspects of social, and of religious, studies.

1.2.3 Social-anthropological

Thus the general historian, speaking of the (urban) universality of (organised) religion, raises questions regarding its presence and form in other situations. Likewise, the general folklorist, demonstrating historical and rural-urban continuity, raises questions regarding structure, as well as survival. So the anthropologist, whose speciality is to be a generalist of the relatively microscopic, produces studies which serve as models for similar studies of the *Sitzimleben* of implicit religion within contemporary society. These can take the form of studies of particular localities (cp Chapter 5), or of particular socio-cultural contexts (cp Chapter 4), or of particular units of personal life and their core-themes (cp Chapter 3).

Model studies of particular groups, some emphasising their religiosity, include G Bateson and M Mead, 1942; E R Leach, 1968; G Lienhardt, 1961; and S F Nadel, 1954. Studies which concentrate upon a particular theme, across several such societies, include D Forde, 1954; W E H Stanner, 1956, and 1963; and M Wilson, 1971. (The latter specifically enquires as to the "standardised nightmares" of contemporary society, which parallel the fear of sorcery in African societies.) Others study a single aspect, of one or more of the Great Traditions: for instance A Ayrookyuzkiel, 1975: R N Bellah, 1957, and 1964; P D Devanandan (ed), 1961; C Geertz, 1960; C P & Z K Loomis, 1969; P Y Luke & J B Carmen, 1968 (and others from the neglected series of "World Studies of Churches in Mission"); G & L B Murphy, 1968; R Oliver, 1952; P C Wiebe, 1975; & C K Yang, 1967.

There are, now, a growing number of studies of particular communities in western societies. Some of the more important American and European studies are outlined in C Bell & H Newby, 1971. To these, however, from the present point of view, should be added R Frankenberg, 1966; E W Martin, 1965; E Z Vogt, 1955; and W L Warner, 1961.

There are also studies of particular aspects of such communities; such as R Linton, 1924; J Loudon, 1966; and E Z Vogt & R Human, 1959.

Comparative studies also exist. Cross-cultural ones include R Horton, 1967; and F B Welbourn, 1968b. "Cross-temporal", diachronic ones include J B Bury, 1913, and 1928; F Heer, 1966; and R Williams, 1958, 1961, and 1966. Cross-temporal, "inter-saecular" ones include P Walcot, 1970 (above).

Yet few of these studies grant their subjects the honour of some degree of attempted phenomenological penetration, either at the overall, human level or at the more specifically religious level. Only the "foreign" anthropological studies that have been mentioned seem to attempt that. W L Warner *et al.* (1959, 1961) drew methodologically upon his studies abroad, but makes few comparisons. E Z Vogt (1955; cp W A Lessa & E Z Vogt, 1965) is familiar with the entire field, but also refrains from comparison.

R Horton (1967) compares the function of natural science concepts and concepts of spirits, but refrains from placing this phenomenologically or structurally in the wider context of religion. F B Welbourn (1968a) does, indeed, make a start in this direction, but within the limits of a volume intended (cp C G Martin, 1968) for school use (which may account for its neglect). J E Harrison, 1908: chapter V, however, had already compared the "pernicious" Keres with bacilli, for a generation oriented towards the classics and biology, anticipating Welbourn's comparison of atoms with ancestors, for a generation oriented towards physics and chemistry; but with a similar failure to pursue its possible wider significance.

Suggestions for studies of this kind have been made in the past. Thus C Geertz, 1971: 73 commented that, "Common sense is not a series of techniques or technology, rather it is a frame of mind, a way of conceiving life"; and went on to describe its assumptions as embodying a religious world-view, which inevitably involves a leap of faith. In similar vein, H Garfinkel, 1967: 75 said: "The study of common sense knowledge and common sense activities consists of treating as problematic phenomena the actual methods whereby members of a society, doing sociology, lay or professional, make the social structure of everyday experience observable".

More specifically, F B Welbourn, 1969a, suggested:

Is it necessarily more rational ... to regard spirits and witches as symbols for "endopsychic or social drives and forces", than to reverse the equation? It is difficult to regard an Oedipus complex as any less "mystical" than a paternal ghost - ESP is generally rejected not ... on any rational ground, but on the sacred ground that action at a distance must obey the inverse square law [cp S H Mayor, 1960] ....

If we are studying religion in a unitary society, we are studying not one institution over against others, but the dimension in which all institutions relate to uniqueness. If we want to study the same thing in our own society ... we shall find it in the "untouchable" (E Durkheim, 1961: 213) and often unacknowledged commitments which these activities express.

In F B Welbourn, 1969b, he concluded with the plea:

African independent churches ought to be studied, not as "religious" phenomena, but as examples of social schism in whatever form. Political parties [anywhere] cannot be properly understood without reference to their charter-myths and their Thou-commitments [cp M Brecher, 1959: 76]. Unitary societies have to be analysed in terms applicable to communism and nationalism but not to plural societies. African witchcraft beliefs are strictly analogous not to contemporary British covens but to our attitude to coloured immigrants. African cults of the living dead are comparable not with Western spiritism but with Churchill memorials and the Patrice Lumumba University. "Spirit-possession" is matched by pop sessions, exo-psychic mythology by Freudian concepts (Christological controversies by arguments about the nature of the ego).

If we are concerned with contemporary British ontology - with what in contemporary Britain is most akin to "traditional religions" - what is needed is a massive study of unrecognised commitments as they are expressed ... in unrecognised myth and ritual.

1.2.4   Cultural-anthropological

The headings given to these sections are somewhat arbitrary, reflecting the character of a selected theme rather than any official designation of the authorities cited. Yet even institutional titles are contingent upon national traditions and generational emphases: *academe* itself is pluriform. The current section therefore begins with a "historian of morals". Indeed, it may be noted that, with P E Hammond 1980 (in R N Bellah & P E Hammond, 1980), and R N Bellah *et al.*, 1985, such phrasing as *moral* in the sense of *morale*, and *civil* in the sense of *civility*, has regained respectability.

In 1894 (chapter VIII, and p 155), W E H Lecky outlined much of the area that is here alluded to as "implicit religion".

> The heroic virtues, the amiable virtues, and what are called more especially the religious virtues, form distinct groups, to which, in different periods, different degrees of prominence have been assigned; and the nature, causes, and consequences of these changes in the moral type are among the most important branches of history.
>
> There is no more important task devolving upon a moral historian, than to discover in each period the rudimentary virtue, for it regulates in great degree the position assigned to all others.

The concept of a "rudimentary virtue" has many synonyms and approximations. Chief among them may be "principle" and "value". Thus S A Cook (1918: II, 27) speaks of the "unifying and necessary principles". D van Oppen (1960; cited in H Cox, 1965: 175f) speaks of the "integrative principle" (of organisation, in contrast with mere order). H Becker (1966: chapter II, 5) and S A Tyler (1969: 3) speak of the "organising principles". K F van Moser (cited in S W Baron, 1947: chapter I) speaks of the "determining principle". Recently, talk of "core values" (eg in politics) has matched that of "core curriculum" in education, and "core business", in management.

The concept of "value" has likewise been seen as unitive of human reality (eg, by R N Bellah, 1957: conclusion), as well as of social studies (eg by M B Smith, 1969: 97-101). Theoretical mapwork in this area has been pioneered, for example, by E M Albert, 1956; H Becker, 1950: chapter I; C Y Glock & R Stark, 1965: chapter I; and C Kluckhohn in T Parsons & C Kluckhohn, 1951. Empirical studies have been reported by G Heald, 1983, and the other publications arising out of the (formerly, "European") Value-Systems Study (M Abrams *et al.*, 1985; S Harding *et al.*, 1986; etc).

Comparable conceptualisations include that of "character" (E Barker, 1927; D Riesman *et al.* 1950, & 1952); that of the "organising categories ... which ... reveal the maximum possible consciousness of the social group" (R Williams, 1971: 13, cited in R Bocock, 1974: 149); that of the "social *eidos*" (C Madge, 1964: 13, cited in E Krausz, 1969); that of the "educational" *paideuma* (Leo Frobenius & Adolf Jensen, cited in U Bianchi, 1975: 98-100), as an extramural "hidden curriculum" outside the schools; of what Levi-Strauss called "the common language which is never heard" (and saw as "binary structuralism"); and that of the *Zeitgeist* (which is capable of quick, widespread and profound change, as well as great continuity).

Similarly "programmatic" significance has been given to ritual, by Monica Wilson, 1971; to "the supernatural", as "instrumental to traditional Chinese social organisation", by C K Yang, 1967: 2; to "the truth about their king [which] affected their lives in every, even the most personal, aspect", in the ancient Middle East, by H Frankfort, 1948: chapter I; and to religion, by, for instance, M Weber, 1947: 267, who spoke of "religiously determined systems of life regulation", and by P Tillich, 1959, who called religion "the substance of culture".

Weber's suggestion that religion is, or was, the organising principle of culture, if not society, in historical civilisations, is plausible, at least. Its independent reality, and its hegemony, are open to question (Freud, Marx, J Thrower, 1980) but its claims were sufficiently reasonable (P L Berger & T Luckmann, 1967; B Wilson (ed), 1970) to be accepted officially (P Vrijhof et al., 1979) by contemporaries. In pre-urban cultures, too, what is akin to such religiosity is likewise significantly or supremely determinative. It is in contemporary, large-scale society that the place of religion *vis-à-vis* culture, is problematic.

The solution lies in acknowledging the variable meaning of religion. In other words, whatever *is* the "substance of culture" (in each particular context) *is* its religion. Some adherents of traditional-type religions may take comfort from this; or, equally, may abhor the presence of rivals. Likewise, some opponents of traditional-type religion may rejoice in the metamorphosis of the concept, or resent its re-emergence. The viability of all such evaluative responses serves to confirm the plausibility and independence of such conceptualisation.

Its advantage lies in its allowing contemporary phenomena to be adequately categorised (without indicating any kind of value judgement). To describe what is ("in fact"), empirically (existentially and politically, for instance), an "implicit *religion*", as a mere "value-system" (using that concept as an end-term), is to restrict not merely the frame of reference in which it is to be considered, but the very data observed, and the range of hypotheses concerning their possible significance. For Values are not only philosophical theories or social facts: if they are valued, they are related to, directly or indirectly (irrespective of the degree to which they are personified), and so function as divinities (or as devils). Indeed, Supreme Values absolutise life, and/or may demand death.

1.2.5   Sociological

M Weber, 1965: 1, opens the way for a non-supernaturalistic, or non-dualistic (D A Martin, 1969: 56) understanding of religion, which may be found to tally empirically with the nature of the implicit religion of contemporary society, when he said: "The most elementary forms of behaviour motivated by religious or magical factors are oriented to *this* world." Indeed, he subsequently states that most religious behaviour has been oriented to this world. Such learned generalisations receive confirmation from the acute observations of A de Tocqueville, 1890: II: "The Americans not only follow their religion from interest, but they often place in this world the interest which makes them follow it". So, to describe religion generally as "practical" (E R Leach (ed), 1968), is no paradox (B Malinowski, 1954), although it may surprise those religious specialists who, rather than "following [a specific] religion", "believe in" a particular theology.

If Weber allowed religion to be simultaneously secular and religious, a generation later V Pareto, 1935: 233 and 276, opened up the possibility that a single society could have plurality even within its official religion:

> In a given people in a given period of history there is a theoretical religion (morality, law) and a practical religion (morality, law). We say a religion, a morality, a law, for the sake of brevity: really there are more than one, even where there is apparent unity [cp Church of England Doctrine Commission, 1979] ... Not only are there various religions, various moralities, various laws; but even if one may say there are various types of such entities [cp R N Bellah, in R N Bellah & P E Hammond 1980: 86-118], so we have to pay due attention to the deviations from them which are met with in the concrete [cp R Towler, 1980].

Weber, then, enabled religion to be an abstract noun, for a qualitative adjective; and Pareto enabled that qualitative adjective to be characteristic of a variety of forms, even in apparently homogeneous religious and social systems. Luckmann, 1967 and 1971, another generation later, outlined, not a definition, nor a description, but a structural history, of what he calls "invisible religion". Coterminous with the meta-biological condition of man as a social being, this "anthropological condition of religion" "is universal in human society" (1967: ch IV). It is subsequently known to history, in institutional social forms.

In contemporary society, however (T Luckmann, 1967: 90),

> [t]he typical process of socialisation no longer includes the "official" model of religion - more precisely, the former "official" model - and only individuals characterised by social or socio-psychological marginality will internalise it as a system of "ultimate" significance. A society in which this is the case is well along the way to a situation in which it is no longer characterised by institutional specialisation of religion ... [This is] a revolutionary change: the replacement of the institutional specialisation of religion by a new social form of religiosity [cp W L Kolb, 1961: 21. n 35].

The characteristics of this new form of "invisible religion" become clearer when he contrasts it with the state of diffused religion in unitary societies:

> The appearance of secondary institutions supplying the market for ultimate significance does not mean that the sacred cosmos - after a period of institutional specialisation - is once again diffused through the social structure. The decisive difference is that the primary public institutions do not maintain the sacred cosmos; they merely regulate the legal and economic frame within which occurs the competition on the "ultimate" significance market .... Diffusion of the sacred cosmos through the social structure characterises societies in which the "private sphere"

does not exist and in which the distinction between the primary and secondary
institutions is meaningless ...

We are not merely describing an interregnum ... but ... the emergence of a new social form of religion characterised neither by diffusion of the sacred cosmos through
the social structure nor by institutional specialisation of religion (1967: 104-5).

A more empirical pointer towards implicit religion, from a sociological standpoint, is R Bocock, 1974. Discerning four types of ritual (religious, civic, life-
cycle, and aesthetic), he recognises that joint membership of the types is possible. He takes intentionality, as stated by the subjects, seriously, not only as
data, but as interpretation (without being bound thereby). Acknowledging that
the concept of ritual spans the religious-nonreligious divide, he posits a more
basic division between the objects of ritual attention, which are "set apart" and
therefore "charismatic" (a term he prefers to "sacred" (cp M ter Borg, 1989),
as being more general), and the profane. Objects of *religious* ritual are further
distinguished by being "holy", as well as "charismatic", since they are "in contact
with or capable of evoking the numinous" (1974: 60).

The main difference between Bocock's work, and the approach of these studies in implicit religion, concerns the areas of concern. Bocock's is more visible,
but (ultimately) less specific. A difference in their presuppositions can also be
gleaned, however, from his assumption that the inclusion of "civic" community-
building rituals (such as the "exchange of the Peace" in the Anglican service of
Holy Communion), in religious rituals, is a concession to secularity, rather than
an (overt, in this case) expression of the sacred (cp W Herberg, revised edition
1960; and J M Yinger, 1961; contrasted with W Herberg, original edition 1955:
280-1, n. 42, and Herberg 1967; and J M Yinger, 1961).

The present approach (as already stated), in some contrast also with that of
F B Welbourn, assumes that implicit religion *may* be expressed in and through
explicit religion.

1.2.6   Psychological

A final group of general studies of the human may be described as psychological
in character. To one who has formulated the concept of implicit religion, especially as a tertiary form of religiosity characteristic of contemporary society,
they all seem to be feeling after such a term (cp A T Embree, 1990), suggesting
the need of such a model, and pointing towards the possibility of such a reality.

Although Freud could find nothing *sui generis* in religion, he opened the
door to the discovery of kindred phenomena, such as ritualism, in the non-
religious sphere (1948-50), by denying the natural-supernatural dichotomy. Yet
those who, whatever they may consider the origin or value of religion, allow
greater reality to the phenomenon itself, can hardly fail to discover in social

psychology (eg T M Newcomb with W W Charters, 1950), or in developmental psychology, secular parallels to religion as a social, Durkheimian practice, or as an individual, Weberian world-view.

A typical instance of the latter emphasis, from the former context, is found in P Zimbardo *et al.*, 1969: 67:

> Cognitive dissonance theory ... is based on a few main assumptions about how the human organism works. The central assumption is that human beings cannot tolerate inconsistency. This means that whenever inconsistency exists in a person, he will try to eliminate or reduce it.

It is true that Freud, like Marx, denied the natural-supernatural dichotomy, by largely dismissing the validity of the latter. Yet the transition can be too easily made from their denial of a God, to the suggestion that they denied all *gods*. Their failure to draw this distinction clearly themselves was understandable, in view of the theological and philosophical climate at the time: Aquinas' careful distinction, following his delineation of each of the Five Arguments, "and that, men call [*nota bene*] God", was generally unappreciated. The Buddha, teaching an ideal Way, had been able to dispense with the theological issue; they, as students of humanity, were unable to ignore empirical divinities, although unable to name them as such.

Jung, with carefully guarded neutrality, acknowledged the reality of this issue (C G Jung, in J Campbell (ed), 1955: 426):

> I fancied I was working along the best scientific lines, establishing facts, observing, classifying, describing causal and functional relations, only to discover in the end that I had involved myself in a net of reflections which extend far beyond natural science and ramify into the fields of philosophy, theology, comparative religion, and the human sciences in general.
>
> This transgression, as inevitably [*sic*] as it was suspect [*sic*], has caused me no little worry.

Or, as A Moreno, 1974: ch III, summarises it:

> Religion, Jung says, is as real as hunger and the fear of death; it is the strictest and most original of all man's spiritual activities; although it is also the activity which, more than even sexuality, or social adaptation, is thwarted in modern man.

R N Bellah (1970: 253f) shares Jung's therapeutic concern, and challenges Durkheim's and Kluckhohn's optimism. He was encouraged, no doubt, by the sort of relativism demonstrated in B Wilson (ed), 1970, and foreshadowed by Weber's remarks regarding diverse rationalisms (and his fears of monochrome secularity).

> The life of the interior, though blocked, is never destroyed. When thwarted and repressed the interior life takes its revenge in the form of demonic possession.

Just those who feel they are most completely rational and pragmatic, and most fully objective in their assessment of reality, are most in the power of unconscious fantasies.

Or (to return, from avowedly sociological, to more officially psycho-analytic viewpoints), as E Fromm (1956: 175) states:

If we are referring to religion in its widest sense, as a system of orientation and as an object of devotion [sic], then indeed, every human being is religious, since nobody can live without such a system and remain sane. Then our culture is as religious as any.

Fromm's apparent definition of "religion in its widest sense, as a system of orientation and as an object of devotion", illustrates the contemporary tendency, noted in the first section of this chapter, to substitute "religion" for the previous "God". Or, as was suggested by the contrast with Aquinas, to confuse the apparent divinities with a putative Divinity, the empirical with an Absolute. Religion as an "object of devotion" might indeed be possible in contemporary society, but in historical societies it would be condemned by religion itself as idolatry, and in small-scale societies would be considered (or excommunicated and outlawed) as eccentric (or incomprehensible and dangerous). (The contemporary terms for such extreme positions are *bigoted* and *fanatical*.)

The boundary between consciousness and self-consciousness, and the priority given to diverse motives, surface in the developmental psychology of Piaget. Describing (1929: 188) as "animistic" the four stages he distinguished in children's thinking, he explained that "this animism is much more a general frame of mind, a framework into which explanations are fitted, than a consciously systematic belief". Indeed (*ibid*: 191), "it is just when an implicit conviction is about to be shattered that it is for the first time consciously affirmed" (cp E Durkheim, 1915).

Piaget explained (1929: 170) that he used the term "animistic" without prejudice to its possible interpretation in terms of souls or spirits, or its possible similarities with the "animism" of simpler societies. Such comparisons may be seen as an alternative (and methodologically more appropriate) form of the older debate about the historical (or prehistoric) origin of religion, and one day may be pursued with profit. For they are relevant to the "confusion" of religious and political phenomena; of religious and moral education (N J Bull, 1969: ch VIII); and of sin, with crime. They are pertinent to the adage that no one doubted the existence of God before people tried to prove it; to the emergence of a "scientific" sociology, following the French Revolution, and the enthronement of nationality-ism; to the dubiety of what "there is no question of", and the fragility of beliefs that "everyone knows to be true"; to true therapy, as well as healthy cognition.

From the present point of view, however, they pose the question whether consciousness, not necessarily of "religion" as a concept, or of the sacred as a category, but of their content, is an essential pre-requisite in order for a phenomenon to be described as religious. Some might see choice as essential to religion (and be prepared to define religion in terms of such deliberate commitments). Others (using the same definition) might see the unchosen, unconscious, unchange-able (cp F B Welbourn, 1965: ch X) as even more important; so that implicit religion must always be more deeply religious than explicit religion.

Each view is equally plausible, and equally partial. The former is working, in an individual, developmental mode, with that understanding of religion as segmented, which flourished in historical societies. The latter is based on an understanding of religion in terms of identity. In small-scale societies, such identity is primarily a group phenomenon; in contemporary society, primarily individual.

1.2.7 Historical-religious

The precise expression, as well as the concept of, "implicit religion", sometimes appeared in the works (which are now unduly neglected) of a number of philosophically-inclined students of the phenomenon of religion, published in the decades about the beginning of the present century. J Martineau, for instance (1899: 28) speaks of the "truth contained ... implicitly or explicitly" "in the experiences of conscience". The expression also appeared, somewhat obscurely, in a more recent, sociological survey of world religion (T F Hoult, 1958: 299-300). One who is, admittedly, attuned to the occurrence of the adjective, might also suggest that "implicit" has gained greatly and significantly increased currency, in descriptions of all sides of human life, during the 1980s and '90s. Concomitant cultural trends, to do with the feminine, the symbolic, the emotional, the intuitive, the expressive, the existential, the local, the traditional (the "post-modern", and the "new age"), might suggest that this is not a wholly distorted view.

This particular term is, however, only one of several score of closely associated concepts. Comment upon some of them may clarify the core meaning, both positively and negatively (E I Bailey, 1978: unpublished paper read at 1st Denton Conference; cp *ibid*, 1983, and 1990b). They may be grouped in accordance with their emphasis upon the historical, social or psychological origin of the phenomenon; or upon its universality; or upon its distinctiveness from, or contrast with, or dependence upon, recognised religion.

Expressions that imply a theory as to the origin and/or extent of the phenomenon tend to have a narrower reference than "implicit religion", in this volume. The implied origin may be, for instance, historical and/or geographical. Examples include "archaic religion" (M A Murray, 1921); "little traditions" (T Ling, 1968: ch VII, part 1; R Redfield, 1955); "primal religion" (J V Taylor, 1963), and "primary religion" (R Hoggart, 1958); and "subterranean theology" or "undertow" (in the context of D A Martin, 1969: 5).

Other expressions imply a theory as to its social origin and/or location. Examples include "common religion" (R Towler, 1974: ch VIII; R Towler & A Chamberlain 1973: 1-28); "folk religion" (M E Marty, 1967; B Reed, 1978: 76,101-8; H-J Schoeps, 1966: part 3); "grass-roots religion" (P Y Luke & J B Carmen, 1968); "humanist religion", and "humanist theology" (R W Hepburn, 1964); "popular religion" (L Schneider & S Dornbusch, 1958); "societal religion" (M E Marty, 1967); "underground religion" (M E Marty, 1967; R Towler, 1974: 147); and "vernacular religion" (R Robertson & C Campbell, 1972).

Other expressions imply estimates as to its psychological origins. Examples of this include "derivations of religious feeling" (U Bianchi, 1975); "natural religion" (D Hume [1779], 1963; T Luckmann, 1967); "neo-mysticism" (P L Berger, 1965); "the religious instinct of modern man" (R C Zaehner, 1959: 402); "spilt religion" (D Hume [1779], 1963); and "unconscious religion" (M Eliade, 1958: 128).

Expressions that imply a particular view as to the universality of religion tend to make assumptions regarding the nature of man. Examples include: "the anthropological condition of religion" (T Luckmann, 1967); "faith" (W L Kolb, 1961; and, as essential to the maintenance of life, in W C Smith, 1964), and "operating faith" (J M Yinger, 1965: 311); "practical religion" (E R Leach (ed), 1968; V Pareto, 1935); and the "religio perennis or common religiosity" (U Bianchi, 1975: 167,n 1; C J Bleeker).

Expressions that imply a defining contrast with (what is described in this essay as) a "recognised" or "named" religion, tend to the opinion that they are, ipso facto, either mutually exclusive, or else, conversely, parasitic. Examples include: "basic religion"; "ethnomethodological religion" (R Robertson & C Campbell, 1972); "lay religion" (M E Marty, 1967); "practical religion" (E R Leach, 1968; V Pareto, 1935); and "real religion" (M E Marty, 1958: ch IV).

Other terms suggest that it is necessarily restricted to a single part of the total religious scene of its host society, whether that part does or does not happen to be the "recognised" religion. Instances of this would be, "civic religion" (P M Harrison, 1970); "civil religion" (J J Rousseau, 1895; R N Bellah, 1967); "political religion" (R N Bellah, 1965: 218); "secular religion" (R N Bellah, 1965; C Geertz, 1966: 370; R W Hepburn, 1964; C L Kluckhohn, 1949: 282); "secular salvation" (E B Koenker, 1965); "societal religion" (M E Marty, 1967); and "unofficial superstition and belief" (B Rosen, 1969: 10).

Others again imply that it is intrinsically dependent upon a more real or more developed form of religion: for example, "inverse worship" (U Bianchi,

1975: 169); "irreligion" (C Campbell, 1971); "para-religion" (U Bianchi, 1975); "proto-religion" (R Robertson & C Campbell, 1972); "pseudo-religion" (G L Kline, 1968: 57; W Stark, 1966f); "religious print" (U Bianchi, 1975: 168); "secondary religiosity" (U Bianchi, 1975: 167); "second religiousness" (Spengler, quoted in E B Koenker, 1965: vii); "secular liturgy" (R Caillois, 1959: 133); "secular mysticism" (R Caillois, 1959: 133). Indeed, some imply a parasitic character, such as (in its context) "new denominations" (C Jung, XI,1: 61, quoted in A Moreno, 1974: 79),"new religions" (H Murray, 1962, quoted in J Havens (ed), 1968), or "quasi-religions" (D L Edwards, 1969: ch VI; K S Inglis, 1963: 330).

Most of these references to such realities lack definition, description or delineation. Yet their allusive character suggests, not only their lack of analytical or empirical content, but also their author's apparent assumption that their validity is easily, widely and immediately recognisable. However, a handful have received sustained attention. Their relationship with the current concept (and the relationship of some of those just listed) will be examined in the concluding part (3) of this first chapter.

1.2.8   Comparative-religious

The pattern of the earlier part of this chapter (1.1.1-4) followed the same sequence as the autobiographical interest (cp Chapter 6.1) which gave rise to these studies. That is to say, religion in the recognised sense having gained substance, the question presented itself, whether what was conventionally described as non-religious, did not itself implicitly contain some form of religion (*apart* from the influence, within the secular sphere, of a professed religion; cp R N Bellah, 1967). A similar presentiment was voiced by D L Edwards, 1969: ch I: "It might be right to define secularisation as the replacement of an old religion by a new one in the allegiance of the masses" (cp G van der Leeuw, 1963). A similar view was voiced by R Panikkar, in a phenomenological (and methodological), rather than historical, vein, when he suggested (1973) that only a religious person could properly understand a truly secular one.

Such a re-interpretation of the contemporaneous in its religious aspect is paralleled, interestingly enough, from a sociological standpoint. As already indicated, both W L Herberg and J M Yinger suggested, on second thoughts, that secularisation might be seen less in terms of the decline of religion (W L Herberg, 1955; J M Yinger, 1961) and more in terms of religious change (W L Herberg, 1955: 280-1,n 42, & 1961; J M Yinger, 1961).

This process, of relativising contemporary "western" secularisation, both culturally and religiously, was developed in the articles by N Tamaru and J Swyngedouw in *The Journal for Oriental Studies*, XXVI, 1, 1987, featuring "Beyond the Dichotomy of Secularity and Religion". Some British sociologists of religion (eg R Bocock, W S F Pickering, B Wilson), however, have tended to equate any change within religion with a decline in "genuine" religiosity, and simultaneously (yet paradoxically?) denied the presence of any real religiosity outside the traditionally religious. (This apparent "blind spot" contrasts remarkably with Weber's *confessed* "tone-deafness" - and yet his deep understanding of, say, Judaism.) A similar tendency to write of religious change, while ignoring the possibility of its religious motivation, can be seen in, for instance, A Russell, 1984.

A similar understanding can be expressed in Weber's terms of "alternative" forms of, and bases for, rationality. As V Pratt, 1970: 4 puts it: "The difference between secular and religious systems of values ... is not that the one refers to ends while the other doesn't, but that the ends involved in the two cases are different". S A Cook, 1918: section 30, expressed a similar point, in a different way: "All such changes", as in the meaning of the action of washing, "are significant for the relations between the psychical states of the individual and ultimate realities" (cp Chapter 1.1.2).

H Becker (1968) saw the essence of the sacred simply in terms of resistance to change. But R Caillois (1959: 135), considered it causally as well. He said: "The sacred persists to the degree that this liberation", of the individual, from psychic restraints, and from protection against them, "is incomplete"; that is to say, "whenever a value is imposed as a reason for being a community, or even an individual".

This understanding, of articulate secularism, or of unself-conscious secularity, as itself a form of religion (whether old or new), is not itself new. From the days between the genius of Comte and the idealism of present-day Ethical Churches, may be cited the more popular publicity of the *Labour Prophet* for August 1893, p 76 (quoted in K C Inglis, 1963: ch VI): "The Labour church is based on the following principles: 1. That the Labour Movement is a Religious Movement; 2. That the Religion of the Labour Movement is .... "

From the point of view of the interpretation of a sphere which is highly articulate, but does not see itself as religious, may be cited G van der Leeuw, 1964: 97: "We do not see theatre and religion, but two different religions, one against another; the ancient fertility religion of *Sacer ludus*, with its candour and sexual symbols, and the ascetic religion of Christendom".

The dynamic aspect of religion (cp R J Ackerman, 1985; cp the Epistle to the Hebrews 11: 1-3)) is overlooked by many of its interpreters (eg H Becker, 1968), but it converts the ideal and the traditional into the practical and the political, and so is germane to this context. A Loisy, 1933: 190-5 (quoted in S W Baron: 1947: 387: n 18) may be cited. He says that a system like the League of Nations "requires a religion of humanity. When the League will have become fully conscious of its unity, it will naturally produce and in a sense be such a religion".

The notion of implicit religion is not, however, simply a key to an alternative, or positive, or phenomenological, understanding of secularity, in its historical, cultural and religious context. It is also a door to the investigation of a common substratum of religiosity existing within and beneath, behind and in distinction from, all the recognised forms of religion. Indeed, without it, W Dupré (1994: chapter IV) has suggested, the study of comparative religion itself is ultimately impossible. It becomes an avenue to the empirical exploration of religion, as a (putative) human universal.

1.2.9   Religious-educational

In the recent fertile debate among British religious educationists, "implicit religion" emerged as a concept which was inadequately developed, susceptible of misunderstanding, and hence temporarily left on one side. Thus the Schools Council Working Paper No 36, entitled "Religious Education in Secondary Schools", like the Avon Agreed Syllabus (1993), contrasted the "implicit religion" approach (ch III, part 2) with the "explicit religion" approach (ch III, part 3). The former was said to see "religious education primarily as an unrestricted quest for meaning in life in terms of actual experience" (1971: 34). It named R Acland, 1963, and H Loukes, 1961, 1965, as examples.

The concept may have lacked development, in religious education circles, because those who were most clear as to the meaning of religion (in the explicit sense, of the historical civilisations) were least clear (and most suspicious) as to its presence in less conscious forms in other spheres; while those who were most clear as to its presence outside the institutions that bore its label, were least clear as to its nature within those institutions. This left room for the former to reject the notion as unreal, and for the latter to reject it as covertly confessional. While it could be both, it did not need to be either. The inchoate, and even the inert, can be immoveable; the inarticulate, or even the undeveloped, may be the seed-bed of a myriad different flowers (or weeds).

In the absence of any such positive pedagogy, however, implicit religion in the educational context came to be seen primarily in terms of the transcendental experiences of individuals. This was not surprising, in view of the age of the pupils, and the non-ecclesial character of the context. Typical (and highly significant, in themselves) were such studies as T Beardsworth, 1977, D Hay, 1982, G B Miles, 1981, and M Paffard, 1973; and, of course, their classical progenitor, W James, [1902] 1960.

The temporary overshadowing, in the 1980s, of this restricted, educational use of the term had its advantage, however, from the point of view of the present studies. For these, longer term, studies understand the expression as applying to any and every level of the personal: the inter-personal, small-group,

social, societal and corporate, as well as (the subjectivity of) the individual.
They are likewise just as concerned with those aspects of experience which are
not necessarily conscious or self-conscious (because unusual or transcendental),
but on the contrary are unchanging, ordinary, and permanent. Yet neither
would they rule out as irrelevant such momentary experiences of heightened
awareness, not merely in group situations, but on the part of groups as such
(eg E I Bailey, 1986a; E Shils & M Young 1953; H Smith, 1968; O E Klapp,
1969, and a host of studies of *sect*arian religious experience).

1.2.10   Religious-anthropological

The listing of pointers towards the concept of implicit religion, from the direction of the history of religions (in Chapter 1.2.7), gathered to itself a considerable number of suggested conceptualisations of the area. So the consideration of
pointers from the sphere of the anthropology of religion (in this section) may be
allowed to gather together a number of pointers (from academic disciplines with
various labels) that have a common theme. Following the example of Charles
Birch's phrase, "the God of the gaps", the common theme may be described as
that of a "gap", existing at or near the level of human consciousness.

The underlying assumption (which is based more upon the study of unitary
societies than of the human psyche, and so is here referred to as "anthropological"), is that the corporate consciousness, in its inevitable search for meaning
(M Weber, *passim*; V Madge, 1965), "abhors a vacuum". It should be noted,
however, that the assumption is beginning to be questioned: by, eg, T O Ling,
1971 (quoted in R Towler, 1974: 149), A MacIntyre, 1967, and David Martin.

The criticism of an anthropologist may be cited, of those people who "talk
past each other", because they imagine they know the location of each other's
religion (and secularity). Thus C G Baëta, 1965, was earlier quoted in B
Sundkler, 1962: ch V:

> Whatever others may do in their own countries, our people *live* with their dead
> .... Yet when Church bodies make rulings in the matter of funeral observances,
> the reasons given for the repressive measures ... are not even religious reasons,
> but merely such irrelevancies as expense, inconvenience, and waste of time. So the
> decisions get nowhere, and the problems persist.

R Pettazzoni, 1967: ch XVIII, with the Italian experience in mind, makes a
similar point, in a more historical fashion.

> The State is and always was the carrier of a religious spirit of its own, which is not
> that of individual religion [or of Christianity or of the mysteries].

> Normally, the crisis led to the setting-up of the secular State, and to its separation
> from the Church. And thus it would seem as if the age-long conflict was settled,

the conflict which the ancient world had passed on to the modern, which had never ceased in the Middle ages when both sides flew Christian colours, and could not cease until the State declared, although in Christian formulae, as once in pagan terms, its own religious spirit. But now that that spirit was denied by the State itself, the quarrel ought to have ended. Instead, it still went on - between the secular state and the Church, moving from the sacral sphere, from which the State had explicitly dissociated itself, to the profane or secular, from which the Church could not withdraw. It went on because this same "profane", which as such tried to avoid all collision with the sacral, really contained a sacredness of another sort, which as such could not avoid clashing ....

Another demand, closely associated with the [demand that Christianity should return (so-called) to non-political individual salvation,] is that the State should recover consciousness of its own religious character and feel itself the bearer of a religion of its own, not incompatible with the religion of the individual, of which the Church is the bearer, but of a different kind and not capable of being resolved into it, because it is a natural component of the State's existence and life; a religion for which the safety of the State is an end in itself ....

To reanimate the spirit of State religion there really is no need to revive the forms of ancient paganism ... still less to create new ones. For Mazzini's God is an idea (I say nothing of dogma) not different from the Christian God and yet Mazzini's religion is something other than Christianity; its motto is *Dio e Popolo*, "God and the People", and it is thus a religion of the State rather than of the individual ....

Not only the Christian parties [therefore], but the other, secular parties also are religious after their fashion .... [So,] if, in the eyes of the Church, the supreme religious values yet have political reflexes, so also for the State the supreme political values have their reflexes in religion. And if the spirit of religion breathes and burns in the life of the church, it is none the less true that a religion exists in the corporate life of the State, according to the inborn otherness of the two terms of religious duality and their dialectical development.

A third student fastens upon this "religion-shaped gap" in human life, from a social, rather than an anthropological, or historian-of-religions, viewpoint. Charles Booth concluded his seven-volume survey (1903: 424-6) of religion in London at the turn of the century, by noting that other "interests" are "filling ... a place that might have been otherwise occupied by religious interests", and goes on to describe a "conflict" of "character" and "spirit", which also sounds akin to a conflict between two religions (in the sense of *ways of life*).

What then is happening? If the working classes are not becoming more religious, what direction does development take? Are ... their interests becoming more political, or more social, more intellectual, or more material? No conclusive answer can be given. We only know that such interests as trade unions or friendly societies, cooperative effort, temperance propaganda and politics (including Socialism) with newspapers and even books, are filling in the mental life of the average working man, a larger space than in the past, and with some may be taking a place that might have been otherwise occupied by religious interests; but this usurpation and engrossment of the mind, may probably be asserted much more confidently of pleasure, amusement, hospitality, and sport...

In practice, the associations of the public house, the music-hall or the race-course conflict with those of the church and chapel, but there is nothing inherently or theoretically inconsistent between the two sets of interests .... The conflict arises from the character which these amusements have acquired, and the spirit in which they are sought, both of which religion, if accepted, might successively modify.

Finally, at the level of the individual psyche, Jacques Maître accounts (1966) for the consumption of astrology in France in particular, and in contemporary society generally, by precisely this theory of the existence of a gap.

Our central hypothesis is that the limitations of scientific knowledge, whether theoretical, practical or pedagogical, demand an asceticism often experienced as frustration in terms of the felt needs of individuals or groups. The dwindling influence of organised religion aggravates this difficulty, to the extent that a large section of the population now finds itself forced to turn to speculation clothed in secular forms to get answers to the vital questions left open by science.

Astrology belongs to a large family of divinatory procedures .... a fairly general category of thought processes in which classificatory and combinative systems are a basic tool. The individual or group on whose behalf the interrogation is carried out must participate in some way in the source ....

Between the ground gained by technology and that lost by religion, there remains a no-man's-land all the larger because the new ways of life in turn engender new hazards (accidents, financial speculations) and allow certain traditional forms of risk to loom larger (the perils of romantic love ....)

Actually, we experience in the face of chance a vertigo which lends it the quality claimed for the sacred [sic] by Rudolph Otto: that of being terrifying and fascinating at one and the same time.

In unpeopling nature of the purposes with which our ancestors peopled it, science takes away from many of our contemporaries the means of coping with the subjective aspects of human events. Astrology goes along only half-way, for it does not fall back upon spirits to explain events, while at the same time it does not endorse the asceticism that forces us to abandon the idea that all the happenings that impinge on a life from the outside are "all of a piece".

It is hard for a student who is not attracted to "playing the machines" (cp Chapter 4.2.2) to know the inner experience of those who are (cp Weber's confession that he was "religiously tone-deaf"). However, it may be suggested that Maître over-estimates the extent to which the *tremendum* pole in the divinatory procedures reflects that to be found in the face of change in "reality". The *fascinans* pole, however, is by no means exaggerated. It may likewise be suggested that, to the dwindling influence of organised religion, should be added the dwindling influence of "unorganised religion", in the shape of proverbial wisdom for instance (cp Chapter 3.3.5).

However, the possibility of such additional comments is a tribute to the presence in this instance of empirical observation.

1.2.11 Religious-sociological

The "religio-anthropological" approach gathered together students from various disciplines (not necessarily anthropological by name) who shared a holistic concern, which led them to posit a "religion of the gaps". This could, of course, be extended to cover all functional understandings of religion, according to the received opinion; although it may be questioned whether a distinction can rightly be drawn between such "functional" definitions, and "substantive" ones (cp Chapter 6). This "religious-sociological" section gathers together various students (regardless of academic designation) whose approach shares a common concern, not with a possible gap in the cultural cosmos, but with a gap in the social consensus.

The thinking behind this approach was stated by J P Williams (1962: 14): "Our society is often called secular .... [Yet] a society whose major values do not correspond to the values of its religious denominations may possess a very strong societal religiousness". M Weber, 1965, similarly describes every group as *ipso facto* possessing its own religion. Durkheim would see it as indicating the extent to which it was a group at all.

Interpretations of this kind do not assume total social coherence: conflict models of pluralistic societies, for instance (eg J Rex, 1961: 131), are not precluded by them. A civil, or at least a civic, religion (cp part (3.2) of this chapter), may exist alongside a rival religion (civic or canonical) (cp E C Bianchi, 1972).

Stanley Cook, 1918: part II, sections 27-28, elaborates this point:

> Every group and every collectivity which can be regarded collectively as a unity has its unifying and necessary principles .... The fundamental ideas, partly of common responsibility, partly of a profound inter-connexion, re-appear in ritual, ethical and other forms, in the ideas implicit in "magical" control or in "religious" prayer, in explicit curse or appeal, in vague denunciation or adjuration, in instinctive ideas of retribution and recompense, and in emotional, political and aesthetic feelings of man's kinship with nature or with the universe. And notably in law and justice, and in the instinctive resentment to what is felt to be inimical to human welfare, the individual is no longer an "individual", but as his "brother's keeper" implicitly associates himself with the progress of the universe as a whole and with the upholding of its principles.

Harvey Cox begins to draw the sort of distinctions with which the present studies are concerned.

The relativization of values does *not* make impossible human society with its pre-requisite of some degree of social consensus. What it *does* is to force man to reconstruct that consensus on a wholly new basis...

If the "post-religious era" makes any sense at all, it is a theory about the emergence of a very different style of social integration in our epoch, a type of integration which lacks certain of the characteristics previously thought integral to religion (1965: 111).

Bryan Wilson likewise said (1969: 10), "At least the terms of non-rationality have changed. It is no longer the dogmas of the Christian church which dictate behaviour, but quite other irrational and arbitrary assumptions about life, society, and the laws which govern the physical universe".

Alasdair MacIntyre (1967) explained the continuance of British society, not in terms of its foundation upon Christianity (whose survival he explained as due to the non-appearance of any ideology of similar stature), but in terms of the growth of "secondary virtues". These included the readiness to compromise, the willingness to admit error and the possibility of error, tolerance, and respect for the rule of the law. They are "rules of the game", rather than values arising from the nature of ultimate reality. This "parasitical morality", so far from being religious in character, declares "ends" to be outside its remit (cp Chapter 1.1.2). Incapable of arousing personal depth, or aspiration to moral height, or apprehension of the nature of life, it is militant only against "moral exclusiveness".

The consensus which is thus posited as the framework for ideological pluralism, and basis for institutional specialisation, operates at about the same level of human awareness as the "of course" which was so frequently noted by R S and H M Lynd (1937). It is more conscious than at least the first three stages of the four stages of Piaget's animistic thinking. It approximately parallels the stage when Piaget's children first verbalise their belief. It could be compared, from the point of view of identity, with clothing that is natural, proper and taken for granted, rather than with the skin, without which independent existence is impossible. If it be considered a substitute religion, then it will tend to be a substitute for the kind of "denominational religious preference" (cp W Herberg, 1960: chapter XI) that is relatively conscious, and is chosen because it "fits" best. However, the present approach opens up the possibility of studying such a consensus as an expression and outcome of a fundamental and vital identity, for individuals and/or groups.

It is consensus of this deeper character that R N Bellah (1967) described, in his famous essay on "civil religion". Although in his definitional opening he was slightly equivocal about its specifically religious character, he subsequently made claims, based upon its self-judging transcendental quality, which bore out his opening, more extreme interpretation. (Indeed, in Lincoln it had a prophetic theologian, who excelled, he suggested, any of his denominational contemporaries.) Thus:

> There actually exists alongside of and rather clearly differentiated from the churches an elaborate well-institutionalized civil religion in America.... This religion - or perhaps better, this religious dimension - has its own seriousness and integrity and requires the same care in understanding that any other religion does ....
>
> What I mean by civil religion, is a set of religious beliefs, symbols and rituals growing out of the American historical experience interpreted in the dimension of transcendence ... It is my conviction that any community of people with a strong sense of its identity will ... interpret its experience religiously .... What Christians call the Old Testament is precisely the religious interpretation of the history of Israel .... Both Judaism and Islam over most of their history and in several forms have been civil religions.
>
> [1969 footnote: I conceive of the central tradition of the American civil religion not as a form of national self-worship but as the subordination of the nation to ethical principles that transcend it and in terms of which it should be judged. I am convinced that every nation and every people come to some form of religious self-understanding whether the critics like it or not. Rather than simply denounce what seems in any case inevitable, it seems more responsible to seek within the civil religious tradition for those critical principles which undercut the ever present danger of national self-idolization.]

1.2.12   Religious-psychological

It has been seen that students of unitary societies, especially in their religious aspects, have sometimes been led to postulate the existence in contemporary society of a functional parallel to religion, in order to fill a gap that would otherwise occur in the cosmic circle of human consciousness. It has similarly been seen that some students of differentiated societies, especially those concerned with religion, have felt it necessary to postulate the existence of a "horizontal" structure, "under-lying" or "over-arching" the specialised institutions: a consensus that can "stand in" for a traditional religion that has now become, from the point of view of society as a whole, merely another "service industry". In a similar way, students of humanity, in its individual and subjective aspects, and especially those who have attended to its avowedly religious experience, have sometimes been led to postulate the widespread, if not universal, existence of phenomena which do service for the functions performed previously by overt religion, where that no longer appears to operate in this way.

As with the other approaches mentioned above, this conceptualisation has rarely been developed *in extenso*. In particular, it rarely seems to have been developed in an explicitly integrated manner, synoptically documenting previous insights and models, or to have been used as the specific framework for

major, empirical, published, research. The main candidates that are known
to the present author are mentioned in the concluding section (1.3), of this
chapter. Meanwhile, five theoretical conceptualisations may be summarised.

Comparisons may also be made with this study's understanding of the concept of "implicit religion". Such comparisons can be pursued in this section, not
because of any special affinity between the concept of implicit religion and the
religiosity of individuals (as distinct from groups), but because the abstracted
individual can sometimes provide an easier model to work with, than total
social, cultural or religious systems.

In some ways, the study of religion may have a longer pedigree than is sometimes acknowledged. The founders (and not only Mohammed), prophets, leaders, scholars, apologists, missionaries, converts, and opponents, must all have
been analysts of some religious dynamics, as well as seers of the "objects" of
at least some religious phenomena (cp A C Bouquet, 1954: chapter I; A de W
Maalefijt, 1968: chapter II; W C Smith, 1964).

However, one of the first recent analysts of religion, humanistically, to concentrate upon the nature of religious experience itself, was C P Tiele. He also
merits attention for simultaneously giving consideration to the nature of what
lay outside the field thus defined; and (which is all too rare) to the nature of
the relationship between the two fields (cp Chapter 1.1.3).

"The characteristic aim of all religion", then, Tiele says (1899: 190-203), is
adoration. This is a mixture of awe and longing (cp R Otto, 1917), and combines the transcendent and the immanent. It is the same in its nature as that
veneration given to finite heroes, saints and relations, which can therefore become *adoration* (and idolatrous). But, when it is religious, it is "a creation of
the imagination, an ideal that is objectivised in this or that personage".

This distinction he develops:

> What is idolatry? I do not now use the word in its figurative sense, as applied,
> for example, to such idols as money or honour, art or science: the pursuit of such
> objects has really nothing in common with religious idolatry .... I would define it
> as religion under the influence of intellectual aberration .... Religion only becomes
> idolatry when the conception of the deity upon which it rests ceases to satisfy our
> moral sentiment or our religious needs, and when we have advanced so far in our
> religious evolution as to perceive that the adored object has ceased to be adorable.

If the religious virtuosi were also analysts, of religion and of life, so, it may
be remarked, can students of religion be "among the prophets". Indeed, we
may add: they (like the "fundamentalists" within each tradition) cannot avoid
contributing to the traditions, if only by their own definitions and descriptions.
In this case, though, the notion of implicit religion would be seen as embracing
both "religion" and "idolatry", adoration of the infinite and of the finite (as

well as the more appropriate *veneration* of the latter), both idealisation and "intellectual abberation".

The concept of implicit religion is evaluative, in the sense of demanding the exercise of that empathy which is a necessary methodological instrument in the apprehension of its object of study; but it is not in the least evaluative, in the sense of ethical or ontological judgement. It affirms the equal possibility, and desirability, of each aspect of the phenomenological *époché*: inter-subjectivity, and the bracketing-out of presuppositions.

James Leuba, secondly, specifically sets out to map the "psychological origin and nature of religion".

> The adjectives *passive* and *active* might be used to separate amorphous [religion] from organised Religion ie the [general] feeling-attitude from the [self-committing] believer. "Passive" used in this connection, would mean simply that the person does not actively seek those advantages the gods might procure, but is content to be acted upon by them ...

> Active religion may properly be looked upon as that portion of the struggle for life, in which use is made of the Power we have roughly characterised as psychic and superhuman .... In this biological view of religion, its necessary and natural spring is the same as that of non-religious life ie the "will to live" [cp Tolstoy's description of faith as that sense by virtue of which man does not destroy himself but continues to live on; the force whereby we live]. The ground of differentiation between the religious and the secular [is] the nature of the force it is attempted to press into service [not a "faculty"].

> Unorganised religiosity must be ... the necessary precursor of organised Religion, it is its larval stage. But it does not by any means disappear from society when a system of definite relations with gods, or with impersonal sources of religious inspiration, has been developed. In all societies there is always a large number of people who live in the limbo of organised religion. They believe in the influence of religious agents, in which they believe more or less cold-heartedly without ever entering into definite and fixed relations with them (J H Leuba, 1909: 10).

If passive believers in Ruling Powers, such as "an African savage or a Parisian Deist", "may be called religious, it is not because they possess an *idea* of the powers, but in virtue of the guiding and inspiring influence these powers exert upon them" (1909: 90).

Bearing in mind the stated referent of his initial expressions, we may prefer to paraphrase their titles as "relational" (rather than merely "active" or "organised") religion, and "dimensional" (rather than simply "passive") religion (cp Chapters 1.1.1, and 6.3).

Implicit religion could be seen as the *heart* of such active Religion (cp the distinction made by H Fallding, 1974, between "religion with and without the capital"); and as being *coterminous* with such passive religion (in view of the influence actually exercised by such powers). The use of the single term, to cover the whole spectrum of the consciousness included in such concepts as "active" and "passive", has the benefit of suggesting connection, and allowing for the possibility of movement, while avoiding unwarranted assumptions as to the ubiquity of development (in either direction).

The turn of the century was a propitious moment in western culture for the analysis of religion, not only on account of the "founding fathers" of what were becoming distinct social sciences, but also on account of various works that are now customarily classified under the philosophy or psychology of religion. Reflecting the later Victorian self-assurance, and fondness for categorising, they combine a holistic approach to human being, with a catholic approach to religiosity. Thus, thirdly, Edward Scribner Ames' *Psychology of Religious Experience* was published in 1910, the year following Leuba's *Fundamental Nature of Religion*. It is no doubt due to Ames' extraordinarily "low-key" definition of religion, that he is able to develop, more fully than most writers, that part of his analysis of religious experience that points towards those areas of particular interest from the point of view of the concept of implicit religion.

"Religion", he says (E S Ames, 1910: vii), "is the consciousness of the highest social values .... These highest social values appear to embody more or less idealized expressions of the most elemental and urgent life-impulses [cp C P Tiele, 1899]. Religion expresses the desire to obtain life and obtain it abundantly [cp J H Leuba, 1909]". Then, developing his particular understanding (E S Ames, 1910: 358-9):

> To the psychologist ... the man is genuinely religious in so far as his symbols, ceremonials, institutions and heroes enable him to share in a social life. It is also psychologically evident that the man who tries to maintain religious sentiment apart from social experience is to that extent irreligious, whatever he may claim for himself; while the man who enters thoroughly into the social movements of his time is to that extent genuinely religious, though he may characterize himself quite otherwise .... Non-religious persons are accordingly those who fail to enter vitally into a world of social activities and feelings.

Examples given of the non-religious include the mentally defective, the delinquent, the irresponsible, the inconsequential, and the criminal; and also those who bifurcate the religious and secular realms, or restrict their life to their own specialism.

Ames' qualitative concepts, such as "highest values", "vital", "elemental", "genuinely", "thoroughly" and "sincerely", are as difficult to sustain, as they are difficult to avoid, in any analysis of *religion*. They also imply a transcendence which his emphasis upon sociality otherwise lacks. However, his description of religious experience does little to encourage the asking of such "consequential" (but cp Chapter 3.3.2) questions, regarding the character of the human relationship with the "objects" of belief, which was one of the particular merits of

Leuba's scheme. The student of implicit religion would also prefer to see the edges blurred, between his non-religious individuals and the remainder of the population; for, on his own definition, the sociality of the criminal can give rise to religiosity, albeit of a minority bent. There can indeed be "honour among thieves".

J E Turner (1934), fourthly, allowed for precisely this. For him, criminals are religious because, and insofar as, they give an "*explicit wholeness* of response". The fact that their view of the world is too restricted for society to tolerate, does not affect its religious character. "Is the man (we must ask) in any moment and in any way acting as an organic whole? Is he more or less explicitly expressing his *whole* nature in some manner or other, in his attitude and relation to the universe?" (1934: 32-33).

He subsequently (1934: 45-51) outlines his view of the religious-nonreligious spectrum:

> This does not mean ... that those "rational, aesthetic, moral and religious" elements, fundamental though they are, can never be suppressed or eradicated. Difficult though this is, it is always possible; nevertheless, it is a radical distortion of humanity. For there can be no such thing as "irreligion", if this means the complete absence of religion. What is ordinarily called such is really only one specific form of religion, provided it is an attitude specifically adopted and not the result of mere apathy.

We may feel that this might over-emphasise the place of conscious choice in religion, and hence in his understanding of "irreligion". However, he considers the religious status of the "irreligious" majority, when he says:

> The absence of religious experience undoubtedly occurs on a very large scale. But this is a privative or negative condition, like complete ignorance or the total lack of a sense of beauty. In all these instances alike, some hostile influence has prevented the natural development of the mind. The "irreligious" or "non-religious", therefore, like the inhuman, is one special and active form which may be assumed on due occasion by the experience of mankind, and is so called simply because it conflicts with the ruling religious systems of the day.

He neatly links this acquired but "unnatural" state of secularity, both with the deliberate cultivation of a nonreligious aspect of life, which itself takes on the aspect of a religion, and with ideological secularism.

> Neglect and apathy of any one aspect of mind may lead to its stultification and mutilation; deliberate specialisation and limitation to any one aspect, on the other hand, if successfully maintained requires support of other aspects and so is "essentially religious".

> So far as any attitude [such as avowed immoralism or theoretical anarchism] is deliberately adopted and explicitly and systematically supported - so far ... as the

person concerned is appealing to some definite intellectual or emotional grounds upon which he is prepared to act at any cost to himself - then I believe we must regard his entire standpoint as his own particular religion, no matter how much this differs from that of his fellows ....

The sole ultimate test [e.g. with Conscientious Objectors] is the sincerity of the individuals concerned. But from the analytical point of view, this "sincerity" consists in the explicit realization of *all* the aspects of experience, together with the readiness to carry these into practice no matter what the result might be.

This broad definition of religion resembles the classical equation of religion with sacrificial systems. His "religiously-deprived" resembles Ames' non-social and thus non-religious category, although far more numerous, and likewise Leuba's "larval" stage, although they are less likely to emerge into a religious condition. He also anticipates the subsequent equation of religion with identity, although the description of the "religiously-stultified" as "unnatural", humanly speaking, sounds both teleological and evaluative. What is lacking in this picture is a positive way of describing apparent unresponsiveness. Subjectivity and judgement may be impossible to avoid, in the very use of such concepts as human or religion (or divine); their use can, however, be widened, so that all there *is* becomes *natural*, whether or not it is desirable.

A final example of an individually-based approach, towards the concept of implicit religion, occurs in one of Mircea Eliade's rather rare (cp J A Saliba, 1976) revelations of his methodological stance (1954: 108-110).

What is called "faith" in the Judeo-Christian sense differs, regarded structurally, from other archaic religious experience. The authenticity and religious validity of these [sic] latter must not be doubted, because they are based on a universally verified dialectic of the sacred. But the experience of faith is due to a new theophany, a new revelation, which, for the respective élites, annuls the validity of other hierophanies.

... the classical example of Abraham's sacrifice admirably illustrates the difference between the traditional conception of the repetition of an archetype gesture and the new dimension, faith, acquired through religious experience ... By this act, which is patently absurd, Abraham initiates a new religious experience, faith .... God reveals himself as personal, as a totally distinct existence that ordains, bestows, demands, without any rational justice, and for which all is possible. This new religious dimension renders "faith" possible, in the Judeo-Christian sense.

As an historian or phenomenologist of religion, Eliade couples Judaism with Christianity, but acknowledges that not all of those who identify with those traditions know them as faith-experience of this kind. From the point of view of the Christian analysis of faith, he is justified in using Judaic data, as does the writer of the Epistle to the Hebrews. However, he ignores the width of the evidence cited, for instance, in that Epistle's classic eleventh chapter: there is no indication that Rahab's faith was as personal or focussed as Abraham's. As a general analysis of religious experience, it unjustifiably restricts historicity in revelation to a single tradition. For instance, "History to the Romans was the story of divine intervention in the affairs of men" (R M Ogilvie, 1969). The dichotomy between faith and religion may be attractive, but it is ultimately as empirically inoperable (cp Chapter 3.1.2) as that between religious and secular, "Church" (of whatever tradition) and "world". It is precisely this kind of absolutised divorce that the concept of implicit religion overcomes.

1.3 Alternatives, Parallels and this Term

1.3.1 Invisible religion, Ultimate concern

The nearest synonym, and the only term that is truly alternative to implicit religion, is Thomas Luckmann's "invisible religion" (1967: *passim*; 1971: 21-28, 135-154).

The two terms are almost twins. Each tries to convey the *double-entendre* of both manifest and latent meaning, in a single adjective. Each does this by selecting a particular human capacity (sight, speech) and using it metaphorically, to form a type-case of what is intended. Each may therefore also be criticised by the literal-minded. In the first case, they may aver that it is pointless to look for what is "invisible". In the second case, they may need reassuring that it is (usually) the religiosity of the evidence, rather than the evidence itself, that is referred to as "implicit".

However, even since the discovery of this alternative, "implicit" has remained the chosen qualifier, because it seems to convey the intended meaning a little more easily, and, indeed, precisely.

The limitations in Luckmann's own use of his expression may arise from the brevity of the treatment he has given it, and from the way in which his essay of that title is not so much concerned (despite its sub-title) with "the problem of religion in modern society", as with the problem of individual identity in modern society. As it stands, however, the use of the concept needs broadening, to include such traditional aspects of the study of religion as the "objects" of belief, the dynamics of sacredness, and, perhaps even more importantly (cp Oman, 1931), the relationships between the "objects" and the believer, between the sacred and the profane (cp Chapter 1.1.3).

The other near alternative to "implicit religion" is Tillich's "ultimate concern" (1959, 1965). As with "invisible religion", the area referred to is, or is capable of being extended so as to become, coterminous with that intended by implicit religion.

However, the present choice is preferred, partly because of the ambiguities in Tillich's phrase (cp R D Baird, 1971: 18-27; W L Rowe, 1968); and, more importantly, because this expression invites the use of religious frames of reference, and the subsequent comparison of the data discovered with the recognised religions. It has the further advantage of suggesting more clearly that the object of interest is not only the individual, but personal life *per se*; that is to say, irrespective of the size, depth, or formality, of the context in which it may occur: familial or national, communal or associational, societal or social.

1.3.2   Common, Civil, and Folk, religion

Attention has also been drawn by Robert Towler to what he calls "common religion" (R Towler & A Chamberlain, 1973; R Towler, 1974: chapter VIII). By this he means, in the European case, the surviving elements of pre-Christian, local folk-religions. Unusually, he gives a brief definition of his intended meaning: "those beliefs and practices of an overtly religious nature which are not under the domination of a prevailing religious institution" (1974: 148).

This reference is more limited than implicit religion, in two ways. In the first place, despite his subsequent disclaimer, by its definition and description it expressly tends to exclude "official religion". The concept of implicit religion, in contrast, allows for the possibility that its referent may, in a particular case, be identical with the official or professed religion.

In the second place, Towler's use of common religion includes an account of its historical origin that is effectively part of the meaning he intends to convey. Implicit religion avoids this limitation, also.

Common religion has two further characteristics, upon which (so far as is known) Towler has not commented, which make it less fruitful. The first is the implication that it is limited in its social location, to the "common people". Indeed, Towler states that it is limited to certain sections of the population, "including, perhaps, members of a residual aristocracy" (1974: 155).

The other characteristic of the term is its possible flavour of *de haut en bas*. Its origin, in the analogy with G D H Cole's & R Postgate's *The Common People, 1746-1946* (1964), which Towler has explained in discussion (at the III Denton Conference on Implicit Religion, 1980) does not eliminate the possibility of this impression.

A second possible parallel is "civil religion". Originating with Rousseau, it was revived and developed by R N Bellah (1967; cp for instance D R Cutler (ed) 1968: 357-393; P E Hammond, 1976; G Gehrig, 1979; and R N Bellah & P E Hammond, 1980).

With this may be coupled "civic religion". While either translation of Rousseau's original phrase, *la religion civile*, is legitimate, in English the two adjectives can be distinguished, and it may be regretted that the distinction in their meanings has been ignored (eg in Bellah, 1965, as he has tacitly agreed, in discussion; also in P M Harrison, 1970; and in Luckmann, in R Caporale & A Grumelli (eds), 1971: 34; and in D Martin, 1978: 1-20; and in M P Nilsson, 1925: 258-261, and 1948). For "civic" could then refer to the formal or official, and civil to the spontaneous or popular, ends of the societal spectrum; placing Bellah's analysis of presidential inaugurals in the realm of civic theology, and analyses of sport (for instance) in the realm of civil religion (E I Bailey, in A Kleger & A Müller-Herold (eds), 1985:104–120).

Both terms, and areas, obviously coincide with a part of what is intended by "implicit religion". Indeed, if they are first distinguished, and then combined, and broadened, in the ways just indicated, they could be said to include all that is societal and social in "secular" religiosity. What is missing, therefore, is precisely that individual, and usually transitory, experience of altered consciousness, to which religious educationists usually refer, when they speak of implicit religion. However, the present usage covers both ends of these individual/social, temporary/permanent, conscious/unconscious, spectra.

A third possible parallel to "implicit religion", is "folk religion". This has been used by Japanese scholars of religion to refer, in a relatively neutral manner, to that congeries of beliefs and customs out of which the named religions grew and grow. It has been used in Northern Europe in a similar, but more historical and corporate sense, to refer to the religion of the people, as a people. American sociologists have initially also used it, but to refer to imported, cultural survivals, akin to period costumes and folk arts. In Britain it has mostly been used by English Anglican clergy, sometimes with a pejorative air.

It is this above all which prevents its being seen as an alternative to "implicit religion". It is not necessary to agree with or approve of what comes under this rubric, but it is considered both essential and desirable to avoid judging, especially its value, in *advance* of knowledge, through its conceptualisation.

"Popular religion" may be considered alongside "folk religion". The use of the expression again reflects the phenomena to be found in the context. Each is to be found in cultures where traditional religion is highly visible, to refer to practices which are on the margins of the canonical tradition. Primary examples include Southern Europe, Latin America, Asia, and increasingly, the past (cp E I Bailey, 1984).

1.3.3   Implicit religion

It will have become clear, not least through these comparisons, that "implicit religion" is preferred as a concept because it keeps its options open with regard to its referent's structural and historical origins, its social and cultural location, its mode of religiosity, and its relationship with other forms of religion (E I Bailey, 1995a:19–25). This agnosticism is, at the same time, combined with an unrivalled breadth of reference.

However, it cannot be claimed that even this phrase clearly and unambiguously includes all that it wishes to convey and excludes all that it desires to deny. Two dangers have already been mentioned: that the data, rather than its religiosity, may be assumed to be implicit; and that an opposition, or at least a disjunction, between explicit and implicit religion may erroneously be assumed.

Other possible misunderstandings may now be laid to rest. First, there is no assumption that any religiosity that is found to be implicit in any situation, will necessarily be identical with any of the existing, recognised religions. (It was partly on account of this fear, that religious educationists found wanting the use of the expression in the Schools Council Working Paper No 36, 1971.) Second, there is no suggestion that "religion" is necessarily "a good thing". It is *posited*, that it is part of being human; but any particular form of religion may be judged by any individual to be true or false, beneficial or harmful, divine or diabolical. Third, it is not necessarily anticipated that investigation of any level of personal life (be it individual or corporate, social or societal, conscious or unconscious) will reveal the existence of a single implicit religion. (Integration, and integrity, are two aspects of a single *rara avis*.)

The greatest defect of the expression, however, is the negative reaction (the word is chosen deliberately) which it sometimes arouses. This reaction may come from one who feels religion is not a reality; or from one who, in view of its concomitants, wishes it were not. Alternatively, it may come from one who feels that religion of the kind implied is not really religious - or else fears lest it be so.

Fortunately, however, such reactions seem to have diminished, almost to vanishing-point, during the twenty eight years of these studies. On the one hand, members of the official religious institutions have largely renounced their would-be monopoly of such realities and concepts as religion, spirituality, pastoralia, divinity, worship, myth, ritual, spirit. On the other hand, both they, in their other capacities, and those who do not profess any such membership, have increasingly come to acknowledge the existence, and even the universality, of such phenomena (E I Bailey, 1994a:863–872). Indeed, such concepts are no longer used merely metaphorically, as literary conceits. Put very simply and traditionally (in western terms), the gods have been re-born - as *empirically* transcendent beings, once again.

1.3.4   Recent developments

A quarter of a century has passed (cp Chapter 6.1) since the general study that forms the basis of the two introductory chapters of this volume, and the three empirical studies that form the basis of the following three chapters, were initiated. During that period a growing number of studies have appeared (or at least have been discovered by the present author) or have been undertaken, that home in upon that "great leviathan" that is here described as "implicit religion". Listing those that, on the whole, have not already been mentioned, alongside each other, may serve as yet another way of indicating and communicating the meaning and reality of the phenomenon that forms the object of this discussion, as well as drawing attention to them, both individually and as a genre or corpus.

Inevitably the list is incomplete, even of those on the present writer's shelves. Equally inevitably, it is bound to become rapidly out-of-date, to judge by recent progress in this field. Likewise, its precise selections, and divisions, reflect considerations that are not subject to extensive explanation in this context. Indeed, in some cases a representative volume has been included, with the very hope that it will suggest the relevance of an entire theme, such as the study of spirituality (religious or secular), or the survival of little traditions or development of local theologies, to the theme of implicit religion.

Central to the interest, then, and containing empirical material, among these additional works, are: N E L Baker, 1990; C D Batson et al., 1982; M M Bell, 1994; R N Bellah et al., 1986; E Bernbaum, 1992; F Blum, 1970; B Clynes, 1990; D R Cutler (eds), 1969; J Ellul, 1975; K G Evans, 1974; F D Goodman, 1988; B Goudzwaard, 1984; J R Haule, 1992; W A Johnson, 1974; J F Meyer, 1991; A Nesti, 1985; A Piette, 1993; J A Prades, 1987; K A Rabuzzi, 1982, 1994; W W Savage Jnr, 1973; L Sexson, 1992; P Sherrard, 1990; J E Smith, 1994; F Staal, 1989; T Szasz, 1977; H N Wieman, 1991; C Williams, 1974; I G Zepp Jr, 1986.

Of closely related import are: C W J Alexander et al., 1977; M Chatterjee, 1989; I Chernus, 1986; M Czikszentmikalyi & E Rockberg-Halton, 1989; J S Cumpsty, 1991: W Damon, 1990; J D Douglas, 1971; L M Edelsward, 1991; A T Embree, 1990; J W Fowler, 1981, 1985; P Gagliardi (ed), 1990; J P Gunneman, 1979; E T Hall, 1969, 1984; D Heller, 1986; E Martin, 1989; S F Moore & B G Myerhoff (eds), 1977; J O'Brien, nd; C G Prado, 1980; H W Richardson, 1981; J E Wright, 1982; T H Zock, 1990.

The rapidly-increasing apprehension of the phenomena of "implicit religion", would appear to be linked with the "deconstruction" of the barriers around (and particularly between) the "great" religions of the world. This is exemplified in such works as: E Badone (ed), 1990; M H Barnes, 1985; R W Bibby, 1987, 1993; J B Butcher, 1994; J Campbell, 1953f, 1972; W A Christian Jr, 1981; R A Clouser, 1991; G S Cole, 1991; G L Comstock, 1995; R Davidson, 1993; M Friedman, 1982; N Goldberg, 1979; P Gregorios, 1992; W E Hewitt, 1993; D von Hildebrand, 1960; L Hyde n.d.; Genchi Kato (1926), 1971; S B Kopp, 1971; C H Lippy, 1994; C G Martin, 1968; T R Martland, 1981; D L Miller, 1981; C Morse, 1994; R C Neville, 1991; D Nicholls, 1994; W E Paden, 1992; R

Panikkar, 1978; C A Raschke *et al.*, 1977; R Ravindra, 1990; N R Reat & E F Perry, 1991; R J Schreiter, 1985; J Seznec (1953), 1972; A & B Ulanov, 1985; P W Williams, 1980; S Wright (ed), 1988.

A similar "deconstruction", in this case of the gulf between the religious and the secular, or the supernatural and the natural, or the sacred and the ordinary, or the conscious and the unconscious, or the articulated and the unarticulated, or the divine and the human, the mental and the physical (and, not least, the spiritual and the sexual), likewise opens up conceptual space for "implicit religion".

This kind of boundary-breaking can be seen in: N Ayo, 1989; M Ballard, 1975; J Becher (ed), 1990; J S Bolen, 1989; J W·Bowker, 1973; C Boyer, 1994; J B Carmen & F J Streng, 1989; R E Davis-Floyd, 1992; P Diel, 1986; J Evola, 1983; G Feeley-Harnik, 1981; R Fenn, 1987; G Feuerstein, 1992; M Fox, 1988; P Gardella, 1985; T J Gorringe, 1990; J Grahn, 1993; F Graziano, 1992; M Halbertal & A Margalit, 1992; J A Hall, 1993; D B Harned, 1981; M J Hatchett, 1976; C Heyward, 1989; B Hoff, 1992; H M Kallen, 1954; M & B Kelsey, 1986; G Kunda, 1992; B McGinn, 1994; M J Meadow & R D Kahoe, 1984; H Mol, 1976; B L Malina & R L Rohrbaugh, 1992; V R Mollenkott, 1992; E Monick, 1987; S H Nasr, 1981; J B Nelson, 1992; T C Oden, 1969; R Panikkar, 1973; N Qualls-Corbett, 1988; I Reader & T Walter (eds), 1993; K J Schneider, 1993; M Skelley, 1991; L D Streiker, 1969; R M Torrance, 1994; D Tracy, 1988; S Traweek, 1992; W H Willimon, 1979; R Wuthnow, 1992, 1994; L Zoja, 1989.

As is only to be expected of such deconstruction, bridging conceptual gulfs also has practical implications. A few instances of these must, and will, suffice: D Applebaum, 1993; S L Carter, 1993; J G Davies, 1973; T F Driver, 1991; J Duerlinger (ed), 1984; D Feinstein & S Krippner, 1988; E G Hinson, 1993; E Imber-Black & J Roberts, 1987; D Keyes, 1983; E Lewis, 1968; T Moore, 1992; R J Mouw, 1994; W Wink, 1984, 1986, 1992; W A Young, 1995.

Not the least significant development, however, is the foundation of the Network for the Study of Implicit Religion (as a precursor, hopefully, of a professionally staffed "Centre for the Study of Implicit Religion and Contemporary Spirituality"). Eight of the two hundred papers that have been given at its annual academic conferences in the past twenty years are available (in French) in *Religiologiques* XIV, Fall 1996. A number are known to have already been published, while others are being prepared for a projected Anthology. And almost all are available (in hard copy and/or audiotape) from the Network's convenor (the present author).

Chapter 2

CAN IMPLICIT RELIGION BE STUDIED?

2.1 Some Objections Answered

Students of religion have long observed that the apprehension of a divinity as real, is closely linked with its empirical importance, and with its evaluation, either positive or negative. Perhaps these are the two, inseparable, dimensions of all significance; that is, of the degree to which any phenomenon impinges upon the *psyche*. Be that as it may, an awareness of, and identification with the search for, implicit religion, would seem to require the combination, in some degree, of a readiness to entertain the notion, and an acceptance that it may prove operational. It is with the demonstration, in a general way, of this latter quality, that this chapter is concerned. (The following three chapters are concerned with its demonstration in more particular ways.)

Reference has already been made to the first objection of a methodological character. The fear is that, if religion is not clearly differentiated, institutionally and experientially, *every* thing will become "religious", and thus the category will lose its meaning.

The fear, however, is groundless. On the one hand, a religion that was not, in some way and in some degree, relevant to the whole of life would hardly qualify as such, in the opinion of most adherents (or, indeed, critics). On the other hand, the demarcation between the religious and the non-religious is a continuum, even if (and this is by no means proved) the ends are polar opposites.

The second objection is related, and can be similarly answered (that is, by reflecting upon what is being said, and upon the dynamics of the phenomenon under discussion). In this case, the fear is that, if the location of religion is not predictable, *any* thing can be religious. This fear is equally unnecessary.

On the one hand, it is only prior to the study of the situation that the options seem limitless. Once the situation is known, be it individual or social, there seems to be nothing arbitrary about the location, or even about the content, of the religious. A social-scientific viewpoint, indeed, might feel that both were absolutely determined by their context (while an actor's viewpoint might feel that they were both absolutely determined by the exercise of - human or divine - free will). On the other hand, it has long been recognised, especially among anthropologists, that there seems to be no a *priori* limit to what can be religious. One society's sacred is another society's profane; or, perhaps more tellingly, a third society's insignificant secular.

Thirdly, a pair of objections suspects that the designation of a particular pattern of phenomena as implicitly religious will reflect criteria that are primarily either subjective, or evaluative. The response in this case has to do with the nature of religious studies, and religion.

On the one hand, a description of any human phenomenon, with any degree of religiosity about it, which was in no degree subjective, would be an analysis that ignored one essential aspect of its character as human. On the other hand, to categorise it as religious is an interpretation, rather than an evaluation. "Religious" is no more to be equated with valuable (either "good" or "bad"), than, say, "economic" is to be equated with economical (either "efficient" or "miserly").

Fourth and lastly, another pair of objections is more sophisticated and substantial. They suggest that the task is beyond human power; and that the attempt to achieve it is inevitably self-defeating, because it changes the object of the study. If religion be allowed as a human mystery, then the study of religion is itself daring; and the study of what is beyond explicit religion is methodologically either impossible, or self-contradictory.

Both of these hesitations are well-grounded. The search for implicit religion will require the same sensitivity as the study of religion, and the same subtlety as the study of the deepest/highest, sharpest/broadest, and the most intimate/ultimate, in the psyche.

The requirements are not different, however, either in degree or in kind, from those for the hermeneutics of other symbol systems, or for the articulation of levels of consciousness in other spheres. Such demands can be construed as requirements rather than as prohibitions. Above all, though, they indicate, if they do not of themselves prove, that the task is too important to be ignored. If implicit religion be that which integrates human intentionality, it should not, if at all possible, be allowed to remain unavailable – first, for contemplation, and then for appreciation and/or development.

2.2 Some Advantages of the Search

Wilfred Cantwell Smith has made an impòrtant contribution to the history of ideas in his account of the evolution of the concept of religion (1962). If, to his account, is added the analogous but independent medieval concept of religion in the monastic sense (cp Chapter 6.3), and the concomitant concept of the secular (cp Chapter 1.1.2), the path taken by the study of religion, as Europe encountered other cultures in the nineteenth century, becomes comprehensible. It was inevitable that what was termed religious elsewhere, should be what was comparable to (including that which was in contrast with) what was considered religious in the culture of those who wrote, and for whom they wrote.

Fortunately for the emergent science, there was considerable diversity, among both the adherents and the opponents of religion, regarding the definitive elements in the phenomenon within their own home cultures. In particular, a contrast lay between those who saw the common aspect in what was religious as some "objective" element, such as (the confession of belief in) supernatural beings, or ritual activity in relation to them, or an institutionalised solidarity; and those who saw the common aspect as some "subjective" attitude, such as trust or adoration or submission. The gradual inclusion in the nineteenth century of Hinayana Buddhism among the religions has been accompanied in this century by an increasing assumption that the subjective attitude is the constitutive factor of religion, with Communism and sport being seen as recent test-cases. The close link between this and a "spiritual" definition of some kind (cp the Epistle of James 1: 26) can be seen in the recent, welcome inclusion of "spirituality" in both (Christian) theological, and (secular) religious studies.

Religion has thus, like Culture, lost its monolithic, normative character (and its initial capital letter, so to speak). Less "God"-like, it has become, at one and the same time, both putatively universal, and simultaneously relative, in relation to its social-scientific peers and to its setting (cp Chapter 1.3.4). The approach, however, has continued to be, if not prophetic, then at least verbal; if not theological, then at least logical.

The final stage in the emancipation of western religious studies, from its inevitable, original model, may be the recognition, for instance, that it is empirically possible (whether or not it is considered desirable) to be thank-full, without *necessarily* thanking any personalised one or any particularised thing; to pray, without formulating any concept of a being to whom one prays; to be at peace, without even raising the question, let alone suggesting an answer, as to what one is at peace with; to believe, without specific creed (*sic*), to hope, without schematic soteriology, to be loving, without fixed or focused object.

So the search for implicit religion, while retaining the typological advantages of the concept, can release the study of religion from these final consequences of its western origins. Conversely, and yet unsurprisingly, it can also release the study of religion from various kinds of secular imperialism.

Chief among these is the dismissal of whatever is described as, or claims to be, religious, as unimportant, on the grounds that it is really something else: either deliberate hypocrisy, or else unconscious pretence. The search for a religion that is implicit opens up the possibility that explicit religion actually articulates that which is implicit; that, even if the articulation is a mis-match, the actual motivation may still be religious; and, finally, that, if their motivation was, in the accepted sense, secular, the use of this alternative model was nevertheless viable and revealing.

For the time has come to turn the tables on secular imperialism; not by any sort of Counter-Reformation, ultramontanism, obscurantism, or fundamentalism, but by suggesting that wisdom in matters of spiritual discrimination comes from the combination of both interpetations, just as the sense of perspective, with its judgement of both propinquity and distance, comes with the simultaneous use of both eyes. Just as Christian historians have accepted that non-theological (and, more importantly, non-religious) factors played their part in, say, the Council of Nicea; so should secular historians (such as G R Elton) accept that theological (more significantly, religious) factors played their part (for better or worse), not only in the Reformation, but also in the growth of nationalism. Indeed, just as Christian historians may need reminding that theology and religion were among the determinants of Nicea or the Reformation, so secular historians need to consider whether nationalism can be understood at all, except as a kind (new or otherwise) of religion (cp J Allcock, 1991; N Smart, 1994).

A third advantage in this approach may be that this understanding of religion is one that makes "common sense" with the man in the street. The religious-secular division has been with the clerical intelligentsia since the Middle Ages, and with more self-taught intellectuals since Holyoake; but it has not established itself with the ordinary man, and above all woman, in either the western or the eastern street. The former acknowledges the tension between profession and practice, but avers his interpretation of the latter when he says, "She goes to church every Sunday, but her real religion is gossiping". The latter either exclusively follows his own exclusive but unimperialistic dharma, as in India, or else uncomplicatedly follows more than one religion, as in China and Japan.

Being human, for the vast majority of human beings, seems to involve both being religious, in a secular sort of way, and being secular, in a religious sort of way. To be comprehensible to those who are being discussed may not prove that the approach is correct; but it certainly does not prove that it is incorrect.

2.3   The Status of any such Implicit Religion

The study of implicit religion, then, takes the whole of a human context as its agenda, rather than any pre-determined segment of it. However, it has certain quite specific questions, which can be summed up. as, What are the foci of personal life in this situation?

The breadth of these terms is intended. The foci may or may not themselves seem to enter into relationship with those who focus upon them. The personal may be individual or social, and is more than animal ("super-natural"), without being non-animal. Thus, eating is an activity that humans share with animals, but it has more than animal-like dimensions. Life may be quantitative ("existing", "living - but only partly living", in T S Eliot's phrase, 1935); or qualitative ("life, more abundantly", John 10: 10). If it is the latter, it may *or may not* in some way be due to, or caused by, or significant of, a relationship (as in romantic love) with the foci themselves (cp Chapter 6.3).

Only after this process has been pursued, can comparison begin with any previously-recognised religious system. To make such inter-religious comparisons subsequently, in this way, can raise questions, which either reveal differences between the systems, or *lacunae* in the analysis so far achieved. To look for parallels and substitutes from the beginning, on the other hand, is to run the risk of merely finding another system, made in the image of the first one.

Finally, however, it may be objected, that all that has been found is only a "quasi-religion". If we did not have the officially recognised religious system, we would not even possess the category by means of which to describe the newly-discovered, so-called "religion"; just as, if no one had any reason to know what priests or sacraments were, then the Society of Friends ("Quakers") would not be able to say, all are priests, or, the whole creation is sacramental.

Certainly, first the Religious, and then the Religions, have given us the category, and their study has given us a typology (cp Chapter 6.3). However, it could be that the unofficial religion is, for a certain (individual or social) unit of personal life, at a particular moment, perhaps only in specific ways, their real religion; while their *professed* religion is really merely their quasi-religion (cp E I Bailey, 1997), operating say, only at the level of formal identity, or in their political life. On the other hand, each may be empirically true to real life in different situations. Nor, indeed, in the East Asian way, is there any reason to assume that each such unit of personal life will only have two such religions, either conscious or otherwise. Integrity is as rare as integration.

Chapter 3

THE IMPLICIT RELIGION OF INDIVIDUALS

3.1 The Methodological Background to the Interviews

3.1.1 The schedule

The first of the studies in implicit religion to be reported upon in this volume, and the first to be systematically undertaken, used focussed interviews, composed of structured questions (in terms of R K Merton, M Fiske, & P L Kendall, 1956). But the aim of that focussing and structuring was to allow and encourage the interviewee to express those beliefs which (s)he held about life in general. The fifty "questions" are therefore accurately described as "stimuli".

The stimuli originated, first and foremost, with comments that had been heard while the student was an assistant curate (pastor) in a parish in the north-east of England. Parents would say of their children, in a manner that included a moral as well as a fatalistic element: "Well, you can't force them, can you?" Grandparents would say, "They've got to do as *they* think best". An old person would say, "Well, just so long as they're happy; that's what matters"; or, regarding people in general, "So long as you've got your health, that's the most important thing." A young person would say (or, would "look"), "Why *shouldn't* I ['do my own thing']?"

Such statements were reminiscent of the concluding quotation in Richard Hoggart's comment (1958: 93-94):

> Most people in the working-classes appear, therefore, not merely unfanatic but unidealistic; they have their principles, but are disinclined to reveal them in their

pure state. For the most part their approach is empirical; they are confirmed pragmatists. It is an attitude derived not so much from a submission to the claims of expediency, as from a sense of the nearness of personal horizons, and of the folly of expecting too much, least of all from general professions. "Ah [the local, Yorkshire dialect form of "I"] like fair dealings" may seem an inadequate guide to the cosmos and can be self-righteous, but - said by a middle-aged man after a hard life - it can represent a considerable triumph over difficult circumstances.

The first principle in composing the stimuli (cp the following section of this chapter), then, was to ask general questions (eg A2, A5, A7, A9, A10, B1, B2. B3, E1, E8, F4-5), which would enable such apparently long-standing beliefs to be expressed, provided they were both long-standing and available to consciousness. The second method was to allow the citation and criticism of proverbs (eg E1, E2, E3), which could be seen as parallels, within the public culture, to such individually deduced conclusions about "life". A third device was to build on the conversational games of fantasy (eg A3, A4, B4, C1, C2, C5, C6, C7, E4, E5, E9) that are commonly played. A fourth was the translation into verbal, question form, of the observations that had been made upon the attitudes implied by such behaviour as the reading of "news" papers, or going away on holiday (eg A1, A6, A8, A11, C4, C4, C8, D1-6, D7, D8).

Then, as the schedule's compilation was nearing completion, some questions (eg F1-2, F3, F6, F7-8, & F9) were included regarding the meaning of certain terms such as "sacred" and "holy", "true religion" and "God" (suggested in part by such studies as E Durkheim, 1961; E H Erikson 1950, 1968; W James, 1902; H M Lynd 1958; M Laski 1961). As it happens, the responses to these have since proved much more significant than was envisaged at the time (cp Chapter 6.3).

Before each interview began, it was carefully explained that the object was to hear about what they already thought; and that they might not therefore wish to answer every question, for there was no desire to "put words into their mouth" (or, thoughts into their minds). A parallel was always drawn with a political pollster, who might ask, "If there were an election tomorrow, which party would you vote for?", when the truth might be that they were about to found their own party, or that they would not vote at all. To the interviewer's surprise, however, only one question was left answered by a single respondent.

Despite (or because of) the very general character of the stimuli, the interview schedule "worked" extremely well: the respondents were thought-full, the responses gave factual statements (even of ideals), the dialogue flowed naturally (cp E I Bailey, 1974: appendix). Indeed, while the interview was seen to be capable of being completed adequately in a mere forty minutes, most interviews took two or three times as long, and some lasted four hours. The experience, as some of the respondents said, was novel ("no one has ever asked me for my views before": cp D Hay, 1982), taxing ("I wouldn't want to say that

I wouldn't ..."), revealing ("I've often thought about this"), tentative ("but you ought to come back in six months' time, say, and see if I still feel the same"), and enjoyable.

Some of those interviewed said they "enjoyed the chance to talk about these things". By "chance", they cannot have meant merely the possibility of mentioning such opinions, for that was daily within their reach. They meant, rather, the opportunity for such sustained self-observation, and for the description of their consequent findings. The exercise was reminiscent of the artist's joy in creative expression, of the putative "need" (in therapy, as in education) for self-expression (and of the Logos doctrine, in Christianity). For "as long as men are still making their first steps in the art of expressing their thought [they] have only an obscure and ephemeral knowledge of themselves" (E Durkheim, 1961: 116).

By "talk" they did not mean discussion with the interviewer, for he simply conveyed his recognition of the meaning and hence validity of whatever they said, and duly transcribed it. They meant, rather, the chance of "witnessing to their own experience" (R K Merton et al., 1956) without contradiction. They, too, began to feel that "the subjectively important complexes of imperfectly formulated belief ... seemed most illuminating in interpreting the regularities of [their own] personality structure" (G M Carstairs, 1968: 170-1).

The longer the interview, the more likely was the respondent to say, "You know, you ought to come back and ask me these questions again, in six months' time, say". Unfortunately time did not allow these generous offers to be taken up. However, detailed analysis of the responses suggested that they were less affected by the circumstances of the moment than had been feared; and, insofar as ephemeral factors were influential (respondents themselves mentioned the importance of sunshine), the multiplicity of the responses was likely to produce an overall balance. However, the evolution of thought during individual life-histories (cp J W Fowler, 1981, 1985; and, with S Keen, 1978), and of widespread trends in such private opinion (B Wilson 1971, in R Caporale & A Grumelli (eds), 1971), does merit further study.

Only a few of the questions had been expected to "ring bells" with any particular interviewee. However, the "success" of the stimuli included in the pilot schedule led to the inclusion of other questions which might have been considered too "personal", that is, revealing (eg A8, A11, D7), or too "vague", or philosophical. Least predictable, and possibly most productive of all, however, was the final question (F 10), which was the last one to be added before the closure of the schedule: "Who are you?"

A list (cp E I Bailey, 1969: Appendix VII) of additional candidates for inclusion in the schedule could include, for instance, "What would you mean by real life?"; "What do you feel are the basic conflicts in life?"; "Is there anything you feel people shouldn't joke about?"; "If you could re-live your life, would you do anything different?"; "Have you any superstitions?"; "Do you feel you have changed over the years?"; "Is there anything you feel is blasphemous or sacreligious?"; "What do you mean by blasphemous/sacreligious?"

While all these and other such stimuli (E I Bailey, 1969) have been tried and found satisfactory, by the author and/or others, the interview schedule used for the present analysis, rightly or wrongly, left the solidary dimension to the attention of the exercises in actual participant observation reported upon in the following two chapters. For a beginning had to be made somewhere. Moreover, on the one hand, "we know that there is no religion that does not have an individual aspect" (E Durkheim, 1961: Book 2, Chapter IV); while, on the other hand "society [is always present] in the mind" (G H Mead, 1970), not least when that mind is operating in depth.

Such a section, however, emphasising the solidary element in human being, and hence in implicit (as in other) religion, could include, for instance: "Who do you most enjoy being with?"; "Who - if anyone - do you talk with, about your worries?"; "Who do you laugh with most?"; "Who might you cry with?"; "Do you prefer being alone, or with other people?"; "how many people?"; "Who do you feel most *at home* with - what group, or what individuals?"; "If you were one of three people wrecked on a desert island, what kind of people would you prefer to be shipwrecked with?"

Other suggestions for possible stimuli may be found, for instance, in: C Y Glock, B Wilson, & Discussion, in R Caporale & A Grumelli (eds), 1971; L S Jung, 1980; T Luckmann, 1967: Chapter VI; R Panikkar 1973: 70-84; R Robertson & C Campbell, 1972.

While the stimuli were composed individually, before use they were grouped under six headings: motivation, world-view, values, routine, beliefs, meanings. This was done in order to assist the conversational flow. The headings were seen as expressing in a very general way a common element in the stimuli that had been thus grouped together.

In other words, there was no suggestion that the six "areas", or "contents", represented an adequate morphology of any recognised religion, or of religion in general, or the anticipated morphology of any implicit religion that might be discovered. Had such a morphology been devised, it might have taken note of, among others: M Eliade, 1967, H H Gerth & C W Mills, 1954: 241-2, G van der Leeuw, 1963: part 2, and J Wach, 1967. But its production would have invalidated the quest, by pre-judging the structure, and/or eliminating significant elements, of that for which it was searching.

3.1.2   The presentation of the data

Elton Mayo said, "It is much easier to measure non-significant factors than to
be content with a first approximation to the significant" (quoted in J H Madge
1953: chapter II). The same conflict is perennially present in the presentation
of the data arising from open-ended stimuli. However, in the present context,
a practical solution unexpectedly presented itself.

When the transcript made during interviews were written up on library cards,
and comparison was made across the board of all the responses to each individual stimulus, they were largely found to fall into natural groups. These were
formed, not on the basis of some external criterion brought to bear upon them
by the student, but upon the "plain and evident meaning" of the answers themselves. Thus, half the responses might have a single theme. The majority of the
rest might contain a different but common thread. The remainder, with one
or two exceptions, might be summarised in the words of a particular answer,
containing most of the left-over elements.

It seemed possible, therefore, to compose a picture of the respondents, somewhat after the manner of the identi-kit photographs composed by the police.
Just as they take the hair, the forehead, the nose, the mouth, and so on, from
different and actual photographs, in order to form a composite picture of the
person they seek, so it was possible to take three actual responses to each of
the stimuli, and compose a (triple) portrait of the total breadth of the typical
answers given to the questions asked in the interviews. There is, of course, no
a priori reason why the number of answers that should be either required or
significant should be three. However, the total spread from which they were
selected remains available for other students to test the choices that were made.

The advantage of this way of presenting the data is that the evidence remains
direct, both for the student concerned and for the reader (in the following
section of this chapter). There is no barrier between at least some (and they
are those considered to be the most representative) of the responses given (or
their analysis by the interviewer) and their consideration by the public. Their
meaning, interpretation and significance, are thus equally open to estimate by
all.

Certain warnings, however, need to be sounded. In the first place, certain
stimuli were introduced into different stages of the schedule in order to serve as
a check upon each other (eg E1 and E4 upon A6; E3, upon A7, E6 upon A5).
This particular way of presenting the data may therefore reveal contradictions
within the implicit religion thus described; but it does not necessarily allow
any comments to be made about apparent contradictions between individuals'
answers. In the same way, affinities between attitudes may be detected, but
causalities cannot be claimed, at an individual level. Neither can the usual
socio-demographic variables be linked with particular answers: their signifi-

cance consists in their typicality, rather than in statistical specificity.

The picture that emerges, then, is not of a single individual; or even of a corporate one; but of an amalgamated one. Or, to be more precise, it is not of one, or even of three, amalgamations (for there is no longitudinal continuity between the selected responses), but of a triple amalgam. Lacking both the coherence and the artificiality of an ideal type, it is, rather, a "constructed type" (P Honingsheim, in H L Becker & A Boskoff (eds), 1966), showing, in every frame (if we may switch to Van Dyck's portrait of Charles I) both a frontal view and two silhouettes, of *different* stances.

Statistical correlations and multi-factorial analyses were precluded by the context and purpose of the study, the style of the interviews, and the nature of the sample. Thus, some care having been exercised to ensure that (the content of their responses being similar) all respondents are duly quoted from in the data finally presented, the specific source of the saying is not even recorded in the Identi-kit Interview, since the only purpose it could serve would be to prove the width of the selection.

The resulting triple identi-kit interview, however, is composed of pieces that are precise, particular, and representative, at least of the universe from which they were drawn. Thus it might be imagined that, had the respondents themselves been told to select the smallest possible number, to present, in their own terms, their overall views (say, at a series of commissions of enquiry, into each question in turn), they too would have found three such representatives to be both necessary, and yet, within the limits of practicality, adequate. So their successive spokespeople, on every issue, are labelled x, y, and z, in the presentation of the data.

The data thus presented differs from an "average", in that the latter, although also artificial, may bear no exact similarity to any of the individual items from which it is constructed. Likewise, it differs from a "highest common factor", in that no single element has been chosen as common to all the evidence. Again, it differs from a "lowest common multiple", in that there is neither the creation of a new entity, nor the merging and loss of identity among the existing parts.

It may best be described as a "cross-section", in which the analyst has simply had to select the point of the cut into the trunk - but has therefore made similar cuts into the other two limbs of which the tree is composed.

3.1.3   The interviewees

The aim of the interview was to plumb the depths of relatively conscious commitment. The method was to stimulate the description of existing beliefs and behaviour. The anticipated amount of resultant material (which in the event was itself greatly exceeded) precluded interviewing a statistically significant proportion of the population, a deficiency which, on this size of sample, scientific randomisation could not have made good.

Candidates were therefore "selected" for interviewing - on the basis that the student could summon up the courage to ask them, and that they were diverse. As it happens, five individuals, and one married couple, had been approached by other interviewees, acting on their own initiative. However, even in these cases, the final request came, of course, from the interviewer himself. In the case of the teenaged groups that were interviewed, following the interviewer's general request, neither the group nor the individual students had much choice.

Seven such requests for interviews were refused. Of these, only four were direct refusals. Of those married couples in which both partners were interviewed, four asked to be interviewed together. In these four cases, questions were either addressed in the first instance to the partner who seemed more likely to be influenced by the answers of the other; or else to each alternately. Those couples who were not interviewed in each other's presence, are treated as individuals, even when both were included in the sample.

When looking for candidates, the interviewer was aware that the sample needed to be as varied as was possible, in terms of age and sex, educational and socio-economic status, religiosity, and the probable extent of their self-knowledge. Above all, it was necessary to avoid replicating whatever views he might hold.

Subsequent analysis showed that the "top of the pyramid", for either education or religiosity, did not contract so much in the sample, as in the population as a whole. Thus, three-eighths had some form of tertiary education, as against five-eighths with secondary only; while five-ninths had *reasonably* high scores on religiosity, compared to four-ninths with low scores. As it transpired, at least five were Methodist, one a former Roman Catholic, one a Jehovah's Witness, and one a Hindu.

In mitigation of these apparent biases, the student would report that, in his experience, the difference between the generations and sexes, and between the educational and social strata, in this respect, lies, not so much in the opinions held, as in the ability to verbalise them. Likewise, that in this as in other northern European countries, religiosity, even when measured by practice and self-identification combined, bears little correlation with world-view.

More serious factors, then, were the interviewees' personality, the extent of their acquaintance with the interviewer, and, above all, the interviewer's belief that they could and would answer with candour. Their diversity can again be gleaned from the subsequent realisation that he was introduced to seven of those who were interviewed, for the first time, specifically for this purpose, by other interviewees. The possibility that answers were "trimmed" to (so-called) "suit" the interviewer would no doubt have been resented by the respondents, and was guarded against during the course of the interview, by the student's affirming attitude, and by his devoted recording of every word that was said (a facility developed through many years of note-taking in educational contexts).

Statistically, then, the hundred or so interviewees can be summarised as follows:

	Individuals	Couples	Teenaged Groups
Pilot schedules:	26	2	6 (independent school)
Final schedules:	30	2	3 (day-release)
Males:	36	4	28
Females:	20	4	27
Tertiary education:	c. 24		N/A
Secondary education:	c. 40		All (c. 60)
High religiosity:	c. 36		Unknown
Low religiosity:	c. 28		Unknown

The most significant single factor with respect to those interviewed, therefore, may be what they believed themselves to be doing. The original report (E I Bailey, 1969) summarised it:

> When they were first approached, they were told that the interview aimed at finding out what they thought and felt about life in general. The first question. "What do you enjoy most in life?", was often cited as a typical example. If it was apparent that further explanation was desired, it was said that from time to time they must have remarked to themselves that "life was like that", and so on, and the object was to remind them of these views and find out more about them, in connection with a study of such feelings that was being undertaken at the University.

> The actual interview was introduced with the explanation that the stimuli had been deliberately designed to allow them to say whatever they wished. The respondent was encouraged to answer them with a single answer, or several answers, or to dismiss the question altogether if s/he so wished. Nor were they to feel it incumbent on them to supply an answer to every stimulus, if it involved "thinking up" something rather artificially, or if they had personal reasons for preferring not to reply.

The most significant limitation, then, is the size, rather than the composition, of the universe from which the triple identi-kit interviews were assembled. It is possible that had it been necessary to compare many more than thirty responses to each of the stimuli, it might have become more difficult to find a trio of spokespeople who would have been able adequately to represent the whole group. There is, however, no reason to assume, in advance of evidence to the contrary, that these thirty interviews are less suitable material from which to construct a triple amalgam, than the whole hundred would have been; or, indeed, than a thousand might have been.

The restriction of the identi-kit interview to their content, moreover, has allowed comparisons to be made, in various directions (E I Bailey, 1969). This has been done by means of the ninety or so sets of responses that were not so used; by reporting the last of the pilot interviews in full (*op cit*: 63-67); by reporting briefly upon all the other interviews with individuals (*op cit*: 71-100); by reporting briefly upon the interviews with the four married couples (op cit: 101-111); by reporting briefly upon the group-interviews with the teenagers (*op cit*: 112-126); and by giving the full table of responses to the final stimulus in the thirty interviews from which the trio of responses were taken (*op cit*: 68-70). These five checks upon the resulting identi-kit interview thus were, and are, available for comparison.

3.2   The Stimuli and Responses

3.2.1   A: Motivation

1 *What do you enjoy most in life?*

> x: Meeting people, reading, watching a good play on television, operas - mainly light ones, especially Gilbert and Sullivan - and helping people!

> y: There's no one pursuit: it's always things of the moment, like drinking and walking, and it depends on my mood. I like a drink with one or two friends, or walking, especially alone.

> z: The children; and being married; and my husband.

2 *What makes life worth living?*

> x: For me, being married, now, and before that, waiting for it.

> y: To me, now, helping others, because I've realised that I'm not in good health, and many a day I'm not worth a half-penny, but I've got eyes and my daughter Peggy hasn't now - I've got joy in giving.

> z: Understanding that one has a role to play, and so doing the job or performing the role well. I don't feel life is purposeless. In individual situations the individual has responsibilities, and one's job is the recognition of those responsibilities - or doing God's will, in other language.

3 *If you had three wishes, and one of them had to be used on yourself but it didn't matter how you used the others, what would you wish?*

> x: I'd like good health for myself for the rest of my days. And never to be far from my family. And to have the family come to me for help always.

> y: I'd like to do away with all kinds of financial troubles, for myself. And it's worthwhile doing away with wars, like Vietnam, though this is similar, really, because most wars are over money problems, in some way. And to do away with starvation.

> z: I'm so reasonably happy with my circumstances, I don't think of any outstanding wish. I keep saying to myself, I have so much to be thankful for.

4 *If you won a lot of money on the Pools (or the Premium Bonds, or whatever), what would you do with it?*
(If guidance was asked as to how much, or it was apparent that the respondent was thinking merely in terms of a few hundred pounds, it was mentioned that an enormous sum was in mind, and an advertisement on the side of a bus, saying someone had recently won over £300,000, was quoted.)

x: I'd put a small proportion to one side for the children, including their education. I'd invest a proportion for various purposes, including buying one's own house, and so on. If there was any more, I'd want to give it to people, like Oxfam and Cancer Research, but I'd want it to be more personal - it's a selfish pleasure, but I'd want to give it to situations with which I was familiar.

y: I'd spend a very small proportion of it. I'd give ten per cent immediately to good causes - I've always thought about that. The rest I'd put away.

z: I'd look for some property of my own, and have a really good holiday, and see my parents and my husband's mother were all right.

5 *What's the most important thing in life?*

x: My wife, of course. Seeing her happy, and the family happy, and retaining our health, and being able to partake in all my activities.

y: Having a circle of friends with whom I can be absolutely at ease and frank.

z: For me, it's family life; for the world, it's love.

6 *Is there anything you feel really serious about?*

x: Yes, human relationships. The problem is communciation, especially between the generations, but also between dons and students, boys and teachers, and in international relations. It's at the root of all manner of problems facing mankind at the moment. It gets me very angry. It's so difficult for the individual to really achieve anything - someone who's really got ideas, but finds it hard to put them across - the individual is submerged. I saw it in America. Students have to resort to demonstrations in order to make the authorities even begin to listen to them.

y: Every situation in which I find people who do not treat other people as individual persons, but only as a category, of things.

z: Yes, I feel seriously about discrimination, over race, for instance. I always find I tend to be on the blacks' side every time there's a fuss over it.

And I suppose you'd say I feel seriously about people's attitudes - I don't just mean their opinions, they're entitled to those, but their attitudes. Like people saying they "don't like coloureds", without being able to say why, or that "it's a good thing the Americans are in Vietnam", but they can't give you any reason, when you ask them for one.

7 *Does anything ever "get" you, or move you, or "send" you whether*
   (a) angry, annoyed, indignant, fed up, or
   (b) pleased, happy, excited, interested?

a: x People being "snobby"; and people being "silly", like girls on buses giggling, though you know they'll grow out of that, or middle-aged women gossiping and cackling - their laughter, ugh! - when they should know better; and people talking loudly. People being ill-mannered - barging you in the street, or drivers not waiting for you at pedestrian crossings, and so on.

a: y Well I'm fed up with my brothers and sisters at the moment. It's partly my fault, but it's partly theirs, no doubt. And I don't like being told in front of other people about something you've [*sic!*] done wrong when I'm out at work. And I get annoyed with people who are two-faced, rather than straight out.

a: z Yes, pettiness - often it's my own. And the "establishment" - for instance, the examination system in education, and red tape, because it often seems not to regard people - it's meant to be more effective but it isn't always.

b: x Music certainly gets me. It's usually only a small snatch out of a piece, such as trumpets, or an orchestra accompanying hymns. It sends shivers down my spine, as if I'm resonant to certain sounds - such as the plaintive clarinet in Acker Bilk's "Summer Set". In art, there's the odd picture, sculpture or film, when you see something deeper than the paint or the music. I get very turned on, now, to things like drama and films.

Also in everyday life, when suddenly something clicks and a person emerges and says something to you that he means, as an equal person.

b: y Little things please me very much, like someone coming to see me here at work, or at home, out of their interest.

b: z It's mostly things that happen to me through the children now - watching their development. And friends.

8 *What sort of thing do you fear?*

x: I must admit I fear death, because I do, but in a very remote way at the moment, though I've a feeling I will fear it more later. I fear dying at an early age, really, rather than death itself: having to leave this world with all its pleasant things.

And of course I fear being a failure, and so on.

y: Getting old, and not being wanted.

z: Yes - I think everyone who works hourly has the threat of redundancy at the back of his mind, always.

And I'm afraid of being senile.

Otherwise, I'll try anything once.

9 *What do you dislike most about people - when you find it in them?*

x: It's an absence of humility, arrogance, an insensitivity to the opinions of others, self-righteousness, sanctimoniousness, the refusal to recognise that there's a grain of truth in other people's views.

y: I hate people to be unnatural - to be bombastic, or have snobbish ideas - that does strain my tolerance. But I don't worry any more. That's one of the things that has come with age. I've faced so many of the crises that an average person has to face, and have come out all right; but I do sometimes get concerned.

z: I dislike dishonesty of purpose, and of speech - backbiting, for instance. And bad manners, however much the same is true of me. And dirty people.

10 *What do you feel most grateful for in life, or most glad about?*

x: For my health and the health of my family. Because I come from a very poor family, and I never imagined I'd live quietly and happily with all the things I needed - I never ask for what I want, but what I need.

And for the opportunity to serve God - I've always considered that a great privilege.

And for my wife.

y: Meeting and falling in love with my husband, is the great thing, and one's own family background.

z: The gifts one has been given, without any doubt whatsoever. I feel very sorry for people who've been born without any gifts whatsoever.

And for having a home such as I had, and being born on this island, and other things connected with that. And that I came out of the last War - we should feel eternally grateful for that.

11 *Do you ever feel there is anything lacking in your life?*

x: Not really.

y: Before I was engaged, I would have given you a tirade on that! Now there are only things that are lacking in me - maturity, ideas, strength, and a clear idea of where I'm going.

z: I wish there was more contact between my parents and myself - I know it's a common complaint of people of my age. I want to be able to sit down and talk with them, but within two minutes it always becomes an argument between my father and myself. Our views are different on everything we discuss - religion, politics, everything - and he can't stand it.

3.2.2   B: World-view

1 *What do you feel is the biggest problem in the world?*

   x: Managing humanity - I'd go back to Robbie Burns - one country against another, and dictatorship. And starvation - it could be overcome with the right cooperation by people.

   y: Trying to get people of different mentalities to agree, on a common level of love and understanding. What a lovely world it would be if all nations were ... all Christians, if you like. Not that I ever feel hopeless about things; nothing's ever as bad as you thought it was going to be. That's very true.

   z: The colour-bar, and starvation.

2 *Do you feel the world is changing for the better or the worse, or not at all?*

   x: The potentials have increased, but men are not necessarily happier. Still, on the whole, there are more people who enjoy life more, now, than there were in the past.

   y: All in all, for the worse. Man has not reached the emotional maturity that's required to use his inventions and discoveries in ways that aren't dangerous.

   z: People stay the same.

3 *What do you think is the purpose of life?*
   (Guidance was frequently asked as to whether this meant "of the whole thing", or "my purpose", in which case the interviewer always reminded the respondent that (s)he was free to take it as (s)he wished, and suggested (s)he "might like to say both".)

   x: We've been fortunate to have been given a life, and so we should try and make it as deep and as wide as possible, and to try and make other people happy in the process.

   y: I don't know. I used to see things cosmically, but I don't any more. Samuel Beckett had a great influence on me about a year and a half ago. I was in a play of his, and I'm recovering from it still. I can't accept it absolutely, but he says our whole life is just waiting: we're born "astride the grave".

   z: The riddle of the universe is still unanswerable, and I wouldn't be surprised if it isn't always. As a Christian, I would say, To do God's will - whatever that means - it isn't always easy to know.

4 *When would you like to have been born, if you hadn't been born when you were?*
(If the response had not already made it clear, the interviewer would additionally ask, "Who as?, and Whereabouts?")

x: I'd rather not change.

y: Oh, in Victorian times - the clothes.

z: Some time later - now, with so many exciting things in front of you.

3.2.3 C: Values

1 *What would a perfect world be like?*

x: Ha! This ties up with my "wishes". My perfect world would be in a way, selfish. It would be as it is now, but without the tension, and it would be fairly static in population, and in the number of cars, and so on.

y: I haven't any other picture. I don't think it would be primitive: modern technology is better.

Oh gosh! The sun would shine all the time, it would be full of happiness, there'd be no cruelty, everyone would live happily together, there'd be no pain or suffering.

Of course, it couldn't possibly be perfect, human nature being what it is. It wouldn't work, because someone would always be dissatisfied. There'd be nothing to work for, and nothing to overcome.

z: I can't visualise it. "Perfect" is not something you can reach, by definition. If it was perfect by our present ideas, then it wouldn't be so then.

2 *If you could change any one thing in the world, what would you change?*
(If guidance was sought as to how realistic it had to be, the interviewer replied that it could be anything, this was "an *abracadabra* question".)

x: I don't know.

y: Wars - or poverty and under-development. I'd have a universal communism, with no strings attached.

z: A lot of problems would be solved if everybody was the same colour.

3 *Where is the best place to start putting the world right - not necessarily meaning a geographical place, of course?*

x: As an individual, or as the world? In theory, the United Nations sets about doing this, at the world level, and it's the best of what we've got at the moment, though it's fairly unsuccessful so far.

As an individual, the best place to start is where you are.

y: In the home. If only we had some means of making sure that parents, when they married, have a standard home with a sense of reason and proportion - though we don't want to turn out sausages.

z: In schools, with your teaching. Start with the children, and give them the right ideas. What's wrong to a large extent with the present generation is that they don't know what they do want. They must learn about consideration for each other, and helping people, especially those worse off than they are. Many of the youngsters are groping blindly for something to do.

4 Who is most likely ever to put the world right?

x: Not the Government. If people worked in harmony, and did the right thing, they could make it much better.

y: To name Christ would be blasphemous - he doesn't need my vote, he can manage on his own. He is very involved, but we don't understand his role.

So, it's the whole collection of me's.

z: God, through the Church. But that's very idealistic. In practical terms, the leader of the Chinese people - not the present one, of course, but whoever is. There was a time when I put most faith in the United Nations, but that doesn't seem to be doing very well at the moment.

5 What do you think a perfect person would be like?

x: I have come across Christians of whom I would say, "Here's the most perfect person I've ever met up to now." But perfection covers, or should cover, so many things. It's just what you'd expect of really good Christians: general sweetness, tolerance, loving in the widest sense.

y: It's a self-contradiction - we're not like dogs in Cruft's.

z: Very dull.

He would not be arrogant, he would be able to communicate, and he'd have the usual qualities of kindness, humility and humanity.

6 Do you see any hope of anyone ever being perfect?
(If the response had not already made it clear, the interviewer would additionally ask, "Why?", or "Why not?")

x: No, because I always say, when people criticise other people, "We're only human, there's got to be something the matter with us".

y: No, because there is no such thing. The top of the scale must be free, and open. But some people are near it.

z: No, on statistical grounds. It would be like going through the chair you're sitting on. There are too many variables.

7 *What would you like your children (or "your grandchildren", or any other child relatives that had already been spoken of, or "any children/grandchildren that you had") to be like and to be?*
(If guidance was asked as to whether this referred to professions, or character, the interviewer replied that it referred to both.)

x: I would not like them to have the tycoon mentality of grasping and pushing. I'd prefer them to be artistic and musical. I would not want them to be materially ambitious.

y: I don't know. I have no particular ambitions for them. They must be themselves.

z: Just to grow up God-fearing - I mean, if they have a sense of honesty, they can't go far wrong.

8 *What's the most useful job in the world - including a housewife, for instance, as a "job"?*

x: There are so many, and every one hangs upon another - the dustman has one of the most useful.

y: A doctor, or a teacher - in the widest sense of the word, not just a school-teacher. No, being a parent, especially if they're also a good teacher.

z: Something in the medical field. You can live without a politician, but you must have good health.

3.2.4   D: Routine

(This section was frequently introduced with the comment that it had proved difficult to convey the meaning initially, but it now seemed satisfactory, and that it was about the absolutely ordinary, everyday things of life.)

1 *Sometimes at the end of a day, you might say it has been a really good day* (the interviewer checked for comprehension at this point, but it was always satisfactory, after the evolution of the stimulus in this form): *what are the practical things that turn an ordinary day into a really good day?*

x: That I've achieved all the tasks that I set off to do in the morning, without difficulty and without trouble.

y: It depends on the various parts of my job being lively, and when things get across to people, and on one's relationships with people, and lack of tension in one's personal relationships on the day itself. That seems to be capricious - you can't plan it, but it depends a lot on your tiredness.

z: You always end the day happier if you've done a job you've been putting off.

2 *What do you mean by a "really good day" - can you find another word to describe it? I was being deliberately vague, in my usual way: can you find something more precise than just "good"?*

    x: "Satisfying" - because, one's achieved something and used the time well, as well as had good relationships.

    y: I can't say "satisfying" yet, because the moment of satisfaction is still two and a half years away, as I'm doing a Ph D.

    z: "Occupied" - a day in which I've been engaged in living.

3 *Is there any part of the ordinary routine of living which you would really miss if it was abolished - apart from what you need just in order to keep alive?*

    x: No, I don't think there is anything really.

        I'd miss music a great deal, and books, and human company.

    y: The chores - it would be terrible to sit idle and not have anything to do.

    z: Well, living in such lovely country here, I'd miss not being able to go for a walk every day, or not being able to cut flowers from the garden. And I'd miss sitting in the evening and watching television - when it's good.

4 *What is the most important thing you do each year?*

    x: Going away - abroad - for a holiday. I enjoy it too, but it's my husband's chief thing of the year.

        And I like to visit my more far-away relations, and see old friends, which I can usually do each year.

    y: I'm not old enough to answer that one yet - the year doesn't have any pattern. Except that for the last five years, we've had a baby every other year.

    z: Exams have been so far in my life, because I've had them every year for ages now. And Christmas. And my birthday, but that's mainly for nostalgic reasons.

5 *What is the most important thing you do each week?*

    x: I like to go to Church. Once a week's enough, just to keep with it, "in touch".

    y: I wish there was something, but there isn't, because I'm too pragmatic. I take life very much as it comes, and I tend not to look forward to things.

    z: To get by and do my bits of jobs.

6 *What is the most important thing you do each day?*

> x: Trying to get out a decent day's work, so everyone is satisfied. Next, it's finishing work, because that's the start of leisure time - that's what I work for.
>
> I also keep having purges when it's getting up on time, but they don't last long.

> y: I can't single out any one thing that's more important than the others I can think of.

> z: Praying over things. I used to do it regularly every morning before I had any children. Now I do it at odd times during the day, while I'm washing up and so on.

7 *Have you had any embarrassing experiences (as Wilfred Pickles used to say)?*

> x: I'm sure I must have done, but I don't remember any of them now.

> y: Singularly few that I can think of, that were intensely embarrassing.

> z: Frequently, such as wetting your pants when you're a child, or forgetting to do certain things, or saying something about a third party who turns out to be behind your shoulder.

8 *Who do you admire most? As I said before we began, it might be one person, or several people, or a "class" of persons, someone who's dead or alive or purely imaginary, or no one at all.*

> x: I admire George Bernard Shaw: he wrote such characters, like St Joan. And Barbara Castle, because she has the will-power to get on, and she must know she's unpopular. And Prince Philip, because he says what he thinks.

> y: My father, because he's clever, but never scores off anybody. In many ways he's unappreciated - he's a parson - but he always appears contented. He never appears upset, he appears to have no pride.

> z: Churchill. He epitomises what a human being should be like. He had tremendous personality, humour, many talents, ability as a leader which is so bound up with personality, and *at the same time* lots of human frailties, so he was completely and utterly human. We can read about him and chuckle.
>
> In contrast, I also had great admiration for Eisenhower. But he became rather moralising later - he was slightly too perfect, but he was a close second, because he was totally lacking in any sort of arrogance.

3.2.5   E: Beliefs

1 *Are there any things that you would say*
   (a) you definitely do not believe in, or
   (b) you definitely do believe in?"

   a: x I can't think of anything, except for superficial ones, like ghosts.

   a: y I don't like the whole idea of "not believing in" things. I tend to say, "I just don't know". It's just too final – ghosts, and ESP, for instance.

   a: z I don't believe in heaven and hell, as places, in God as a Father sitting up there, in ghosts, but I'm not sure about the supernatural, such as telepathy and ESP, or in the value of violence, as fascism does.

   b: x I believe in God, of course, but I don't understand him. In other words, in a sense I would describe myself as a Christian agnostic, as it's now possible to do so.

   b: y I believe in Christianity; and a sense of humour; and honesty.

   b: z I do believe in the ultimate goodness of men. Basically, given the right circumstances, and atmosphere, a person is good.

2 *Are there any proverbs or sayings that you think*
   (a) are true, or
   (b) are not true?

   x: Half of them contradict the other half. I believe in most of them, that are not contradicted by the other half - "a stitch in time", for instance. There are a lot of wise sayings.

   y: I think a lot of them are true. There are so many. For instance, "a stitch in time", and "never put off until tomorrow what you can do today". They're built on common sense. Often one will flash through my mind - like, "Empty cans make the most noise".

   z: I don't remember any. Being a scientist, I tend to take a rational view, and feel there is some truth in any view.

3 *Is there anything which other people seem to believe in and you wish that they didn't?*

   x: No, let them believe in what they like - who am I to run their beliefs? You can still put your point of view, though. I often do, about ghosts for instance - I watch for them, for the local paper.

y: I wish people didn't believe in Powellism.

And in materialism, though I'm as guilty as anybody else. I mean the belief
that the car or TV or mortgage are the vital necessities of life. It's all due
to insecurity really, and I'm as guilty of that as anyone, but it's the business
of keeping up with the Joneses, of caring too much about what other people think, for wrong reasons, that gets me - reasons of prestige, snobbery,
position, how it affects them.

I wish people didn't form set prejudices, that they had a tolerant attitude of
being prepared to change their views if they're not right. What we need is
the "constant reappraisal" that the Kennedy's talked about.

I wish people thought more about the arts, and education - that they were
more aware of them.

4 *If you were prepared to die for anything, what would it be?*
(If the response had not already made it clear, the interviewer would additionally ask, *Do you think you would do so?*)

x: I think I'm a prize coward, really. I can only see myself dying to rescue my
little boy, or my wife, or parents. I'd like to think I would, in other situations
too, but one must be realistic about these things. I've never been in the army,
but I've thought about that: I can only say, I suppose the best comes out in
people, when the crunch comes.

y: I don't want to die for "any thing", just in general, like that. I'm afraid I'd
make a poor Christian martyr, but I wouldn't want to say I wouldn't die for
that. I could do something constructive, that may result in my death, but
that wouldn't be dying for it.

z: I haven't thought about this particularly, but I think probably the most
likely way would be for a friend, to rescue him, rather than "for my country"
- probably because I would feel my sacrifice was more significant.

5 *Supposing you had a minute, just time to say a sentence or two, in which
to pass on your philosophy of life to a fifteen year old, what would you say?
I say a fifteen year old, because they're old enough to understand what you
are saying, without having had your experience of life.*
(In the group interviews of teenagers, this was amended to, "*someone a year
or two younger than yourself*".)

x: The important thing is the greatest happiness of the greatest number. And
Christianity. And being kind to others. And you can't be happy yourself if
you don't make other people happy.

y: I would suggest he should be considerate, and have an open mind about
things in general, and "if older people suggest things, don't brush it aside but
analyse it and pick out the meat of the advice".

z: Never be afraid of the truth, about anything and everything, and fear God.
     It's so easy to scramble out of things with a little lie, but you should own up.

6 *What is the most important thing in the world?*
   (If questioned, the interviewer pointed out that this was not quite the same
   as A5.)

x: Love and understanding.

y: As a person, I would say good health. For the world, or people as a whole,
     they ought to have a faith or a belief in something really. Each group would
     have to develop its own.

     (*What is your faith or belief, in fact now that you are no longer happy with
     Roman Catholicism?*)

     My way of life at the moment is that I want to try and live at peace with
     people, and be considerate. I have no very strong feelings about anything in
     particular - "live and let live".

z: To the world at this moment, the most important thing is that every single
     body of people has to be better than everybody else - the Americans and
     Russians, for instance.

7 *What is the most powerful thing in the world?*

x: Love, and/or hate.

y: The two Powers, the USA and USSR - their military potential - at the level
     of "might is right". I would like to think it is truth, honest and loyalty, but
     they're not, at the moment.

z: Money, or is it? Is it people trying to do good?

     It's one of them. Of course, money can be used by people to do good - I
     hadn't thought of it in quite that way before.

8 *What is the best thing in the world?*

x: Love.

y: I can't say, except at the trivial level.

z: The things that move me most deeply and make me most happy are all
     related to human loyalty. There are other specific answers, like a Mozart
     symphony. But I'm prepared to forego music, in order that there may be
     human kindness, on the same principle as the Atlantic convoys - that all
     must move at the speed of the slowest.

9 *What puzzles you most about life? What sort of things makes you say to yourself, "I wonder why..." or "I can't understand ... "?*

> x: I can't understand how people can be unkind and cruel to children and animals. I know I just couldn't bring myself to do it. I can't understand their being made like that, that they can be so rotten.

> y: The biggest puzzle to me, and it must be to anyone who thinks, is, Why we're here at all. I often think, there's no reason why there shouldn't be a universe with inhabitants with a much higher mentality.

> z: What a difficult time some people have, and what an easy time others have, though you never can tell, really.

3.2.6 F: Meanings

1 *Is there anything that you might be prepared to use the word "sacred" of?*

> x: Each person's own beliefs.

> y: To me, Jesus is sacred. Our Lord is sacred - he's the most sacred thing in my life.

> z: People talk about sacred places, but I wouldn't use it at all.

2 *What do you mean or understand by "sacred"?*

> x: Something which is personal, which should be cherished, and which you alone have got. This is where I disagree with western religion's organised sacredness together at a set time on Sunday mornings. The Tibetan monk, and the whole Tibetan nation, were so fanstastically devout - they even frowned on civilisation, and the wheel, until 1949.

> y: It's a belief in something that is almost untouchable, or something that has got to be revered in some way.

> z: Those aspects of life which directly, or indirectly, relate to God.

3 *What would you mean or understand by "holy"?*

> x: The "sacred" isn't religious, but "holy" does mean "religious" to me. I could apply it to everybody's religious symbols. But it's not a word I've clarified yet - it just carries the overtone of incense.

> y: It's very close to "sacred", but again I would understand it in other people's terms. I am impressed by people who are able to see something as holy, such as people who draw strength from a grave. I approve - though my approval is irrelevant, of course - of a personally felt holiness.

> z: "God-fearing" - you can't be a "holy" man, apart from religion; it's an attitude.

4 *Have you had any great moments in your life - the sort you'll never forget?*

    x: Yes: entering examinations, and passing them, and getting jobs, and getting married, and being present at the birth of one's children, and coming to decisions about things like the way you live and being a Christian.

    y: Yes, the revivalist meeting I attended with a school-friend, when I was about sixteen, for one. I had a conversion experience. I didn't used to go to Church often, but I took it more seriously than many of my friends who went regularly, and I had an experience of an abyss at my feet, as if the ground was dropping away. But I couldn't help asking myself whether I was acting it all. I took it extremely seriously, but I gave it up about four weeks later, because I was not in real contact with a church, and I was under a constant strain of being over-conscientious throughout the day. But the effects have continued. For instance, I felt more guilty afterwards about not going to church.

        Then there have been some moments in the theatre, even in Gilbert and Sullivan, and with ballet especially - I've sometimes been absolutely raptured then - and in West Side Story.

        Then there have been some moments in Germany that I'll never forget. Like walking up a Tiepolo staircase in a Baroque residence in Wurzburg and suddenly hearing an orchestra rehearsing Mozart. And walking into the Baroque cathedral in Salzburg - the whole thing broke on you, as you went through the door, and there was an organ recital going on too, just as though it was all for you. And very often simple things, like a magnificent view, especially in the mountains, or being up on the moors, by myself, or when you seem to be alone - that's partly because of "Wuthering Heights", which I must have read about eight times since I was twelve years old.

    z: The day we were married, when everyone greeted me in such a friendly way; and passing my exams, and the day I'd heard I'd got the job going to sea; and my husband's face, when we decided we were expecting.

5 *What, if anything, would you say they've shown you of the meaning of life?*

    x: I associate their happiness with some insight into what makes life meaningful, what it's about. Raymond Williams' novel, "Border Country", talks about people who had an answer to that, in my opinion.

    y: No, they haven't shown me anything really. I haven't found anyone with the same views. I've never been able to sort myself out - I haven't really sorted myself out.

    z: Yes. I've learnt the basic pattern of life, from people and from things that have happened. So you learn how to plan your own course.

        The basic pattern is that you should be a good, honest person, an active member of the community. It's not easy to put simply. Someone else might say "To feather your own nest as easily as possible" - that's easy to put. But I don't want to say that, and what I do want to say is not so easy to put.

6 *Whether or not you would use the word "God" yourself, what does the word*
mean to you?

x: I do use the term "God", but it is difficult to define. I'd say, There is a God,
for want of a better word, whether it be the Buddha, Jesus, Thor, or ....

There's definitely a being who is called God.

y: I can't imagine living life without Him. That's enough.

z: In terms of this figure sitting up there watching everything ... I think it's
unimportant, but I can't get beyond thinking it's still up there.

I agree with Blake's idea. He's feeling for it, but I don't think it's accepted
as orthodox by Christians. I wouldn't use the word myself, but I have used
it, to refer to the "spirit of humanity", which I think is what Blake means by
it. It's to do with spiritual communication between people. It connects with
the experience of beauty and so on that we've discussed - with a higher plane
of things.

7 *What would you mean by "true religion", so that you might describe a person*
as "truly religious"?

x: I think what I mean is ... I don't really know. I know what I mean, but I
can't put it into words.

An *attitude* can be very religious, without going to church. You might still
have Church in you, even if you've missed one or two weeks.

y: It's certainly not living in church. It's human acts of kindness and sympathy.

z: I could apply it to someone who's mad keen on cricket. So that means, so
long as he carried his religion into all his life.

8 *Have you ever known anyone like that?*

x: Yes, several - spiritual people. I've great admiration for them. I'm impressed
with the fact that they don't try and thrust it onto you.

y: One or two people.

z: I don't think so.

9 *If a fifteen year old - again! - came to you and asked you to to tell him how*
   he could always distinguish right from wrong, good from bad, what would
   you say?
   (If asked for further guidance, the interviewer said: *"He says, when I was a*
   young child, it was easy to tell the difference, because if my parents told me
   to do something it was automatically right, and if they said, Don't, then I
   knew it was wrong; but now I've no longer got them to tell me, and I've
   moved away from home, into all sorts of situations, and I cannot always tell
   what is right and what is wrong. Can you give me any sort of rule?")

   x: Your conscience will immediately tell you. But you can also ask yourself, Is
        it done by most people or not? If it is exceptional, then be careful; but if
        people you respect do it, then it's all right.

   y: To what extent does it help other people. The good would help many, the
        bad may help some.

   z: If the fifteen year old knew something of Christianity, I'd say, "Is it in accord
        with the will of Christ?".

10 *And finally: Who are you?*
   (If guidance was asked in this case, in fact none was given, beyond slowly
   repeating the question, to allow greater time for it to be comprehended.)

   x: What do you mean by that?

        I'm just another human being. I get the feeling my own family might miss
        me. But I've lived too quiet a life for anyone else to miss me.

   y: Yahweh's answer: I am that I am.

   z: Will my name do?

        I'm the wife of so-and-so, the housewife of so-and-so ...

        I'm a person.

        But what nationality, even, am I, at the moment? I don't even know that at
        the moment.

3.3 The perceived Commitments

3.3.1 The Forty Themes

The evolution of the Identi-kit Interview, in its triple form, may have solved the problem as to how summarily to present the data, in a way which also enables readers to draw their own conclusions, and check those drawn by others. However, it did nothing to reveal what conclusions could or should be drawn, by the initial student or by any other.

The study's aim, and the interview's method, both suggested that the appropriate means of content analysis was *verstehen*, followed by comparison. It was necessary to think and feel one's way into the mind of the speaker, as that was indicated by the response; and then, through one's knowledge of alternative mind-sets, to come to appreciate what it affirmed or denied, or what it simply omitted. By a process of phenomenological *époché*, one would first "go native"; and then, by dint of one's ability to return to other angles of vision, one would begin the process of placing that "subjective-object" of experience, in a wider perspective.

The process bore some similarity to that of literary criticism; although when the language and culture are common to the data and to the critic (whether at first or second hand), it occurs so spontaneously as to be virtually unconscious. It also bears some similarity to the processes involved in meditation, in the Christian rather than the Hindu or Buddhist sense, as recommended for instance in the Ignatian and Salesian methods.

Such an approach may appear to lack the apparent precision and objectivity of statistical methods of content-analysis, such as word-count; yet in the last analysis they too depend upon an individual and subjective apprehension of what is *meant*, either by the words themselves or else by the other resulting data. Whatever the technique, the final check, like the process of communication itself, is provided by the opportunity to be inter-subjective, and hence make an independent judgement. Indeed, the same test is automatically used, at each stage, by the original analyst.

The interview schedule comprised some fifty stimuli, so the resulting triple identi-kit interview was composed of a hundred and fifty responses. Accompanied by, or followed by, the attempt to tease out their implications as fully as possible, each of them must have received an hour's initial reflection, cogitation, meditation. In the course of thus composing one hundred and fifty short essays on the responses, certain elements kept recurring, which gave rise to forty main Themes. These disparate Themes were then grouped into fours, and given ten sub-headings. The ten groups were then found to fall into three areas, which were labelled the Inner Scene, the Outer Scene, and the Other Scene. The latter, which contained four groups of four Themes each, as against the three groups in each of the preceding areas, was deliberately given a crucially ambiguous label, posing one of the key questions requiring analysis.

The manner in which the forty Themes were articulated (first, in the sense of being made explicit, and then, in the sense of being joined up with each other), is, of course, identical with that in which the stimuli were, first of all, individually devised, and, only subsequently, arranged in relation to each other, and, finally, given some kind of heading. It is considered important to record the chronology of this process, in order that the emphasis may continue to be placed upon the individual "bricks", rather than upon the structures into which they have been placed. They may be disparate; to judge by our knowledge of religious experience in other "systems", they almost certainly will be. Yet it is, first and foremost, these one hundred and fifty Responses which are *data* ("given"), and then, clearly in secondary place, the forty summary and interpretive Themes. Thus, their positioning in patterns is (again) for ease of presentation, and is to be regarded as arbitrary rather than as being in any way absolute.

3.3.2   The Inner Scene (i): the Nature of the Self

> (a) I have a self
> (b) The self is human
> (c) The self is sacred
> (d) I have gifts

The search for implicit religion may (but need not necessarily) be thought inevitably to involve a considerable degree of revelation of the self. Certainly, in the absence of any other agreed definition of religion in general, and in the absence of any agreement as to the content of this putative religion in particular, it is a logical place to begin this description of the Themes present in the data. However, it is more than merely logically unobjectionable. Phenomenologically it is imperative to begin with the self (or otherwise, climactically, to end with it).

That every response was self-revealing was to be expected, in view of the nature of the quest and method. What was not necessarily to be expected was the ease with which even the most personal questions (eg A6, A8, A9, A10, A11, C7) were accepted (even when they were hardly answered), without spoiling the tenor of the interview; likewise, the readiness of respondents to accept as personal even questions (eg A2, A5, F6) which, grammatically, were general; also, their obvious interest in their selves; and, above all, the willingness of respondents to share with the interviewer their (hitherto, largely private) subjectivity.

Although some may find it strange to begin an account of a system that is potentially religious with the Self, it is by no means unique. Classical Buddhism, and many current presentations of Christianity, often do so. In each of those cases, however, it is a jumping-off point, from which to be redeemed, rather than, as in this case, the foundation or conclusion - the primary, given, reality.

In this respect the "concrete jungle", with its intense awareness of the self, is reminiscent of the North Indian plains in the hot season: for (R C Zaehner, 1959: Introduction) the primary experience of the Upanishads, with which the historical development of Indian religion began, was the immortality of the soul (cp the indestructibility of the self). Indeed, for Jung "the archetype of the self is the most important element composing the unconscious", and is psychologically indistinguishable from the God-image (A Moreno, 1974: 60f.). P L Berger (1965) offers an explanation: "The other world, which religion [has] located in a transcendental reality, is now located within consciousness itself". In that consciousness an inner and unknowable unconscious, reflects an outer and incomprehensible complexity.

The Nature of the Self cannot be so much described as delineated, for it is, of itself, ineffable. Had such a question been included in the schedule, the response might well have shown that this was the popular view (cp T Luckmann, 1967: 110-111), as with the conception of God (N Smart, 1968: 16; P V Martinson, 1987). The first Theme of all therefore simply states the belief (whether it be called dogma, conclusion, hypothesis, guess, or wish), "I have a self". As R Otto says of "this [numinous] mental state", "like every absolutely primary and elementary datum, while it admits of being discussed ... [it] cannot be strictly defined" (1959: 21). This is the same difficulty as that which "archaic thought" solves by means of "a mythological model", "obedience" to which is necessary "in order to become a man" (M Eliade, 1958: xiv).

The last of the stimuli, "Who are you?", gave the best opportunity of describing the self and its nature. However, respondents divided, clearly yet unpredictably (by way of the customary sociological variables, such as class, education, marital status, or religiosity), into two camps. On the one hand were those who thought the question rather pointless, and answered in terms of categories and relationships which they acknowledged to be obvious (hence their opinion of the question). On the other hand were those who (equally immediately, for it was not new to them) considered the question to be profound, and confessed explicitly, or by tone of voice (neither of which would have been picked up by pre-coded questionnaire), that they ended their efforts by similarly naming the obvious categories and relationships, only because they could find no other satisfactory answer.

Although quiet may be the consequence equally of acknowledging the presence of a vacuum, or of ignoring or denying its existence, the qualitative difference between the two kinds of silence may be as great as that between the respect which inhibits the naming of the holy one, and the dismissal of the very question of its existence as unworthy of serious attention. Unobtrusive though it may be, the interview material is redolent with the former attitude towards the Self. Thus, "Do you feel there is anything lacking in your life?", prompts the answer (A 11: y): " ... Now there are only things that are lacking in me - maturity, ideas, strength, and a clear idea of where I'm going" (cp B2: x and z; C7: x, y and z; F6: x, y and z).

Just as the Self, like most divinities (and all persons), is known by its works, rather than simply through being — so this acceptance of its reality is known through its accompanying attitudes, rather than by explicit statements (had they been prompted). That attitude, as already indicated, varies between reverence, and resignation (or exasperation), within the same individual, in the course of the same interview. The conviction itself, however, must be the primary bedrock of whatever implicit religion the interviews may be held to indicate.

The self is intuited as real, because the facticity of the individual's experience (of it, and of the experience of it, of individuality as a whole, rather than simply of Cartesian thinking), will not be denied. Consciousness includes self-consciousness; I cannot escape from me, or hopefully, even from "I" (cp Psalm 139). The public culture may ignore its existence; the official logic may not know how to account for it; the moral society may not allow its communication; but private experience is responsible for a conviction (cp John 16: 8, and B F Westcott 1958: 227-8) which represents a confessional "triumph" (cp R Hoggart 1958: 94) over public assumption, which is comparable in its significance to Luther's "Ich kann nicht anders".

The nearest possible approach to a definition of the self may be its categorisation as personal, and therefore as impossible to define, and a "confession" (admission) of belief in it. However, its perimeter may be delineated in triangular shape, in the form of "its" being simultaneously human and sacred, and "my" possessing gifts.

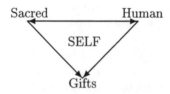

The "humanity" of the self is mainly moral, and yet is ambiguous. Of considerable practical importance, it cannot be understood without prior consideration of the nature of a yet more fundamental apprehension. It must, therefore, be considered in conjunction with its paradoxical contrary: its sacredness. Whether the self is seen as human and nevertheless sacred, or as human and therefore sacred, it is certainly seen as both human *and* sacred.

An intuition as fundamental as the possession of a Self is usually (if not always) both evaluative and ontological. Thus, in the "classical" period of the study of religion *per se*, R Otto insisted that the specifically holy (the numinous) was "prior" to the apprehension of both the real and the moral. Durkheim similarly insisted that the experience of the sacred was the *sine qua non* of all other categorisation.

That the debate was allowed to lapse into commentary upon the "founding fathers", was no doubt due to a combination of the ambiguity in the priority they accorded to religious experience, and to the dangers inherent in either agreement or disagreement with them. Was the "priority" chronological, or phenomenal? If it was chronological, was religion therefore a necessary universal, or outgrown? If it was phenomenal, should it be encouraged, or discouraged? It was no accident that two of those (P L Berger & T Luckman, 1963) who criticised sociology for ignoring religion (and lamented the degeneration of the sociology of religion into mere ecclesiastical market-research), should also have pioneered the return of the study of religion to the centre of attempts to understand society.

Be the fundamental apprehension as it may, by the time it reaches the light of day, so to speak, the Self can be described as both human and sacred. Both "secular humanists" (eg A J Ayer, 1968; J Huxley, 1964), and "Christian humanists", may be inclined to assume the affinity of those two adjectives. The interviews indicate, however, that each of them is evaluatively ambiguous, and their conjunction, paradoxical. If the existence of the Self is sensed as *mysterium*, then its character, as immediately apprehended, makes it simultaneously *tremendum et fascinans* (R Otto, 1959: chapter IV).

With only one possible exception (and that, E4: x, was reluctantly admitted), the concept of "human nature" and of "human", throughout the identi-kit interviews, is always associated with "human weakness", and therefore with fallibility. Two examples may be quoted:

> "Of course, it [the world] couldn't possibly be perfect, human nature being what it is" (C1: y)
> "... We're only human, there's got to be something the matter with us" (C6: x)

Indeed, if some network could eavesdrop on the entire nation's conversing, it would show that "human" was most often used in conjunction with "only", in the sense of "merely". Indeed, an entire industry, of politicians and writers, is devoted to proving that golden idols have feet of clay. Thus, ideological Humanism is far removed from the everyday understanding of human-ness, in England if not throughout the United Kingdom. The highest claim for humanity that this usage can be said to make, is to hint that it is a biological species with a difference; that, though part of nature, it is yet unique; that "human nature" is, as well as natural, somehow super-natural.

Yet "human" is not simply a pejorative term. Eisenhower might be admired because he is (unpretentiously) human; and Churchill is admired because he is (richly) human (F8: z). Each is, therefore, "so" human (cp the Greek *arete*, the Hindi *pukkha*, and the Christian concept of purity). Eisenhower allowed others to be human, by giving them space to become so; Churchill enabled others to be human, by vicariously involving them in his own humanity.

To be human thus becomes the basis of a solidarity. It progresses (qualitatively, rather than evaluatively) from "common humanity", in the sense of uniformity; through a warmer sense of sympathy with fellow-feelings, fellow-suffering, and fellow-sinners ("humanity in common"); to an explosive joy and common participation in "a shared humanity". Thus, Churchill's "foibles" prevented his "richness" becoming a put-down for his fellow human beings, without detracting from his achievement which (for one interviewee) was primarily his *joie de vivre*.

Upon reflection it is this high valuation, of a humanity which is simultaneously errant, and yet transcendent of both errors and achievements, that allowed such questions as A8, A10, A11, D7, E4, E9 to be asked; and thus allowed verbal games to be played, and the self to be used as evidence in the entire exercise.

The ambiguity in the popular evaluation of the human ("anthropology"), although reminiscent of Biblical usage, may provide further scope for consideration in the context of the modern history of religions. The ambiguity in the evaluation of the sacred, on the other hand, is better known to students of religion than to contemporary practitioners of it, or to popular usage. The latter require the scholar (or the traditionalist) to point out that the admirable, the desirable, the love-able, is not all there is to the sacred. It also contains that which is off-putting (if not "down-putting"); that which is *in*imitable and untouchable; that which simply is, whether it is love-able or not.

At the time of the interviews (1968-69), it was commonplace among the more *avant-garde* Christian clergy and theologians, that industrial man did not use or understand the word "sacred", because he lacked the experience which it described. Levitical prohibitions on touching the Ark of the Lord, therefore, were described as archaic, esoteric, anthropological data, on a ritual par with cosmological beliefs about a flat earth or spatial heaven. It came as a matter of some interest, therefore, to discover that even those who would not use the term, did understand it; and that they understood it in terms that practitioners and students of religion the world over, and throughout history, would recognise: as meaning, respectively, "personal" (i.e. existential), "untouchable", and "relating to God" (F2: x, y, z).

"Beliefs" were shown, explicitly in the dominant answer and implicitly in the others, to be primary locations of sacredness. Asked, "Is there anything you might be prepared to use the word *sacred* of?" (before, as usual, being asked in a general way what it meant to them), the three representative respondents said:

"Each person's own beliefs"
"To me, Jesus is sacred. Our Lord is sacred - he's the most sacred thing in my life"
"People talk about sacred places, but I wouldn't use it at all". (F1: x, y, z)

Just as the Self overcomes its ineffability and becomes available for discussion, in a relatively relaxed or "profane" (better, *secular*) way, through the concept of "human nature", so it becomes available in a manner more demanding of respect, through the concept of beliefs. The sacredness that is attributed to them is wholly unrelated to any abstract quality of objective truth. It derives entirely from their closeness to the self. They are its property (almost in an Aristotelian sense), chosen and possessed by the individual, and yet obligatory and possessive of him, revelatory of his inner being (and of his judgement upon himself). The negative dimension that unavoidably accompanies such a positive as the sacred, is vividly illustrated in the opening passion of response E3: x: "Is there anything other people seem to believe in, and you wish they didn't?": "No, let them believe in what they like - who am I to run their beliefs?"

These beliefs are, in the first instance, religious beliefs. This must seem strange, in view of the low importance attached to theological doctrine in this culture. On the one hand, however, even less importance is given to religious cult or community; and on the other hand, these beliefs, although seen as religious, are primarily ethical in character, not theological. "What does the Lord require of thee, but to do justly, and to love mercy, and to walk humbly with thy God" (Micah 6: 8), would find ready acceptance, as morally demanding, spiritually humble, and theologically unpretentious - if, indeed, it were not simply taken for granted, as obvious.

It is their ethical character that makes them so revealing. "I believe", if sincere, is always a statement of fact, about the believer, if about nothing else. Faith is always thus "confessed", just as sin is. Both confessions are of facts, personal revelations. They are also dangerous, although blackmail about the faith that is confessed ("I thought you said you were a Christian"), is easier to get away with socially, than blackmail about sins. Both are therefore hostages to fortune, requiring trust in the hearers, if not in the gods. All this is intuitively sensed, at least in part. So confessions are difficult and embarrassing to receive and hear, as well as to give and speak (cp Chapter 5.3.6.2).

This double observation, that beliefs are sacred because they are revealing of the Self, is borne out by the acceptability of expressions of belief on the part of professional believers, such as clergy and politicians; but only so long as they restrict their statements to their professional interests. Otherwise, the expression of belief always runs the risk of becoming "insincere", "wearing your heart upon your sleeve", "being hypocritical". They are classic instances of how, "to be personal", has come to mean "being private": that is, only available for sharing under strict safeguards, with intense emotion. Thus the greatest credit is given to the individual whose behaviour not only matches his beliefs, but whose acts of kindness match his charitable ideals - at least in *both* being kept secret. (Whether as cause or effect, such dominical sayings as Matthew 7: 15-20 or 21-23, and Matthew 6: 2-4 or 5-6, find immediate *rapport* in this culture.)

The positive and negative, inviting and inhibitory, participatory and private, open and closed, aspects of the sacredness of the self, which become available for description and analysis through the contrasting concepts of humanity and belief, reappear united in the fourth Theme of this initial quartet: the acknowledgement, which is a little less intense than a conviction or a confession, that, empirically, "I have gifts". The two that appear in the identi-kit interview are neither impersonal *data*, nor personal achievements, but simply "life" (B3: x) and "health" (E6: y; C8: z also stresses the importance of health, but without the same implication of its being a gift). This, then, completes the triangle that surrounds the ineffable *mandala* at the heart of the interviews.

Stimulus A10 allowed for a distinction between a theistic and a naturalistic approach: "What do you feel most grateful for in life, or most glad about?" The distinction may not have been meaningless to all the respondents, but it was in fact ignored by all but one of the chosen trio; although even he, in the course of giving his answer (A10: z), seemed to decide to ignore it.

There is, therefore, the making of a paradox, logically speaking. The natural properties and assets of the Self are widely seen as gifts (cp also B3: x). This may appear to suppose a giver, even a personal one. Yet the respondents would hesitate to posit any super-natural donor, upon the basis of their own reception of life and health. At most, they would wish to thank such a being for what "nature" had "given" them.

Just as the sacredness of the Self does not extend, without diminution, to all the properties of the self, so the interpretation of some of these assets as gifts, does not extend, without diminution, to the feeling of gratitude and belief in a Giver. However difficult institutional practitioners may find it to understand, people find it possible to feel, and be, grateful, *without* saying "Thank you"; just as it is possible to "pray for", without praying verbally, or to apologise, without feeling guilt. In the same way, a conviction in the existence of a sacred Self does not necessarily lead to a similar apprehension of any pre-existent self, either human or super-human. "Yahweh's answer: I am that I am" (F 10:y), would be seen as describing the human situation, not underlying it.

3.3.3 The inner scene (ii): the Life of the Self

> (a) My self is on a conveyor-belt
> (b) My self has a life of its own
> (c) I am content with my round
> (d) I am happy if I can get by

The conviction of the Self's existence, and the conceptual space it occupies, in terms of its innate sacredness and ideal humanity, and its necessary "gifts", were described, in the first quartet of themes, in static and self-contained terms. Into this outline picture must now, in this section, be woven the temporality of the Self, and, in the following section, its relationship with other Selves. Respondents were highly conscious of both dimensions, not only because of their theoretical significance, but because of the extent of their observed influence upon them. Thus, time is the background of all these four Themes.

The first two Themes of the quartet express lessons that have been drawn from this life-long experience, and from the self-observation that has been in process since around puberty. If "proverbial wisdom" is usually concerned with life outside the self, such as other people and the seasons, then this might be better compared with "spiritual direction", or a popular form of autopsychotherapy. (Indeed, the time has come for an account which not only treats traditional Eastern religions as psychologies, after the manner of G & L B Murphy, 1968, but treats Western religions in the same way – and also treats modern psychologies as spiritualities, and treats unofficial psychologies as empirical, albeit unsystematic, wisdom, neither ignoring the uniformities, nor disguising the discontinuities.)

The time-orientation of contemporary culture, both as reality and as value, is conveyed powerfully throughout childhood. "Growing up" seems the supreme goal. "Be your age" is, perhaps, the supreme rebuke. Certainly, "Stop being childish: grow up", is too serious to be said by one adult to another (however appropriate it may sometimes seem). It comes as no surprise, therefore, to find awareness of the temporal dimension throughout the interviews. Examples, according to approximate ascending age, include: " ... I know it's a common complaint of people of my age ... " (A11: z); "I can't say *satisfying* yet, because the moment of satisfaction is still two and a half years away" (D2: y); " ... Samuel Beckett had a great influence on me a year ago. I was in a play of his, and I'm recovering from it still..." (B3: y); "I'm not old enough to answer that one yet ..." (D4: y); "If it was perfect by our present ideas, then it wouldn't be so then" (C1: z); "That's one of the things that has come with age" (A9: y).

The Theme was articulated as, "My Self is on a conveyor-belt", because the image conveys the sense of relentless movement, independent of the self. In the middle of the present century it had the same symbolic but ambiguous fascination that the microchip has in the latter part. The attraction is that perennially exercised by the concept of perpetual motion, and currently by the television screen: by experience of constant flux, thus asserting life and developing identity. The fear is that of being swept along, and chewed up by that which moves, so that separate identity disappears. The relationship with this passage of time, and the knife-edge quality of the difference between "identifying oneself with" and "becoming identical with", is reminiscent of the medieval western distinction between revering the creation and adoring the creator.

The second Theme, "My Self has a life of its own", bestows upon the self a matching sense of independence and movement. It is this "schizophrenic" distance, and the equal reality of each pole in the life of the Self, that allows "I" to exercise pastoral care of "me". For, just as the self cannot un-discover itself, neither can the Self of which it is conscious be entirely subject to its control. The classic instance must be the almost-universal mythology of "falling in", or "out of" (romantic) love. It is at this point, focused in the concept of the unconscious, that the fatalism that must be present, in any culture with a notion of cause-and-effect, strikes home in contemporary society. The interviews indicate that, at least in this country, the "deeper" self is not so much manipulable (as P L Berger 1965 tends to suggest), as determined by factors, often within its own past, which are beyond its control.

Two responses in particular demonstrate this "fatalistic" acceptance of unpredictability in the life of the Self. (That "the spirit" thus "blows where it wills" indicates, on empirical grounds, that even "science" does not have the last word: that the Self transcends it.) D1: y and A1: y discuss the causality of experience which, although ordinary, is nevertheless highly valued: "a really good day", and "what" "you enjoy most in life". In each case certain causes, which have obvious subjective significance, are specified: "one's relationships with people, and lack of tension", and lack of "tiredness", in the one case; and, "things of the moment, like ... a drink with one or two friends, or walking, especially alone", in the other case. However, in each case a space is left, in the web of causality, for an element which is critically important, yet unpredictable. It is subject to its own law, rather than to any outside control, even by the individual concerned; yet (s)he can hardly know that law.

The individual thus becomes the *object* of his/her own subjective life. The inner life is all-important, but (in contrast at least to the typology of D Riesman *et al.*, 1950) it is not ultimately "inner-directed". The two respondents already cited, say that "a really good day" seems to be capricious - "you can't plan it, but it depends a lot on your tiredness"; and, "it [enjoyment] depends on my mood". "Fatology" (to borrow the expression of S C Brown, 1969) is thus an existential matter: "fate", if named at all, is not so much an independent reality, as a way of referring to that which is natural but unknowable.

Relatively speaking, their adherents, although so numerous, are justified in saying that they "don't take the stars (D Newton 1980, 1982) [or mechanical games of chance] seriously". They are known to have been "fixed", mere games, artificial mythologies and rituals. Nevertheless, they appeal as *parables* of the infinitely complex, natural chains of cause-and-effect.

Contemporary life is sometimes pictured as being both conformist and yet competitive, and its participants as being both alienated from, and yet ardently committed to, their routine, of work and television, chores and outings. However, the other pair of Themes in this quartet suggest that this picture is inadequate, and indeed inaccurate. One Theme, "I am content with my round", suggests that respondents were, if not enamoured of it, yet far from hostile to it. The other, "I am happy if I can get by", suggests that they are, if not passionate about its goals, nevertheless pleased if they are able to keep "in the swim", with their heads above the water.

Society may not fit the individual (or vice-versa) as comfortably as a glove, but, according to these interviews, their relationship is neither a "drama between individual needs and social realities", nor a "balancing act between fulfilment and frustration" (P L Berger, 1965). The individual is aware of his individuality, but pleased to play the roles allotted to him. Thus (D3: x, z):

"Is there any part of the ordinary routine of living which you would really miss if it were abolished ...?"

"No, I don't think there is anything really. I'd miss music a great deal; and books, and human company."

"Well, living in such lovely country here, I'd miss not being able to go for a walk every day, or not being able to cut flowers from the garden. And I'd miss sitting in the evening and watching television - when it's good".

This air of contentment with the ordinary round is partly due to the fact that it is seen as a challenge. Role-playing is like juggling: simply to keep all the oranges in the air at once, is success, of a kind. Survival remains an achievement. Life remains critical; that is to say, a constant crisis, in which judgement is delivered, in a psychological, spiritual and moral manner, if not sociologically, religiously, or theologically. This knife-edge quality is clearly established by school days, continues throughout working life, and by no means ceases upon retirement. Examples may therefore again be given in an ascending age order.

"Exams have been [the most important thing each year] so far in my life, because I've had them every year for ages now ... " (D4: z).

"Trying to get out a decent day's work [is the most important thing each day], so everyone is satisfied ... I also keep having purges when it's getting up on time, but they don't last long" (D6: x)

"Of course, I fear being a failure, and so on" (A8: x)

"Everyone who works hourly has the fear of redundancy at the back of his mind, always" (A8: z)

"To get by and do my bits of jobs is the most important thing each week" (D5: z)

" ... I don't worry any more. That's one of the things that has come with age. I've faced so many of the crises that an *average* person has to face ... but I do sometimes get *concerned*" (A9: y).

In the past it has been suggested (eg M J Bayley, 1973) that most pastoral care, including counselling, is exercised, not by official agencies, either statutory or voluntary, but by unorganised "neighbouring". It may now be suggested that there is, however, a still larger volume of pastoral care, which is exercised by the individual, of his or her own self. It qualifies for inclusion in the same category because, far from being simply self-concern, self-defence, or self-regard, it is exercised consciously, conscientiously, and self-consciously, critically and self-critically. The self that is so real and so valued, is watched and learned from, guarded and tended.

Time takes its meaning, then, not from the working-out of an historical or divine purpose, but from the development of the life of the interviewee's Self.

3.3.4   The inner scene (iii): the Relationship of the Self with other Selves

        (a) The self comes to life in relationships
        (b) An economy of inter-dependent selves
        (c) An ethic of acknowledging self-hood
        (d) A working principle of "from I to the other"

The space occupied by the inmost self was sketched round in the first group of Themes, and given its temporal dimension in the second group. In this group it is placed in the context of other, similar entities.

Respondents frequently spoke of relationships (that relatively lengthy and abstract word itself was frequently used), and of the pleasure they derived from them. Indeed, their view is expressed in the first of these four Themes: "The self comes to life in relationship" - a "life" that, more than mere existence, is qualitative in character (cp John 10: 10). Thus, however superficial the *public* psychology, *popular* wisdom in the *private* mode would seem to be close to much traditional thought. This is neatly illustrated by K Cragg: "Solipsism, for the African view, contradicts what it states. There is no *ipse*, no man himself, that is *solus*. One cannot be, without inter-being" (1968: 150).

The responses exemplifying this Theme are too numerous for all of them to be reproduced, and too plain in their meaning to profit from further commentary. They are, however, capable of distinction, according to the "object" of the relationship specified. This includes: other people (eg A1: x, y and z; A6:

x, y and z; A7a: x, y and z; A7b: y and z; A10: y; and D1: y); nature, both cultivated and wild (D3: z); the Divine (F6: y, and D5: x - "important", in this series of stimuli, being intended, and taken, as existential rather than moral); and their own (A1: y).

The kind of social psychology present in the interviews goes well beyond Hobbes's struggle of all against all, or Locke's marriage of mutual convenience. It is, however, social, rather than corporate: each depends upon others, and each may become "party to" (a limited number of) others; but neither the whole, nor any of its parts, is dependent upon either the individual or the totality, for its existence and identity. The order of the day, according to this widespread private wisdom, is neither corporatism nor individualism (each of the poles being an imaginary abstraction), but (to coin a word) "societism". Thus, sociology has come into its own, because it studies, neither society *tout simple*, nor any particular society as a whole, but an entity of indeterminate boundary, which is yet large enough to comprehend all these particular experienced relationships.

This Theme is expressed as, "An economy of inter-dependent selves", because it is from the economy (in the narrower sense) that illustrations can most easily be drawn, to illustrate a principle that is seen to apply to (what used to be called) "the divine economy". Two responses to the same stimulus will illustrate the point (D8: x and y), before turning to the other pair of Themes in this group.

> "What's the most useful job in the world - including a housewife for instance, as a job?"

> "There are so many, and every one hangs upon another - the dustman has one of the most useful."

> "A doctor, or a teacher - in the widest sense of the word, not just a schoolteacher. No, being a parent, especially if they're also a good teacher."

Whatever the precise relationships of ethics and religions, the intuitions upon which ethics are based will always be important for accounts of implicit religion. Not least is this so in this country, whose religion "passed straight from the mystical to the moral without ever being sacramental" (C H E Smyth: book review in the "Church Times", about August 1974). Indeed, J Baillie speaks (1929: chapter VI: 4) of their "single psychological source"; and K Marx (1859: Preface) of morality as being more fundamental than theology. Clerics (or their opponents), then, should not be surprised when the British public shows that it wishes to retain religious education in schools, yet understands by it mainly moral education.

The heart of the ethical insight which is apparent in the interviews may be expressed as, "An ethic of acknowledging self-hood". G Gorer likewise speaks (1955: 286) of the importance given to "consideration and delicacy for the feelings of other people". Its seriousness as an ethic can be seen in its use as a criterion for self-judgement (eg A7: y and z). Indeed, the passion and the fluency of the evidence for this Theme (eg A6: x, y, z; A7a: x, z; A7b: x, y, z; etc) may be seen as evidence of its close connection with the very sacredness of the self.

That this Theme so often received negative expression suggests it is the taboo side of that coin, or that they are "Siamese twins". The all-important part to be played in the study of religion by evidence of a negative character, on account of the inability to speak more adequately in a positive mode of that which is ultimately ineffable, was, indeed, deliberately allowed for in the interview schedule.

Closely linked with such an ethic, is an epistemology that underlies it and therefore much else. This can be expressed, in the words of the concluding Theme of this group (and of the area described as the Inner Scene), as, "A working principle of *from I to the other*". The principle expresses, and is based on, the belief in the common humanity of every self. Similarly, the ethic of acknowledging self-hood expresses, and is based on, the sense of the self's sacredness. Both the epistemological and the ethical principles, like the economic paradigm, arise out of the empirical observation that the self comes to life in relationships.

Descartes' systematic and universal doubting, to the point where he could not deny his own intellect and hence existence, has been seen (eg B Russell 1946: 580-591) as the epistemological point of take-off for modern knowledge and philosophy. Here we have its religious companion. It extends the Cartesian *cogito* beyond the cerebral, and adds to the concern with the existence of the individual's self an equal concern with the existence of other selves. Thus, *cogito, ergo sum*, becomes *Cogito* (or *sensio*; or *scio*; or *praesto me: I feel* - with all the ambiguity of the English verb; or *I know*, with the same ambiguity; or *I accomplish*; or *I stand before myself); ergo omnes sunt* (therefore they all are).

Examples of this pair of Themes (colloquially put: If it hurts me, it must hurt him) are legion. The ethic is evident in responses A6: x, y, z; A7a: x, z; A7b: x, y, z; A9: x, y, z; C7: y. The epistemology is evident in responses A5: z, & E9: x. That response, indeed, may be quoted to illustrate both Themes: "I can't understand how people can be unkind and cruel to children and animals. I know I just couldn't bring myself to do it ..."

So, following the example of some "explicit" religions, the ontological and evaluative aspects of the Inner Scene which have been enumerated in these three groups of Themes, may now be summarised in credal form, as:

> I believe in my self,
> in the all-pervading influence of time,
> and in other selves as in mine.

3.3.5 The Outer Scene (i): the Received World

(a) Proverbial wisdom
(b) A square-shaped world
(c) The Atlas effect
(d) Money

The three groups of Themes that comprised "the Inner Scene", progressed outwards in their concern: from the core nature of the self, via its temporal character, to its relationship with its peers. The three groups of Themes that comprise "the Outer Scene" move in the contrary direction: from the "received world", via that "psycho-social reality" which spans the self and other selves, to the individual's overall conception and judgement of his or her Outer Scene. In those areas that are most "personal" in their significance, and thus impinge most deeply upon them, however, repondents' interest is as intense as it is in similar parts of the Inner Scene. Thus, in the first group of Themes, the private experience of carrying something of the world's sufferings upon one's shoulders ("the Atlas effect") is more significant than the traditional emphasis of the public culture upon proverbs, or the new emphasis upon television, or the accustomed emphasis upon money.

Proverbs have always been an important medium for the transfer of human wisdom. As important in the history of religion, as they are in human culture, they have bridged the gap between popular and official culture, between implicit and explicit religion. However, their true home is with the people; for both their inclusion in scripture, and their contradiction by prophets, are acknowledgement of their pre-existing authority.

Collections of them have been made, from the time of King Solomon, to that of W G Smith (ed), 1935, for instance. Histories of them, individually and as a *genre*, have been written (cp J E Heseltine and references in W G Smith (ed), 1935). Particular sayings have likewise been analysed (eg in S C Brown, 1969, and B Dunham, 1962). However, their overall place in continuing cultural and religious life may have been under-estimated. Perhaps they have fallen into a no-man's land, somewhere between studies of traditional folk lore and dialect, and studies of contemporary culture and slang. Yet Howard Becker gives the title "proverbial" to the first of his four "constructed types" of society (H Becker & A Boskoff (eds), 1966).

The main concern in this context is with proverbs that are "bywords" and "commonplaces", rather than with the *sententiae* and *exempla* of the wise individual. The canonisation of such sayings in earlier times is peculiarly significant in the Semitic traditions, with their emphasis upon history and revelation, novelty and individuality, "Thus saith the Lord", and, "But I say unto you". Comment upon them (eg I Samuel 24: 13, Ezekiel 12: 22 and 18: 2, or Matthew 16: 2-3) is itself an exercise in comparative religion, albeit a judgemental one: a comparison between elements in contemporary priestly or prophetic, canonical or folk, explicit or implicit, religion. Subsequently, their low-key, apparently secular, approach has sometimes seemed to call for an apology, for their inclusion in sacred scripture.

However, they exhibit three of the distinguishing characteristics with which religious phenomena are generally credited. They describe areas of reality, which may be inherently unquantifiable, with an air of finality. They prescribe and proscribe specific behaviours, while leaving the actor to apply the principles. And they balance these potentially divisive characteristics with an integrative power: they integrate contemporaries with one other, with their own life-histories, and with departed generations.

All three responses to stimulus E2 profess respect for proverbs. Yet the respect is matched by an almost parallel, good-natured disrespect. The combination is reminiscent of the admiring affection, yet bantering informality, which characterises the attitude of many Jews towards Judaism, Italians towards the Papacy, Irish Catholics towards the Church, French Catholics towards the clergy, or Anglicans towards the Church of England. To be "at home" with the official sacred in this way, may suggest either its profanation, or the existence of a personal identity that is so confident in a reality lying beyond symbol, that the sacred does not have to be idolised (or vilified). Thus, students of proverbs may cause amusement, on the part of those who use them, by their apparent reverence for them.

The respondents claimed to see them as neither more, nor less, than the "tentative hypotheses" of contemporary science: would-be generalisations, hopefully based on the empirical evidence to date. Their function, as end-stops in the perennial process of recurrent rationalisation, is not, professedly, the result of a supposed infallibility; nor is it on account of their antiquity, anonymity, or popularity, or their status as proverbs, or of the status of their carriers and propagators (chiefly children's mothers, quoting their own mothers).

Their mutual contradictoriness, as the responses show, is itself "proverbial". It is this that simultaneously prevents their being taken too seriously, and yet allows each to become a proved half-truth. As hypotheses with a built-in non-obsolescence, as dogmas without doctrine, as panaceas without pretensions, they encourage the individual to venture into those areas, such as human relationships, decision-making, the future and the weather, where s/he might hesitate to tread alone.

In addition to their descriptive and prescriptive function, their appeal lies in their brevity and memorability, each of which is enhanced by such verbal devices as the use of internal rhyme ("... time ... nine") and doubling (" ... tomorrow ... today"), and the use of active verbs and concrete nouns. As (it may be) with all the "best" symbols, they combine an immediate clarity of literal meaning, with an intriguing mystery regarding their wider intent. This last characteristic can give rise to straightforward ambiguity. Thus, the interviewer realised that one respondent meant, by "Still waters run deep", what he would understand by, "All that glitters is not gold". As well as communicating messages (wisdom), to be analysed, therefore, they also *function* as symbols, evoking the smile that indicates a sense of community.

However, one cannot leave this particular Theme, without raising the question of the future of proverbs. For it was noticeable in the interviews that those who, "despite" knowing least proverbs, had least respect for them, were the young urban males. A two-fold question therefore arises. Is this a passing phase in the life-history of such individuals, comparable, say, to vandalism? Or is this a trend which will stay with them throughout their lives? If it is the latter, then it suggests that the loss of proverbial wisdom is a "secularisation" process, so far as traditional folk religion is concerned, comparable to that "secularisation", where ecclesiastical religion is concerned. That has also been most marked among young, urban males.

The ground that has been lost by all that proverbial wisdom stands for (the influence of tradition, mediated through the older generation), has been gained by that culture which is mediated by television and by the peer-group. Indeed, the formulation of the second Theme in this group is intended to convey three impressions: that the world that is received is that conveyed by television; that the world is conceived as being the one that television portrays; and that the image is hardly distinguished from the reality.

The triple identi-kit interview, being verbal, cannot report the initial evidence of the close identity between the screen of the television set and the world. For the interviewer kept finding that when questions (eg B1) were asked concerning the "world", respondents' eyes repeatedly went towards the television set, if there was one within sight (although it was always turned off); and if none was physically present (for instance, in the place of work, in the case of a cobbler, an ironmonger, and a storekeeper), then the respondent still diverted his eyes, as though to facilitate the recollection of a television set, presumably at home. It was as though the respondent was re-playing what he had seen on the screen, in order to make a judgement (about the world, not the programmes), and thus be able to give his answer.

The picture on the screen, then, like an Orthodox ikon, has something of the character of the reality which it portrays. Other students have commented that even people and places that are known personally are more real on the screen, and that, once they have been on the screen, they somehow become more "real" in the flesh than they were previously. As a consequence of broadcasting, the present writer has been able to observe that adults' reactions in this respect are not different in kind from those of children.

Consciously, in a culture which draws (or used to draw) an exaggerated dichotomy between symbols and reality, programmes may be dismissed as "merely" good or bad television. But unconsciously, whether fictional or otherwise, they continue to satisfy the unavoidable hunger for an understanding of reality. So, if "fundamentalism" be defined as the equation of the medium and the message (in reaction against the utter denial of significance to symbols), then this equation of the screen with the world is a secular form of epistemological fundamentalism.

The meaning of the world that is received through television is simultaneously holistic and selective. On the one hand it is global, even cosmic, and (the signs were already present, in 1969) ecological. On the other hand, it is limited to this planet, and in the main to the human aspect even of that. The extra-terrestrial and the sub-human have little place, apart from their significance for humans. Existence is channelled through the lenses of reality as seen by metropolitan man, whether he be the producer, cameraman, or viewer. So the "world" tends to mean, (other) people (with selves, like mine).

All of the responses to stimuli B1, B2 and C2 illustrate *in toto* this wide (so-called "global"), yet restricted, understanding of the "world". Examples of the virtual equation of "life" with humankind may also be found in the responses to A1, A5, and A10. Respondents to C3 tended to confirm the same Theme, first by asking whether the stimulus meant "my purpose, or "the purpose of the whole", and then by their failure to provide any answer for the second half of the distinction they had drawn.

In Greek mythology, Atlas was the giant who held the world up, on his shoulders. So, apparently, the mountains to the north-west of Africa and south of the Mediterranean were given his name. His name is borrowed in the third Theme of this group to express the feeling, which interviewees repeatedly communicated, that they bore a very considerable burden of the world's problems, and people's consequent suffering, about with them. In this case, the "world" is not that of physical geography, but of personal distress.

The recorded responses to stimulus B1, "What do you feel is the biggest problem in the world?", show something of the intellectual content of this "Atlas effect". Probably, however, they should have been introduced with a line of dots, to denote an initial silence. This pause, during which respondents took a deep breath, did not indicate a purely intellectual problem, such as the difficulty of identifying a single candidate when so many were potentially fatal. It was, in part, a spiritual response, as consideration of the stimulus brought to the surface an unmitigated succession of *problematiques*, of conflict, and of suffering. Yet the reaction was not simply one of bewilderment and despair: it included a sense of other people's tragedy, and of steadfast endurance.

The last Theme, under the heading of "the received world", describes the place of money. The findings indicate that this is one of the major instances of the disjunction between the public culture and the private one; for, contrary to the expectation of the interviewer, although respondents recognised the "games" borrowed by stimulus A4, they were not prepared to consider the spending of huge sums. Twice the cost of an average house would represent their maximum, while sums ten times that size were at that time being won on the pools. (It remains to be seen how far the institution of a National Lottery, and its cultural reinforcement, will change this.)

Because of the many and varied limitations on freedom of choice in actual expenditure, the valuation placed by respondents upon their outer world may be indicated more faithfully by the drawing-up of ideal budgets, than by the recording of actual expenditure. The semi-statistical character of the question allows the overall responses to be "averaged". Thus, one-tenth of the money was going to be "spent" immediately, on "the children, including their education", and "a really good holiday". Another tithe would find its way "to people, like Oxfam and Cancer Research", "to good causes", or to "my parents, and my husband's mother". The rest was going to be invested, with the purchase of a property particularly in mind.

The responses demonstrate the existence of a continuum. But it does not run from, say, immoral self-indulgence, through morally neutral investment, to the positive morality of giving to charity. It runs, rather, from the relative immorality of expenditure, which is dark grey in proportion to its impulsiveness, to the relative morality of investment, which is a lighter grey because self-denying. The choice, or conflict, is not seen as lying between either asceticism and charity (cp A4: y), on the one hand, and consumerism on the other; but between consumerism and capitalism (cp C Campbell, 1986). It is perhaps this admiration for abstention from immediate self-gratification which is responsible for the reluctance even to consider sums of the size that the stimulus suggested.

3.3.6   The outer scene (ii): the Psycho-social Reality

> (a) The social archipelago
> (b) The I-they encounter
> (c) The involvement of the individual in the "other"
> (d) Steady-state marriage

The interviews reveal awareness of an experience, which is here referred to as being of a psycho-social reality, that is almost completely without conceptualisation in the public culture of contemporary society. The absence of any such conceptualisation can lead to the sort of puzzled nihilism expressed in such statements as, "There's no such thing as society; there are only individuals - and families" (which must be the sociological form of total atheism). This awareness is not, however, to be confused with the kind of corporatist thinking which says, for instance, "England [or even, "we"] won the Ashes", referring to eleven players selected by the Marylebone Cricket Club; or (in 1945), "the only good German is a dead one".

The social sciences themselves seem to be increasingly coming to identify this area of experience. G H Mead's "Society in the Mind" (1934) was a precursor. P L Berger and T Luckmann (1965), coined the concept of "inter-subjective reality". V W Turner used the concept of *communitas* (1969), to describe some of its dynamics. E I Bailey (1990) lists a number of religious concepts that have proved to be of value in this process.

Practice likewise increasingly recognises its reality. The Royal Air Force has long acknowledged the special needs of twins. Management now takes great account of "corporate culture". Politics and journalism likewise recognise that our opponents (if not ourselves!), need to "save face".

The first Theme, The social archipelago, in this quartet, stresses the prime importance for the individual of those small groups, even the transitory ones, that are formed by his succession of face-to-face contacts. This, the truly social dimension of his life, has a greater significance than is usually realised. Thus the "mass media" (by which is increasingly meant simply television) are consumed neither *en masse*, nor yet by the masses atomistically, but in the main by individuals in small groups. Most of the individual's personal life (the part that matters most for her or him) is lived at the hub of a relatively small number of relatively long-lasting direct contacts with other individuals and such small groups. Thus human being, speaking empirically rather than evaluatively, continues to be an archipelago, stretching ultimately around the world.

The importance of this level of contact is demonstrated by a number of responses. The most enjoyable things in life are, respectively (A1: x, y and z): "Meeting people", "a drink with one or two friends", and, "family life". Its influence may be seen in all four of the Themes headed "the Relationship of the Self with other Selves"; and, it may be suggested, in that ultimate conviction that, "I have a Self".

The second Theme suggests that this level of reality does not generally take the form of an "I-Thou" encounter (M Buber, 1958). That is a useful description of those individuated areas, or moments, in life, in which inner-direction and intense devotion (as in romantic love), predominate. But the interviews point to the way that most of life is dominated by the experience, not even of an "I-You" encounter (as H Cox 1965: 48-9 suggested), but of what is best described as an "I-They" encounter. The last Theme of this group, and the Themes concerning Religion in the final group, will also suggest that something of this kind is true even of the most "personal" (individual) relationships. It is madness to lose one's Self - save for the sake of one's Self (cp Chapter 5.3.3).

The existence and importance of the "I-They encounter" come to light, above all, in the responses to stimulus A5, "What's the most important thing in the world?" The second response expresses this attitude perfectly: "Having a circle of friends with whom I can be absolutely at ease and frank". The third response opens: "For me, it's family life." Even the first response, beginning, "My wife, of course", conveys the same approach, as it explains itself: "Seeing her happy, and the family happy, and retaining our health, and being able to partake in all my activities".

Phenomenologically (that is to say, in terms of the subject's own experience), the relationship described by this Theme differs from the classical I-Thou encounter of devotional religion (N Smart, 1968), and from romantic love, in failing to draw such a sharp distinction between one item within experience and the rest. It is not, however, the same kind of relationship as that experienced in traditional small-scale society, for it does remain an "encounter". "I", having and being a self, am highly individuated, even if the object of my encounter remains fairly general. The typical questions running through the mind, remain, for many adults, those most often voiced in adolescence. They are not only, "What do I feel about him/her?" and, "What does he/she think about me?", but also, both prior to and after that, "What do I seem like to them, what is their image of me?", and, "How do I feel about them, how am I relating to them?"

The involvement of the individual in the "other", the third Theme, must be understood in the light of what has just been said about the nature of that "other" which "I" encounter. Even when it is single, and sharply differentiated from the rest of "them", it remains less individuated than the self which "I" know within my self. The discovery of a particular "Thou" does not evacuate all other selves of their meaning. Rather, it stands as a representative of "them", just as it affirms the reality of my own self.

The content of this Theme develops out of the experience summarised at the beginning of the third group in the Inner Scene: the Self comes to Life in Relationships. The Theme, however, suggests that the self is involved, not only in the relationship with an other, but within the life of that other subject which is the "object" of the relationship. This distinction may seem either subtle, or tautologous. Yet it contradicts many of the assumptions that have prevailed in western culture in the last couple of centuries, such as those behind the concept of "encounter" itself. For the self is not experienced as self-contained. It is the existential aspect, basis, evidence, and consequence, of that epistemology and ethic of acknowledging other selves as being as sacred (real and valuable), as I know mine own to be.

The clearest description of this kind of relationship occurs in the third response to stimulus A7b, "Does anything ever *get* you, or move you, or *send* you ... [making you] pleased, happy, excited, interested?": "It's mostly things that happen to me through the children now - watching their development". The same attitude may be seen, but more ambiguously, in three other responses: A1: z, A5: x, and A9: y.

There is no desire to deny that such pleasure, in the progress of children for instance, may sometimes owe much, and may always owe something, to the projection of the self; so that the other becomes a source of acceptable self-adulation. There is, indeed, ancient tradition for the understanding of all relationships in terms of mutual "possession", whereby the own-er is himself "possessed", spiritually, by that which he "owns". ("Own-ing up" could be seen as synonymous with articulating a religion that was hitherto implicit - with confessing faith/sin.)

The question that is raised by this evidence, though, is whether all such relationships should be so described, *in extenso*. It may also be relevant to point out that such a view of human motivation, which is often cynically advanced, would not even be considered pejorative by many of those being discussed. Indeed, not to "take a proper pride" in the achievements of others would itself be considered inhuman, unnatural, and deplorable.

The plea is therefore being made for the recognition of the secular possibility of a non-manipulative co-inherence of the spectator in the other, akin to that described as contemplation within the Christian ascetic tradition (cp C Butler, 1960: 248-272). A similarly unpossessive pleasure, or distanced empathy, of the kind sought by counsellors (P Halmos, 1965), may characterise the relationship with sub-personal objects, not only in nature and in high art, but also in gardening, with machines such as cars, and with systems, of all kinds. Thus, even "watching their development", which can so easily be seen in egotistical terms, can also be interpreted (and, the context suggests, much more plausibly) in terms of receiving pleasure from a good with which I am familiar, because of our relationship, but for which I am not claiming credit. There can, indeed, be additional pleasure in the realisation that life continues to be lived, when *I* am not directly involved.

The last of these Themes finds, in what it calls "steady-state marriage", a particular instance of this psycho-social reality. The final response to the opening stimulus puts the point with a clarity of concept, and matching simplicity of expression, that gives it a beauty of its own. "What do you enjoy most in life?" "The children; and being married; and my husband".

The public comment might suggest that the husband only appeared as an after-thought. Certainly, the "logical" sequence, be it chrono-logical or bio-logical, has been reversed. The order does, however, record the sequence of recall. It reveals the empirical psychology, the existential ontology, in which the husband is "taken for granted" (*datum*), as the *sine qua non*. "Being married", a verbal noun, expresses a living continuity, to which neither the legal "marriage", nor the personalist "living with - ", could do justice by themselves. "Contract" has become "status".

Not all these thoughts are in the respondent's mind, of course. But she was analysing her experience, in order to answer the question, not analysing her answer to it. Consequently we see signs of a psychic reality which, based on the premise of the self, comes to life in relationship; encounters a generalised plurality of similarly unique beings, more often than an all-absorbing singular Thou; lives, and gradually discovers itself to live, in such others, usually following the discovery of a single, similar, Other; and finally may find itself fused with that Other, and others generally.

The significance for the individual of this range of experience accounts for the widespread substitution, in a society with problems of identity, of Tillich's term "acceptance", affirming the goodness of being, in place of the "forgiveness", which is more appropriate to reciprocal relationships. M Weber (1965: 206) also commented upon modern man's "distinctive type of guilt and ... godless feeling of sin ... He feels that both he and the others are inhuman, because there is no significant possibility of *forgiveness*, of *his unalterable idiosyncracy* [that is, that] *he is as he is*".

3.3.7   The outer scene (iii): Polarity without Dichotomy

(a) The individual and "people"
(b) Change and continuity
(c) Good and bad
(d) Satisfaction and dissatisfaction

The four previous Themes described a progressive penetration into that psychosocial reality experienced by the interviewees. This group contains three parallel examples of polarities that are present within their consciousness, while the fourth describes the absence of any unifying and overall, ultimate polarisation.

The first of these Themes draws attention to the polarity between the individual and *people*. Regarding the importance of the former, suffice it to allude to all of the preceding Themes, and to the "naturalness" with which respondents witnessed to their individual selves, epitomised in such expressions as, "For me ..." (A2: x), and " ... there are only things that are lacking in *me*" (A11: y).

The reality (albeit phenomenologically secondary) of the other pole ("people") has likewise been described, as very general and yet highly restricted, in connection with "the received world". To label this pole "society", as the mass media might do, would be too impersonal, and too holistic, to represent unstimulated consciousness. To call it "humankind" would be too corporatist. To use a species term, such as "human beings", would exaggerate the extent to which it is seen in the context of other species. "People", therefore, most accurately portrays the polar opposite of the individual.

The term represents a general and unbounded extrapolation, from the self and its face-to-face connections within the social archipelago, through its lesser associational contacts, to what is, effectively, infinity. It combines the grouping of individuals, with the personalising of masses. It gives rise to expressions such as, "... it often seems not to regard people" (A7a: z), " ... it could be overcome with the right cooperation by people" (B1: x), or, "Trying to get people of different nationalities to agree" (B1: y).

The polarity of these two realities comes out in such responses as, "For me ... for the world ... " (A5: z); in the query, "As an individual, or as the world?". (C3: x); or in the conclusion, "... I'm just another human being" (F10: x). Yet, as that last quotation suggests, the polarisation is far from complete.

The self may be unique, but it is what the individuals that comprise "people" all possess. Far from being "opposite", to each other (in reality, as opposed to conceptually), the poles are not even mutually exclusive. Hence the epistemological and ethical principles, and the relatively seamless quality of the psycho-social reality. "The best place to start putting the world right", therefore, is with "the whole collection of me's" (C4: y; cp C1: x, and A11: z).

The second Theme also finds a non-absolute dualism in the concepts of change and continuity. The former is seen as a fact of history, as accelerating in the present, and as utterly inevitable in the future. The responses to stimulus B2 are typical of many conversations in small groups, such as the family and the public house. In such contexts, the concept of "change" gives way to that of "progress" - and is almost always pejorative. "But that's progress, I suppose", implies a recognition of change as inevitable, and therefore to be accepted (a new form of fatalism), combined with a strong disapproval of many of the forms that it takes.

Yet the cultures of the little societies in the social archipelago show a matching awareness of continuity (cp T Harrison 1961: 42, regarding "areas of unchange in Worktown ... in everyday gesture, pub behaviour, love life, kids' games").

The relationship between these two poles may be gauged from the fact that the "opposite" of change is continuity, not permanence. "*Plus ça change, c'est la même chose*", may be quoted as a comment upon the mystery of history (or of Idealism and the doctrine of universals), but it is not taken literally. Neither change, nor non-change, is illusory (*maya*); nor, on the other hand, is either of them the only reality. Their phenomenal polarity may be the occasion of phenomenological strain, but the sense of the interviews is that they are mutually interdependent, rather than mutually exclusive.

The third Theme focuses on a polarity which was especially evident in connection with an "ethic of acknowledging self-hood". Stimuli such as B2, "Do you feel the world's changing for the better or the worse, or not at all?"; or stimuli directed towards their existential reactions, such as A6, "Is there anything you feel really serious about?", or A9, "dislike", or A7a and b, "*get* you, move you, *send* you", or such as D1, " ... you might say, it has been a really good day" – all gave rise to the expression of strong convictions. (The occasional critical stance, in C1:z, C5:y, C6:y, E1a:y, or E3:x, towards the possible assumptions of the questions, by no means nullifies this comment.) Yet respondents themselves would rarely use such abstract concepts, with such absolute evaluations, as "good" and "bad". If they did, they implied the presence of inverted commas, in order to make clear their recognition that this is a "personal" opinion.

The presence of a relative moral polarity, and absence of an absolute moral polarisation, is reflected in the responses to the stimuli with which the interview opened. They also indicate something of the character of the criteria which did accompany, and did not accompany, the distinction between the poles. The fact that A2, "What makes life worth living?", was not seen by anyone as a repetition of A1, "What do you enjoy most in life?", suggests that enjoyment was not seen as sufficiently legitimating by itself. The fact that the division between the individual and the totality in stimulus A3 ("If you had three wishes, and one of them had to be used on yourself but it didn't matter how you used the others, what would you wish?"), conveyed little meaning, confirms the earlier suggestion that the self and "people" are distinguishable, yet not seen as fundamentally in conflict. The fact that respondents declined to win a really large amount on "the pools", suggests that the material world was seen, not as bad in itself, but rather as having potential for evil in its consequences.

The test of morality, therefore, centres neither on happiness and unhappiness (the pleasure-pain principle), nor on selfishness and unselfishness (the skin boundary). It centres rather on self-hood. This is no more to be equated with an easy way out of moral struggle, than with selfish disregard of others. What it does mean is that to look after oneself is not automatically to be condemned. The denial of pleasure, or self-sacrifice, are not necessarily self-authenticating. This feature of popular psychology, spiritual discernment, and moral judgement, long pre-dates Freudian theory.

The final Theme in this group is concerned with "satisfaction and dissatisfaction". It suggests that respondents were critical, but not ultimately alienated. Indeed, they were more dissatisfied with the world-situation, and more satisfied with their own life-situation, than the public culture of the media seems to suggest.

Their unwillingness to spend vast sums of money (in response to stimulus A4) suggests basic satisfaction with their own situation. This view was in

fact voiced by one respondent to the previous stimulus regarding their wishes
(A3: z): "I'm reasonably happy with my circumstances, I don't think of any
outstanding wish. I keep saying to myself, I have so much to be thankful for".
Dissatisfaction on the individual's own account, therefore, was more personal
than material. It included "things that are lacking in *me*" (A11: y), and the
desire for more "contact between my parents and myself" (A11: z), and the
fear of "having to leave this world with all its pleasant things. And ... being a
failure", "Getting old, and not being wanted", and "redundancy ... and ... being
senile" (A8: x, y and z).

Dissatisfaction on the world's account mixed material concern with personal,
but the material was valued on account of its personal significance. The general
motivation was pity in the face of suffering. "Wars ... and ... starvation" were
wished away (A3: y). "Wars - or poverty and under-development", and "colour",
were the "one thing" respondents would change (C2: x, y and z; cp B1: z).
However, a more passionate strand in the motivation seems to have been anger
at people's failure to agree (B1: x and y; cp A6: x, y and z). This was once
expressed as, "Why can't they behave like grown-ups?"; that is, as selves who
can acknowledge others' selves (cp Chapter 4.3.6).

Yet the dissatisfaction felt on behalf of suffering "people" was also limited.
Of the nine wishes recorded in the three responses to stimulus A3, only two
(from the same respondent, A3: y) were global, or even social, in character.
The first respondent, who "could change any one thing in the world", answered,
"I don't know", when asked, "What would you change?" (C2: x). Neither did
stimulus C1, "What would a perfect world be like?", produce much in the way
of a vision or blue-print for utopia.

This apparent absence of any absolute quality of satisfaction or dissatisfaction is further confirmed by some of their "internal" evidence. Many show a
marked moderation in their desires (eg A3: x, 7 and z; A4: x, y, and z; A11: x,
y and z; D1-D7; E1-2; E4-5). Others explicitly identify themselves with those
traits they deplore in others (eg A7a: y and z). Two sayings in particular (C1:
y and B1: y) show a similar approach globally.

"Of course, it couldn't possibly be perfect, human nature being what it is. It
wouldn't work because someone would always be dissatisfied."

"Not that I ever feel hopeless about things; nothing's ever as bad as you thought
it was going to be. That's very true."

So, following the precedent of the Inner Scene, the Themes of the Outer Scene
might also now be summarised, credally and briefly:

As the world is in me, and I am in those I know,
So I distinguish, but I decline to divide.

3.3.8 The Other Scene (i): Moral

(a) Happiness is an Imperative
(b) The List
(c) The "Alexander principle"
(d) The primacy of the individual

It will be desirable in this concluding section of the interview analysis to indicate what the adjective "other" indicates. Are the themes merely miscellaneous, or in some sense in contrast to those in the preceding two sections?

The Themes in the first group describe Moral principles that are present in the consciousness. The second group concern what is commonly called Religion, and topics that are commonly associated with it. The third is entitled Salvific, because its Themes are concerned with the amelioration of life (including the criteria of such amelioration). The final quartet is headed simply Parameters, because its Themes concern divinity, and dying, and therefore most obviously raise the question as to whether they are miscellaneous, or transcendent.

As the first theme in this quartet says, happiness is an imperative, as well as a value, in the interviews as elsewhere (cp Chapter 3). Thus, response B2: x makes it the criterion of the world's progressing. A11: x likewise describes "a perfect world" as "full of happiness ... everyone would live happily together". That it is a goal to be striven for, as well as (like the "bliss" of explicit-religious tradition) a blessing to be received, is confirmed by the "philosophy of life" which might be passed on to a fifteen year old (E5: x): "The most important thing is the greatest happiness of the greatest number ... "

The intimacy of the enjoyable and the moral is revealed by all three of the identi-kit responses to D2. "Another word for a really good day", is, neither "happy" nor "enjoyable", in any of the responses, but "satisfied" (D2: both x and y), or "occupied" (D2: z). The three respondents amplify their meaning: "Because one's achieved something and used the time well, as well as had good relationships"; "the moment of satisfaction is still two and a half years away, as I'm doing a PhD"; "a day in which I've been *engaged* in *living*".

For happiness by itself cannot, it seems, be allowed an unqualified, absolute value: it is morally ambiguous. Thus "to give [the surplus money from the win on the pools] to situations with which I was familiar, *is* [emphasis added] a selfish pleasure" (A4: x); and, "My perfect world would be, in a way selfish" (C1: x). The conflict is resolved in ways reminiscent of the Scout Law. Thus, the fifteen year old who had been told that, "The important thing is the greatest happiness of the greatest number. And Christianity. And being kind to others", is finally advised: "And you can't be happy yourself, if you don't make other people happy".

Their own spiritual self-direction seems to have shown that happiness must be mutual and reciprocal, because the self coinheres with other selves. In this way self-righteousness and moral pretentiousness are avoided, in a culture which is both moralistic and anxious to avoid appearing smug. As respondent A2: y said, "What makes life worth living", "now ... is helping others ... I've got joy in giving". (This element within the Great Traditions has been largely over-laid in the general culture through their use of the traditions as schoolmasters.)

The second Theme, "The List", demonstrates this moralism. The interviews revealed how widespread, and burdensome, is the mental list of "jobs" that respondents need or want to do, which this society carries around within its head. If it is not too bothered about the danger of nuclear war, it may well be because it is more concerned about that "mushroom-shaped" cloud, about which the individuals can do something. Thus the question of whether "it has been a really good day", was no novelty to them.

The seriousness of the issue, and at the same time the sense of challenge and achievement and pleasure to be derived from their response, is seen, above all, in four responses to three stimuli.

"... *What are the practical things that turn an ordinary day into a really good day?*" (D1)

"That I've achieved all the tasks I set off to do in the morning ... " (D1: x)

"You always end the day happier if you've done a job you've been putting off" (D1: z)

"*Is there any part of the ordinary routine of living which you'd really miss if it was abolished?*" (D3)

"The chores - it would be terrible to sit idle and not have anything to do" (D3: y)

"*What is the most important thing you do each week?*"

"To get by and do my bits of jobs" (D5: z)

So what the "Atlas effect" does, with respect to "the world", is paralleled by The List, with respect to the individual. However, the "Atlas" of the interviews bears a spiritual weight, about which he can do very little. It would only become a moral issue if he were to try to repudiate such vicarious suffering. The List, on the other hand, although in part self-imposed, consists of items which the individual acknowledges he can and should do something about. It is therefore the moral dimension of that earlier Theme, in which the successful juggling of social roles was described as, "I am happy if I can get by".

The voluntary element in The List may suggest a game-like quality. Neither the seriousness with which it is approached, nor its moral aspect, contradict this possibility. Its reciprocity with the real world, not simply of pitches and gravity, but of people and the passage of time, render its interpretation as a religious ritual more realistic. It is the daily devotion, of believers in a prag-matic moralism.

It is said that the future Alexander the Great used to remark wistfully to his tutor, Aristotle, when news reached them of yet another victory won by the boy's father, Philip of Macedon, that there would be nothing left for him to conquer. The story has frequently come to mind when discussing the problem of evil, especially with teenaged boys. For they have shown a strong feeling that evil not only must exist in order to demonstrate the character of goodness, but also that it must be available, in order that it might be overcome, and goodness developed.

A similar conviction, which has already become apparent in the analysis of the interviews, that goals are *ipso facto* desirable, is therefore the third Theme in this group, and is called the "Alexander principle". Two responses (y and z) to the same stimulus (C1) illustrate the conviction.

"What would a perfect world be like?"

"... it couldn't possibly be perfect ... There'd be nothing to work for, nothing to overcome."

" ... *Perfect* is not something you can reach, by definition. If it was perfect by our present ideas, then it wouldn't be so then."

Such an "Alexander principle" has much in common with what is sometimes called an "achievement orientation". However, it lays greater stress upon the desirability of goals as such, and correspondingly less upon the attainment of particular goals. So it opens up the possibility of selecting goals that are seen to be impossible to achieve, and nevertheless (or, therefore) of insisting on the use of ideal methods which are consonant with them. Reinhold Niebuhr's teaching (1941) on "the relevance of an impossible ethic", and Gandhi's application of the ethics of means and ends, come to mind; and, indeed, the interviews contain numerous protests (eg C7: x; A7a: x; C7: y) against "the tycoon mentality", of grasping and pushing. Thus, "ambition" is invariably a derogatory term. (The 1980s' deliberate emphasis upon "enterprise" tacitly acknowledged this.)

The principle assumes the self's existence on the conveyor-belt of time, and places in a wider perspective the Themes concerned with the "round", and "getting by". Its most constant and mundane expression is The List. It is, indeed, the generative power responsible for the latter's almost infinite capacity for self renewal. It is this will-power that "keeps me going", to borrow the phrase of a once-famous comedienne.

The primacy of the individual is the final Theme in this quartet. Its existence could have been deduced, from the combination of such other Themes as the sacredness of the self and the Alexander principle, even had there been no direct evidence for it in the interview data. It is, however, the moral application of the ethic of acknowledging self-hood, and requires separate articulation on account of the clarity and frequency with which it is expressed.

Three of the responses to, "Where is the best place to start putting the world right?", and "Who is most likely ever to put the world right?" (C3, C4), pin the responsibility directly upon the individual. Thus: "The best place to start is where you are"; "... if people worked in harmony, and did the right thing, they could make it much better"; "... it's the whole collection of me's" (C3: x; C4: x; and C4: y). The other three responses name either the individual(s) in the best position to influence the largest number of people, or the individual(s) with the role to exert the deepest influence upon other individuals. They say: "In the home ... parent ..."; "In schools ... Start with the children ... ", " ... the leader of the Chinese people - not the present one, of course, but whoever is" (C3: y, C3: z; C4: z).

While the last of these stimuli was partially oriented towards an individual-istic response, there is little evidence in the interviews that social or corporate levels of human being were apprehended as having a reality comparable to that of the individual. General scourges, such as war, poverty and racialism, weigh heavy, and the United Nations Organisation was named; yet the reason for the impatience with "statesmen" was that they would not sit down and talk together, like individual adults. Responsibility, for amelioration and for the lack of it, lay with technology and those who use it or fail to use it. For, at bottom, the "world" was simply "people": "the whole collection of me's".

3.3.9   The other scene (ii): Religious

> (a) Religion is infinitely individual
> (b) Christianity is "established"
> (c) God is a high God
> (d) The supernatural is the super-scientific

Asked whether they had ever known anyone who was "truly religious", the three representative respondents replied (F8: x, y and z): "Yes, several ..."; "One or two people"; "I don't think so". The first response was amplified: "... spiritual people. I've great admiration for them. I'm impressed with the fact that they don't try and thrust it onto you."

That description itself echoes the representative responses (F7: x, y and z) to the previous question, "What would you mean by *true religion* ...?" The flow of their thought, and relative homogeneity of their content, calls for their sequential reproduction: "I think what I mean is ... [pause] I don't really know. I know what I mean, but I can't put it into words ... [pause] An attitude can be very religious, without going to church. You might still have Church in you, even if you've missed one or two weeks." "It's certainly not living in church. It's human acts of kindness and sympathy." "I could apply it to someone who's mad keen on cricket. So that means, so long as he carried his religion into all his life."

Religion, properly speaking, then, is a matter of basic attitude. Visible acts of kindness, it is present and influential in all areas of life. Given the opportunity, even in 1969 (long before "spirituality" became a recognised concept, in the 1980s), "spiritual" could be used (F8: x), because the need was felt for a term to describe the inner core of the person. (By 1974 the Labour Party called itself "the Party with a soul"; while the expression, "the life and soul of the party", in a purely social sense, had never lost its meaning.) The insistence that such a spirit could not be guaranteed by, or gauged by, or equated with, liturgical participation or doctrinal position, came out of a conviction, both conscious and unconscious, in terms of the Christian tradition, that this spirit of holiness was to be sought in humanity in general, rather than being peculiar to any particular category, however defined.

Not the least significant aspect of these responses, however, is their ready understanding of the concept of religion. Cantwell Smith (1964) has usefully documented the spread of the concept; but our position is like that of Cnut, when he deliberately demonstrated his own impotence. In contemporary society, the word is meaningful, because the concept is understood, and the concept is understood, because the phenomenon is apprehended as real. Certainly the academic use of the word needs up-dating, in accordance with an intuitive understanding which is based on widespread observation and judgement (cp Chapter 6.3). But to expect its abolition is as unrealistic as to anticipate the disappearance of its referent, in any and all of its forms.

Religion, then, in the interviews, as in popular speech outside them, is believed to exist; and can be "believed in", or otherwise. While Eisenhower's classic statment of this creed has been questioned on text-critical grounds, what M E Marty has reasonably said (1958: 67) of the United States, is also true, although less obviously, and less exclusively, of Britain: "The religious aspect of our culture ... is an attitude towards religion. Elevated to ultimacy, this attitude has become a religion itself. Indeed ... it is no doubt already *the* prevalent religion."

However, one of the ways in which religion has changed its meaning, during the two millenia of its conceptualization, is from a social, civic or corporate emphasis, towards the opposite extreme of individuality. Thus, if "religion" has become a periphrasis for God, it has also become the symbolic expression of the sacrality of the individual. It was seen as the locus of divinity; it has become the focus of identity. Thus, freedom of religion has been the first and foremost freedom, because it means the freedom of the individual to be individual. Whereas once it meant the freedom of the group to practice a ritual, or the freedom of individuals to propagate an ontology or follow their conscience, it has come to mean the freedom to be intuitive or subjective, and so to "be one's own [*sic*] person".

The particular pair of stimuli that specifically referred to religion, were individualistic in their assumptions. Although none of the three respondents in any way questioned that assumption, further direct evidence of this individualistic understanding of the concept may nevertheless be sought. It may fairly be said to be found in the responses to the earlier pair of stimuli, concerning the possible reference and meaning of the word "sacred". The first response (F1: x; F2: x) in each case said: "Each person's own beliefs"; and, "Something which is personal, which should be cherished, and which you alone have got ..." A similar individualism is likewise apparent in the responses to the following stimulus (F3), regarding the meaning of "holy".

All three concepts (religion, sacred, and holy) are widely understood, and highly regarded. It is, however, as expressions of the self that they are both apprehended and valued. It, rather than they, are icons of any kind of transcendent divinity.

Constitutionally, legally and historically, the Church of England is said to be "Established". This has never meant that the Church in question was a "State Church", for instance, receiving money via the Government from taxation; but even its lesser meaning, which might be summarised in terms of a publicly recognised corporate chaplaincy to the nation, becomes more attenuated, or at least more general and cultural, with each successive generation. The term has, however, been widely borrowed, to refer to the "establishment" of a sociopolitical cultural network (eg A Sampson 1966).

The second Theme suggests that "Christianity" is similarly "established"; not so much legally, as phenomenologically. This means that the expression is widely used; its referent is generally understood to exist; and it is valued positively. This is explicitly stated once, and implied many times, in the interviews. Thus (E1b: y): "Are there any things that you would say ... you definitely do believe in?" "I believe in Christianity; and a sense of humour; and in honesty." To some extent, the respondent probably saw the second and third items as subsumed in the first.

The concept takes much the same place in this country, as "religion" in the United States; like being "against sin", it is difficult not to concur with it. They are, no doubt, the modern successors to the place held in previous generations and cultures by such expressions as the Church, Christendom or Islam (the territory in which Allah was acknowledged), or the Way (A C Bouquet, 1941: 12). While all these terms acutely reflect their *Sitzimleben*, none of them is purely religious, in a liturgical or doctrinal sense.

It is not only "the religious", in the monastic sense, for whom religion means a rule of life; and it is not only the "religious community", for whom the *Opus Dei* has ritual, as well as ethical, overtones. But for those who believe in "Christianity", or "religion", that rule is not clearly articulated, or ceremonially adopted. Its "ritual" expression is primarily ethical, and takes place within the symbolism of natural human life rather than in tailor-made contexts. It "helps a little old lady across the road", where others may "help at Mass". "Service" has a different, first meaning, in this religion.

A similar ambiguity, or, perhaps better, breadth of reference, can be detected in the concept of *dharma*, which is used alike of those who conscientiously follow the norms of that station to which they have been born, and of those who consciously adopt a *yoga* or *bhakti* which denies the world, at least to the extent of representing a new order or way.

The belief in "Christianity" finds its position expressed by Keble, in a poem reproduced in most of the standard hymn books used in the Church of England:

> If on our daily course our mind
> Be set to hallow all we find,
> New treasures still, of countless price,
> God will provide for sacrifice.
> The trivial round, the common task
> Will furnish all we ought to ask,
> Room to deny ourselves, a road
> To bring us daily nearer God.

A parallelism may be sensed between, on the one hand, the individuality of religion, and the "establishment" of "Christianity"; and, on the other, between the sacredness of the self, and its characteristic "humanity". In each case, the inner core has its outward ramifications; the ineffable expresses itself mundanely; ultimately, simply in kindness.

Subsequent Chapters, reporting other studies, will in part explore the content of this conception of Christianity (in particular Chapter 5.3.6.2). Here it will suffice to quote another observer (J Loudon, 1966, in M Banton (ed), 1966), of a rural parish in South Wales: "Although organised religion plays a relatively small part in the life of the community, ideas about behaviour spring from an outlook of a religious kind which is basically Christian in character". D Martin likewise says, provocatively (1967: 55): "A broad assent exists to what is perversely believed to be a *Christian* morality" (cp T Parsons 1971: 216-7, especially n.11 on 217-9, in R Caporale & A Grumelli (eds), 1971).

If the individual is the most basic theme in this religious group, Christianity is next to it, in the depth and breadth of its significance. While "God" is associated with "Christianity", the belief in "him" is not as inclusive as the belief in it, nor can it be so easily and publicly affirmed. Other than as an expletive, it is almost impossible to name him, outside a context in which he has been deliberately included.

The contrast in this respect is not so much between this country and the United States (R N Bellah, 1965), as between the role of the Prime Minister and the President. Mrs Thatcher's quotation of the so-called "Prayer of St Francis", upon her first election in 1979, could not escape the appearance of moralism and/or insincerity; whereas the Queen may legitimately reveal a little of her own self, because, like the President's role at his Inauguration, her fundamental role is to be symbolic, not executive, an inheritor, not a suppliant.

"Christianity", then, is second only to the individuality of religiosity, both in its comprehensibility and comprehensiveness. "God", though readily available, except in contexts when he has other meaning (as an expletive, which somehow works, for instance), can only be used when his personal significance to the speaker puts sincerity beyond doubt. The interview situation allowed this. Indeed, the responses to stimulus F6 went out of their way to affirm their commitment to, and conceptualisation of, God.

The third Theme of this group articulates that content. In view of the notorious silence of the religious tradition in this culture (still, in 1969) regarding what Christian theology knows as the doctrine of the Spirit, the most striking characteristic of the responses is their feeling for what is sometimes called a pneumatic approach. The terms only occur in the last response: "... the *spirit of humanity* ... It's to do with spiritual communication between people ... " However, the apprehension is present in the first two responses: "... There is a God ... whether it be the Buddha, Jesus, Thor, or ... [pause]"; "I can't imagine living without him ..."

Also notable is the juxtaposition of ineffability and certitude. Such a combination not only makes each of them more easily comprehensible, but also more convincing. As it happens, these explicit religious questions were placed last, partly to avoid misunderstanding, but partly because they were seen as an appendix and a precaution. However, it is possible that, had this been the main object of the interview, only in this position, and after such an introduction (by way of other "mundane", "empirical" questions), could this degree of self-revelation have been achieved.

This combination, of experiential knowledge but conceptual ignorance, is present in all three responses, although especially pronounced in the first two. Thus: "I do use the term *God*, but it is difficult to define ... There's definitely a being who is called God"; "I can't imagine living without Him. That's enough": "... I think it's unimportant, but I can't get beyond thinking" "in terms of this figure sitting up there watching everything ..."; "I wouldn't use the word myself, but I have used it, to refer to the *spirit of humanity* ... a higher plane of things."

A degree of development may be detected, in that a growing apprehension of the reality referred to by the concept leads to an increased personalisation of its object, and turns the apprehension into a relationship. Otherwise, what stands out about the "object" of such a relationship or belief, is not only its imprecision, but the absence of any common ground between the various responses. With certitude is associated not only ineffability, but variety. Indeed, the first response (F6: x), with its conclusion, "There's definitely a being who is called God", echoes and illustrates Aquinas' empirical, and almost sardonic, conclusion to each of his famous five "proofs" of the existence of God : "... and *that* men call [*sic*] God".

The fourth Theme in this group, The supernatural is the super-scientific, concerns a concept which did not have a stimulus which even touched upon it. Indeed, although the study of religion contains much empirical evidence of what either the actors or the observers would consider to be supernatural, there seems to have been no full-length study of its meaning, comparable with the works of Durkheim, Otto and Cantwell Smith, regarding the sacred, holy and religion, unless it be J Oman (1931). While studies of what different cultures have meant by "natural" (including eg R Horton, 1960) form essential ancillaries, they cannot be primarily analytical of experience that is by definition excluded from their area of concern.

The inclusion of such a stimulus in the interview was considered, but rejected, in particular on the grounds that it may suggest that the exercise was covertly based upon the kind of dualistic understanding of reality that has received such a high profile in the popular image of western religion. It was also thought that the question was relatively unimportant, and the answer relatively obvious, and known.

As it happens, the very year (1968-9), in which the interviews were conducted seemed to see the re-emergence of the supernatural as a widespread area of interest, using that very term. This was facilitated by its relative independence of official religion: neither effectively condemned, nor theologically exploited, it was available for "naturalistic" consideration, as a re-discovered *genre*, an alternative kind of science-fiction.

Nevertheless, the concept was volunteered in one response (E1a: z), ambivalently and yet revealingly.

Are there any things that you would say you definitely do not believe in, or you definitely do believe in?

"I don't believe in heaven and hell, as places, in God as a Father sitting up there, in ghosts, but I'm not sure about the supernatural, such as telepathy and ESP, or in the value of violence, as fascism does."

This respondent's train of thought progresses from the specific issue of ghosts, to the general concept of the supernatural, although on the face of it his grammar excludes ghosts from the category. As it happens, all three respondents to this stimulus mention ghosts: they are marginal, and yet significant. It may be that their existence is increasingly accepted, and thus decreasingly considered a *super*-natural matter. They do (or do not) "believe in" them, not in the same way as they believe *in* Christianity, nor yet as they believe *that* two and two make four. Although far from totally absorbing or demanding, there is a personal commitment, to a position that is, however, merely ontological in character: they do now believe in (the *existence* of) ghosts.

The supernatural thus occupies a midway position between science and religion, a no-man's-land between two orthodoxies and "establishments". In varying degrees, for different individuals and groups, it possesses something of the *tremendum et fascinans* of the forbidden and unknown, the taboo. However, the intellectual prohibition is scientific rather than theological, leaving religion (in the form of "Christianity") to supply the moral dimension.

Positively, such a "supernatural" appeals because it indicates that "there's more to life than meets the eye": "there are more things in heaven and earth, than are dreamt of in" the philosophy of a narrow, school-laboratory science. It cocks a snook at human omniscience. Yet it would be a mistake to see it as a prolegomenon for (explicit) religion. The assumption, and faith, is that it is, in principle, and one day in practice will be, the subject of science. It is a "matter of fact"; part of "the system".

So the validity of religion, as unobjectivated value-system, is mirrored in the reality of science, as unsubjective knowledge; just as the insubstantial self stands out in, and and stands out from, the hard world.

3.3.10   The other scene (iii): Salvific

(a) The world is gracious
(b) Improvement is individual and gradual
(c) Perfection is a private notion
(d) Truth is mainly personal

Change, even within the self, is accepted as inevitable, a "permanent fact of life"; but not all change is "for the better". Indeed, conscious reflection upon the general concept tends to issue in just the opposite opinion, albeit with a degree of resignation and element of humour: "But then, that's progress, I suppose", has become a (pejorative) cliché. However, not surprisingly, the analysis of the data threw up four Themes which can be designated as salvific. The first pair refer to the "way the world is", and the second pair to how it might be.

The interviews' contrasting attitudes towards the world are reminiscent of the ambiguity towards the concept, that is present in both Biblical religions. In this case, the contrast is between the world regarded as a "box-full of problems", as suggested by several of the Themes in the section on the Outer World; and the world as reckoned to be gracious, at least to the individual respondent. In the Biblical case, the root of the paradox lies in the ability of personality to hold together, what logic sees as opposites: for instance, that Divinity can love what offends, or that humanity can use images as icons *or* as idols. In the case of the interviews the root of the paradox lies in the use of a single term to refer to more than one area of meaning. The "outer world" consisted primarily of "people", in the aggregate, who bedevil their own situation. The "gracious" world is that conglomeration of biology and history that has given rise to my individuality, my Self, and which therefore gives grounds for hope.

The areas of reference are distinct, although connected. The contrasting attitudes can likewise be seen to be connected. As usual, though, their difference is a distinction, not a dichotomy.

On the one hand, respondents clearly felt that the world had been gracious to them, as individuals. None of them questioned the assumption made by the first stimulus, that life is "worth living". None of them had any difficulty in producing a short litany of things for which they were "grateful" or were "glad about" (A10). Even items that others might see as misfortunes, were regarded as redemptive (A2: y). They had difficulty, even playfully, in spending their three wishes (A3), or their giant win on "the Pools" (A4). This sense of satisfaction comes out in two characteristic sayings: "We've been fortunate to have been given life" (B3: x); and: "[I] would like to have been born" "some time later - now, with so many exciting things in front of you" (B4: z).

This satisfaction, on the other hand, is not to be confused with self-satisfaction, with complete complacency regarding even their own *status quo*. When asked (A11), respondents were able and willing to name things that were lacking in their lives. They wished to emphasise that some of the laments which they criticised in others' behaviour were also present in themselves (A7a: y and z). Nor, indeed, was even the "world of people" all problematic. Reduced to arithmetic, their answers to the question whether the world was "changing for the better or for the worse" (B2), averaged out at zero. Likewise, "People stay the same" (B2: z).

The individual character of the blessings received from a high God by means of the impersonal processes of nature and history, is reflected in the tendency to see power as inherent rather than as designated, and as mostly good, rather than as sorcery or witchcraft of any kind (cp M Marwick 1970: 380). In this particular culture, this leads to a decline in the occurrence of questions of theodicy, at least in the classical, monotheistic form (cp E E Evans-Pritchard 1929, and M Weber 1965: 138). The conclusion of E Z Vogt 1958, though drawn from an apparently small-scale society (but lacking in long-term tradition) is relevant to this evidence, with which it shares much culturally: "Continued optimism in the face of repeated failure is related to the future time orientation".

The description in the second Theme of the salvific element as "improvement", is not only indigenous, but itself indicates its individual and gradual nature. In comparison with many explicit religious (or political) traditions, it is characterised by a series of negatives. It shows little or no sign of an overall strategy, or victory; it is not revolutionary or apocalyptic, complete or cosmic, final or eschatological. However, its "piecemeal" quality endears it to the "English", and makes it very English.

Responsibility for this creeping process of improvement is neither divine nor messianic, in the classical sense of an external saviour, but individual. Thus, "the whole collection of me's" is "most likely ever to put the world right" (C4: y). Otherwise, if a choice must be made, it is those classes in society (or rather, to be more precise, those categories of individuals) who are in the best position to influence others (individual others). Moreover, whether that opportunity is used to the best advantage, itself depends upon each particular individual.

Examples include "the leader of the Chinese people - not the present one, of course, but whoever is" (C4: z), while "the Government" is definitely ruled out (C4: x), and, based upon experience, the Church, and the United Nations, albeit somewhat wistfully (C4: z). A question about "the most useful job in the world", brings to mind "so many", including "the dustman" (C8: x); "a doctor, or a teacher - in the widest sense of the word, not just a schoolteacher. No, being a parent, especially if they're also a good teacher" (C8: y); and, "something in the medical field" (C8: z). The comfort with the categorisation of individual jobs, assumed by the question, is matched by a desire to insist upon their widespread inter-dependence.

It is true that some of the stimuli (eg C3) which provide evidence for this Theme are themselves oriented towards the individualistic and gradualist. Likewise, stimuli of evidence of the preceding Theme, such as B1 and C1-4, are oriented towards a beneficent view of the world. To invalidate the data for that reason, however, would be unduly hasty.

On the one hand, any interviewer, both consciously and unconsciously, uses language which experience, and the pilot study, suggest makes "common sense" with the interviewee, as far as possible. On the other hand, respondents were quite capable of informing the interviewer when they did not agree with the assumptions of the stimulus (eg C5: y, C6: y, E3: x, and F9: z), and of ignoring even probes which they did not care to pursue (eg A3: z). These considerations are confirmed by the homogeneity of the responses to such stimuli as C3 and C4, which allow for precisely these differences of approach, between the social and the individual, and between the human and the superhuman.

Thus the soteriology of this implicit religion (indeed, the implicit theodicy [cp N E Baker, 1990; K Millard, 1995] of that vast activity which comprises contemporary society, economics, culture, and politics) is natural rather than supernatural, pragmatic rather than dogmatic, and individualistic rather than social. On the other hand, if such empiricism is given its due weight, then such a faith, in what is natural, pragmatic and individualistic, may suggest that these various aspects of life have themselves become, albeit simultaneously, super-natural, doctrinaire, and messianic, in a sense that is, strictly speaking, collectivist (rather than corporate).

There is respectable precedent for this empirical approach to what subsequently appears esoteric. Thus J M Kitagawa, 1968: 276, in P G Kuntz (ed), 1968, suggests that "man's understanding of his own nature and destiny ... determines to a great extent the differences of various religious traditions, not so much in philosophical speculation as in soteriological outlook". Even more telling, M Weber 1947:278, states: "Psychologically considered, man in quest of salvation has been primarily preoccupied by attitudes of the here and now". Or, as he says elsewhere (1965), most religion has always been "secular". From a different standpoint, that perceptive observer of the recent world scene, M A C Warren (1965: chapter III), noted: "The ability to conquer poverty will *de facto* be accepted as warrant that the Mandate of Heaven has been conferred, in the new nations."

B Malinowski's analysis (1925) was acute in recognising that the distinctions, and in particular their institutional differentiation, hitherto made between magic and religion (and science), though valid and inescapable, were only legitimate if they were simultaneously recognised as anachronistic. S C Dube (1955) was similarly acute (whatever his students' methodological deserts) in his observation that Indian villagers became fatalists only when all else failed. There is no longer any reason to limit the reference to other cultures.

The third Theme could be seen as describing that utopia towards which the soteriology must, however implicitly, be pointing. The concept of perfection was used in three stimuli (C1, and C5-6). They were remarkable for the sheer speed of the responses which they drew, and for the negative character of those reactions (for such they were). The laughter which twice greeted the concept of a perfect world might have been (but was not) a gloss to prevent self-revelation. However, the denial of the possibility of a perfect person was uniquely unanimous (C6: x, y and z).

Yet the very speed of the reaction shows that the concept was comprehended. Indeed, both that characteristic, and the content of the responses, show that its consideration ante-dated the interview. As a consequence, its desirability was denied, on grounds that were themselves moral (C6: x; cp E1a: y and E8: z), or its conceptualisation was denied, on grounds that were theoretical (C5: x, C6: x, y and z).

This finding echoes that of N J Bull, 1969: chapter I: "The ... Ideal Person Test" has been "used now for seventy years, in which subjects are asked to nominate the person they would most like to be. The most striking development over the years ... is the increase in the number of young people who choose to remain themselves". While there is ample evidence in the public culture of what is popularly known as "idol worship", not only among the young, the present study would confirm the validity of that conclusion, in the private worlds of individuals.

Such a finding has obvious significance for implicit religion in the individual dimension. It may suggest either the lack of a model, myth, or vision; or it may suggest the lack of an inner bifurcation. Socially, however, it is even more ambiguous. It could suggest that the culture fails to supply a common hero, stereotype, or archetype, at least at the conscious level, with which its carriers can identify themselves. This could mean that they are alienated from each other. Alternatively, it could mean that they identify with each other directly, say at the level of the ultimate self, rather than through some third party.

The fourth Theme attempts to portray what is, in effect, the other side of the utopian coin: truth itself is mainly personal. In other words, what *importantly* is, as well as what should be, at least in these interviews, is what "impinges" most. Advertisers, politicians, preachers, and all who wish to convert other selves, are concerned with this "impingement" factor, whose "momentum" can be described as a multiple of intrinsic weight and personal attraction. This double-dimensionality, of objective importance and subjective appeal, of independent existence and the power to move selves, can be properly expressed in terms of meaning, significance, and the symbolic. Such phenomena and concepts are crucial to the discovery and study of implicit religion.

Beliefs may be objects of commitments, and hence more than merely metaphysical. They may likewise be expressions of commitment, and hence themselves simultaneously ontological and evaluative. If this study were concerned primarily with implicit philosophy (rather after the manner of M Douglas (ed), 1973; H Frankfort *et al.*, 1948; R Horton, 1967; J Piaget, 1929; and R P P Tempels, 1959), it would be willing to accept "worldview" or "value" as its field of concern. Indeed, implicit religion and implicit philosophy converge, as they approach the primal, whether that be seen in terms of the development of individuals or of society, or of some trans-social, species evolution, or in terms of priority in the apprehension of reality. What is (factually), is also what ought to be (morally); just as what should be (eschatologically) tends to become what already is (proleptically).

So, beliefs which are both the objects and vehicles of commitment may be listed, on the basis of the responses to stimuli E1a and E1b, as: agnosticism (as contrasted with negative dogmatism) (twice), the limited value of violence, God, Christianity, a sense of humour, honesty, and the ultimate goodness of men. They range widely, but all are personal in their reference, as well as in the character of the commitment to them.

Beliefs, however, are only one kind of object or vehicle of commitment. Stimulus E8 evoked expression of the kind of commitments, of which beliefs are the explicit developments. Routines, and Solidarities, which (in the accepted wisdom of the tradition of religious studies) are the other major expressions of commitment, will therefore be the subject of the final part of this section.

3.3.11   The other scene (iv): Parameters

(a) Death, Dying and Ageing
(b) Dying Voluntarily
(c) The Religious Location of the Divine
(d) The Non-religious Location of Divinity

Of the three main sections into which this analysis of the interview data is divided, one alone (as already mentioned) builds ambiguity into its title: the *other* scene. Of the three sections, it alone also contains a fourth group of Themes. It is tempting to describe them simply as "other elements", thus continuing to avoid the issue whether they are seen, by the respondents or by the analyst, as set *over against* the rest, or as merely "miscellaneous".

Insofar as they are coherent with respect to each other, and transcendent in regard to the rest of reality, upon which they also bestow a certain coherence - then they may be deemed religious, in the manner of the major recognised religions. Insofar as they are phenomenologically unrelated to each other, and are simply categorised by the observer as sharing their oddity as a common characteristic; and insofar as they are exceptions and eccentricities within reality as a whole, without bestowing even the unity of common relationships with each other - then they are religious in the manner of little traditions suffering from obsolescence (ie "superstitions"). The concluding section of this chapter indicates this latter approach (as does the following section of this chapter).

Before reaching either conclusion, their status may be acknowledged as parameters. This is not to suggest that other parameters, which are not dealt with here, are not present in human life; or even that they are not to be found in the triple-identikit interview material. For, it will be recalled, the forty Themes emerged from the interview material, not as a result of attempting to answer particular questions regarding the existence of an implicit religion within the data, but as fundamental themes within the consciousness which was there represented. So the parameters that are grouped together here, therefore, happen to take two forms only: death and divinity.

The only reference to what happens after death was the negative and limited statement, "I don't believe in heaven and hell, as places" (E1a: z). Indeed, the only mention of death (as such) came as an example of what was feared, and was then both amended from noun to verb, and also brought further forward in time: "I must admit I fear death, because I do, but in a very remote way at the moment, though I've a feeling I will fear it more later. I fear dying at an early age, really, rather than death itself: having to leave this world with all its pleasant things."

This pre-mortem, rather than post-mortem, emphasis is characteristic of the evidence. For, although there were no specific questions in the schedule regarding death or what happens thereafter, there was ample opportunity for comment on each of those topics (eg B1, C1-2, E1, E5, and, above all, E9).

The total silence on the actual moment of death may be seen as cause and/or effect of the contemporary seclusion of that transition from the majority of the population.

The inevitability of death, or rather of the approach of death, on the other hand, frequently occurs. It is named in all three of the responses to the question about fear (A8). However, two very different fears are described. Whereas the first response, just quoted, talks of, "Dying at an early age. Having to leave this world with all its pleasant things", the other two speak of, "Getting old, and not being wanted", and "being senile". It is likely that the possible continuation of life far beyond its prime, weighs more heavily than the possible loss of life in its prime. The prominence of this fear must have increased with increased longevity, and especially with the institutionalisation of the elderly.

If the most significant aspect of death, then, is the process of dying; so the most significant part of dying is its preliminary, ageing. It is feared, and acknowledged as such; by all age-groups, including, as it happens, teenagers.

The possibility of dying voluntarily, on the other hand, only appears in the data in response to the stimulus (E4) that specifically raises it. The third respondent volunteers that he "hadn't thought about this particularly", but the middle one gives the impression that (s)he had, while the first one says that this is the case. All three answers are, nevertheless, unusually alike.

The respondents begin with a self-estimate, which can be described as realistic, in being neither simplistically idealistic nor cynical. The third response implies what the other two specify: "I think I'm a prize coward, really ... I can only say, I suppose the best comes out in people when the crunch comes"; and, "I'm afraid I'd make a poor Christian martyr, but I wouldn't want to say I wouldn't die for that".

Respondents then proceed with a negative statement. They do not see themselves as saying they would die "for any *thing*, just in general like that". To die "for my country", which was already a conscious issue, perhaps due to Remembrance Sunday observances, was often seen in similarly impersonal terms, as dying for an abstraction, rather than for actual people. Propagandists no doubt share this intuition, when they personalise the state in terms of "*la patrie*" or "*das Vaterland*" or the regnant monarch, or when they personalise society, in terms of each member's nuclear family or the "royal family"; and when they "green" the nation or country, in terms of its "countryside".

Finally, however, respondents *can* see themselves "dying to rescue my little boy, or my wife, or my parents" (E4: x), or, "for a friend, to rescue him" (E4: 2). Behind each of these particular examples probably lies the general distinction drawn by the other respondent (E4: y): "I could do something constructive, that may result in my death, but that wouldn't be *dying for it*".

The stimulus posed the question in non-moral terms, as usual. Respondents, however, were coolly predictive regarding their own likely behaviour, on the one hand; and, on the other, expressed moral judgements. These run in two directions. For, while they were divided on the morality of "dying for one's country", they did not condemn themselves (sometimes, quite the contrary) for their unwillingness to die for "causes" (E4: y and z, by implication). Here, then, is confirmed the initial emphasis of this report, upon the overriding sacredness of the existent Self.

In this connection it is interesting to note that, whenever Christian martyrs were mentioned, they were seen as dying for a cause (rather than for the sake of their own integrity, their witness, their neighbours, or Lord, or God). Yet the unsubstantiated equation which turns a concept such as "Christianity", into the absolute object of martyrdom, is likewise apparent in statements that confuse particular patriotisms with a general abstraction such as "nationalism". Thus, C J H Hayes, 1960:171, says that "the best and final proof of the religious character of modern nationalism" is "its devotees" laying "down their lives on battlefields in the last one hundred and seventy years". The intended hypothesis is important indeed; but precision probably precludes any individuals dying for *nationalism*, that is, for patriotism in general.

If death is the common subject, of one of the pair of Themes to which the title of "parameters" has been given, the divine is the subject of the other pair. Like death, as such it did not appear in the schedule of stimuli. However, this facilitates its application to all those responses that were concerned with such related concepts as the meaning of God, and of true religion, the sacred, and the holy. The divine, then, is associated, first, with such traditional locations as the gods and the founders of religions. Thus, "God" is "the Buddha, Jesus, Thor" (F6: x). "Our Lord is sacred" (F1: y). The second association of the divine is with the simple conviction: "There's definitely a being who is called God" (F6: x). With this experiential yet non-intrusive approach may be coupled: "I can't imagine living without Him" (F6: y).

A third group of associations is "with the spirit of humanity ... spiritual communication between people... the experience of beauty and so on ... a higher plane of things" (F6: z). With this may be coupled the description of the sacred as: "Those aspects of life which directly, or indirectly, relate to God" (F2: z). So the divine is associated with that in humanity which comes under the heading of religion (or, rather, of "true religion").

The religious location of the divine can be further elaborated. The sacred is one form of the divine dimension (F1: y, F2: x and z). Sacredness is especially associated with that which distinguishes the individual, his beliefs being the outstanding instance of this (F1: x, F2: x). But divinity is also associated with beliefs through its being, typically, the object of such individual beliefs (E1a: z; E1b: x and y; F2: y; and F3: x and y, since "symbols" are seen as things that are "believed in"). Thus the self can be identified both with its beliefs, and with the object(s) of its beliefs: my "deity" is the personification of my "identity". Such a focus of belief is, however, the source of the sacredness, neither of the belief itself, nor of the self. On the contrary, it is the self that bestows sacredness upon both belief and its content.

The holy is religious in a more specific sense than the sacred, and therefore even more closely associated with divinity. "A *holy* man" has a "*God-fearing* attitude" (F3: z). Everybody's religious symbols are also "holy" (cp "sacred places", F1: z), and so, directly or indirectly, are locations of divinity (F3: x and y). With this may be coupled the definition of the sacred as "something that is almost untouchable ... that has got to be revered" (F2: y).

These various aspects of divinity, then, indicate a "high God" who is closely associated with religious phenomena, both for those who are thought to identify with them and for those who do not. But, strictly speaking, he is not so much the subject of religion, as its object; or, to speak in more usual ways, he is not so much the object, with which relationship can be entered into, as the theme or topic of the specialism.

The special status accorded to religion is less on account of its god, than of its significance for its adherents. Thus, it is not only "the existence of the Jews" that "proves the existence of God", but the existence of belief in divinity generally, that indicates the reality of the divine. That significance is primarily seen as emotional, akin to a capacity for auto-hypnotism, but it is a matter of some public interest (F3: x, y). However, its ultimate criterion, as being both true and beneficial, lies in the fixed personal attitudes apparent in the realm of non-religious relationships.

For divinity is located in the non-religious as well as in the religious realm. Thus, without any mention of religion, a question about their "definite beliefs" prompts mention of God in two out of six responses: "I believe in God of course" (E1b: x), and, "I don't believe in ... God as a Father sitting up there" (E1a: z). The concept of "doing God's will" is also volunteered twice: once in connection with "what makes life worth living" (A2: z), and once as "the purpose of life" ("although it isn't always easy to know" what "that means": B3: z).

The other three occasions on which the non-religious location of divinity is demonstrated are also all of a conative rather than a credal character. One respondent is "grateful" "for the opportunity to serve "God" (A10: x). Another would advise a fifteen year old: "Never be afraid of the truth ... and fear God" (E5: z). A third assumes that it is the will of "God, through the Church" to "put the world right", but feels that "that's very idealistic" and so puts the thought aside (C4: z; cp C4: y).

So this final section of the report on the interviews' Themes may be summarized credally as:

> Conscience commands, Christianity helps, and the world is kind;
> but ageing is fearful, and God is distant.

3.4   The Integrating Foci of the Interviewees

The elucidation of the forty Themes seen as present in the interview data makes no claim to be exhaustive. Indeed, it is to be hoped that others will wish to add to, amend, or challenge the validity of, this list: such a process should be facilitated by the reproduction *in toto* of the evidence from which they have been developed. As well as serving as hypotheses for others to improve upon, however, such Themes have the merit of beginning to articulate (in both senses: to verbalise, and to integrate) their content. It is now therefore possible, and indeed necessary, to articulate those integrating foci that are present within the identi-kit interviews as a whole: to articulate the underlying themes of the forty Themes.

Four such integrating foci can be discerned. They are "the round", of everyday life; the experience of "an alternative reality" (or alternative realities); the "priestly" functioning of various phenomena; and the commitment to what is called "Christianity". The particular study reported upon in this Chapter will conclude with the description of these four foci. The report on two further studies in the following two Chapters will likewise conclude with descriptions of the integrating foci distinguished in other contexts within contemporary society (in the United Kingdom). Only subsequently (Chapter 6.2 & 3) will an attempt be made to integrate these three sets of integrating foci, and to gauge, from them, the character of the implicit religiosity (if any) of contemporary society.

3.4.1   The "round"

Several of the stimuli were concerned, not so much to elicit detailed description of the "round" of everyday life, as to discover which were its most important constituents, and how important they were. The paucity of references to it in the table of Themes is explained by the lack of uniformity, both in its constituents and in the meaningfulness of those constituents. Its significance does, however, account for the emergence of the two Themes that said: "I am content with my round", and, "I am happy if I can get by". It is also related to all those Themes that were grouped together under the heading, The Relationship of the Self with other Selves, and with other individual Themes, not least, "The List".

Despite its heterogeneity, the practical meaning of the Round, for the respondents, must first be sketched. Thus the question about "the most important thing" they did "each year" (D4) produced at least five, disparate items. However, a common element in both halves of the first response involved "going away", either "for a holiday", or else "to visit ... relations and old friends". This orientation towards the cessation of one part of the round, itself routine, is echoed in the first response to the question regarding "each day": "Next, it's finishing work, because that's the start of leisure time - that's what I work for" (D6: x).

The question regarding the weekly round, on the other hand, elicits only two items, "I like to go to church" being the first of them (D5: x). This realm of activity finds an echo in the first response to the preceding question, which named "Christmas" as one of the (three) "most important" things each year (D4: z). It was also echoed in the third response to the succeeding question, which described "Praying over things", as the "most important thing" "each day" (D6: z). Again, a "going away" may be discerned: not so much in terms of physical residence, as in spirit. Again, also, this recurrent exodus is seen as itself part of the Round, within the overall routine of living.

A third commonality finds a ready expression, in the first response to the question regarding "each day". This respondent said: "Trying to get out a decent day's work, so that everyone is satisfied" (D6: x). This emphasis, upon work (or, rather, upon its completion), was anticipated by the other positive response to the preceding question, which said that, "to get by and do my bits of jobs", was "the most important thing" of "the week" (D5: z). The Round is thus dominated by "work", whether it is imposed by others or self-imposed.

Whether the whole Round can be described as expressing a Protestant (or a secular) "work-ethic", is however, another matter. Max Weber (eg 1930: 70) was intrigued by the apparently non-transcendental love of work (cp R Bendix, 1960: chapter III). Tom Harrison even gave the name of "Worktown" to Bolton, Lancashire, in his 1961 study (cp P L Berger, 1961; G Gorer, 1965: 71; G Lenski, 1955: 93-97). There were, however, signs by the time of the interviews that the economic necessity, or religious legitimation, or social advantages, of this emphasis, were disappearing (cp R Hoggart, 1969, in W R Niblett (ed) 1969; H Cox, 1965: 185-6; V Packard, 1950). Jeremy Seabrook, 1967, saw a subordination to "meaningless things", giving way to a "dead" ritual.

It comes as no surprise, therefore, to find in the interviews a fourth, and equally prevalent strand - of agnosticism, regarding the "most important thing" that was done each day, week or year. It appears in three of the nine responses: "I'm not old enough to answer that one yet - the year doesn't have any pattern" (D4: y); "I wish there was something, but there isn't, because I'm too pragmatic. I take life very much as it comes, and I tend not to look forward to things" (D5: y); and, "I can't single out any one thing that's more important than the others that I can think of" (D6: y).

Thus the most important characteristic of the Round is its very existence, as a Round. Or, to put it another way, the most significant aspect of the routine of ordinary life is that it, including its variety, is repetitive. Phenomenologically, this seems like saying that the "usual" way of life is seen as both natural and normative (inevitable and proper); and that it contained, *within itself*, contrasts which are nevertheless mutually inter-dependent (dichotomies that retain a reciprocity).

The parallels with the situation before the (self-conscious) Founders of the religions (A C Bouquet, 1954; E Durkheim, 1947; W C Smith, 1964) is apparent. Hesitation in formulating a hypothesis based upon this similarity, however, arises from the difficulty in knowing which elements within this cultural cycle to identify with the sacred, and which with the profane. Thus D3: y says she would "really miss, if it was abolished", "the chores and it would be terrible to sit idle and not have anything to do". Likewise, D5: z says, "To get by, and do my bits of jobs", is "the most important thing" she does "each week". On the other hand, D6: x says "finishing work" is "the most important thing" he does "each day" (after, "trying to get out a decent day's work, so everyone is satisfied"): "Next, it's finishing work, because that's the start of leisure time - that's what I work for".

Yet the difficulty arises from an over-simple attempt to transfer understanding regarding religion, and its relationship with the total social setting, in small-scale societies, or even in historical societies, to contemporary society. ("Fundamentalism" may, as so often, have been first characterised as a religious trait; but it is a common, human characteristic.) Just as we should not necessarily expect to find religious life in contemporary society restricted to those institutions which were designated as religious in historical society; so we should not assume that all its members will share the same valuation of the two sides of the work/leisure division, or of whatever division they experience as basic. (It is possible that simpler societies themselves were never so simple, or simplistic.)

The deepest expression of this fundamental distinction may likewise be spatial, rather than temporal: a contrast between the subjective qualities inherent in different buildings, personnel, or records, rather than in seasons or activities. Thus D3: x does not "think there is anything really", in "the ordinary routine of living which" (s)he "would really miss", if it was abolished; yet points to certain strands, rather than events, in volunteering that (s)he would "miss music a great deal, and books, and human company". D3: z says she would "miss not being able to go for a walk every day, or not being able to cut flowers from the garden. And I'd miss sitting in the evening and watching television". Even D4: x implies that "going away - abroad - for a holiday" is "the most important thing" she does "each year", not, primarily, because "I enjoy it ... but [because] it's my husband's chief thing of the year". D5: x suggests an instrumental, yet non-magical use of overtly religious ritual (what the Church of England's 1559 Book of Common Prayer itself described as a "Use"): "I like to go to Church. Once a week's enough, just to keep with it, in touch".

The Round, then (as that designation implies) has an integrating influence, upon individuals, as upon society generally. It also contains some (or all) of the fundamental categories present in consciousness. It is, however, as erroneous to look for any single item, be it event or institution, within the Round, as the source of its unity, as it is to look to overtly religious activities or organisations for that function. There is no single template, in secular contemporary society. (It is legitimate to ask whether there ever was, empirically, save in the official religious model, of the official religion, in past societies.) The absence of a single unifying item, within the Round itself, does not mean that all religious experiences (in the official or unofficial sense) have become private, however; any more than that all human experience has been privatised. It simply means that none of them have the kind of "pull" over the remainder of experience which is associated with such miniaturised models as a holistic sacrament, or totalistic "microchip".

Indeed, the Round as a whole has only a relative, rather than an absolute, pull over its individual devotees (or officiants). They, like society, sit somewhat loose to it. It is relatively integrating, but does not bestow complete integration. This, of course, does not, in itself, prevent its being a form of religion: religions express, legitimate, and enhance, divisions as well as unity, within individuals and society.

In this case, however, there is one reality which is present throughout the Round, and which is related in a common manner to every item within it. That Self, which is thus immanent, is therefore simultaneously transcendent - even over the individuals' *loci* of the sacred.

3.4.2   Alternative reality

Analysis of the interview data constantly suggests that another integrating focus might possibly be the apprehension of an alternative reality. When considering the candidature of the Round, it was necessary to weigh the evidence of the interviews themselves. In this case, it is sufficient to concentrate upon the Themes, of which this might be the underlying theme. For, whereas the Round was a whole universe, albeit with distinctions, Reality is experienced as already split. The existence of its Alternative half is therefore a foil to the apparent contentment of the Round, and may be conscious.

The Alternative Reality is, in the first place, posited as contrasted with the prevailing public culture. The primary instance of this repeated but private conviction is the belief in the existence of the Self, which is capable of being distinguished from all the "accidents" by which it is known. Thus it can find its own life, not just in relationship with an other, but within the other, with whom it is capable of being "substantially" united, for instance in marriage.

The second set of contrasts is not with the prevailing public assumptions, but is shared with them. It is the contrast between possible, and present, realities. Thus improvement is seen as possible and desirable, albeit gradual and piecemeal. The world is seen as capable of bringing salvation of various kinds; for, while goals are desirable in themselves, they are also in part attainable - and therefore in need of re-formation. To give, or at least risk, one's own life, in order to save someone else's, is at least conceivable, and was indeed conceived of, before the interview experience.

However, just as the Round proved to be less than fully integrated, so the vision of an alternative Reality turns out to be less than fully integrated ("an") or dichotomous ("alternative"). Thus respondents could name "great moments" quite easily, but only one respondent (F5: z) could clearly affirm, "Yes", they had shown him/her something "of the meaning of life". However, it is doubtful whether even s/he had ever previously articulated that meaning, even privately. Likewise, no radical change in life-style could be conceived, even in play. Indeed, in view of the near-duty to be already "happy", such pipe-dreams would be self-indulgent and shameful.

At the deepest level, the Self was, and would remain, "only" human; and "I" had little power to change its nature. My, or its, beliefs were similarly unlikely to change. Answers as to identity were in keeping with this: either one knew who one was, so that the question was unnecessary, or one did not know the answer, and was unlikely ever to discover it.

Global attitudes were not dissimilar. The world is a problem, and change is real, but endless. Polarities exist, but are not dichotomous. The relativities are not clustered, and should not be absolutised. Christianity holds out a hope, or at least the ideal, of a better way, but is unlikely to help those who do not already find it helpful. Religion, being essentially private, cannot help, socially or corporately. God is too distant (or sometimes, too close?) to be of assistance, except in moments of crisis. Life has purpose, but its purpose is a puzzle. Perfection is a moral concept (or possibly an immoral notion), but anyway is private.

No doubt there are individuals for whom the apprehension of an alternative reality is a consuming interest. No doubt there are groups of individuals for whom a vision of an alternative reality is an integrating focus, at least in aspects of their lives which they share with each other. While there are signs, especially of the former, in the identi-kit interviews, methodologically they were concerned less with individuals, in the totality of their lives, or with groups, in their group-life, than with elements of personal significance across society as a whole. However, the theoretical possibility remains that there may be one or more foci, based upon apprehensions of an alternative reality, which serves to integrate some areas of that individual but repeated reality with which the identi-kit interviews are concerned.

The only candidate for this role is that named in the first theme of all ("I have a self"); or, perhaps more fruitfully, the inter-dependent pair immediately following ("The self is human", and, "The self is sacred"). The depth of the conviction with which they are held, and the depth of such convictions, is matched by the breadth of their influence. They are linked (as cause, or consequence, or simply in consonance with) the dismissal of such alternative realities as all-round progress, universal panaceas, or redemptive collectivities. They determine (or express) the "this-worldly" character (cp A de Tocqueville, 1890) of this culture, and of any and all religions that are "at home" in it (F B Welbourn & B A Ogot, 1952).

The ultimate expression of the power of this conviction may be the refusal to participate (described in the following Chapter as the solidarity of individualism). Its influence is inevitably primarily private, negative, and ineffable. It nevertheless safeguards, enhances and proclaims the basis for the conviction that "I" am the steward of my self: its devoted master. Its future (unknown, but not entirely open-ended) is the only alternative reality to the present.

3.4.3   Possible priesthoods

A third candidate for the position of integrating focus kept presenting itself during the analysis of the interview data. It too could be described as a theme of many of the Themes. For the moment (cp Chapter 6.3) it can be characterised simply as "the human". It is demonstrated most clearly in the responses to stimulus D8.

The "human" has a different function and meaning in this case, than in the preceding section, where the self was described as sacred but "only human". The emphasis in this case is upon the human as an existing reality, as the present sign of a great glory, as an experienced vision, a *fascinans* exercising its innate power of attraction. This use of the word differs from that in the previous expression ("only human") in being so complimentary, in its expressing admiration rather than resignation, in its statement of glee rather than sympathy. In it, the present and the personal "are met together ... have kissed each other" (Psalm 85: 10, Coverdale translation).

Its description as a "possible priesthood" is intended to emphasise its *modus operandi*: by the revelation of incarnation, by existential attraction, by inspiration (to adoration and thanksgiving); in contrast to a visual aid, illustrating an independently conceived ideal, or an empirical example demonstrating a law of personal dynamics. In this case the experience always outstrips the understanding; just as the response exceeds the expectations. For the worshipper is affected, either by that which is worshipped, or by the relationship experienced, or both.

Various human priesthoods within contemporary society have been posited. The television industry was analysed for a volume (published about 1968) under the title, "the new priesthood", but without elaborating on the reasons for this choice of phrase. The British Humanist Association has a representative role, ideologically, and legislatively; however, there is no evidence in these three studies (and little elsewhere) of a continuing sense of communion with it (or even awareness of its existence). In the following reports, the Manager and Barmen, or the Rector and congregation, have some sort of corporate (and incorporating) priestly role. They give their respective institutions a "human face"; but it is "only [too] human".

Better candidates for this priestly role might be the politicians and Government. Does their legitimation not lie in their representative capacity? Are not their researches geared to finding out how they can best fulfil that function - in every way, from policy to fashion, from world-view to "private" life, from ethical stance to accent? Yet, for these very reasons, among others, they too are seen as "only human". In the contexts of the succeeding pair of studies, they can be seen to integrate a proportion of the population, both with each other and within themselves, especially at election-time. The attitude of the bulk of the population, however, is better illustrated by the identi-kit interviews, which portray them less like a priesthood, and more like a guild of witches, against whom the best defence is cynicism. They are integrative, but inversely.

Other particular groups to emerge from the interviews as a possible priesthood tend to do so in response to stimulus C8, "What is the most useful job in the world?" The answers named "a doctor", or "something in the medical field"; "a teacher", or "a parent"; or "a dustman". However, the tenor of the responses matched that of the stimulus: more utilitarian, and appreciative, than enthusiastic, or religious.

A better candidate than such categories was the general and global "humanity", as a whole. Yet in practice this humanity, in the mass or in the abstract, becomes "only human". The integration of the individual seems to require smaller frames of reference. Humanity only becomes a priesthood when it is both specific, and not average. Three main examples are to be found in the interview data: children, small group situations with face-to-face contacts, and certain public figures. Then the human becomes truly human (as well as "only human"); the truly human becomes real; and the real becomes significant because human. This significance can be known, and responded to, but never adequately described or anticipated.

Such manifestations of what it can mean to be human become revelatory "moments" (in the sense of momentous, rather than momentary). They may or may not be seen as a theophany: the response to them shows that they are *hiero*phanies. That which was (and remains) "only human", is simultaneously seen to be gloriously, richly, splendidly human. The self is given a quality which all have, yet also long to possess. An "anthropophany" has taken place.

Religious experiences, in contemporary society, would seem to include this type of occurrence and insight. The fact that not every member of society will be integrated, internally, and externally, by the same anthropophany, is only to be expected in a mass and pluralistic society; and is by no means novel. However, contemporary culture also contains its own checks and balances: individual identity will fall for charismatic characters with finite groupings, but will no more stand for universal hero worship than for panaceas. The truly representative and integrative is the anonymous, replicated and unknown, soldier (as after 1918), victim (as of terrorism), or child (as in famine).

3.4.4   Christianity

The final candidate for the post of integrating the data of the interviews must be Christianity. It would, of course, be seen in this role by many of the respondents. It is also connected with many of the Themes, including (in the belief of many of the respondents) those to do with the self, and those to do with inter-personal relationships (hence the desire for religious education, conceived as moral education).

The meaning of "Christianity" will be more fully explored in the report on the parish (Chapter 5.3.6). Meanwhile, the interviews show that it is Christianity, rather than Christ, the Church, or God, which is the possible integrating focus of the consciousness they reveal.

Certain limitations upon its integrative influence may also be noted. Thus "Christianity" has little to do with the Received World, or with salvific themes (although they are not altogether outside the realm of God, apparently inactive though he be). It is also in some conflict with the valuation placed upon the self, and the truly human, for that is loveable and laughable, while it is ideal, perfect, uniform, schoolmasterly, lifeless, and disapproving of the Self.

Historically, a parallel might be drawn between this popular understanding of Christianity, and Homer's "humanisation" of the gods, for the city-states of the Greek archipelago, in contrast to the religion and theology of such formal, centralised empires as Egypt; likewise with the Aryan contribution to Indian religion, followed by the village versions of the "Great Tradition" of Brahmanism; and similarly with the contemporary, polycentric renewal of the world-religions, through the emergence and re-emergence of "little traditions" and "local theologies", new or old.

The Round, alternative Realities, possible Priesthoods, and Christianity, may for the moment be allowed to stand, as foci of the interview data with varying powers of integration. In the concluding Chapter they will be compared with those foci found in the other two studies to be reported here: of the life of a public house, and the life of a residential parish.

Chapter 4

THE IMPLICIT RELIGION OF A PUBLIC HOUSE

4.1 The Methodological Background: Participant Observer

Concurrently with the holding of the interviews, two other sources of data were utilised. A national political party was joined, at the most local level possible, that of the Ward. This led, with surprising rapidity, to membership of committees that were responsible for choosing parliamentary candidates for the constituency, for liaising with other institutions, and for governing schools. While a record, in the form of a diary, was kept of what was observed, and of its apparent meaning, this source of data will not be formally and separately reported upon in this context.

Two impressions from that experience, may, however, be mentioned: that people generally did not so much work or vote for a party, as *against* another party (there being only two parties of popular, national standing, at that time); and that people did not so much vote against a party's policies or platform, as against its *culture*. As it happens, these reflections were shared with the other active members of the party in the Ward. It was found that they were immediately acknowledged as true; not merely, it seemed, of the general public, but of themselves. (Indeed, had the student felt able to suggest that this "culture" represented some sort of "implicit religion", without thereby revealing his personal agenda, the validity of that interpretation might also have been recognised, even in 1970.)

The other source of data that was attempted was a public house. Again the student simply visited the nearest one to his own address (at that time) as a customer, approximately weekly, over a period of six months. This led to a number of conversations of interest, with individuals. Again, a "diary" was kept, of observations and analysis. In contrast with the Interviews, however, the productivity of such visits was little greater than it was in the case of the political party. Whether it was due to the self-conscious concern of the party with public opinion in the first case, or to the absence of decision-making in the second case, or to the relative inexperience of the observer at that stage, the time taken was hardly matched by the depth achieved.

In undertaking these alternative methods of collecting data, it was hoped to avoid situations in which the student was in danger of influencing, to any serious extent, the situation that was being observed. For this had been anticipated as possibly being a major drawback to the interview procedure. As it transpired, however, that fear was ill-founded. Certainly, the interviewer provided the particular stimuli. He also contributed the "listening ear", without which the interviewee would hardly have engaged in the labour of self-description. Yet there was (surprisingly, it is admitted) little evidence that the responses were geared to him, in any way other than the desire to communicate, as accurately and truthfully as possible.

That the interviewee (as well as the interviewer) understood his or her own word to be the last word upon the material itself, was confirmed by the similar lack of influence exercised by those other interviewees that were present, in the case of the three married couples who preferred to be interviewed as pairs; and in the case of the eight groups of teenagers, who, for practical reasons, had to be interviewed in small groups, of about half a dozen.

Indeed, this material not having been used in the composition of the existing "triple identi-kit" interview, remains available, both for individual comparison, and for the compilation of further, including independent, identi-kit interviews in the future.

The two additional sources of possible data (the Ward, and the pub – as a customer) were abandoned, then: partly because they did not provide sufficient contrast with the individualistic character of the interview situation, and partly because the observer did not consider he was influencing the character (as distinct from the nature) of the data being elicited in the interviews. Another avenue of activity was therefore explored: that of *working behind the Bar* of (as it happens) the self-same public house. This provided the desired contrasts, and proved highly instructive. It therefore forms the basis of the second study to be formally reported upon, and the subject of this chapter.

The public house in question was owned by a brewery, and run by a Manager (rather than a landlord). It was his practice to appoint five assistant Barmen. They worked for four sessions, of four hours, each week, in the evenings on week-days, or at lunch-time or in the evening at week-ends; except for one week in four, when they worked three sessions only, on Friday evening and twice on Saturday, or on Saturday evening and twice on Sunday. By this menu they worked an average of fifteen hours per week, in each four week month: between 1966 and 1971, had they worked sixteen hours, their employer would have become eligible for Selective Employment Tax. Just over one hundred sessions, of four hours each, were worked in this way, between November 1969 and July 1970. The observation thus acquired was supplemented by some twenty visits to the same public house, as a customer, before, during and after this period. All were duly recorded and reflected upon, initially in diary form.

The public house was chosen as a suitable *venue* for participant observation within a *social* situation, for reasons that are well-known to all who are familiar with this institution, and its meaning in English society and culture. First, it is open, by law as well as tradition, to all who are of sufficient age, provided only that they purchase one item, and their behaviour does not constitute a nuisance to the other customers and require the manager to exercise his discretionary veto. It is therefore the classic *locus* for straw polls, by journalists for instance, of public opinion in general. Secondly, the context is (within certain limitations that will be noted) egalitarian, both socially and culturally. Indeed, tradition has it that, "You get all types in a pub", and each is "free to say what he thinks". Thirdly, not only does each and every public house contain a broad spectrum of individuals, but in England it is a social institution, even more, perhaps, than in other parts of the United Kingdom. Individuals may and do enter and remain alone; but one's very presence invites personal interaction, if only with the staff, through the necessity of engaging in a purchase. Finally, although this is clearer with hindsight than was anticipated by intuition, it is social, not just in the sense of individual and social inter-action, but in a corporate sense: it has continuity and character, a "life of its own", that exceeds that of the mere sum of its constituent parts. It not only possesses the "face-to-face" situation, and the "continuity of social relations", which T Luckmann (1967: chapters III-IV) sees as required for the "fundamentally religious process" of "[constructing] meaning systems": it is also a community of some sort in its own right - as became, and will be made, clear.

In this respect at least, it may not be as unique as is sometimes suggested, either by its participants or their compatriots, or by its foreign admirers. The café in France, or in Greece and Turkey, the beer-cellar in Germany, the platform in front of the house or around the *banyan* tree in India, may all provide comparable social settings. Whatever may be true in their case, however, "little research of a serious-deep sort has been carried out in the pub: one of the key institutions in British life" (T Harrisson, 1961: 168; cp also N Kessel & H Walton, 1965: 48, and their references to T Hopkinson, 1945, and S B Rowntree & G R Lavers, 1951, and a survey during the War by Mass Observation). Indeed, pride in the antiquity of its origin as an institution, and the longevity of some particular examples, may be suspected of "ruling out of court" any investigation or suggestion regarding the extent of change, or the comparative novelty of some of its "traditional" aspects.

To do more than raise such questions, at this point, would, however, be to anticipate. This report will begin by briefly describing the life of the public house: its external setting, the internal scene, the "members" who people it. Once the *Sitzimleben* has been thus sketched, its religious aspect will be investigated: first, the place of explicit religion, and then the place, character and nature of any implicit religion that may be felt to be present in it.

4.2 The Life of the Public House

4.2.1 The setting

4.2.1.1 The catchment area

The public house in question lies a little over a mile (nearly two kilometres), to the north of the old (medieval and eighteenth-century), and recently redeveloped, centre of Bristol. Its doors open onto the pavement by the side of the A38, the ancient trunk road from the south-west peninsular of England to Cheltenham, Gloucester, and the Midlands conurbation. At the time of this study, just prior to the completion of the M5 relief road, it was constantly passed by commercial travellers' cars, heavy lorries, and, at week-ends in summer, by holiday-makers' caravans. The overwhelming impression outside the building was one of noise, and petrol and diesel fumes, and litter, for the conjunction of the main road, and three minor roads, produced unbroken acres of tarmac in each direction. However, the lack of parking facilities, the urban setting, and the absence of historical nostalgia, precluded this house from catering for the passing traffic.

So the public house's *clientèle* nearly all lived, or at least lodged, locally. Up on the hillside behind the building lay a suburb whose development spanned most of the nineteenth century. The older, larger houses at the top of the hill, with their Bath-stone *façades*, had all been divided into flats, and many of them sub-divided again, into bedsitters for students at the nearby university and other colleges. Some of the smaller, Victorian houses, near to the main road, were still occupied by owners who had lived there all their lives; but even they had taken in lodgers. Up the hillside on the other side of the main road lay a much more uniform suburb, built in brick about the turn of the century. The residents from both hillsides came down to "the Cheltenham road" to shop.

The names of "pubs" form a *genre* which expresses an important part of the institution's character. It accounts for the attention paid to them (far exceeding the dedications of any other local institution, such as the church), and to the sign bearing the name. Without a knowledge of medieval liveries, hunting lore, or the symbolism of the Apocalypse, the frequent references to "arms", the "golden hart", or the "lamb and flag", can become an occasion for a public acknowledgement of puzzlement, even mystery, in the face of a tradition which is now entirely mundane. In this case, the "Beaufort House" made no pretentions, beyond seeking a fictitious association with the largest landowner in the region, the Duke of Beaufort.

4.2.1.2   The building

The "pub" itself was built in 1939. One of the "regulars", at the time of the study, could remember stepping over the threshold the day it opened. Of brick, edged with a little decorative Bath stone, it had distant reflections of pre-War "contemporary", and post-war "neo-Georgian". Perhaps it could best be characterised as being, simply, conspicuously unremarkable, deliberately (presumably) unostentatious.

The entrance is almost as utilitarian as it is possible to be. Notably insignificant, its lack of enticement is reminiscent of the more recent betting shop, just beyond the railway viaduct. It consists of a gap, large enough for two red-doors in the *façade* fronting the pavement. Their being open or shut indicates whether the *house* is open or shut, for they lack both handle and knocker.

The porch into which they give access is likewise functional, to the point of utilitarian. The doormat says "George's", the name of the brewery that built the pub, before it was taken over by Courage's (and Courage's, later, by Charrington-Bass). However, as it is not even large enough to unfurl an umbrella, for instance, it is necessary to go out onto the pavement first, in order to raise an umbrella against the rain. So the real purpose of the porch is indicated by the sign at eye-level on the wall opposite the door, directing the customer into the Public Bar on the left or the Lounge on the right.

In Britain the "public" house has not only been licensed to sell alcoholic beverages and food between certain hours that are agreed locally, but obliged by law, for the sustenance of the travelling public, to make them available for purchase for a certain number of hours each day. Beer traditionally being a standard sustenance, its price in the public Bar is therefore controlled by government, whereas in the Lounge it is "free" (of control). So it is the "public" "side" of the house which is definitive of the institution historically, legally, and socially.

In this case, then, pushing open the door on the left and entering the Public Bar, the customer immediately finds himself up against a small round table and so has to turn right, round the edge of the door, which is now springing shut behind him. Looking down the length of the room in front of him, he sees it is about three times as long as it is wide. Along most of the right-hand wall runs the fine wooden Bar, about two feet wide. In the middle of the long wall opposite to it is a fire. Round most of the rest of that wall, and of the shorter end walls that back onto the road and onto the "yard" at the rear, runs a bench, with tables and chairs set at intervals in front of it. At the far end of the bar (room), beyond the Bar (in the stricter sense), and beyond the entrance to the gentleman's lavatory, is the darts board and its score-board; opposite to them is the "machine" or "one-armed bandit", backed up against part of the bench.

Each section of the bench has a long cushion, covered in yellowy-brown plastic. The chairs round the tables, and the stools at the bar, are covered with the same material. The table-tops are covered with a light brown formica, streaked with white, in cursory imitation of the grain in timber. All the real woodwork is likewise painted brown, and the cream gloss on the walls and ceiling has also turned a light brown. The floor is covered with a brown linoleum. Even the curtains, which the Manager's wife has introduced round the frosted-glass windows at each end, are black, red and brown.

Should the customer decide that the Public Bar is too large, too long, or too soberly brown for his liking, he could return to the porch and push the opposite door. This time, looking left round the edge of the door, he would see a room which was only half the length of the other, and so approximately square-shaped; for the portion of the building beyond it is occupied by the Ladies' and Gentlemen's toilets. To his immediate left, behind the door, is a table, followed by the fireplace, and then the Bar, which in this case is semi-circular and has a glossy surface. Between the doors to the "Ladies" and "Gents", on the wall away from the road, is another rectangular table. Between the tables (and the "one-armed bandit"), on the wall opposite the fireplace and bar, is another door, this time with leaded, opaque glass and marked "Private": it leads upstairs, to the Manager's flat. On the side abutting the pavement are two more tables, with one of which our visitor nearly collided, as in the public side.

This room also has a bench running round the walls wherever possible. It too is covered with a plastic cushion, like the chairs and bar-stools. However, on this side they, and the table-tops, are all red, as is the carpet with which the floor is covered. The walls and ceiling have been painted in cream on this side, too; but with a matt finish, and more recently perhaps, because the colour has become less mellow. The curtains over the windows have frills above them, and are of a heavier material, with a quieter pattern.

The contrast between the two "sides" of the pub, therefore, is discreet, but marked and consistent. Considered as an architectural shell, devoid of people, one is a bar room, containing the Bar, reminiscent of an old-fashioned school-room, or the kind of drill-hall that the Territorial Army used to meet in. The other is a room, modelled on a modern, or recently-modern, petit-bourgeois sitting-room.

On the public side are the black handles of the "pumps" for the bitter (beer), and the barrels and gas cyclinders for the Tavern Keg, laager and Guinness, and the sink for washing up the glasses (below the bar-top). The beer bottles on that side are open to view, behind the bar; in the lounge, they are hidden from view, below the bar. The glasses for long, bottled drinks on the Lounge side have a stem, and a gold rim round the top, with a red-and-white "Courage's" logo (a cockerel) on the side: those on the Bar side have neither stem nor decoration. The casks of sherry, and all the bottles for short drinks, are kept on the public side, above the back of the bar space, where they provide a colourful back-cloth; the lounge bar has a table lamp with a red shade sitting on each end of it. Cigarettes are kept on the public side, cigars in the lounge. However, most of the cigars are sold to customers on the public side, and so are carried through, one by one.

The "doorway" epitomises the relationship between the two sides exactly. As it happens, there is a curtain at each jamb, but no door. Once there had been a bar across the door, unconsciously recalling the original purpose of the "bar", when refreshment was being served from, or in, what were basically domestic premises, with the "bar" across the entrance to the private quarters, barring access to them. Only when this bar had proved insufficiently roomy for customers to stand by, had the semi-circular bar been introduced into the lounge (at the expense of some of the sitting area).

Customers in the lounge are more conscious of, as well as more articulate about, the existence of (what they usually call) "the other side". They will use the doorway (which is easier for them, for they cannot avoid being closer to it) to see who is on the other side, and what kind of life is going on there. Some will say that customers on their side must obviously be pleasanter to serve than those on the other side.

Customers in the public bar virtually ignore the lounge and its customers. "George the painter", who sits opposite the "doorway", cannot avoid seeing through it, and from time to time will remark that the Manager spends too long talking to customers through there. "Young Martin", his son, ordering a drink between turns at the dart-board, will also half-humorously accuse the assistant barmen of paying too much attention to orders in the lounge, in order to draw attention to his empty glass on the counter.

When friends spy each other through the "doorway", it is nearly always the one on the lounge side who first sees the other, and likewise acknowledges him, and orders a drink for him. Usually, indeed, he carries his own drink through to the public side, via the porch, or else asks the barman to take it through, while he walks round to the "other side".

The traditional pub, so beloved of advertisers, and many tourists as well as natives, is in many respects of rather recent origin. The Lounge, for instance, when it was introduced in the 1920s, had the glamorous, even suspect, air of a *rendez-vous* for journalists and other sophisticates who were "no better than they ought to be". By 1970 it had apparently been forgotten that they were ever new. (In contemporary society, as in the Domesday Book, "time out of mind" seems to be about forty years; cp Lord Raglan, 1936). During the period of observation, suspicion was voiced, however, that "really" the breweries wanted to do away with the public side, so they could charge what they liked, for bitter as for other drinks. By the 1990s further changes have again taken place, with the provision of rooms and garden furniture for children, an increased emphasis

upon food, and the appeal of a social centre for the family, accompanied by
the relaxation of licensing hours.

Nevertheless, in the pub as in public attitudes and in religion, change, although it may be both profound and relatively fast, takes place over decades,
rather than overnight. After all, voluntary participation means personal identification. Thus the current Manager's wife had introduced curtains for the
first time, into at least the Bar; and the "machine" had clearly been installed
in each side, also probably in the 1960s, certainly since the benches had been
designed (in 1939). Likewise, soon after the period of observation, in the 1970s,
a new Manager did away with the coal fires, and installed a second "machine"
on each side, up against the redundant fireplaces. Indeed, by the end of the
1980s, a dark, "late Victorian" décor, with low-hanging lamps over each table,
and "frilled" red-glass light-shades, attempted to double or treble the building's
actual age.

4.2.1.3 The passage of time

It is possible, however, that the temporal dimension remains more stable than
the spatial. For the pattern of the day, week or year, is less subject to the
brewery's marketing director or architect, or even to statutory changes, than
is the physical environment.

The Beaufort House was open every day, during the period of observation,
from 10.30 am to 2.30 pm, and from 6.0 pm to 10.30 pm; except on Sundays,
when it was open from 12.0 to 2.0 and 7.0 to 10.30. Assistant barmen were
required every evening, but at lunch-time only on Saturdays and Sundays.
However, a few additional visits, as assistant or as customer, at lunch-times on
week-days, were sufficient to confirm that the assistants' customary working
sessions were the times when the pub really came to life, and set the pattern for
the house. Most of the customers at lunch-time on week-days are "looking after
themselves", simply. They are working locally, and have come primarily for the
food and/or drink. They are somewhat hurried and businesslike, take little
notice of other customers, and restrict their conversation to the conventional,
like the lift-operator who asks every lift-full of passengers in turn, "what the
weather is like outside".

The evening pattern includes great contrast, but in regular sequence, although variable timing. Soon after 6 o'clock some men, mostly living alone,
come into the public bar for a quick drink on their way home from work. Some
retired couples also come into the lounge then, and may stay for up to two
hours, mostly drinking a sucession of "shorts". (Twenty years later, following
the relaxation of the licensing hours, these were the target of the "Happy Hour"
half-price drinks, following the American technique.) At 7 o'clock the men in
the bar leave to complete their homeward journey, and the two assistants on

duty that evening are due. Once they have both come, the Manager goes "up-stairs for tea", indicating by that message and the invitation to, "Ring the bell, if you want anything", which of them is in charge.

The assistant barmen wash the glasses that have gathered since opening time, and replace all the bottles that have been used since closing-time the previous evening. As it is quiet, they rarely need to ring the bell by the "doorway", but "anything" includes additional help with serving, information about the price of an unusual drink, awkward questions about the quality of the bitter, or the need for further supplies of the crisps, cigarettes or spirits, which, for the sake of quality or security, the Manager keeps under his own control.

Work is slack until at least 8 o'clock, and sometimes 9 o'clock. Despite the difference in the size of the two sides, the number of customers is fairly equally divided between them. In spite of the late arrival, probably, of one of the assistants, and despite the thoroughness with which they arrange the stock on the shelves, they can find no more work to do. So they converse at length with one of the customers across the bar, or (on the public side) join him at a table, or they play the "machine", or a lone game of darts, or read one of the newspapers.

The "busy time" should start at about a quarter to nine. If it is still quiet at 9 o'clock, or a quarter past, the assistants start watching the clock, because (they acknowledge) they are bored, and they politely compete to serve each customer who returns to the bar for another drink. The "regulars" also start bemoaning the general decline of the pub, complaining that they have "never seen anything like it before".

The Manager returns downstairs about 9 o'clock, or whenever the banging of the two doors suggests that "the busy time" has begun. Trade always does "pick up", at least by comparison with earlier in the evening, even if it is not until 9.30 or 10 o'clock, and even if the barmen are not completely "rushed off their feet" at any stage of that particular evening. Usually, however, they are fully occupied for the last hour or hour and a half, and they are watching the clock, in that case, to "ring the bell" at 10.25 ("last orders"), and again at 10.30 ("Time, gentlemen, please"). By 10 o'clock, indeed, the atmosphere may be so smoke-laden, and they may be so warm, that they are looking for an opportunity to collect the empty glasses from the tables, in order to pause in the porch, while changing "sides", for some "fresh" air.

Just as the use of artificial light and power, and the spread of shift-work and "flexi-time", have diminished the contrasts in the course of the day, in society generally; so the contrasts in the pattern of the week have been reduced, since the last century, by the mechanisation of housework, and the emptiness of many homes for much of the time. However, some pattern remains, and it is not that of rural society. The life of the public house likewise contains a weekly flow.

Monday may no longer be "wash-day" at home, but in the pub it still *feels* like the start of a new working-week. Most of the regulars (and there are few others, on a Monday) come in more quietly, remain more serious, and leave more subdued (even than on Sundays). On the other hand, because it is a quiet night, it is the League night for the darts team, so there is some air of excitement. Either the team has a "home" match, or else they meet here, before walking to an away match at a neighbouring pub.

By Tuesday work has become habitual again: it no longer dampens the spirits. Also on Tuesday the "Off Licence" (*licensed* to sell intoxicating liquor for consumption *off* the premises) next door is closed all day; so some of its would-be customers come into the pub, to buy cigarettes or beer and cider. Although they take them away to consume, they add to the general air of activity.

Wednesday is a little quieter, which is no doubt why it is the manager's "evening off", when the number of assistants is increased to three. This time the quietness is presumably due to its being the end of the wage-week. However, any reference to pay-day, which was already becoming more flexible, is extremely rare. It is the contrast with the following nights which suggests that it retains significance. Only once in nine months did a customer ask this barman if he could pay for his drink "after pay-day".

The rest of the week saw a great many more five-pound notes being produced - at a time when the one-pound note was still standard, and the ten-shilling note was just in the process of being phased out in favour of the fity-pence piece (in readiness for decimalisation). This indicated, among other things, that the customer had received his pay, in the form of cash - and that the pub was a convenient place to change the inconveniently large notes beloved of the wages clerks.

Thursday evening is more active and efficient, but Friday is the more relaxed and expansive evening. It marks the end of the working week. Saturday lunch-time is quiet, but includes some men coming in after finishing work at 1 or 2 o'clock, and a few customers who are fitting in a drink and a sandwich, between shopping trips and household chores, before going home for lunch proper. The atmosphere is not as individualistic and hurried as on a week-day at lunch-time, but it is more earnest than on the previous evening; so lengthy discussions may be heard, regarding the afternoon's sport, or the extent to which homosexuality or drug dependence can be inherited, for instance. Saturday evening is relaxed again, like Friday evening, yet more gleeful; for instance, it may include accounts of parties held the previous evening.

Sunday midday can produce one of the most remarkable atmospheres of the week, especially if the weather is sunny and a trifle bracing. Many of the regulars are occupying the same seats as the previous evening, but now the men are newly shaved. They are bathed, smartly dressed, in holiday mood, not merely friendly, but positively welcoming. In the evening, the loss of the first hour makes little difference to turn-over, as indicated by the description of the daily pattern, especially as there is hardly anyone finishing work at that time on a Sunday. Indeed, despite the late start, at 7 o'clock instead of 6 o'clock, trade both "picks up" earlier, and customers leave earlier, many of them between 10 o'clock and 10.30. There is a distinct feeling that Sunday evening is not only the conclusion of the week-end, but the eve of a new working-week.

An annual pattern may not be quite as marked as the daily and weekly pattern, but is nevertheless apparent. November is said to be well-known in the trade as a very quiet month, due to "people saving up for Christmas". When the quiet evenings continued into December, they were put down to "people getting ready for Christmas". By the evening before Christmas Eve (which was just beginning to become an additional holiday at the end of the 1960s), expectations were duly fulfilled and the pub did become busier. Customers dashed in and out in the course of their shoppping, which, rather than present-wrapping or home-decorating or cooking, was the main form taken by Christmas preparations (or, at least, by discussions about them, among the men who came to the pub). This impression was borne out by the readiness of most customers on Christmas Eve, when the licensing hours were extended to 11.30, to stay for the whole evening, and even then to have no Santa Claus duties to go home and attend to, apparently.

The Christmas Day hours were as for a Sunday. The numbers at lunch-time, and the mood, were also as for a Sunday, but the evening was "very quiet". On Boxing Day the hours were extended, as for Christmas Eve, and there were almost universal enquiries, at the re-assembly of the pub's "family", as to whether "you've had a good Christmas?" An affirmative reply was virtually universal, and possibly almost de rigeur. However, one man said simply, "Don't speak to me about Christmas", in such an imperative manner that his friends did as they were told, without further question. (The observer subsequently learnt from another source that the boiler at the school for which he was resident caretaker had burst.)

When January was "quiet", the Manager explained that "people were getting over Christmas". "Quiet times" in February were blamed on "the weather". In March they were "doing things about the house"; and in April, "about the garden". In May people were "going out for the day in the car", and in June they were said to be going on their holidays. However, the high summer months promised to be at least as busy as the winter; or rather, almost as busy as the winter ones "should have been".

Easter passed almost unremarked-on in the pub, apparently. One exception was a newly-qualified and newly-married young Irish doctor, who had forgotten to go to the Bank before the holiday, and so (before the days of cash-points) did not welcome the prospect.

Somewhat surprisingly, ecclesiastical Pentecost, as distinct from the recently introduced, fixed, Spring Bank holiday, received more attention than Easter, due to its combination of Church and secular festival. At Easter there had been some guarded conversation about "more shops opening on Good Friday", and some jocular comments about people taking too much wine at Communion. However, at Whitsun people seemed anxious to show that they knew of the existence of both the different "festivals", even though they found the separate dates hard to remember.

4.2.2 The scene

The catchment area, the internal lay-out, and the temporal pattern, together compose the stage upon which is set the "scene". This may be now be described in terms of the three roles, of manager, barmen and customers; of the three visible actions, of entering, being served, and watching the entertainment; and of the three aural forms, of the radio, conversation, and silence.

4.2.2.1 Roles

The Manager finds explanations of a climatological, sociological or economic kind for each "quiet" time (much as clergy and regular churchgoers do). The "regulars" blame him on the other hand, in comments to each other, or to the barmen. He is said to be "not interested": structurally, "it stands to reason, [because] he's only a Manager", not a tenant or landlord. "You can tell he doesn't care", for instance, "by the way he slams down your change." Personally, he is also thought to be more suited to a pub in the country, and to be incompetent for an urban type of house; because, for instance, he has difficulty in working out the required change quickly. As it happens, he and his wife both came from rural Somerset, and dislike living "in the centre of the town".

The Barmen are "hired and fired" entirely by the Manager. He places an advertisement (repeated, if necessary, sometimes more than once) in the numerous "Small Ads" pages of the Bristol Evening Post. In consequence, twenty or thirty may come and apply within a couple of days, even at a time of low unemployment, such as 1969-70. About twice a week, when there is no advertising, a man, usually young, will come to the bar, on the public side, and enquire whether there is a job going. If, as the Manager explains, he "likes the look of him", he will note his name and address for future reference, in theory, although partly perhaps out of simple politeness. The first female assistant for a number of years was employed in 1971: this was an event of some note, "but she was quite all right".

There are always five assistants. A carefully designed rota means that each is "on" (duty) three or four times a week; and that each is "off" for most of the following week, if he worked two or three sessions at the week-end. All are willing to arrange exchanges to help each other. Sometimes they are willing to do an extra turn simply because they have little else to do, or would like to earn a little extra money. In order to avoid liability for Selective Employment Tax (introduced in 1966 and repealed in 1971), which became operative at £4 per week, the brewery insisted on payment at 4/9d (23p) per hour, or 19/- (95p) per session, for a maximum of four sessions (sixteen hours) per week, totalling £3/16/- (£3.80p).

In seven months of regular, intensive observation, between November and June, there was a considerable turn-over of assistants. The senior barman, who had devised the complex rota, was married, over fifty, and had been there several years, but left at short notice in January, officially for family reasons, but reportedly to play the piano and earn more money for less hours at a club. Two bachelors, both in their late twenties, had already left before Christmas, after giving good notice. One wanted some free time, before going to New Zealand as a maintenance fitter on an oil rig; the other worked for a builders' merchants which had been taken over, and he found he was becoming "too tired" to do his main work properly.

The customers noted this rapid turn-over. It broke up a certain stability, and followed the Manager's return from sick-leave, when a Relief Manager had been "put in" by the brewery. There was no evidence, however, of any causal relationship between any of these movements.

A period of instability ensued. The first replacement's blonde good looks aroused suspicions of homosexuality. After working two evenings, he failed to appear again. After three such non-appearances, the Manager felt he could look for another replacement. The second appointee was in digs in Bristol, preparing to begin teacher training in the autumn. The manager seemed to be equally drawn by sympathy for his tiredness, and admiration for his lack of hurry.

The next two appointments were each in their thirties, married, and had pleasing personalities. The Manager came to suspect one of them of "fiddling the till". Each left separately, without explanation. The following pair of recruits had the same first name, but little else in common. One had been a full-time barman in the City of London, and left, with a girl he had met in Bristol, to go and work together in Devon. A student was then recruited.

After seven months, therefore, only one of the pre-existing team of five was left. The three of the original team who had left, had all given due notice; three (all of them married men) of the four others who had gone, had all disappeared without warning, and at least one more was about to go soon.

The pub's patrons, in their specific role as customers, are easily divisible, as most of the world knows, into the "regulars" and (presumably) the occasionals. The latter need not be considered further at this point, for the simple reason that they neither "belong" to the pub, nor it to them.

Each "regular" is absolutely consistent in what he drinks. Some alternate between two different drinks; the second of which may be used to "top up" the first, when it is half-drunk. In either case, their choice remains uniform, regardless of such factors as the time of the day, the state of the weather, or the condition of their palate. So the Barmen can often refer to them, when talking among themselves, by naming their accustomed drink.

However, a customer can be identified by the barmen, with equal ease and accuracy, by the manner in which he relates to them. Some, in the Lounge for instance, only gather their friends' requests after they have been served, place one order at a time, do not know what they want for themselves, use terms that are ambiguous or unknown in this area, and wait until they have been given their change, before asking for a further item such as a packet of cigarettes or crisps. Others, in the Bar for instance, call out their order, intending that the Barman should see to it when convenient, but forgetting that his head is already full of orders, arithmetic and faces, and then complain because he did not remember their particular preferred type of glass.

Others again, appreciating the difficulty of catching orders against the background noise, remove their pipe and raise their voice, buy the barman a drink, either when he has time to enjoy it, or to encourage him when he is "rushed off his feet", and consistently refrain from attempting to display their superior knowledge or efficiency.

4.2.2.2   Actions

Turning from role to action, the actors on this stage engage in three pieces of "business". The first is the "entrance". Entrances are "made", especially on the public side, but also in the lounge. While this difference may be connected with the different clientèle on each side, and with the semi-circular shape of the bar, which allows the back to be turned upon everybody else, it particularly reflects the size of the room. Those entering the lounge only need to use the techniques familiar in the traditional railway compartment: proceed with the task in hand, control one's own movements, and appear to ignore other people's presence. They, on the other hand, know he cannot move out of sight, and can inspect him later.

However, the "public" side presents more of an ordeal. For instance, every night of the week, and at least one lunch-time at week-ends, one young man reveals an underlying shyness as he walks the whole length of the public bar, down to the darts fraternity, looking neither to right nor to left. Indeed, despite the reassuring prestige involved, he seems to be genuinely oblivious both to his friends' calls, and to the barman's enquiry as to his wanting his "usual" (a "brown split"). As a regular himself, he knows that the bench around the outside wall is occupied in preference to the chairs around the tables, because they give a better view of the "scene", in particular of the bar and the door, and that the regulars in the nearer half of the room never fail to look up whenever the door opens.

Customers are aware how revealing their "entrance" is. The retired actor, the "life and soul" of the small group that know him well, enters regularly at 8.12 pm, with eyes downcast. He places his order, as though no one would have noticed his presence or absence, and appears genuinely surprised that his pint is ready waiting for him by the time he reaches his stool. A man of similar age and stature, but with an habitual policy of compensatory truculence, will walk to his place half-way down the bar and, despite his much less frequent attendance, expect his order to be ready by the time he reaches it. Similarly, the owner of the ex-service clothing store on the other side of the road (who employs the shy young man) always walks in, confident that eyes are upon him. Likewise, the tall young darts player, who later in the evening will call attention to his empty glass on the bar, at first marches tensely down the public side, with his eyes fixed upon his group. So, as each "finds his place", virtually every entrant is sensitive to this ordeal.

The "entrance" serves to indicate that the customer can "look after himself". In the Bar the reference would be to the potentially aggressive stares directed at the entrant. In the Lounge the reference would be to watching one's dress and expenditure, and keeping one's self to oneself. The same contrast is apparent in the converse phrase, "offensive behaviour". The ordeal of entering the bar implies the ability to stand up for oneself, should anyone else engage in such behaviour. The test in entering the lounge is the ability to avoid giving any kind of offense oneself (cp D Riesman et al., 1950, 1952). The object of the first fear is primarily physical and "anti-individual" behaviour; of the second, primarily cultural, and "anti-social" behaviour.

The second piece of business, as already indicated, follows on quickly from the first: negotiating the "service". The tension of the exchange indicates that the orders, the disbursement, the payment, and the reimbursement, though real in themselves, are also vehicles of the sort of spiritual realities that go to make up a relationship. Thus a customer who regularly omits the courtesy of saying (or, by his manner, implying), "please", can be corrected, by supplying the missing word *sotto voce*, as though from his own mouth. Not only is the lesson never forgotten, but a positive relationship can thereby be established. Should the manner, as well as the matter, be at fault, then the lesson can be conveyed if the change is lightly slammed down on the counter, before visibly turning to the next customer and demonstrating how a barman treats a *gentle*man, and *vice-versa*.

The importance of such inter-personal dynamics is underlined by the prevalent innocence and ignorance regarding the monetary aspects of the transaction. The compulsory display of the price list has not changed this fundamentally, because the culture or ethos of the public house is not financial. It is geared to extravagance rather than economy, an open hand rather than a tight fist, a *potlach* rather than the "protestant ethic", sacrifice rather than calculation.

A regular will know the price of his own drink, and (even if he does not drink it) of a pint of bitter: it serves as a bench-mark. If he buys a drink for a friend or two, he will know how much they should be, if only because he did the same an hour before. Beyond that, he probably has hardly any idea. He will probably not be a regular, at least here; and if he bought a round earlier in the evening, it was probably composed differently. The barman, on the other hand, will state only the conclusion of his arithmetical addition, and the change due.

This apparent carelessness is nonetheless significant. Few customers check that the change they are given tallies even with the barman's summary statement. Even less customers have the nerve to enquire the cost of the individual items, or attempt to do their own sums. Their attitude is accurately demonstrated in their initial handing over of a note, even when sufficient change can be seen in their hand. Such notes, even at the time of observation, could include not merely £1 notes, but £5, £10 and £20. (The only other time they were met, by this observer, was when bridegrooms were settling their wedding fees.) Having spent the week, "in the counting house, counting out the money", now they are "king". To "count one's change" is, at best, prudence; at worst, miserly. Socially, and individually, such behaviour is largely "out of place", in a *public* house.

The third "action" on this stage consists of the "entertainment". About twice a week, a man will come in, apparently for a drink: for he will order it, pay for it, drink it, and go out again, without another word. But most people come for some kind of social life and entertainment; wherein does it consist?

There is, of course, the specific entertainment of the drinking itself. It provides work for the oral muscles, sensations for the palate to savour, questions for the sophisticated mind to ponder, and the primitive satisfactions of a distended stomach. However, the "company" is at least as important, as many customers will say at once.

Other attractions, as already mentioned, include the coal fire on each "side". They must also include the "fruit machine" in each of the rooms. On the public side there were also the darts, the crib-board, a few newspapers, and the radio. However, with the possible exception, in the case of one or two students, of the fire, they do not come for any of these individual items.

The most important component of the "entertainment", then, is the presence, simply, of the other people. They go to the pub in order to drink, as the simplistic ritual ideology puts it; but they also have to drink, in order to go into a pub. As E Durkheim 1957: 25 (quoted, for instance, in F A R Bennion, 1969: Chapter XIV) nicely said:

> When individuals who share the same interests come together, their purpose is not simply to safeguard those interests .... It is, rather, just to associate, for the sole

pleasure of mixing with their fellows and of no longer feeling lost in the midst of adversaries, as well as for the pleasure of communicating together, that is, in short, of being able to lead their lives with the same moral aim.

The function as entertainment of this third act was clearly demonstrated on occasions when a party of half a dozen young people came into the Lounge. They tended to be students, or to be hairdressers, say, one of whose number was leaving to get married. Seated at the round table in the middle of the room, and nowhere near the extreme of bohemian or bucolic behaviour, they provided such an evening of spectation for the rest of the clientèle that a cabaret in a night-club might envy them their success. Often it was conscious, if not deliberate.

For the regulars come, not so much "to see and be seen", as is said of the higher echelons of Society, as to "see, and see themselves seeing". It is often said, with pride, "You get all types in a pub, don't you?" It appeals to the arm-chair anthropologist, "interested in human nature", to the informal sociologist, "wondering what the world is coming to", and to the amateur psychologist, marvelling that "there's nowt so queer as folks". It appeals to the *voyeur*, in most, if not all, of us. They enjoy being, if not "where the action is" (for there are only these three actions), but being on such a stage, in such a heterogeneous company. It is live soap-opera.

4.2.2.3 Noise

Description of the aural aspect of the Scene must begin with the radio, for that dominates the earlier part of the evening. It is switched on before the barmen arrive at 7 o'clock, and stays on until Closing Time, although it is not heard at all once the "busy time" begins. It is a relay system, which allowed a choice of all four BBC stations plus Radio Luxembourg, but it was always switched to Radio 1 or 2. So a typical evening's broadcasting, before its existence is lost in the hubbub, runs: music, news, bingo, music.

Occasionally a programme penetrates through to the consciousness of a cus-tomer who is sitting in silence. Otherwise the programmes are seldom actually listened to, even when they are audible. Hence the calling-out of a succession of numbers, for a game of bingo that no one is playing, never strikes anyone as superfluous. Even the news bulletins are only half-heard, and seldom give rise to any comment, partly because no one can assume that anyone else also heard it.

The only kind of programme that consistently provokes a (negative) reaction, is the singing of grand opera: a soprano spanning the musical and emotional scale evokes mirth, mimickry, and mockery. Otherwise classical music is in an ambivalent position in the public bar: probably, in the process of becoming

acceptable. Indeed, the super-star status of Pavarotti, thanks to his association
with fooball, by 1991, suggests that this was indeed the case.

The only programme that universally evoked a strong positive response, in
a hundred evenings of observation, was the commentary on Henry Cooper's
World Heavyweight boxing match (on Thursday 19 March 1970). Although
the loudspeaker, like the controls, is situated towards the "darts end" of the
bar, the volume had to be turned up, so that those by the door could hear.
This also allowed those in the lounge who wished to hear, to crowd round the
bar. During the commentary, a young couple who were playing darts together
(not members of the team or its fringe) were told by the regulars to keep quiet.

On Sunday evening the programmes are so different that the observer wondered whether the Manager had changed station out of respect for the day. A
check in the *Radio Times*, though, revealed that Radio 2 remained the order of
the day. A succession of popular tunes of a generation ago, may be followed by
the melodic strains of Grand Hotel, and then by community hymn-singing, and
popular classical records. Any comments (complaints) are easily quashed with
such jovial rejoinders as, "It'll do you good, you heathen". The almost total
acceptability of the output, even in the public setting of the bar, confirms the
acumen of the programme planners. Indeed, during the first hour or two after
opening (at 7 o'clock on Sundays), the programmes receive more attention than
at any other time of the week, although that attention is given in lone musing
(or "meditation"), not in conversation.

Conversations are, of course, the second, and main, aural item in the pub's
life. At the beginning of the evening they are like those at lunch-time on week-
days: short and practical, to do with physical and external topics. Insofar as
more personal topics are broached, the adopted attitude is cautious, agnostic,
or sceptical. This is the kind of conversation evoked and repeated (as indicating
"public opinion") by journalists and by motorists.

During the interregnum, between 7 o'clock and 8.30, there is little conversation. Customers are few, and scattered singly about the bar and the fireplace.
They know each other, but are not very interested in each other, and tend to be
quiet generally. Conversation of any length or depth is therefore discouraged
by the paucity of candidates, and by the accompanying publicity.

The lounge may have as many inhabitants at this stage, in half the space.
But conversation there is also difficult, because the married couples are sitting
on the bench along the walls, while single customers may be reading a book,
by the fire or the bar. So the barmen may do most of the talking, arranging
their many exchanges of duty. This process may take up to an hour, and may
be aided by a visit from one who is off-duty that evening, but has a request to
make of one who is "on".

The publicity of conversations conducted in the quiet period may encourage
animosity on the public side, or greater caution and consensus in the lounge.

During March 1970, for instance, the bar saw a lengthy, and eventually heated, discussion, regarding the relative contributions of the Navy and the Army (by which was chiefly meant the Glosters Regiment) towards the Allied victory in the Second World War. The chief protagonists were two men who were more notable for their highly unusual desire to have each drink in a fresh clean glass, than they were for their own standards of cleanliness. The slimmer, taller one maintained that the navy had protected the convoys and enabled the British Isles to eat, and suggested that the Glosters wore their cap badges at the back as well as the front of their berets because they were always running away from the enemy. (In fact, the custom commemorates an occasion when the "fore and afts", as they came to be called, were attacked from in front and behind simultaneously.) He pressed at least the former of his arguments with such seriousness that none dared contradict him too overtly. Even his short and fat opponent, not lacking his own bellicosity usually, preferred to keep his sharpest wit and repartee until after the other had left, in something of a huff.

By way of contrast, a lengthy three-cornered conversation was held across the lounge, while the newspapers were discussing the possibility of a June election, by three regulars, with ages ranging from 40 to 70. All three agreed that politicans will promise anything at elections, but the voters forget their promises; that prime ministers always hold on until they think they can win (Mr MacMillan being cited as a specific example); that few electors ever change their allegiance, and that those few only matter if they live in a marginal constituency; and that, whichever party won, a majority of about 40 produced the highest standard of government. Throughout this discussion, the political neutrality of their personal hopes (rather than any objectivity, for personally they were highly involved) would have done credit to, say, a BBC documentary programme. The content of their discussion also anticipated television's subsequent education of its public in politics and psephology.

During the busy time of the evening, or the lunch-time sessions on week-days, conversation is rarely so sustained, even among neighbouring customers. Neither, of course, can the barmen participate or listen so consistently. However, some lengthy discussions are known to have taken place, of some sensitive topics. The range of concepts and themes can be indicated by listing some of the expressions overheard while serving customers, mostly during the two months of January and February 1970. From this list, however, are excluded all the conversations involving the more obviously "educated" customers, such as the newly-qualified Irish "medic" (already mentioned, in connection with Easter), the chartered accountant, the three customers (of varying degrees of regularity) who read the *Financial Times*, or the pair of men who spent two hours at the public bar discussing the Third programme's musical output.

Terms used in the pub, then, by this section of the wider base of the social and educational pyramid, included: "atmosphere" (with reference to the pub); "relationship" (referring to the barmen); "the team" (similarly); "rough" and "respectable" (cp D Marsden, in A S C Ross (ed), 1969); "inherited"; as against acquired, characteristics; "snobbish"; "education"; "university"; "philosophy"; "conception" (of ideas); "fluent"; "phonetic"; "forgive"; "sacrifice"; "sacrilegious"; "scenery"; "tropical"; the meaning of dreams; "rate-payers"; "news" (as distinct from what the newspapers actually publish); "inferior" (of immigrants); "apartheid"; the Bristol Docks Bill; canals; and public parks.

The sources of noise in the pub are numerous. Some conversation is usually taking place, even if the rooms are nearly empty. Someone is usually putting tokens into one of the two fruit-machines, causing the cylinders to clank round, the "ducks" to blast, and the tokens to fall, with attention-seeking clatter. The radio will be on; or one of the regulars will wake up to its absence and ask a barman to "see what's on" (as a result of which it always stays on all evening).

The barmen contribute to the noise by bumping full bottles onto the shelves, and clanking empties into the cases and dumping them in the yard. They fairly constantly ring up the takings in the two tills, which then slide open, but have to be banged shut again. Likewise, the door keeps being pushed open, and springing shut. Outside, the noise of the traffic is a fairly constant roar, and so is easily overlooked, but it is punctuated from time to time by a heavy lorry applying its air-brakes, or by a motor-bike or sports car or old "banger" accelerating, virtually unsilenced, or (with the homely regularity of church bells out in the country) by the siren of an emergency vehicle.

Nevertheless, the third aspect of the aural dimension in the life of the pub is, paradoxically, silence. Indeed, many customers come to it for the sake, not simply of the scene, or of the company, but of the opportunity for a kind of solitude and silence. Thus, at one extreme a customer said his wife did "nag so"; so that their daughter had married, partly in order to avoid it, and their son would not visit home when his mother was there. At the other extreme are the men living alone, in "rooms" that are probably no more attractive visually, than they are socially or domestically. They seem to enjoy an unplanned "think" (cp G Bateson & M Mead 1942: 3, 68) in front of the fire, or over their first drink. Again, for the first half-hour on Sunday mornings, the lounge will usually be populated by three or four readers of the "posh Sundays", although less posh ones may also be noticed underneath the unread parts. On Sunday evenings, as already mentioned, a similar number of men will let themselves be lulled by the music programmes.

Indeed, with the possible exception of the young man playing darts (and excluding from that group for the moment the wife, the girl-friend, and the other female partner, who accompany three of its members), there is not a single regular customer who does not spend a considerable proportion of his or her time, sitting or standing in silence, "lost" in "thought" (or feeling). Few mind being disturbed out of their reverie into conversation; but almost no regular wishes to converse without pause all evening, or throughout the whole of their time in the pub.

The place of silence in the life of the lounge is epitomised by the two married couples (one husband retired, the other working) who spend up to three hours there each evening, each pair sitting side by side, with their backs to the wall. Although divided from each other's sight by the machine, each commands an unbroken view of the "stage" lying between the entrance and the bar, in front of the fire. However, even when there is nothing specific to spectate, they still spend the time simply sitting musing.

On the public side the fondness for a solitary or interior silence in the midst of the pub's life is epitomised by the numerous men (some married, but perhaps relatively more, single) who sit, gazing straight in front of them. Insofar as they are looking at anything, they are watching either the fire or the barmen. In either room, if anything happens of interest, the silent sitters see it; but they are not consciously watching or waiting for anything to happen. They are, they would say, "perfectly content"; unless and until one of them decides, in due time, that "it's quiet this evening", meaning, too quiet.

4.2.3   The people

A sociological, or a market research, study of a public house might describe its clientèle, or customers, purely in terms of their social or economic characteristics. Something of these has already been indicated, by reference both to those in the two "sides" of the pub and to the catchment area of its surrounding district. However, to pursue this approach further would be to miss the point of the pub. For the pub is, and knows itself to be, an environment in which such distinctions are comparatively insignificant. Indeed, the very attempt to discover such data would be to do violence to its nature. It would also discredit the observer. Its methodological inaptness (or ineptitude) confirms precisely what has already been suggested regarding its character as a "human community".

Nevertheless, some way must be found (some ways have already been utilised) of describing the units, whether individual or social, of which this community is composed; for its ultimate components are, themselves, (at least partially) self-mobilising, self-motivating, willing beings.

They may, therefore, be described in three different ways, placed in an ascending order of self-consciousness. First, they can be described in terms of the groupings in which the life of the public house is largely lived. These are of the essence of its attractiveness for its members, and of its social organisation. Next, they will be described in terms of the individuals, many of whom compose those groups, but some of whom (visitors usually but including some regulars), comprise a class rather than a group. Such individualism is itself an important aspect of the life of the pub, for its ideology centres round the right of everyman to enter, and his consequent freedom to be himself. Finally, the observer will attempt to describe the "types" of human personality he discerns in the lives of the members, as they reveal their life within the pub itself.

4.2.3.1 Groups

Those who come to the pub, as individuals or as members of a group, mostly do so in order to become part of a scene, it has been suggested, in which they see themselves mainly as spectators, but are of course inevitably among the actors. (Indeed, their role is, informally, that of participant observers.) They come as part of the audience which is nevertheless glad to be sitting in the wings of the stage itself. Enjoying the sight, as objects, of other subjects, they can side-step the degree to which they themselves are the object of others' gaze.

The point at which this cannot be avoided, however, is when making the Entrance. Motivation for going through such an initiatory procedure is provided, for a couple of visitors a week (as already mentioned) by the desire for physical refreshment and sustenance (and perhaps the myth of the pub). For the vast majority, however, it lies in the knowledge that inside the public house is one's own group; or else one comes, as a member of a group that enters together; or else in the knowledge that one will be part of a scene (and perhaps in the hope of acceptance into a group).

The pub, then, is a kind of community theatre, largely peopled by small groups, in which the individual is free to come and go, and to be himself between those times. Mentally, this group or communitarian aspect comprises three parts. The public bar is fundamental to, and definitive of, the whole. The lounge receives converse and particular self-definition, from the public side: for the latter is that which the former is not, but requires the public bar for the positive reason of being linked with it, as well as for the negative reason of being different from it. The third part of the communal life consists, of course, in the manager and barmen who constantly go between the two sides, and service the whole. So the small groups, which form one of the two kinds of biological-like cells that go to make up that whole, may be briefly sketched in that order.

Socially, the public bar is rarely a single room. The only exception, during the period of observation, other than when it was simply unpopulated, was during the commentary on the Henry Cooper fight, already mentioned. For the length of the room is accentuated by the projection of the bar itself along most of the length of one wall, while the room's uniform brownness emphasises its bare, shell-like quality. So its constituent sub-groups require to be mapped in a geographical fashion, spatially.

The most cohesive, and the most noisy, group, are the darts players, in the far corner beyond the bar. The core of this group consists of the darts team.

Men, mostly aged between 25 and 30, and all between 18 and 45, they are approximately equally divided between the married and the single, but rarely will any of them miss a single evening session, or either of the lunch-times at the week-end.

They stand while waiting for their turn. However, there are a number of non-playing "supporters", including the three women related to individual members of the team (as girl-friend, partner or wife), and some irregular customers who use the board before the team members arrive. These position themselves on the bench around the wall, or on the chairs by the door into the "yard", or on the stools at that end of the bar itself. So for them the game (or its players) are effectively "the scene". They are not part of the general scene, as those at the round tables in the centre of the lounge side are. Their presence is simply part of the background, like a piece of living radio, whose own volume indeed tends to keep pace with the general noise.

A second group has a considerable life of its own, and is well known to the barmen, without necessarily being in the centre of a visitor's consciousness. It consists of men who are mostly in their fifties and married. They may stand at the bar itself for a while, then, when their friends arrive, retire to the table by the fire (on the side nearer to the entrance and away from the darts board), assuming it is still vacant, where they chat, and sometimes sing, while playing cribbage and dominoes.

Two members of this group are "pillars" of the pub's overall community, and the "salt" of its life, by reason of their unfailing attendance, and their observant, teasing *rapport* with the barmen. The others may on any single occasion include the son-in-law of one of those "pillars"; the pub's lone accountant (a garrulous joker and drinker, who "doesn't act like an accountant"), and his son-in-law (a young, good-humoured decorator); a large and elderly motor-cyclist; a man who looks as though he could be a family doctor; up to three sleek, executive-looking young men; a pair of brothers who specialise somewhat in cribabge; and any of half-a-dozen other lone men between 50 and 65, or a lone woman, or a married couple. The half-dozen who compose the group on each occasion therefore represent something of a confederation of sub-groups, linked by their physical nearness and their overlapping memberships. Their drinks are usually bought in twos and threes, reflecting their marital composition, and the lines of their current dialogue.

The other "groups" on the "public" side might perhaps be better described in terms of relationships. For instance, for a very large part of the evening, half-way along the bar, there sits a painter who was made redundant when he was 59, and now has only a year to wait until he is 65 and so qualifies for a pension. His unmarried son is one of the leaders of the darts team, while a married son also plays darts sometimes. This, and his slight deafness, may account for his situation midway between the darts team, and his friends, especially the two "pillars", in the confederation just described.

Each evening at 9.30 a man comes in and positions himself next to the painter, on the side nearer the entrance. At 10 o'clock he is joined by another man, but those two do not know each other's names or addresses. Behind them, and exchanging courtesies as they place their successive orders, by the side of the fire in winter and of the fireplace in summer, sits a man with an artificial leg. He has become friendly with a retired actor, a result (he has explained) of once deliberately leaving the bar to join him by the fire. At the other table, between them and the "machine", sit two married couples. These four people are all small of stature, and always order half-pints.

So the list could continue, but the description would be of sub-groups rather than groups, numerically if not phenomenologically. They help to set the scene and they watch it, but they do not themselves prescribe the tone or life of the whole. That is done by the younger, cohesive darts players at the far end of the bar, and the ageing pillars and their confederation between the fireplace and the entrance door.

The Lounge being more compact, and the décor more attention-seeking, the physical geography of the groups within it has less influence upon their relationships to each other.

A group, consisting mostly of men, who come alone and in some ways remain alone, stands round the bar proper. They are united by their apparently common desire not to speak (beyond the odd pleasantry), unless spoken to. One of them may spend the entire evening reading, one of Sir Arthur Bryant's histories for instance, or at lunch-time on Sunday, the *Sunday Times*. (Several of those men may be found of a weekday morning reading the papers in the nearby public library). They monitor their surroundings for personnel or behaviour of particular interest, but do not wish to be drawn into the life of any other individual or group. They are friendly with the staff, and tend to have one particular barman from whom they order, and with whom they will discuss (as with the traditional barber) affairs of the day, sometimes at great length. But they never "hear" each other's conversations, unless explicitly drawn in by their immediate neighbour.

If those round the bar merit group status, more by dint of their simultaneous common propinquity and social distance, than by reason of any developing common life, then the second category is likewise defined by certain characteristics that are common to them individually, rather than by a life together, which is common to them as a group. These are the married couples. They sit along the bench, for up to three hours, in pairs, side by side. They are very regular in their habits, neat in their appearance, and "proper" in their relationships with (what they regard as) the "junior" staff (the assistant barmen). They never use the "fruit machine". Viewing the "scene" would appear to be preferable in some way to viewing television at home, presumably because they are in a larger social context, it is "live", and they can do the "editing". But they exchange few comments with their own spouses, and even less with each other, and prefer to leave at the first sign of the room becoming busy.

The third category includes true groups, but, so far as the pub is concerned, they are visitors, albeit with a corporate existence. These are the parties who come in sequential series, especially towards the end of the working week, and sit round the tables in the centre of the room. Such parties tend to include at least one married couple, and two single men. Geographically and socially, they become the main act in the scene while they are present. Often they also establish some degree of relationship with one of the married, "grand-parental" couples sitting on the outside of the room, through asking to "borrow" the chairs on the nearer side of the table that they are using for their glasses.

The fourth and final category is similar to the third. It consists of the occasional party of young people, such as the five hairdressers, and the fiancé of one of them, who came in to celebrate the pair's forthcoming marriage, with an uninstructed proliferation of drinks, including much vodka. They are always referred to as "students", by the regulars in the first two groups, because their hair and clothes follow different fashions. However, they are well content with this description and image. The hairdressers' attire was not as spectacular a part of the scene as with the usual run of "students", but their high-spirited screams ensured their receiving a similar degree of attention.

The third location contains but a single group: the manager and the assistant barmen. Each individually builds up a special relationship with particular customers. Together, they are employed to be the more functional representatives of that largely symbolic role which is the manager's vocation. However, neither of these can be altogether separated in practice from their inter-personal relationships with each other. One indicator of these has been mentioned already: their willingness to exchange duties, almost regardless of the time and effort required to arrange it. Another indication was a somewhat dramatic incident that occurred one evening in February 1970.

A lorry-driver, who is married, a "regular", and usually friendly, but is recognised as being, on occasion, "touchy" and belligerent, came in just after 7 o'clock, on his way home and so still in his working clothes. The previous evening an item on television had drawn public attention for the first time to "Paki(stani)-bashing" by "skinheads". His reference to the incident was "broadcast" (in both senses: to no one in particular, but everyone in general, for few are present at that hour), with considerable feeling and volume. Standing immediately in front of the speaker, on the "business" side of the bar, was the large, middle-aged, and most senior of the barmen at that time, who consistently avoided mentioning his (almost certain) Anglo-Indian origin.

All those who had suddenly heard the customer's forthright statement of opinion thought he had spoken with approval of the skinheads' activities. All froze, but none gave any kind of answer. In spite of, rather than because of, his own background, the barman standing opposite the speaker quietly demurred. His propinquity enabled him to protest almost privately (and the bar-top discouraged any physical reply), while his length of acquaintance with the speaker, and his seniority in the pub, no doubt enhanced his willingness to take a risk. The other assistant concurred in this remonstrance, despite his relative youthfulness and recent arrival, but no doubt encouraged, in his case, by his *not* knowing the speaker personally, and by his obscurity, as he crouched behind the bar re-stacking the shelves.

The "broadcast", as it transpired, had been misunderstood. The speaker was appalled by what he had seen on television. However, the incident was significant in showing that, in those circumstances, the barmen had felt able to protest, when others seemed to be reduced to silence. This willingness to express their opinions was encouraged by their central, even if subordinate, position in the community; by the greater *and* by the lesser degree of their acquaintance with the speaker; by their careful conversion of an intensely personal view into the more objective and less passionate key that is characteristic of contemporary culture; by the degree of community developed by members of a work-team, and by the degree of self-revelation, necessitated by the desire to exchange duties.

Similar characteristics can be seen more continually, if less dramatically, in the face of customers' criticisms of the manager. No assistant appears to invite or confirm such comment.

If the life of groups within the pub is very real in some cases, but overall rather limited, as a whole a pub is frequently said to stand for the freedom of the individual to be himself; meaning, above all, regardless of his role(s) in the wider community. "A dustman may drink with a duke" would sum up the belief. In that sense, each one, having gone through the initiation ceremony, is re-born into a new society, an enclosed enclave, into which he may bring his views, but not his prohibitions. In the pub, a cat can look at a Queen.

4.2.3.2   Individuals

The individuals in the pub, like the groups, will be described in three stages. In this case, some of the visitors, who both come and go as individuals, will be mentioned first. Then, two portraits of individuals will be sketched: from the public bar, the redundant decorator, who is friendly with most of those around him and yet a member of no group; and from the lounge, the customer who stands at the bar, night after night, reading rather than talking.

Long and illuminating conversations have been held at various times with new arrivals to the pub, who did not become either members of any group or regulars, and who often turned out to have been visitors for that single occasion (so far as the observer could tell). To report upon them is to record not only who arrives in the pub, but what can be discussed there. These conversations were all held with men: women who came in as visitors came in with and talked only with their companions (male or female). Women with whom any length of discussion was held, therefore, were regular customers.

These conversations have been held with: a man who said he had had a cough ever since 1916; a Welsh kitchen porter, who said that Enoch Powell was "his man", because "he speaks out"; a Southern Irishman, who "blamed" the Civil Rights movement on "Blacks", that is (in the Irish situation), "people without any religion"; a young electronics officer who worked for Shell, and held forth on the political aspects of "high finance"; an illiterate, who described himself as unemployable, and attended the Salvation Army citadel in nearby Stokes Croft, because it gave him company, and said he would go to any similar gathering, "even if it was organised by Communists", if the Salvation Army closed down theirs, and who also said that murders and wars were caused by the devil entering into people's bodies; a motor mechanic, who now blamed himself (without naming the reason) for the fact that his wife had gone off with another man thirty years ago, and who thought everyone required disciplining until they were thirty years old; another motor mechanic, who claimed he had left the employ of the local branch of a national chain of garages, because he was expected to issue road-worthiness certificates, despite his not being qualified to issue them and the vehicles' not being road-worthy, and who now therefore worked in zinc-smelting; the manager of a local greengrocery, who had previously been in turn a male nurse and a laboratory technician, and who had been jilted by his first fiancée without any explanation, but so that, it subsequently transpired, she could marry the son of the owner of a well-known chain of chemist's shops in the area; an instrument mechanic, who in 1961 went out to South Africa because his fiancée disappeared three days before their wedding, never to be heard of again, by him or by her parents, and who was now hoping to return to South Africa, as it had no disadvantages, "so long as you were not too outspoken"; a keen supporter of Gloucestershire Cricket Club, who said he "hated blacks", because "they're all so dogmatic"; the secretary of the students' entertainments committee, at a branch of the local polytechnic, who lamented that a thousand students could only produce a single football team; a young salesman for Lyons, and another for Avon Tools, and another for garden sprinklers, who all fervently believed in the value and worth of the products they were engaged in selling; an employee of the Boots chain-stores, who had changed to stock-taking from counter-work, in order to "get out of" quiet Axminster; a man who regretted putting about five pounds a week into the "machine", whenever he started using it, which he said was about once a week; a man who wore the "old boys' tie" of possibly the second most prestigious school in the land, and claimed to have "earned it"; an elderly man who had been reminded, by reading about a sex-change case in the paper, of an occasion when he was about eight years old, and had heard his mother talking with another woman, who was unable to tell how she should dress her child; a self-confessed passer-by, whose son was "much more settled", now that he had left the staff of St Mary Redcliffe School, in order to teach at Oxford Technical College, and for whom this fact was clearly much more important than the various (repeated) statistics about his son's hard-earned degrees, and his salary of £1500 per annum for eleven and half hours' teaching per week; an engineering graduate of Manchester University's Faculty of Technology, who began working for himself, because £1500 a year, after a three-year degree course, was "mere buttons"; a poorly educated young man who had persuaded his father to "move up to" the *Daily Telegraph*, but who now "often" buys *The Times* on his way to work, because he has some shares and so wants to be able to follow the stock market; a youngish man, who admitted to some embarrassment over reading *The Financial Times* on the public side; and another, younger man, who often read *Hansard* and thought Oswald Moseley "a genius".

Returning now to the "regulars", the "portrait-sitter" on the lounge side stands by the little semi-circular bar each evening (despite having stood at work all day), and drinks his alternate pints of bitter and of EIPA ("East India Pale Ale"), while reading his book (and unobtrusively monitoring all that goes on). He is tall and slim, his hair is almost white, and he wears dark-rimmed spectacles. His florid countenance, the smell of his breath, and a peculiarity of speech, may suggest a degree of alcoholism; but he denies this, and says he has more than once had hospital treatment for a throat defect.

He has charge of the bedding department in a large local store. He was the manager of a furniture shop, in the recently re-built city centre, until it was "taken over". Previously he ran his own employment agency in London's West End. Two previous wives having died, his present wife is his third one. She still lives in London, but comes to spend the week-end with him in his flat nearby, "roughly once every two months". He remains friendly with the three children of his previous marriages, but seldom sees them, as they are all married and living elsewhere.

He is friendly towards other customers in the pub, and (it has been observed) towards his colleagues at work. He can be irritated by what he considers to be unnecessary stupidity or rudeness, and he is prepared to show that irritation when it serves his purpose. Despite his good-mannered affability, and his ability to combine character with reserve, he does not, however, appear to have any particular friend in the Bristol area (unless it was eventually this barman).

One of the first conversations of depth, between the observer and this customer, arose from the behaviour of a certain visitor. This customer hailed from Lancashire, but was working temporarily in Bristol, and came to the pub daily for a fortnight, and offended against the *mores* by both drinking and talking

too much. Our portrait-sitter found this behaviour so irritating that he transferred himself, complete with his glass and book, round to the other side, until
such time as the visitor ceased to visit the lounge. When the visitor (whose
anti-Bristolian comments also failed to endear him) transferred himself to the
public side (whence the Manager soon expelled him), the subject of this pen-
picture returned to his accustomed place by the lounge bar. He described to
the barman, by means of an autobiographical parable, the usual and proper
way of introducing yourself to a pub (and possibly any other small community
in England, certainly in the recent past).

One winter, he said, he had been staying in a Butlin's chalet near Maidenhead, and used to go each evening to a pub in the nearest village, which he
said was some miles away. He always greeted the locals, who were farmers and
labourers, as he entered, but, after ordering his drink, talked only with his wife
or the landlord. Eventually there came an evening when the "locals" (ie the
regulars of this "local"), being short of a player, asked if he could play "Spoof"
(sic): the point being, that "they had seen I could hold my own". By way of
contrast, the man from Bury in Lancashire had been constantly buying drinks
for other people in this pub, and glibly introducing himself all round.

It was not hard to envisage the self-effacing reply that he would have given the
locals near Maidenhead. Indeed, as he claimed he won the game that evening, it
is even more certain that he would have disclaimed any skill, beyond the barest
familiarity with the rules. But as a consequence, of course, he and the players
had become the best of friends, with invitations to him to shoot where he liked,
and to call at their farmhouse for lunch any day he was in their vicinity. Again,
by way of contrast, he said that other visitors "walked into the pub, bought
them all drinks, and then were ignored". The moral lay in the need to "prove
yourself", "to stand your ground", without trying to open up conversations that
were not wanted.

That particular conversation took place on Thursday 11 December 1969,
soon after the beginning of the period of intensive observation. From another,
entirely independent conversation, towards the end of the period (Tuesday
12 May 1970) may be quoted a sentence which his father wrote for a local
Eistedfodd (Welsh festival of arts), when our customer was a boy aged twelve.
It had always stuck in his mind, he had always believed in it, and he felt he
had lived up to it. (No doubt the previous parable was sensed as confirming its
truth). In English, its translation would run, "Seek grace not to demean any
man".

The portrait-sitter on the other side occupies an equally central position: in
space, as he occupies a stool in the centre of the bar; in time, as he sits there
for several hours each evening; and in the society and culture of the public
side, by his attitude and character. Again, two particular conversations, from
almost opposite ends of the main period of observation, are illuminating. The

first of these (Saturday 17 January, continued on the 24th) directly concerned the life of the pub.

This is the redundant decorator, whose short, modest, bearded, unmarried "boy" (aged about thirty) plays in the darts team. Whenever it is his turn to buy the darts players' round, he nearly always gestures towards his father, saying, "And see what the old man says"; and the father nearly always says to the barman, "A bottle of three-star brandy"; and "settles" for a bottle of Home Brew to "top up" his pint of bitter; and might be pretending he has no knowledge whatsoever of its source, for all the attention he gives to the donor.

"The old man", then, as already mentioned, is sixty-four, slightly deaf, completely bald, and a little difficult to understand, for anyone not familiar with a strong Bristol accent. He still does odd days of painting when they come his way, no doubt skillfully and conscientiously. He readily joins in discussion, and loves a leg-pull, which he always concludes with a kind wink.

On two Saturdays in January there was enough time to make it worthwhile to break the unspoken custom of the barmen, and follow up his complaints about the manager and the state the pub was "coming to". There was also enough noise to avoid embarrassment, and yet not so much as to render the conversation inaudible or incomprehensible.

It emerged that he had been coming to the pub since 1939, being one of the first people to come through its doors. But the present manager, who had "only been here about four years", "didn't care": "how could he? He's only a manager, after all. Not like a landlord". Last night, for instance, "he slid the glass over to me", instead of putting it on the mat. So, "it's only logic, isn't it?", that people should go elsewhere. It became apparent that he, and those like him, came in spite of (if necessary), rather than because of, the manager of the moment. It might be added that they have years of emotional investment (braving the "entrance", for instance) in this particular community; where else, for instance, could they say what he had just said? So managers "may come and [managers] may go", but the life of the pub, as a community, (like "The Brook") "goes on forever".

The other conversation, on Sunday 7 June 1970, may have been encouraged (but was not tailored) by its taking place on a Sunday, and by the now growing awareness among the regulars that this barman was also a minister of religion. The initiative, however, lay entirely with the customer, from start to finish. Beckoning to the observer to lean over the bar-top, so he could speak to him quietly, he asked if the barman had "seen that?" Another customer, the ex-naval one mentioned in connection with the argument about the "Glosters", had just won twenty tokens in "the machine". Yet now, having put them all back in, and lost them all again, he was following them up with further sixpences.

The attitude of the customer who had observed this sequence was one of sheer condemnation. It was reasonable to put back three or four of the tokens, for the fun of it - they were a kind of good-luck gift; but to replace even half of them .... As for putting them all back into the machine ... that was just plain daft. The only possible cause of such behaviour, he said upon questioning, must be "greed, sheer greed". A note of disgust entered his voice. It expressed, not simply a criticism of such imprudence; not even a condemnation, of such (im)morality; but an abhorrence, of a sort of blasphemy. It seemed to have contravened, not merely a virtue, but some kind of reality.

4.2.3.3   Types

To describe the people of the pub in terms of groups, and even more as individuals, was closely in line with the pub's own ideology. Curiously, to describe them in terms of types, is also in keeping with a self-image, in which it takes considerable pride. "You get all types in a pub, don't you?", is frequently said. The understanding is by no means superficial.

As with the groups, and as with the individuals, the division will again be into three. The first of these three typologies is one that is based entirely on the life of the institution itself, and is of immediate, objective relevance to each barman: the type of glass that customers prefer. The second, that of age, is one that is widely used in contemporary society, including the pub itself, not least at the time of this period of observation. The third is a modification of that, which allows for greater accuracy (and, since its original development, has been found to be similarly relevant in the life of a residential community): an attitudinal division, between "Mono-men" and "poly-people".

Pint drinks are mainly of either bitter or EIPA, or of draught Guinness or anything that is "split" (with half a pint of bitter), or of shandy or Keg Tavern. They could be served either in a "tankard" (ie a glass with a handle), or in a "sleever", although by law the Keg Tavern had to be served in a special glass tankard, allowing room for the froth.

There are no privately-owned, metal tankards in this pub. The brewery's glass tankards are either referred to as "handles", or else indicated by pretending to hold an imaginary tankard next to the cheek. Alternatively they may be referred to as "jars", by customers who convey the impression that they are anxious to show what (they believe) they are called in this area. The thumb-sized indentations which cover their vertical surface are reminiscent of the half-pint Victorian beer-glass, which had a stem but no handle, and was made of equally thick glass.

J A H Murray, 1888, does not link a "handle" with either beer or beer glasses, but E Partridge, Vol II, 1967, records that in Australia a pint has been known as a "handle" of beer since about 1920, and here since about 1950. In the pub, though, the word and the mime refer primarily to the type of glass.

A sleever is a tall glass which bulges a little over half-way up, before contracting part way in again. Its general shape and design is reminiscent of an Edwardian working-man's "snug". It is made of thin material, and so breaks easily, but labour was cheap, when they were made by hand. However, it is possible (to judge by advertisements for pubs) that today the breweries wish to discourage their use, presumably on account of the cost of replacements.

As well as being called a sleever, it is also known in this pub as "a glass", "a tall one", "a straight one", or "a slim one". This last expression may refer to the thinness of the materials, rather than their overall shape; because customers will sometimes, with a strength of feeling that is sufficient to overcome obvious embarrassment, state that they dislike the feel of the thick material of a tankard between their lips.

J A H Murray, 1888, says a "sleever" of beer contains about three-quarters of a pint, and cites an alleged Welsh origin for the *measure*. E Partridge, *op. cit.*, and P B Gove, 1971, are not familiar with any related uses in this country. It is therefore possible that the term is relatively local, and indeed of Welsh extraction.

Regular customers assume their preference in glasses will be remembered, apparently to a greater extent than with their choice of drink. This is because they tend to forget that there is any choice of glass, and so fail to specify their wishes. Even should a barman feel he can anticipate their choice, he may think it advisable to check, since quite strong feelings are involved. Should he guess wrongly, the regular may ask for the liquid to be poured into the right kind of glass, rather than waiting for his next pint before putting the matter right. He will say he would rather not drink it, than drink it out of the wrong kind of glass. It is safer to enquire, than to predict a new customer's preferences.

Nevertheless, a general, although not infallible, scheme of preferences may be discerned.

Sleevers are chosen by older men, on both sides, by middle-aged men in the public bar, and by the younger men playing or watching darts. Some young men will say they "don't mind", but older men appear more sophisticated. They are chosen by "the working classes": that is, those with a working-class origin, and/or those whose own self-image is working-class. They give the impression that they consider the handle a frivolous encumbrance.

Tankards are preferred by younger and middle-aged men in the lounge. They seem to be selected by those whose self-image ties in with that catered for by the industry's advertising; that is to say, those who will feel that the tankard is both the manly and the traditional vehicle for drinking beer from.

Even a long drink, for a woman, is usually, not draught, but one from a bottle, and therefore a half-pint. However, most women prefer the thinly-made half-pint glass, to the glass tankard. This is true, even on those rare occasions when a woman has a draught half-pint, which should legally therefore be served in a tankard. A few female visitors to the lounge, however, will ask for their half-pint to be served in a tankard. The impression is given that they, like their male company, feel this to be the proper, manly and traditional way of drinking beer in an English pub.

The feelings involved in the choice of glass seem to be a combination of the aesthetic (the feel of the glass between the lips); of inner identity (how the customer sees himself, and what he is accustomed to); and of "inter-identity" (how he wishes others to see him, and in particular the maintenance of his individual identity in the consciousness of the barmen).

As it happens, the two portrait-sitters fitted this typology exactly: the departmental manager preferred a tankard, and the painter a sleever. However, no very accurate system for prediction became apparent, either during or following the period of observation.

A second possible typology, therefore, must be according to age. This is more obvious in the lounge than in the public side. There are several reasons for this. For instance, when groups of young people come to the pub, they are more likely to be composed of a fairly equal mixture of the two sexes: as the lounge is where women can feel at home to a greater extent, their wishes are more likely to prevail. (An all-female group, of any number, always chooses the lounge.) If they are fairly numerous, they are likely to require one of the two free-standing tables in the centre of the room, so they can draw up other chairs. This, as already mentioned, makes them the inevitable centre of attention for the older couples, who are already occupying the benches around the outer wall. However, it may also be added that the older regulars in the lounge possibly enjoy watching, wondering, criticising, and even disliking, these younger people, more than their contemporaries on the other side would do, as indicated by the third typology.

The young, as the catalysts of this second typology also, may be considered first. The uniform sign of their vaunted nonconformity (with, that is, the prevailing fashions among the old), and the identical badge of their identity as individuals, is that element of the body over which the human being has most control: the hair. It may be long or wild, or both. Clothing, including ornament, being the nearest non-biological element in visible identity, becomes the second characteristic. It may be carefully careless, or exotic, but not usually both (speaking of the period of observation). The care that thus goes into even a relatively careless self-presentation is such as should appeal to the older spectators around the edge of the lounge; it is not, however, appreciated.

On the rare occasions that the archetypal young enter the public bar, such statements of personality as are made by hair and clothing are ignored, in obedience to customary canons of politeness. If they wish to enter into a conversation, and follow the usual rules, then their overtures are accepted in the usual way. When they have left, their appearance may indeed give rise to laughter. However, it is reasonably good-natured, and genuinely humorous. It may also be slightly paternal and affectionate.

In the lounge, though, the personal statements they make through their attire and hair, are nearer to the heart of their target, what they may refer to as "the system". In extreme cases the response is one of disgusted, blatant staring, and barely concealed, hostile comment. So long-lasting is this reaction that it may be concluded that the scene would lack both interest and enjoyment for its proponents if it were not for those who "shouldn't be allowed ..." etc. For the reaction is deeper than, say, that of children watching the monkey-cage at the zoo. There may be little of Otto's *tremendum*, but there is much of his *fascinans*, with such breaking of the taboos (R Otto, 1959: chapter IV).

The "old" are simply so described by way of contrast with the young. (The "elderly" would be euphemistic, and misleading, for the age in question is relative, not chronological.) They have already been described, in the persons of the regulars, on each side; and in terms of their reactions to the young. All that needs adding is that their uniform is very often a suit, except at weekends, when very clean, casual sportswear may appear; that their hair is cut short, clearly parted, and usually oiled (in the style described by M Weber, 1930: 274-5 as "that of the ridiculous Roundheads"); and that their (unvarying) drinks cost in total far more than the promiscuous mixture consumed to their disgust by the young people. Such older people, in the lounge, usually want the barmen to show sympathy with them on the more dramatic of these occasions. However, the staff appear to find themselves agreeing with their regular patrons in direct proportion to their overall responsibility, and their own age; and appear to fail to agree whole-heartedly, in proportion to their own youth, and the length of their own hair.

It will already be apparent how close a typology based on a difference of age is to a typology explicitly based on contrasting attitudes. Certainly, age like the length of hair, or the colour of skin, is fairly easy to gauge. However, it is not always an accurate indicator of that which is actually relevant and sought. Thus, in the public side, many of the old took a tolerant, and even friendly, view of the young; while many of the younger members in the darts team (who chose sleever-type glasses) would have sided with the rest of the "old" in the lounge.

The form taken by an attitudinal typology, then, is a contrast, as already mentioned, between the Mono-man and the poly-people. The differences in punctuation, and in category, are intended to convey, at the expense of symmetry, the essence of the meaning of each. Thus, the Mono-man is capitalized because it sees itself as normative. It is restricted to a single gender because it regards the whole as included within that part.

The Mono-man type assumed a single, and therefore normative culture; which can therefore be initially capitalized, as (a High, or indeed the only true) Culture. It can be seen as a social and historical extension of the former educational assumption that the "classics", in whatever sphere of human creativity, were necessarily Graeco-Roman, or else their Western European descendants. Similarly, its art is expressed in, and its arts are restricted to, the Beaux Arts, which are defined by their purely aesthetic purpose, and are otherwise non-functional. Thus, the achievement of a straight furrow is hardly a work of art, and artistry is not involved in ploughing, because "artists" do not plough, or perform such useful work.

This culture should be assimilated by the young; otherwise, "what will the world [as we know it] come to?" It is so assimilated by "the up-and-coming" (meaning, those who are "coming-up"), who "know what's what" (from the point of view both of reality and of value). "Bringing-up" can therefore take only one form; to be "badly brought-up" is not to be "brought-up badly", but rather to be not "brought-up" at all. Such "training" consists of internalising (the correct form of, that is, proper, meaning both real and right) manners, dress-sense, language, spelling. (Indeed, "everyone needs disciplining until they're thirty", as the visitor, already quoted, said.) As it happens, each one of these four aspects of life was uni-form (the word is itself typical) in this country at least, between (say) the introduction of compulsory elementary education in 1890, and the (highly up-setting) award of the MBE to the Beatles in 1965. Private interviews and public examinations were, therefore, highly appropriate methods of assessing such assimilation.

Poly-people, on the other hand, see culture, like personality, as an inevitably variegated phenomenon, in a world that includes more than one nation-state-society, or religion-culture-race. No single culture can therefore be capitalized, for none is normative; with the paradoxical consequence (as in Hinduism, or the Roman Empire) that tolerance becomes *de rigeur*. Following (significantly) the academic anthropological example, and the popular understanding in the United States of America, culture becomes a non-normative, generic category, with a plural reference: everybody has their own culture(s), music(s), etc.

A similar contrast, in small-scale societies, is described by P Brown, 1970: 22 (in M Douglas (ed), 1970), when speaking of the Accuser and the putative Sorcerer. "The accuser", he says, "is usually the man with the Single image. For him there is one, single, recognised way of making one's way in the world. In rejecting sorcery, such a man has rejected any additional source of power .... The sorcerer, by contrast, is seen as the man with the Double Image" (cp R Horton, 1967 on the "closed society").

F W Dillistone, 1973: 162-3 similarly and usefully distinguished between "an exact, univocal, one-track system of conventional *signs*, and ... an open system ... expressed through a system of *symbols*", which he described as "the most striking division in the scientific world today". It may also be the most striking division in the pub, and in contemporary society, and in the contemporary world (including contemporary religion). Thus, when Mao Tse-tung said, "Let a hundred flowers bloom", he was departing from the missionary Marxism which issued, for instance, in Walter Ulbricht's "Ten Commandments of Socialist Morality" (1958; quoted in E B Koenker, 1965: chapter III), and the apocalyptic view of the world as seen from the ghetto, and was returning to a traditional Chinese high-culture view of local cultures (so long as they were Chinese).

These two world-views are not only bordering on the necessarily religious themselves, but, by reason of their awareness of their contrast and antipathy, come close to explicit religious confrontation. Thus, for the Mono-man the normative (and capitalized) Culture closely approximates to both Truth, regarding the way the world is, and Value, regarding what is and/or should be. To express their meaning, each must again be capitalized, as there is only One, and that is Absolute. Indeed, the movement from the "facts" (a characteristic expression) of life, to Morality ("ethics" are potentially pluralistic), is achieved by means of a Logic which is equated with reason, and itself is of a single mode, and operates mechanically, consistently, and universally. It was often taught in connection with (the grammar of) an alien and almost defunct language, Latin, as another subject ("object" might have been more accurate) to be learnt.

Poly-people feel and/or say (rather than think and/or assume) that there are at least as many truths as there are people or indeed phenomena. For each truth is dependent both upon the functional situation of the "object", and upon the extent of penetration of it by the subject, and each such relationship potentially requires its own language.

Unsurprisingly, it is in theory and practice that such contrasts are pinpointed. For the Mono-man, the truth is plain, singular, rational, objective, factual, and to be "mastered", by hard work. For poly-people truths are three-dimensional, their unity is inevitably beyond the experience of any individual, their apprehension is mystical rather than moral, and their "discovery" is a kind of revelation. So the Mono-man teaches a subject, while poly-people put children "in the way of learning". "School projects" are virtually "pointless" to the Mono-man, because unsystematic parts of a non-syllabus, but "personal" to poly-people, because forays into the depths of totality.

Mono-men belong to a single Society. It can be awarded an initial capital, because (high) Society is often seen as its pinnacle, goal, and ideal representative. It is linked by "breeding", both biological and Cultural. Its renegades therefore are either "bastards" or "uneducated". Initiation into it, through progressive forms of assimilation (bodily self-control, avoiding anti-social behaviour, respect for cultural norms, success in some valued field, and replication of the pattern in the next generation) is a *cursus honorem* (both terms being significant).

Should either the birth-right or the desirable degree of acculturation be lacking, it is possible to achieve membership through excelling in one dimension only. Thus "blue-blooded" aristocracy can dispense with cultural forms ("indulging" in youthful "high jinks", or adult eccentricity) and still retain their position. Likewise European Jewish immigrants (such as Rothschild, Disraeli, Mark, Siegler) can gain entry through incontrovertible success in some area, if allied to assimilation. Likewise, those who excel in other respects can ignore either the central moral norms (Edward VII, Edward VIII, Bertrand Russell), or the possession of blatantly inappropriate biological inheritance (Lord Constantine).

Polypeople, on the contrary, are aware of belonging to numerous groups, none of which embraces all the others, or even includes all the significant others. Entry is by dint of present existence, or location, or participation, rather than by birthright. Although they, or membership of them, may be transient, they are highly valued, but as much for their degree of community, as for the tasks they perform. Thus evidence constantly comes to hand of people leaving jobs for these, rather than for financial, reasons. Groups are valued less for their contribution to an overall, normative Culture, than for their contribution to the individual member's fulfilment, and the sense of well-being or identity they bestow upon their members generally.

The emphasis, however, is upon "*doing* your own thing" (cp M Fish 1969, in ASC Ross (ed), 1969), rather than the Aristotelian concept of virtue (*arete*) or the Hindu duty (*dharma*), for there is little awareness of a coherence belonging to the individual or social whole. For, while there is considerable awareness of the world outside the individual (as already mentioned, in connection with the interviews), that world in theory has no edges, because there is no viewpoint upon which to stand, in order to transcend it. So, honour goes to those who appear to achieve maximum fulfilment.

This may be for themselves or for others. At least as far as the Colour Supplements go (and Sunday remains a day for middle-class reflection upon life-styles), this is measured by the number of groups that one belongs to, the number of individuals who are touched, the number of spheres of life that are influenced. The quest is not for an external uniformity, as in the Great Chain of Being (cp A E Lovejoy, 1936), or even an external unity, as in a self-definition by one of the Great Traditions of religion; but for an interior identity, which can encompass conflict and contradictions. Thus disagreement is acknowledged, and even expected, within (for instance) the Cabinet, political parties, the "body politic" (and the body social). (In the Church, *episcope* becomes constitutional and collegiate.) Such pluralism is met with incredulity, and scorn, on the part of the Mono-men: for them, it is an abdication of moral responsibility, with practical social consequences.

Characteristically, the pub's regulars are Mono-men, who (like the clergy, doctors, teachers, police, politicians) maintain one of the institutions and "fill" the public role, so that the poly-people can participate in it temporarily. In this contrast lie the seeds of a potential conflict which can be moral in nature. For those who "make use of" such "public conveniences", also disapprove of that possible monolithism which says "If you ain't got it my way, you ain't got it at all".

Mono-men cannot envisage there being more than one way of being moral (except immoral; although a-moral might just be allowed, of the morally-handicapped). It means *doing the right thing* (all four terms are significant). So it is activistic, individualistic, and almost positivistic, in its fundamentalist simplicity. The acknowledged Community (or Society) becomes both the totality, and the criterion, of morality - and thus can be above it. In practice, however, immorality receives the greater emphasis - and is largely equated with deviations from sexual norms.

Poly-people inevitably see morality as situational. It does not consist of easily-apprehended rules, learnt in childhood, for all such rules are relative; but its own quality, as demand rather than command, remains absolute. Its criteria lie in the sphere of personal motivation and social consequence. The tendency is to emphasise experience, fulfilment, happiness, and what seems right to and for those involved. It therefore becomes literally impossible to "lay down" any precise guidance for another. It is only possible to suggest "what, if what you say is true, and, if I understand you aright, I think that I, if I were you, would want to do, if I were in your situation".

In view of the depth of meaning of the moral in this culture, when considering morality we begin to move out of the general, human description of the public house, and into that particular area designated as the religious, whether explicit or implicit. This portrayal of the contrast between two types of attitude may, however, conclude by specifically describing their respective theologies, as they largely symbolise and encapsulate the different wholes.

The Mono-man's beliefs about, or belief in, God, can, as is well known, gain independent significance. However, the belief in One God is clearly the pinnacle of all other monolithisms. It is possible to be monolithic in various other respects, and ignore, or deny, monotheism; and it is possible to be a monotheist, and a believer in, and advocate of, pluralism; but when monotheism and monolithism are found together, they possess an "elective [if not determinative] affinity".

The God of the Mono-man is transcendent by reason of His (the capitalised pronoun is again in keeping: indeed, it says just about all that can usefully be said) antiquity: His association with the heights (of all kinds) of human Cultures, and the limits of the Cosmos, and His very "distance" (not least "His" impassivity) of every kind. Socially, therefore, He may become impersonal; but by means of identification or projection, this can be coupled with an intense, inner awareness.

Thus the pub is not a situation in which He can be easily named, in public (except as an expletive, which is usually not intended to be meaningful). It does not give rise to that kind of community. (Individuals who have entered together may, of course, name Him.) It is, however, possible to call other (regular) customers, "You heathen", because it utilises exaggeration to produce a cloak of jocularity. It is also humanly-oriented and limited, even negative, suggesting the breaking of mere rules, rather than a denial of vision and vista, without an end.

Poly-people do not so much disagree with the content of the Mono-man's theology, as find it foreign, and potentially threatening. Christianity has met similar situations in the Roman Empire, and Hindu India, for instance: toleration, as a self-conscious goal (or god) must always look askance at any quasi-absolute, lest it become dictatorial, monopolistic, or totalitarian. Polypeople believe "everyone has their gods", meaning that everyone has their *different* god(s). In that sense, gods are very real, empirical beings. So polypeople would tend to meditate, where Monomen supplicate. However, the possibility of inner or outer dialogue with the divine is no more acknowledged, *publicly*, by the one type than by the other.

It will be seen that the two attitudes have much in common. Not the least important are their assumptions regarding individualism and instrumentality. So the conflict is a civil war, rather than a foreign one; hence its moral passion. Perhaps the battle began, and the war was lost, when marriages ceased to be "arranged", and were instead decided, upon subjective grounds, by the parties directly involved: "they have to decide for themselves" seemed to ground policy and morality in a holistic view of "the facts of life".

4.3   Its Integrating Foci

4.3.1   The place of explicit religion

In the course of describing the life of the public house, as "a human institution" (neither more, nor less), reference has (inevitably) been made to the place of explicit religion in that life. Reference has also been made (equally inevitably) to certain characteristics of its life which, in the present context, will be clearly seen to link with the concept of "implicit religion". This, the third and concluding section of this particular study and chapter, will consider these two topics in turn.

The place of explicit religion will be described in the first place in terms of its reputation in the public, spoken life of this particular community; then the pub will be looked at as a parallel institution to the Church, in some ways identical, and in other ways, mirror-like, reflecting it in reverse. Then the question of a possible rivalry with the Church, will be raised. Next, the place of implicit religion will be looked at, first from the point of view of certain popularly accepted hypotheses regarding the meaning of the pub; and then in the light of empirical observation of its life, describing its focal points - and lastly their own focus.

Non-Christian religiosity was occasionally mentioned in the pub, in 1969-70. Judaism did not receive mention, within the observer's ambit, but jokes involving Jewish people were told, in very carefully controlled situations. The owner of the neighbouring ex-Services clothing store was also heard describing Hitler's gas-ovens, to a young couple in the nearby darts group - at some length, due to the listeners' incredulity and questions. Otherwise, the only reference was the blanket (and semi-jocular) expression, "you heathens", said to customers who were heedless of Radio 2's community hymn-singing on a Sunday evening. Should the meaning of the metaphor have been analysed, then "heathen" would have been equated with "worshipping idols". A complete absence of a religious adherence, or even of denominational self-identification, would not have been entertained, spontaneously.

In 1970, probably no other religious system could have been named by many of those present. (By the end of the 1980s, Islam certainly could have been.) So, had the matter arisen, it would have been assumed that those who were "English born and bred" (and white), were, almost *ipso facto*, Christians (with a nodding acceptance that certain intellectuals called themselves "secular", which seemed like a rather combative, logic-chopping sort of popular Christianity). Conversely, it would have been assumed that the two Chinese men from the fish-and-chip shop opposite, who came in most weeks, and the odd Indian or two, and the West Indians or Africans who came in twos or threes and spent hours together in conversation, were all non-Christians. However, as their possible religions could not have been named, and as they all behaved "themselves" (that is to say, "so well"), they might easily have been awarded the title of "Christian", or "civilised", or "English"! It was "as if" they were each of those.

4.3.2   The place of Christianity

Behavioural (spoken or acted) evidence of the place of Christianity in the public culture of the pub, therefore, is almost lacking. When friends "toast" each other, there is neither conscious nor unconscious reference to the Last Supper. Had the Salvation Army come round with the week-end's edition of the "War Cry", it would have been allowed, and would have been bought, although by individuals, as with the students' Rag Week magazine. Corporately, the only commitment was to the freedom of the individual; the only limitation, lay in the liberty of others to disagree, or abstain altogether from commitment. However, it does not necessarily follow that the individual members of the pub (even, the majority of them) are lacking in such commitments (even, at a deliberate, self-conscious and articulate level). Indeed, it could be such individual commitments (even if held in private) which are, together, responsible for the careful corporate commitment to agnosticism and silence.

Certainly, the best (and, perhaps, the only) evidence for the place of Christianity in the pub will derive from the pub's own understanding of the term. For that, a considerable amount of empathy, and imaginative articulation, will have to be exercised. A four-fold association of ideas was, however, suggested, at the conclusion of the period of observation.

This sequence, of immediate reactions to a mention of the concept of Christianity, would have run: Church, in the sense of buildings and services; Clergy, in the context of family gatherings for christenings, weddings, and funerals; "Bible-punching", and restrictions upon personal habits, especially external behaviour, such as drinking, swearing, and the expression of sexuality; and finally, the Golden Rule, especially, in its Silver, or negative, form.

This, last, would be the individual regular's own conception and evaluation of the meaning of Christianity. With it, he would readily identify both himself, and the tradition's founder. In that sense, he would, in the appropriate context, willingly confess, "I believe in Christianity" (cp Chapter 5.3.6). The avoidance, so far as practicable, of any public imposition of this or any other belief, was conceived as a part (and indeed as the test) of the reality of this faith (cp Chapter 3.3.9). If such "tolerance" was the conscious, contemporary validation of the dominical adage of "turning the other cheek", then, less consciously, it also emulated the dominical warning about public confessions of faith. "Uneducated" may be the worst insult; but the possibility of hypocrisy, which any confession of faith opens up, is almost beyond mention.

Tolerance, in this context, can itself appear negative. However, the situation is one of close personal proximity, and (as has been shown) is intensely social. To "keep oneself to oneself", to pretend not to notice, to ignore (politely) dress which is deviant, or behaviour that is anti-social, or views that are provocative, becomes a positive act of toleration, as well as a would-be example and object-lesson to the miscreant. To "walk by on the other side", when the other has *not* been left for dead, can be gracious. Final responsibility, moreover, lies with the Manager: his *diktat* should be a safeguard against the community being "held to ransom" by its own rules (terrorised by deviants).

A particular incident is illustrative. On a Tuesday evening when the "off-license" shop next door was shut, a complete stranger entered, to buy some bottles of a certain brand of cider. The pub did not stock the type in question. The would-be purchaser became very voluble, and lectured the barman concerned, and the public side at large, on the "impossibility" of this brand not being available: he knew, because he also worked for the very same brewery, and so on, and on, and on. The protest was allowed to run its course, until the man departed. Both while he was present, and afterwards, the accompanying politeness (expressed in silence) was exemplary, by its own standards, at least. Its achievement was also encouraged, rather than discouraged, by his Afro-Carribean origin.

Excessive drinking, and deliberate swearing, were frowned upon. This disapproval had a moral flavour. Had a reason been requested, it might or might not have been explained in such terms. Had "anti-social" been proffered, as a possible explanation, it might have been gladly accepted. Yet it was deeper than that. Indeed, the difficulty in articulating the "reason" is indicative of both its depth, and of its potentially or implicitly religious character. For the objection was fundamentally to signs of an absence of self-control.

Drinking only became "excessive" when it impaired self-control: there was no other criterion. Swearing was only wrong when it suggested the speaker was suffering from a reduced sense of decorum: his use of sexual, rather than theological, expletives, for instance, or their volume, showed he lacked the personal tact to avoid embarrassing his neigbours. His irresponsibility towards them was the side-effect, or index, however, of the basic fault, which was his apparent lack of responsibility *for himself*.

On the other hand, the idea that "all drinking", even "drinking in moderation" was wrong, would have been considered "out of this world". Such ideas would have been dismissed as utopian ("nowhere"), rather than as "ideal". Had they been given sustained consideration, however, they would have been judged as non-Christian, rather than Christian (even though known to be held by some ardent, self-confessed Christians); for (it would have been felt) they ignored the function of the drink, including the alcohol element which the phrase refers to, in opening and maintaining individual peaceability and inter-personal communication. As for ordinary, automatic, swearing, to single that out was to mistake the trees for the wood, the letter for the spirit, the mote for the beam. Yet such things were not, in point of fact, said, it would appear; for (emphatically, and not only as an escape-route, out of difficult territory), "Of course, everyone's entitled to their [own] view".

4.3.3   Comparisons with the Church

The Christianity that is believed in, therefore, is an individual (although not entirely private) matter, with an intensely spiritual emphasis. Yet the public house itself is highly institutional. It therefore begs comparison with the Church, in its local manifestation, as the official institutional form of Christianity. The possibility must exist that the local pub is a parallel to the local Church; that the public house is seen as such a parallel; that it is itself seen as an institutionalised expression of that same spirit of Christianity; and that it (consciously or unconsciously) rivals the Church, either through duplicating, or else through reversing, its characteristics.

The lounge, as already indicated, seems designed to be a place to "feel at home", but in a larger and more public place than the lounge at home. The public side being larger and more public still, and both more traditional and more masculine, seems to lack any such domestic pretensions. One of its models, on the contrary, might be an old-fashioned school-room, or drill-hall, or church hall; or, indeed, a church, especially a nineteenth century nonconformist chapel. There is, of course, no suggestion that this was the only "model": the public bars of other public houses obviously had significant influence. Nor is there any suggestion that this parallel was conscious, let alone deliberate. Yet it is present.

Thus the bar, in the most specific sense (taken from the bar that was put across the door into the private part of the house, from which the drink was served), bears a functional resemblance to a communion rail, and an aesthetic resemblance to the holy table or altar. Two inches thick, over two feet wide, made of teak, it is undoubtedly the most splendid object in the room. Phenomenologically the resemblance is striking, too; for customers come up to, or sit up at, the bar, just as they come up and kneel at the rail or altar. The bar stools, high and lacking any support for the back, preclude lounging at the bar; yet the "up" is also expressive of considerable respect, in the pub as in the church. For the bar proper is a fine piece of timber, its appearance represents a work of art, it is constantly "wiped down" by the barmen and/or the customers, it is a matter for pride. Customers have surreptitiously stubbed out cigarette ends against its hidden under-side: but its top, the bar itself, is always treated with total respect.

If the bar is understood in its middle-range meaning, to include not only the counter but the space enclosed by it, and the wall behind that enclosed space, then the parallel becomes even clearer with the "sanctuary" of a church, the space containing the altar and the communion rail, in which the official ministers chiefly serve, and within which the most respect-able or symbolic clothes (contemporary or antique) are usually worn. In each case the space in question, and its furnishings and functioning, are the centre of attention for the whole unit, and indeed its *raison d'être*, a veritable *sine qua non*.

True, in the bar the attention passes across the horizontal plane of the counter to the verticals of the human assistants and the illuminated bottles of coloured liquids behind them, whereas in the church the eye may be stopped by the verticals of cross, candle-sticks, and flowers, or pulpit. Yet the parallel is close, experientially. The resemblance between the bottles with their coloured contents, lit up by strip-lights above and below, and reflected in the mirrors behind, and the coloured glass of the stained glass windows, lit by external light, which are often to be found above and behind the altar, is in itself merely accidental. Even the element of mystery regarding the contents of the bottles, most of which are never used (not even the Manager was conversant with their contents), and a similar possible ignorance regarding the actual subjects of a church's stained glass windows, is not centrally pertinent. What is undeniable, and significant, however, is that the bar (and its bottles), and the sanctuary (and its painted glass, or similar) are in each case the high-light of the whole room, literally and phenomenologically. In the bar, the colourful, brightly-lit bottles form the reredos in front of which, and in the context of which, the ministers and the customers perform their standardised functions.

This reredos is not only prominent: it is also closely observed. Reaction is immediate, when some Christmas decorations are placed on the glass shelves; when the darts cup is placed on top of the wooden canopy that surmounts the whole *ensemble* (or is removed again); and when "special offers" are displayed. These are matters for broadcast and truly shared comment, usually of genuine admiration.

The comment may also be made that the darts cup needs cleaning; but then explicit religion also inspires similarly down-to-earth, easily understood, "secular" comments among its adherents. It is always easier to discuss the "sensible" (what the sense are able to indicate), such as the length of the sermon, than the numinous, wherever and however and if ever, we may happen to "sense" it.

The second obvious parallel between the local public house and the local church is between the role of the Manager, and the role of the Minister. Despite the variations within the methods of appointing each category, both have an element of authority that is external to the local institution, yet must rely on the goodwill of clients, whose participation in the life of the institution is entirely voluntary. Each has some kind of charge, not only of a "ministerial" team who are largely or wholly of his appointment, but also of the entire community, meaning both the regulars and the visitors. This charge is not restricted to periods of duty and physical presence: when the Manager is "upstairs" he still "presides" over the house, in spirit, as is indicated by his availability at the push of a button, and his deliberate appointment of his personal deputy. He is always, as some of the "tankard" sort of men frequently *like* to say, "mine host". He gives the building, its activity, and its community, a human face; he successfully embodies its spirit (or fails to embody its ideal). Minister or Manager, he is an incarnation, willy-nilly; he should be "the" incarnation (of the object of desire).

Managers receive training, and their responsibilities are indeed many-sided. Yet their personality, which includes their competence and acceptability, is their most important qualification. Assistant barmen receive little instruction: this one had two minutes of instruction from the manager, who pointed out that the prices of most of the "long" drinks were written up on the shelves, while the price of most of the short drinks was identical, and that anyway he himself was "always available to answer any question". Colleagues answered other questions, and were themselves keen to perform the more complex actions, such as changing the kegs.

Thus, personality again seemed to be the main qualification of the barmen. Hence the Manager's criterion: whether "he liked the look of him"; no doubt bearing in mind his regulars and others, whether "he will fit in" and they will "like the look" of him. Their relationship with him is functional and personal, rather than formal. The total web of their inter-relationships "make" the pub, especially for those sitting up at the bar, watching, just as similar relationships "make" the local Church, for those near the centre, "in the know".

The Manager's wife also takes part in this ministry. She must run her household in such a way as to fit in with her husband's prior commitment, publicly-speaking, which is downstairs. It is taken for granted that she, rather than the daily cleaners, will polish the darts cup. She comes into the bar, always on the working side, and therefore able to help with the serving if required, but mainly, it seems, to talk with the customers, and (it seems) because she is lonely otherwise. She is treated by the customers with a combination of the respect accorded to the Manager, and the leg-pulling that is reserved for the "joker" of any society (cp G van der Leeuw, 1963: 81; H Rahner, 1964). This latter is reminiscent of the place of the curate: his "egg", his "Adam's apple", his nervousness, naivete, gaucheness, idealism, innocence, childlike qualities. Her relationship with the barmen is more informal, friendly, personal, jocular, maternal and yet coquettish, than that of anyone else in the building: she is its president's *alter ego*.

A third parallelism may be seen, as already indicated, between the two ministerial teams: between the assistant barmen (with some slight extension to the regulars, who may ask for a "wiper" to dry off the top of the bar), and the lay leaders of the local Church. It is true that the former are paid; and that some of them will say the money comes in handy. Yet it is unlikely that they really work *for* the money. It seems more likely that it helps them to explain, to themselves and to others, why they are there, in terms of a psychology all can appreciate; and it enables the Manager both to hire them and fire them, to count on a commitment and terminate their assistance. In fact, though, they are probably there, because they enjoy it.

In the same way, some part-time officials in the local Church may be paid honoraria (the organist, the sexton, the secretary), but they do the work because they want to do such work, in such company, in furtherance of such a cause.

A parallel is often drawn between the function of the bar staff, and the function of ministers within the active Church community or in the parish at large. For it has often been noted that the former hear something akin to "confessions". The comparison tends to be made by observers who may exaggerate the extent of this aspect of the Christian ministry, especially since about 1960. They may also minimise the extent to which other human beings will take other opportunities that are available to them to talk about themselves. The context of the pub, however, encourages such talk, through the consumption of alcohol, and through the lack of personal accountability. At the same time, it discourages it (as already indicated), through the speed of the transition from inhibiting quietness to prohibiting busy-ness.

Nevertheless, certain conversations, of a more personal nature than those recorded when discussing the "visitors", may be mentioned. Thus, numerous confessions were made of addiction to "the machines", and one, of a mild gambling mania. Some confessions were also made, of difficulty in reaching decisions. For instance, a customer in the lounge, who found he was having to make fairly frequent trips to Derby, admitted that he found the problem of whether to spend an extra three or four hundred pounds, on exchanging his Ford Anglia for a superior car, "a worry". The accountant, among the regulars in the bar, shared his grief at having to attend the funeral of his friend next day; but appeared again the following evening, without ever referring to the matter again.

The shared item may be more positive in character. A man may be received back into a fuller fellowship, following a period of intermittent attendance, due to "woman-trouble". A young salesman may come in to "celebrate", and indeed "proclaim" (the eucharistic phraseology is deliberate) the success achieved during his first day's "travelling". A new barman, recently arrived in Bristol, may come in, following his first day of work in new surroundings, to recover himself (his sense of identity) among those whom he has already come to know slightly.

Complaints, about other people, are also quite common. A woman cleaner in a mental hospital had been "sacked on the spot", "for giving a patient a cigarette", "after fourteen years' service". (She was subsequently reinstated.) A lorry-driver appeared, aggrieved. He had driven to Wales and back by 3 pm, because he had been told he could use the lorry to "move house" for the rest of the day; but upon his return he was told the vehicle was "now wanted for another job". A store assistant, in the lounge, was irritated by the incompetence of his ageing superior, who had lost him a sale by "conversing socially for twenty minutes" with a customer, who had already said she was short of time.

Philosophical questions are rarer. However, one woman asked (and the question was neither merely rhetorical, nor boasting), why her "friends and relations always expected [her] to pick up the phone, and go and see them", and why they never felt an equal obligation to maintain contact. More practical, or political, topics, however, are less rare. At the time of the observation they centred round immigration, young people, demonstrations, and the world's troubles generally.

There is, however, very little questioning of the institutions of public drinking. There is criticism of the Manager, as already mentioned; there is suspicion of the designs of the breweries; there is occasional "wonder" at "why I come here", when "I've already got everything I want to drink at home"; but the basic institution is beyond criticism.

The Manager's and assistant staff's more "liturgical" functions are, of course, the economic raison d'être of the pub's existence. Their role is more than merely technical, however; just as the pub's function is more than simply biological.

Thus, the way the glass was "charged", and conveyed to the customer, and the change was given, were all noticed. The choice of glass was not only a serious matter, but, it would seem, a question of identity, rather than aesthetics. The preference for a glass, which only just contains a pint, and so is filled to the brim, rather than for a tankard, with a margin for the froth, must also have symbolic significance; for it is certainly the reverse of an economic motivation. Presumably the explanation lies in the extravagant air of luxuriant celebration due to its being "filled to overflowing" (cp Luke 6: 38).

The preference for offering notes, in as large denominations as possible, rather than coins, suggests the presence of a similar appeal. The use of the black-handled pumps likewise suggests the presence of subterranean lakes, from which the pint is pulled; just as the pouring of short drinks into a measure, before their transfer to a glass, simultaneously suggests prosperity and precision. Indeed, the way the barman has his back to the customer, when measuring out these expensive, and often foreign, liquors, may be reminiscent of the medieval attitude to the crafts and mysteries (including the need for trust, on account of the opportunity to give short measure).

Finally, the ecclesiastically-minded observer might note points of similarity between the customers, and the congregation at the different services of a local Church. In the lounge, especially, they appear "respectable" (D Marsden, in A S C Ross (ed), 1968), authoritarian (T W Adorno et al., 1950), and "monolithic" (see above), as congregations at non-sacramental services did, at the time of the observation. As the meaning of the expression seems to creep up, to mean anything up to retirement and pensionable age, they might be described as "middle-aged" on average, looking "quite content" (cp the Themes from the Interviews) and "at home".

They have not, however (despite the usual terminology) "come [just] for a drink". If they had really been thirsty, they would have drunk it more quickly. If they had wanted several drinks, they could have had them far more cheaply at home. The drink, then, is the "excuse" which legitimates their coming, the practical and tangible reason, which they and others can name and comprehend, and are thus helped to build community around. The nourishment, for which they have come, therefore, is spiritual, rather than physical. For most of the customers in the lounge, it is to see, and to be part of, the Scene; for those up at the bar it is to be in the midst of a fellowship of "mystic, sweet communion", which goes so far, and not further.

The regulars in the bar (and there are always some visitors in the public bar, in the course of the evening) are more varied than those in the lounge, and less like a congregation in a church. "Respectable" themselves, they are not so anxious to impose their standards of respectability upon others. Less articulate about a pub containing "all types", or the world needing "all types", or the need to "live and let live", it is, rather, an habitual way of life for them "to keep themselves to themselves". Their diversity is less of philosophy or practice, than of age, class and status. So the chief difference between the public bar's clientèle and a church congregation is the presence of members in and around their twenties, and of the older blue-collar male (this side's "regular" par excellence) - and (by law) the complete absence of children.

Mention of both similarity and dissimilarity between regular customers and regular churchgoers inevitably raises the question which popular mythology, institutionalised in restrictions on Sunday opening hours, already postulates: the extent to which the public house is a rival to the public church. The phrase, "demon drink", no doubt originating with the theologically-oriented, suggested comparability, as well as hostility. In tightly-knit villages or back-streets, each institution offered a legitimate change from home and family for one of the sexes; but, back together again, each partner was liable to resent the lure of the other's venue. Such rivalry, however, may go far deeper than time and money; or rather, the competition for their adherents' time and money may indicate a rivalry of attraction which is spiritual, representing a rivalry which can only be adequately understood if designated as religious.

G van der Leeuw (1963: 50-56, 97-100) spoke of the theatre as a religion (cp R Bocock, 1974: 151), a point which can be daily observed merely by listening to the enthusiasm and hyperboles of those involved. The limitations upon licensing hours owed much to opinion within the organised Churches.

For instance, the 1901 Bill has been described as "perhaps the most unpopular measure ever introduced into the House of Commons" (R J Evans, 1950: 301). But in 1909 the Church of England Temperance Society, alone, had 639,233 members (G M Trevelyan, 1952: 110n.) The 1872 Act, which closed public houses at midnight in towns and 11 pm in the country, owed its passage to the United Kingdom Alliance of temperance movements (G K Clark, 1965: 199), but caused rioting in some of the towns. The afternoon gap was introduced in 1916, to prevent workers, unaccustomed to regular employment, hindering munitions production through malingering in pubs after their lunch-break (A J P Taylor, 1965: 37).

The motivation was in each case no doubt primarily religious, but the intention behind the week-day limitation was humanitarian in a philanthropic sense, while that behind the Sunday restriction was humanitarian in a explicit-religious sense. For Sunday opening was forbidden before midday and before 7 pm, precisely in order to prevent its clashing with times of public worship.

The present context, however, raises the issue of the rivalry between the two institutions, phenomenologically, empirically, and microscosmically, rather than historically, ideologically, and nationally. In which case, the most distinctive feature of such potential rivalry must be the degree of community engendered by the pub. While this is under-pinned by the mythology of the surrounding culture, it is a very present local reality. Just as this community sense provides the parameters within which the individual is free to be himself, within the walls and opening times of the public house, so it provides the parameters within which individuals decide whether or not to come and participate in its life at all.

The power of this communal spirit is seen most clearly and most often at the end of a session, especially at week-ends, when leisure-time presents the greatest freedom of choice. Members will ask each other, or one of the barmen, whether they "will be here this evening", or "tomorrow morning". The question may look like formal, polite rhetoric, a concluding parallel to the opening enquiries regarding the health of the individual or the state of the weather. It sounds, however, more like the application, to a particular individual, of a general and super-personal principle: the desirability of the other's company. Yet there is no suggestion that the questioner's attendance is dependent upon an affirmative answer. The tone implies: I shall be here [doing my duty] - will you be here too?

It may be the best possible indicator of the "authentic" character of the community's strength and authority over its members. If no minister would dare to speak to the members of "his" church in such a way, that might indicate either a weaker sense of community within the Church, or else a recognition of a deeper, unspeakable seriousness in the commitment.

There are other ways in which the sense of community reveals its commanding position. Many of these have their parallels in the life of local Churches, and no doubt in many other kinds of voluntary association. There is, for instance, the concern over the future and fate of the community itself. Praise of yesteryear contrasts with the annual round of laments over the poor attendance, for which, first, foul weather, and then, fair weather, excuses are found. Ultimately, however, the Manager is to blame. Such scapegoatism, or negative election, is itself an index of community. Conversely, a new Manager would put the situation right. Indeed, the Relief Manager, who, due to the illness of the Manager, took over from December to January, did no wrong at the time, and in retrospect could do no wrong.

Messianic figures may create community (through *charisma*), but messianic roles arise from within community (through institutionalisation). However, the supreme demand is that the Manager be a person, *persona*, personal. He is to be concerned for the welfare of both those present and those absent, the *representative individual*, the one whose job it is to be "sincere". His role is to be more than a role, to be a Manager without being managerial, to be himself but according to a desired pattern, to be the human face of the institution.

Members themselves are hardly aware of any rivalry between their belonging to the pub, and membership of the Church. There was hardly any evidence of interaction between members of the two organisations. As already indicated, they see little or no conflict (whatever others may say) between the "Christianity" which they believe in, and the joyful, communal, tolerant, self-fulfilling, life of the pub. They would see them as parallel, celebratory institutions, oriented (and restricted) to the enjoyment of the optional, leisure aspects of life.

They do, however, sense and speak of certain other rivalries. One of these was domestic pressure: what the returning customer referred to as "woman-trouble". Another could be called "isolated individualism", in contrast with the social or communal individualism of the pub: the beguiling *indolence* of staying at home "alone" and watching television. In this respect, too, the pub was another voluntary association, like the Church, resisting the growth of sybaritic secularity or privatised consumerism.

4.3.4 Alternative foci

The suggestion that explicit religion was not (certainly in an explicit way) the integrating focus of the life of the pub will come as no surprise. There are, however, certain other possibilities that should be considered, as inevitably occurring to the mind of the enquirer.

While religion, and the Church, as such, have only limited, conscious influence, the integrating and focussing power of a specific form of religion, or, rather, of belief in what was considered to be that form, was duly acknowledged. In other words, Christianity, conceived as a moral system or attitude, exercised a moral influence, not only upon individuals, but upon the *mores* or norm of the institution as a whole.

4.3.4.1   A kind of Stoicism

One particular aspect of this moral influence, which, for a variety of reasons, may be picked out in its own right, is a kind of Stoicism, or at least the dislike of passion. The context is oriented towards conversation, so the confession of intense conviction must always be private. For public speaking is almost always *anathema* in the pub. The only exceptions are the Manager's greeting (not the barmen's) of a customer, but even that is only "overheard" by the remainder; and the concluding, legally required, traditional phrase, "Time, Gentlemen, please", but even that contains the double *placebo*, "Gentlemen, please". Comments are made, upon public issues, which might arouse passion, but they are usually simplistic in character, and probably represent antennae put out in the search for community, like hands groping for the first touch of each other under cover of darkness. Indeed, on one occasion such an opinion was politely but plainly contradicted by this barman, and was immediately replaced by its exact contrary, without any appearance of embarrassment.

Any attempt to change the opinion of someone not known personally (that is, outside the pub), is to speak "publicly" (that is, to say, not to a large number of people, but to a member of what, from the speaker's point of view, is simply a member of the public). The rationale for the hostility aroused by such "public speaking" might run: "I didn't come here to submit myself to your views, with your desire and demand that I change mine. I just came here to enjoy myself; that is, to drop all the roles I have to fulfil in life outside the pub, to be myself. Of course, I know I still have to play at various roles, just as I'm insisting you do, by my apparent but obdurate concurrence with everything you say, but here I can play the roles I choose, without their necessarily having any relevance outside this enclosed, artificial world. So I'm going to be the self I want to be, without having you push your self down my throat."

This dislike of "passion" (ie of the expression of any intensity that requires significant change on the part of the individual in the world outside), has already been seen, in the reaction to the visitor from Lancashire who forced his drinks upon the other customers, whom he did not know, and in the reaction to the West Indian, who insisted his type of cider must be available. Another instance occurred when a fairly regular customer came in for a bottle of sherry to take away with him. He thought he had put down on the bar, among the other coins, a fifty-pence piece, but the barman, who by then had put them all in the cash register, insisted it had been a florin (a two shilling, or tenpenny, piece). The customer became angry, but (being fairly regular) did not talk loudly enough to be heard by all those in the bar side. He eventually agreed to "rectify", what he still did not consider to be his mistake, and departed, muttering darkly. Only then did his neighbour, sitting at the bar next to where the purchaser had been standing, authoritatively confirm to all who might be listening that the barman had indeed been right.

The apparent desire "not to get involved", was not simply due to fear of his neighbour's wrath, though that no doubt played some part. Nor was it just due to a desire to save the customer from having to make a public climb-down, though that probably also played an intuitive part. Nor was it necessarily due to a general desire to lead as untroubled a life as possible; for the susbsequent comment was offered entirely voluntarily, yet without any sign of malice towards the departed acquaintance, or of desire to curry favour with the barman involved. Had he been asked whether he had observed what coins had been put down, he would have answered at the time. As it was, he followed the community's *mores*, by ignoring the passionate outbreak, and dispassionately rectifying in tranquility the mistake that had been made in passion.

All these *mores* would be seen as consonant with the Christianity of (the negative form of) the Golden Rule. To the historian of religions, or of ethics or philosophy, they may appear to have more in common with the founders of Stoicism than of Christianity. However, Christianity, especially in the form of the "public" schools and Sunday Schools between 1830 and 1950, has been in large part their propagator in this society. Whatever their origin, this "dominant value" (A I Richards, in P Mayer (ed), 1970) is reflected throughout the evidence regarding the Beaufort House, and accords with much comment upon the surrounding culture. (Thus G Gorer, 1955: 13 regards the "problem of aggression", and its unusual control, since 1850, as "the central problem for the understanding of the English character".) It must, therefore, be regarded as another integrating focus of its life, in its own right.

4.3.4.2 Sexuality

A third candidate, that must be considered as a possible integrating focus, is sexuality, which is clearly no less profound in its significance, nor less extensive in its influence, than alienation and the other biological bases of human life. The fact that the pub is, to a large extent, a man's club, has been seen by some as proving the validity of such an interpretation of its life. It is, however, by no means necessarily so significant. Single-sex contexts, as in university accommodation, and fraternities or sororities of all classes and ages, can give relief from the strain of emphasis upon gender, without themselves being sexually-oriented. As it happens, even at the time of the period of observation, it was said that, increasingly, women were "now able to enter a pub" (meaning, either alone or in male or female company), "as they wished".

Nevertheless, only once, in four hundred hours of observation, were women ever seen entering this pub without the company of at least one man. On that occasion, two quite young women entered the lounge about seven o'clock, when it was quietest, and stood by the bar for their drink, clearly feeling "out of place".

Specific instances of sexually-oriented behaviour included one barman telling another barman, in January, to leave open the hinged door in the side of the bar underneath the hatch (through which the staff came and went), as the young woman sitting on the opposite side would provide an intriguing "leg-show" when she had had a few drinks. In February, the Manager allowed the university students' "Rag Mag[azine]" to be sold in the pub (in aid of various charities). It was purchased almost universally, the purchase being justified in terms of its "dirty jokes", a matter which each year gave rise, outside the pub, to criticism of the university authorities. Another time, a middle-aged bachelor referred, while playing darts, to his war-time experiences with women in Italy.

Several other instances need to be taken into consideration, however, before interpreting even those three. Thus, one evening, the accountant mentioned, to anyone who might be within earshot and interested, that he had been "taken to a strip-club at lunch-time". But he had been "put off" and lost interest, he said, when a dancer had pushed her pelvis forward towards him, and said, "he could see more for ten shillings". His statement had something of the air of a "confession", or of a subjective self-discovery: as though he had been surprised to find (and wished to share the finding), that, when presented with such a blatantly sexual opportunity, he had found it repellent. His hearers seemed to understand and sympathise with his reaction, as well as wishing to appear to do so.

A similar attitude seemed to be revealed just before Christmas, when a customer brought a calendar in for a barman, at the latter's request. Two groups of customers, who had been standing by the one who brought it in, were allowed to inspect it, but no one else. They reacted to the pictures with an interest that soon gave way to boredom. While the latter may well have been defensive on the part of individuals, it nevertheless demonstrated (like the restrictions on viewing) that the public consensus (whatever the psychological reasons) prohibited sex from becoming an integrating focus.

A bachelor in the lounge, and, on another occasion, the Italian war-veteran, sought confirmation of their "right" not to marry, if they did not wish to under-take the "responsibility". Each of them said their married friends kept telling them that not to marry was "selfish", and also warned them of the approach of old age. They sought support, therefore, for their counter-argument: that to marry, especially as an insurance in readiness for old age, could be just as selfish. Equally serious, but in this case, only between customers who had en-tered together, were various secretive conversations between young, apparent bachelors, which were oriented towards sex.

Returning however, to the public culture of the pub, two further incidents can be recorded, which indicate the place of sexuality, and the interpretation placed upon it. The first was entirely conversational. A middle-aged spinster, who always entered the pub with a married couple she knew, but who often sat at the bar alone, asked one of the barman if he knew any more "dirty jokes", because both her landlady and her office colleagues had so enjoyed all those he had told her the previous evening. The expression, "dirty jokes", however, suggested glee, rather than gloating. Undoubtedly, the interest, humour and hilarity of the stories depended upon their "dirty" (ie sexual, and usually genital) character. Yet there was a moral innocence about the request, and, it would seem, at least as she understood it, about the pleasure given by the earlier collection.

The second incident involved the lounge side, but no conversation. A young woman had come from the public Bar side, via the porch, to visit the Ladies'. As she emerged again, it was apparent to all who glanced in her direction, as she crossed the lounge to re-join her friends outside, that she had inadvertently tucked the back of her mini-skirt inside her pants. It was quite clear that the reaction to this very public display was one of genuine and innocent amusement. If there was any undertone at all, it was one of irony, that what was intended to be concealed had thus been revealed, and of the poetic justice involved in wearing such a short skirt.

The place of sex in the pub, then, may seem paradoxical. It is a fundamentally masculine, or rather mono-sexual, world, which women enter on those conditions. However, it is a mistake to assume that it is therefore oriented towards sexuality, of any kind. On the contrary, especially but not only at the public level, sexuality is carefully kept at arm's length. It is not denied, but it is kept in a communal perspective.

The resolution of this paradox may lie in the position of the previously identified integrating focus. For the asexual character of this sexism safeguards against the lure of that "passion" of which sexual emotion is the type-case. Indeed, these two principles came into visible conjunction one week when a young boy and girl came into the public bar three evenings in quick succession, and sat on the bench along the wall, facing the bar. Eventually they felt sufficiently at home, to give each other long and passionate kisses. The Manager was temporarily nonplussed, but it was eventually agreed, by him and the nearby regulars and the senior barmen (in that sequence), that the kissing must stop. However, he neither wished to instruct them publicly, from behind the bar, nor did he wish to disturb their privacy by going over to speak to them. Eventually, though, they were told that this was "not the place for that sort of thing", and they left, shame-faced.

The public house, then, as its name implies, is an open society, a club whose only conditions of membership are the purchase of a drink, and the observance of its unwritten rule, that anti-*social* behaviour (whether individual or à *deux*), such as passionate behaviour of any kind, is prohibited.

4.3.4.3 Work

A fourth candidate for the position of integrating focus must be work. The Interviews demonstrate that this is a more serious matter for more people in contemporary society than might be imagined. Observation in the pub confirms that it is a serious value for individuals, and so is acknowledged in the more intimate type of relationship. However, it is not acknowledged in the public culture of the pub, any more than (at least at the time of observation) it was in the surrounding society.

This may, indeed, explain the widespread belief that no one, except the speaker himself, of course, and possibly his audience, any longer "believes in hard work". By its nature, however, the public house is an unlikely venue for the public expression of a "work ethic", for its legitimation depends upon the conception of leisure, which is defined as the absence of the compulsions of time and role. Its influence, on the other hand, is noticeable, inversely; as with sexuality, and (for the lounge) of "the Other side". A would-be salesman, like a would-be lover, or a would-be evangelist, would be not only exploiting the community's tolerance, but abusing it. Such tests reveal the limits simultaneously of the width of its toleration, and of the depth of its community.

4.3.5   The seven foci

Certain empirical foci have been discerned in the life of the public house. Certain of them may be sub-divided, or amalgamated, but the designation of seven owes less to any adherence to precedent (or numerology), than to the desire to avoid capitulation either to the Scylla of a particularity which denies the phenomenological meaning of similarity, or to the Charybdis of a generality which is externally imposed.

The "idea" of the English or British pub is the first such focus. It operates within this pub, as in the nation generally, not least at the cultural level. Thus, customers say, and do so with pride, "You get all types in a pub, don't you?" The breweries' advertisers build on this when they use the slogan, "Let's all meet at the pub" (N Kessel & H Walton, 1965: 47). S B Rowntree & G R Lavers said, "Taking public houses as a whole, their customers thus tend to be a cross-section of the male population" (1951: 48-9). Indeed, the pub is used as a symbol for the British way of life, for people in other countries. Thus it was regularly reported, around the time of this study, that a "pub" had been included in the "British pavilion" at international exhibitions. Similar gratification (satisfaction, tinged with humour) greeted reports of the proliferation of "British pubs" in New York and other American cities in the 1970s.

Part of the attraction of this idea (its mythological character) lies in its being a "local". You "get all types" in a pub, although many individuals will seldom or never enter one. Most of the population, however, will know the names and whereabouts of those in their own locality. It was therefore a commonplace that, "If you ask the way to somewhere, men will direct you by pubs - and women by churches". Likewise, it is said, every village (meaning every community) should have at least one pub (and church, and school, and general store with post office).

However, there was no evidence that even the observer's various neighbours, living a hundred yards away from the Beaufort House, regarded it, or any other public house, either as *their* pub, or as *their area's* pub. Neither does an individual public house make any precise territorial claim, or overt claim to undivided allegiance, in comparison with its neighbouring competitors. The fact that a customer "used to go to the Prince of Wales", or that another customer has gone there this evening, or that a former customer now goes there regularly, may not be flaunted before the Manager: but it is said to an assistant barman, with only a little embarrassment.

The physical presence of the pub, the designation of the building, the existence of such an institution, may be the first of the integrating foci; but the "idea" of a pub includes much more, as is abundantly clear. The inner environment, in its spatio-temporal dimensions, is simply the setting for the people, and their activities. Indeed, as with the wearing of uniforms, individual personality seems all the more diverse and conspicuous, when other factors are thus "controlled"; so that decor becomes the necessary antidote to the absence of spontaneous community feeling. Indeed, one influential group within the Beaufort House will talk of "my pub"; and it is conceivable that, should the occasion for it ever occur, they would speak of "our pub". This identification with the community within its matrix is daily reinforced by the legal right of entry and the testing rite of the entrance, and over time by the waiting period and procedures for entering into dialogue, so that eventually to change one's pub would involve a considerable dis-investment of tension and emotion, of successful negotiation and accumulated goodwill, of longevity, seniority, and respect.

This sense of community overflows to the lives of at least its own members, outside the walls of the pub itself. This is particularly noticeable in the case of the staff, who serve both sides of the institution. They may meet while shopping, but if either party has been missing from their accustomed place, then some indication that they have been missed, will be valued. An enquiry after his health will be concerned primarily with his own welfare, not with his particular role in the economy of the public house. It will be followed by a similar exchange of news regarding mutual friends, and, of course, the Manager. Such shared, personal commonalities are recognised as forming the content of communication, and the means of restoring and developing communion.

The idea of the pub, then, contains a pair of integrating foci (the building and the clientèle), one of which is inevitably more apparent to the non-participating neighbour and the other to the regular. The third integrating focus (the doorway between the two sides) is likewise accompanied by its obverse: that of each side in itself.

Both the wall, and the hole or doorway set in it, had functional purposes of the strictest, most utilitarian kind. Some kind of division was legally and commercially necessary, so that the brewery could designate the space in which bitter was sold at the controlled price, and that in which it could be sold (like other drinks) at a price set by the brewery. Likewise, had there been no opening, each side would have had to have its own staff and range of products.

Both the wall and the doorway, however, had functions in the realm of meaning. Customers on each side are aware of the division, and value it positively. Both groups, however, also appreciate the existence of the way through (and thus of common staff, and common consumeables): it symbolises, expresses and maintains their over-arching (or underlying) unity. An unbroken wall, without the doorway, would subtract an important characteristic from the pub. Indeed, it would hardly be a public house any more; just two clubs. The resentment aroused by the suspicion that the breweries were "trying to do away with the public side altogether in some pubs now", was not primarily financial, but ideological. The coexistence of the two sides to the public house proved that categorisation by class was secondary to their uniformity as people. Their very differentiation reinforced their inclusive commonality. If the American dream included the belief in equality, and in the openness of the future of all, the British dream included the freedom to classify one's self in the world of the pub, and its demonstration of reciprocity.

The fourth of the integrating foci, are the "bars" that capture the attention in the two sides. Whether or not they imitate or reflect or rival, consciously or unconsciously, the sanctuaries of churches, they are clearly major elements in the life of the pub, and thus presumably of any indigenous religion which may be implicit in it.

A fifth focus is the "busy time": the period between the advent of the majority of the customers, between nine o'clock and half past, and the calling of "Time" at 10.30. This is not a separate part of the evening, but the climax of the whole, when the pub really comes to itself, into its own, to life. It is the time for which the regulars, who have been complaining how "quiet" it is, and the barmen, who have been complaining they were "bored", have been waiting, consciously and unconsciously. One or two married couples in the lounge "like to leave early, before it gets too busy", and do so; others, who say they like it best when it is "quiet", somehow seem to stay on, if not until closing-time, at least until it becomes "busy".

The assistants would rather be "rushed off their feet", than have "nothing to do": it provides or restores purpose, excitement. The regulars would rather have something to watch, even if it does mean waiting for service: it provides or restores action, liveliness. The ritual may be demanding, financially, for the customers, and physically, for the attendants; but it is an accepted, and hence acceptable, way of passing the time of day (or of evening, until the night). The business, and such busy-ness, restores identity to the whole, and function to each role.

The sixth of these integrating foci is the Manager, and, as extension of him, his staff. His presidential role in and over the house as a whole, and his (and their) pastoral role, *vis-à-vis* individuals, have already been described. Both aspects are demonstrated upon the arrival of a regular, whom he will personally greet, and attempt to serve. Should he be "on the other side" at the time, the omission will be made good, if necessary by calling a greeting across from the bar to the table where the regular is sitting. The bestowal of such accolades, or, more precisely, the relationships and reciprocity they indicate, are "of the essence" of the institution. Indeed, they are of more moment for the Manager than his contacts with the brewery, for the latter are restricted to a monthly meeting for consideration of common problems, and the daily delivery of the barrels. The regulars are likewise a more important focus for the assistants, than is the Manager himself.

Nor is the form of welcome (the personal greeting) restricted to the regular customer. The visitor will likewise be greeted by the Manager in person, if he is not too preoccupied, due to the rush-hour, to notice - and it would never not be noticed, eventually. It is the Manager's recognition, in the name of the community, of the customer's presence and right to be there. Meanwhile one of the assistants, as delegated carriers of his presidency, will serve the customer, since he cannot be everywhere at once, and they are, after all, only visitors. Indeed, during a quiet time, the barmen may vie with one another for the job of serving a new arrival; but if he is a regular, there is an unarticulated acknowledgement, if the Manager is not available, that certain barmen have prior claim to those customers they know best.

The last of the seven integrating foci to be listed here is the "trans-action" of "giving" the drink and "giving" the money. Just as the wall and doorway confirmed both the distinction and the community between "them" and "us", so this action simultaneously re-affirms and yet relates and relativises the difference between the barman and the customer. For some, at least, it integrates not only within the public house, but also life outside it. "What else has the working man got?", used to be said after each Budgetary increase in the price of beer or tobacco; or, as the gentle, bachelor Scot, who sits at the bar for two or three hours each evening, once said (with reference to his "tubbiness"): "But if you don't eat and drink and have a smoke, what is there left in life?"

To describe the transaction as a "purchase", sounds inappropriately formal and "hard" (cp M Mauss, 1970: 69-70). The "mutual exchange" may regularly include the offering of a comment, or, in one case, of a funny story, on each occasion. It also involves, not merely the two parties most directly concerned, but also many of the others at the bar, who watch. Progressing with time, it also has a dramatic quality. Tension may be involved, in getting the terms, like the glass, "right". It becomes the mythic bearer of all the weight attached in contemporary culture to the simple ideogram of "getting myself [or, ourselves] a drink". Despite the relative privacy of the two consenting adults involved, it is an integrating focus, not simply by reason of its repeated and legitimating character, but by reason of its representative quality. All agree that "you can drink at home", but that "it wouldn't be the same, would it?" As a small *entrepreneur*, who was a regular at the public bar, put it, "I always keep a couple of bottles of everything - gin, whiskey, sherry, the lot - in the house; but I never drink at home, when I'm alone", meaning, with his wife, but without "company".

The integrating power of the seven foci that have been enumerated should be apparent, to those unfamiliar with the life over time of any pub, let alone this one, from the description given previously. The criterion for their selection has been phenomenological, as with the responses to the interview stimuli: What has most (depth of) meaning, and/or most (width of) relevance, for the greatest number of people? Again, the categorial unevenness arises, not from the inconsistency of the subject, nor from the illogicality of the analysis, but from the nature of the empirical material observed: it is a life-style. Nevertheless, at this point some common thread, or common threads (whichever may be more appropriate to the data) should be sought out and tested, and conclusion(s) formed; upon condition that such unifying understanding avoids doing violence to the reality it seeks to interpret. Contradictions cannot necessarily, for instance, be explained as paradoxes, without transmutation.

4.3.6   Their integration

So far, then, the integrating power of explicit religion has been seen to take the form of a common, but private, and to a lesser extent a common and shared, belief in Christianity; by which was understood a relatively modest, but nevertheless taxing, constellation of moral and spiritual demands, mainly concerned with peaceable co-existence. This *ethos* could be seen as finding its expression in a local institution, which was comparable in some ways to a local Church. On the other hand, that comparability could be interpreted in terms of rivalry, although few of its members saw it in that way.

Alternatives, largely based upon widespread interpretations of human motivation, were then also tested against the evidence. The notorious British or English cultivation of "reserve" and a "stiff upper lip" were seen as achieving prominence in the pub, in the form of avoiding public passion. Not to be confused with an other-directed (D Riesman *et al.*, 1950, 1952), or a "laid-back" attitude, it was closer to that Stoical tradition which has been the form taken since the Industrial Revolution, by the post-Renaissance amalgamation of Christianity with classical culture. With it was indeed linked the sexual character of the public house, for this was not so much orgiastic or Bacchanalian, as ascetic and contemplative. The work-ethic, or economic motive, only appeared on the public stage of the pub, in order to be denied: an officially licensed *potlach*, to which the universal response is a slight snigger (as though at something mildly naughty), it is a sort of protest, an anti-economy, a system, but one of sacrifices. (This does not prevent its members being well aware that its owners have different ends in view.)

These three "alternatives" happen to coincide, in what has (recently) usually been seen as a non-religious key, with much of what was said above regarding the relationship of the pub with explicit religion; for the repression of passion is seen as necessary for "Christian" tolerance; the cultivation of togetherness is seen as comparable to, but unconnected with, the Church; and the pursuit of celebration is seen as rivalling, or indeed contradicting, Church life.

Seven integrating foci that had been empirically noted, were then described: the "idea" of the pub, dividing into, firstly, the presence of the building in the locality, and, secondly, membership of the community within it; thirdly, the physical distinction between, but the valued conjunction of, the public side and the lounge; fourthly, the actual bar and its background in each of the two rooms; fifthly, the "busy time" of the evening; sixthly, the Manager and his assistants; and lastly the "trans-action" involved in obtaining the vaunted drink itself.

It is now suggested that the common element, or ultimate concern, or inner meaning, or all-but-ineffable essence, of the world, the society, and the culture, of the pub, is its own sense of community. Thus the moral system that was described with reference to explicit religion and its alternatives, is not so much itself integrative, as a "public philosophy" (cp W Lippmann, 1956). It is the rationalised articulation of a deeper phenomenon, that of belonging or identification. This is internalised through the daily initiatory rite of the entrance, and nurtured through the hourly ritual of the transaction, renewing the charter. Together they allow the constellation of supporting foci to perform their integrative work.

The moral pressure which the community is able to exert through, and upon, its members, was described earlier. Christianity has something of the same character in this micro-society, but that must be phrased negatively, and humorously, no doubt because of its very combination of extreme idealism, final judgement, and ultimate allegiance. Within the pub, moreover, it is inevitably an import, a stranger: not constitutive of the community itself.

The strength of this community feeling, pressure and spirit is (perhaps inevitably) fully demonstrated and revealed only at the critical hour of closing. Something of its character can be gleaned at lunch-times, especially at the week-end, but naturally it is the evening closure, with no further prospect of re-opening in sight this day, which is starkest. The short interval between the climactic "busy time", in the hour leading up to 10.30, and the shutting of the doors upon the community, only adds to the drama; but such is the nature of the sequences in all art-forms that work in the dimension of time, be it musical, dramatic, or liturgical.

After calling "Time [Gentlemen, please]" at 10.30, it is customary (and legal) to serve alcoholic drinks only to those customers who have already indicated their desire to order (or to serve tobacco to those who are leaving). Legally, by 10.40 all glasses should be empty, and by 10.45 the building itself should be empty of customers. These precise rules and times were not known to the customers, or to the barmen, or (it seemed) to the Manager himself, but a judgement was given by Lord Chief Justice Parker, just after the period of observation began, and was widely reported, although ignored. The tendency, on the part of one or two of the assistants, to abide by these times was, however, not welcomed by the Manager, who feared they would offend the regulars: a fear that was justified.

Yet the regulars' desire was not simply to linger over their last drink; nor merely to out-stay the legal limit. It was, by doing both, to "prove" the reality of their place within the community of this pub.

The regulars in the lounge were a little more punctilious in their time-keeping and observance of the law, as they were in their role-play. However, there were groups on each "side" who knowingly and deliberately hung on to their drinks, until 10.45 or 10.50. The most extreme cases were the male, and mostly unmarried, darts players, who, having placed their last orders at 10.29, at 11 o'clock turned back to "play the machine" - and then requested cigarettes. A parallel suggested itself, with a child testing its parents' love, wishing to confirm its place within the family, tempting the maker of a covenant, making trial of the strength of community.

The fundamental importance of this feeling of community is illustrated by the case of a particular customer. A regular up at the bar in the lounge, he always wore the same tie. Upon being asked by a barman, he explained that the badge on it was the emblem of the Gloucestershire Cricket Club, whose ground was hardly a mile away. He was clearly surprised that the barman had not recognised it. One evening, in the usual search for communion through conversation and commonalities, the Gloucestershire supporter expressed his opinions regarding the "students" (and others) who were demonstrating their feelings regarding South Africa's policy of *apartheid*, by trying to "Stop the Tour", by that country's cricket team, during the summer of 1970. The barman adopted, by turns, a tentative, agnostic, neutral, or "both-and" position. Yet, however much he affirmed the good intentions, the sincerity, or partial justification, of both sides to the argument, the more his colleague in the discussion saw him as contradicting his own position ("unilaterally", so to speak, rather than as "bilaterally" sympathising with both sides).

It became apparent that, regardless of what was logically viable, any intermediate position was psychologically impossible. "The role [of hero and villain, were not only] dualistically conceived ... supplying the imaginable limits at the two extremes of moral belief" (W L Warner, 1959: 85; cp J Seabrook, 1967: chapter II), but were conceived as mutually exclusive. Indeed, as it happened (and a link can only be surmised), soon afterwards, this hitherto frequent customer ceased coming to the Beaufort House. While the particular, moral community under discussion had been that focussed in the County team, there can be little doubt that its apparent schism within the (aptly named, in the circumstances) Beaufort House had spoiled the latter (its taste) for him. There can be little better index of the strength of such community feeling. The insignificant may be ignored, the erroneous may be tolerated: it is all-but-impossible to embrace the diabolical, those in respect of whom we identify ourselves as against.

A question-mark may, however, be placed against the prevailing use of the word, "community", in this type of context. "Solidarity" may be preferred, to describe this kind of undifferentiated kinship, or fundamental homogeneity. For "community" suggests a unity which is experienced, in spite of or because of, heterogeneity. (The "Athanasian" description of Christian Trinitarianism may be seen as a type case.) In view of this distinction, the spiritual culture of the public house is not so much characterised by a rather superficial community, as by a profound solidarity: the former has hardly been explored, the latter is daily apparent. It describes the kinship of those who *define* themselves as fundamentally alike. This includes defining as *not* part of themselves (individually, socially or corporately) that which would make them seriously different.

So the fundamental integrating focus of the pub, beyond the apparent sense of community, and the actual sense of solidarity, is the idea, ideal, and ritual possibility, of "being a man". For the pub's society is instrumental to the individual's self-fulfilment. The definition of such man-hood lies, of course, not in any contrast with a supernatural being, in any of the ordinary sense which that word has in contemporary society, for instance in the pub itself (although in a certain sense every ideal, such as this one, is itself super-natural). Nor is it seen as being in contrast with the natural environment. It may, indeed, be distinguished from the opposite sex; but, as has been seen, it is not to be defined primarily by such a distinction. It may likewise be distinguished from younger age-groups, who are forbidden entry, but, again, such a negative *definiens* is far from exhausting its meaning.

Positively, then, "being a man" consists, first and foremost, in the ability to "hold your own". The phrase no doubt originates in the various kinds of (serious or simulated) face-to-face combat, such as duelling, cudgelling, fisticuffs, and wrestling. Here it is expressed in terms of physical propinquity, its accompanying conversational procedures and restraints, and eye contact. It means holding your own position and treating others as equals (and assumes the ability to "hold your liquor").

Secondly, it consists in the ability to allow others to pursue the same goal as you, with you. Thus, the Lancashire visitor's gift of indiscriminate rounds could not be refused, without giving offence, but itself offended, and could only be met with hostility among one's peer-group, in order to preserve *amour-propre*: otherwise, it was a "put-down". Only a relationship based on friendship outside the pub, plus the *promise* to "have one on me, next time", enables a reciprocal and equalising round to be refused, without causing offence The drink itself is all-important; not because it is thirst-quenching, or gastronomically attractive, but because it is the visible, shared, miniature and dramatic sacrament of the community. (The fact that a non-alcoholic drink, at the time of observation, was some cause for embarrassment, confirms the greater suitability of describing the spirit thus discerned as one of "solidarity".) Similarly, the wholly acceptable barman demonstrates, by coming into the bar on his evening off, as a customer, "for a drink", himself, that he does not work for the money, and does not wish to finish when the law says he may and must. Hence the laments that the Manager never buys a "Christmas round", like any other member of the community; for he fails to allow us to bestow the same manliness upon him, by receiving his round, that he bestows upon us, through receiving the drinks we individually buy for him.

While the nature of the religiosity inherent in contemporary society will be discussed at greater length in the concluding Chapter, at this point it may be remarked that the implicit religion of the pub, in common with explicit religion and other types of "personal" behaviour, has three facets: the solidarity of the initiates, the ritual of "having a drink", and the rationale of "being a man".

Chapter 5

THE IMPLICIT RELIGION OF A RESIDENTIAL PARISH

5.1 The Methodological Background: Observing Participant

The public house provided a social setting, of particular significance within contemporary society in this country. By working as an assistant barman, the observer was able to be at the centre of its life, yet with as little power to influence it as he had desire to do so. In both these ways it provided an excellent contrast with the interview situation. This contrast had been sensed, through visiting it as a customer, albeit for purposes of observation, while the interviews were still in process.

The third and last of the pieces of systematic observation, that have been extensively analysed, likewise began before the conclusion of the preceding period in the public house. It came about through offering (just before he began work in the pub) any help that might be required with an occasional Church service. He was immediately asked to help in a parish whose clergyman was unwell. Soon afterwards he was asked to look after the parish's Sunday services, and the "occasional offices" on week-days, until a new incumbent was appointed. As it seemed that this would provide a useful "third leg" to the main thrust of the observation, the invitation was accepted, though for "not more than two or three months". At the conclusion of that period, however, an invitation that he himself should become the next Rector, was accepted (with the proviso that he should maintain his interest in these studies).

Twenty-six years' residence has confirmed the original intuition. For the parish is a relatively large community, of seven thousand people; and it is not, at least to the extent that the pub is, a self-selecting community. Everyone has to live somewhere, even if only temporarily; so in a parish "you [do] get [nearly] all types". Indeed, "you get" both sexes, and all age-groups, as well.

The method of study has again been by participant observation; although in this case the sequence might be changed, to "observant participation". Likewise, the daily recording of events and reflection has been mental and verbal, rather than written: the keeping of a daily diary has had to give way to the systematisation of such observation, and their sustained analysis, on a cumulative, approximately annual, basis, spread over the past twenty-plus years.

Just as the functions of the Manager and barmen needed some description, so the position of the Rector requires some explanation, in this methodological introduction to the report. For the Rector of a parish in the Church of England, to a greater extent than is the case in most other Churches in England, or in most of the other autonomous provinces in the Anglican Communion, is the Rector (or the Vicar: the terms are usually equivalent) of the entire parish and its population; he is not simply the Minister of the Baptised members of the Church of England in that parish, let alone of the regular Communicants. The Lutheran Churches of the Nordic countries may supply the closest parallel to this situation today. This is a matter, not merely of legal history, or of ecclesiastical ideology, but of popular attitudes.

Likewise, his concern is not only with the religious sphere within life (whether that be defined as the sacramental or the moral, the spiritual or the evangelistic), but (ideally and potentially) with life as a whole and for its own sake, albeit on the implicit assumption that this holistic and intrinsic concern is demanded theologically. This approach is not seen, primarily, as concealing an ulterior motive ("he might get me to come to church"), but as fundamentally inherent in every situation ("God is already active here"). Thus, it has often been assumed that, if the Rector was writing something about the parish, it must be either its (general) history - or else, possibly, the history of its church building. The ubiquity of this understanding of the clerical role in the Church of England is in fact justified by the number of parish histories produced by clergy in the past, and by the quality of current, clerical, holistic observation of "their" parish.

So the role seems to have proved fruitful. For the Rector has potential access to virtually every single individual *and group* within the parish, as well as to the community as a corporate whole. (In twenty-six years of visiting homes, by himself, and by his colleagues and by lay volunteers, access has been refused on only one occasion.) Secondly, the potential inter-face between his interests and theirs, is likewise relatively unlimited. The exigencies of time and personality impose limitations upon the social and cultural areas of contact, but the role itself can combine the width of friendship with the intimacy of counselling - and the longevity of neighbour-hood.

This realisation causes less surprise now, than it would have done a generation ago. Then, the academic, or the journalist, tended to assume that the "priest" or the "minister of religion" (for they were not taking sufficient cognizance of the situation of the English, Anglican, "vicar") would find his contacts restricted to discussion (not action), of religious (ecclesiastical) topics, with involved Church members (or guilty backsliders), who would be kindly disposed (or wish to appear so). But experience shows that in one parish (and others may not be very different), this is a gross under-estimate of the sense of dignity of virtually every inhabitant. (The only exceptions are *some* of the men in the former Reception Centre for "men-of-the-road", who wanted financial help.)

This erstwhile assumption may also be said to overlook the priest's or minister's experience, dealing with thousands of groups and individuals over the years, in gauging their degree of commitment to attitudes and opinions of every sort. No doubt it is possible, for a clergyman who wishes to "play at being Church" (as children play at being mothers and fathers), to find a few like-minded friends to play the game with him; but given the number and variety of group meetings in the contemporary community and Church, it would be difficult to maintain such a façade and not be detected.

It may be methodologically useful to report a "false start", as part of the background to this report. For an initial attempt to report upon this sphere of study under the headings of "explicit" and "implicit" religion (as in the concluding part of the study of the pub) had to be abandoned.

On the one hand, it was clear that certain overall activities, such as worship, or the meetings of the Church Council, fell into the former category; but, at the empirical, specific and detailed level, it was by no means so clear, either that the motivation, or that the topics, did so, even in the case of such events. On the other hand, apparently secular activities, such as party politics or home improvements, could be undertaken in apparently (or avowedly) secular contexts, by those who did or who did not participate in "explicit religion"; and yet their motivation may be, not merely implicit-religious, but (consciously or unconsciously) explicit-religious.

The difficulty arises from part of the nature of the (actual experience of the) sacred: that it is symbiotically linked with the remainder of (experience of) reality. The relatedness of the sacred and the secular, in many if not all cultures, has sometimes been neglected. Certainly it seems likely that the difficulty experienced in this instance must be frequently encountered, whenever religion is placed *in Sitzimleben*. Studies of popular religion, or in the anthropology of religion, of such "micro-religion", bring all abstractions down to earth, and result in a *problematique* that is seen in other attempts to define the specifics of "incarnations".

The approach subsequently adopted in the report, therefore, was to sketch the *meaning* of the parish. It is a "community study", primarily from the point of view of its contemporary consciousness; there are only the briefest references to the geological, botanical, agricultural, historical, fiscal or other factors. Then, the parish will be described as having a number of integrating foci, spanning the explicit/implicit religious gamut. These include the resistance both to integration, and to explicit religion. Then, in the final Chapter these observations can be compared with those reached in the other two reports, and assessed from the point of view of the wider study of religion.

5.2 The General Consciousness

5.2.1 Its identity identified: the four meanings of Winterbourne

In the general consciousness of the parish, the name "Winterbourne" has four possible meanings or references. Firstly, there is the ancient parish church, thought to have been begun about 1190, and usually said to have been "finished" (*sic*) in 1380. The building is next to Winterbourne Court (where a court used to sit), and is surrounded by a hamlet of half a dozen dwellings. It is often assumed that the "old" (original) village of this name was there, by the church, but aerial photography shows little sign of there ever having been more dwellings than there are now (and several of these are recent conversions of farm buildings).

Secondly, half a mile or more away to the east, there is the settlement on the High Street. In the high Middle Ages the weekly market and annual fair were held here. From the fifteenth century on, the stone from the adjacent quarries was used for building. This settlement centres upon a pair of pubs, and some shops, at the southern end of the slightly elevated and fairly straight stretch of road, which at this point traverses a plateau. No doubt it owed its development to its arterial character, and to its midway position between Bristol, to the south, and, to the north, Chipping Sodbury, and the old Fosse Way (the Roman road to the Midlands and East Anglia). Indeed, it is still, to some extent, an example of "ribbon development": two sites on the west side were still undeveloped in 1995, while behind the single line of buildings on that side lie fields, down to and beyond the church. However, the five-branched cross-roads, the pubs and shops, make it the parish's best candidate for the title of "town-centre".

Winterbourne, in the sense of this High Street settlement, has an opposing "pole": Watleys End. This is reached by going half a mile, to the northern end of the High Street (where there are again two pubs, on opposite sides), and then branching off to the right (east), down Watleys End Road, for another half-mile. The name of this settlement, and the road to it, is never explained, or questioned. No doubt it demonstrates the dominance of the High Street viewpoint; for this was part of that millennial process of internal and external colonisation, that followed the break-down of the Roman Empire and still goes on, giving rise to such comparative names as Middle Wallop or New Hampshire. "End", however, seemed natural and apt, as late as the 1970s. For, until the road was straightened and widened, it led, round alternately projecting gardens, to (almost) a "no-through-road" area of narrow lanes, with blind, right-angle bends.

This hamlet or village was mainly settled in the eighteenth and nineteenth centuries. "Factory Road", "Salem Road", "Common Road", "Beaver Close", "The Gully", commemorate its origins: in the recognition that a house built during one night upon common land gave right of possession; its dependence upon the manufacture of hats, and the mining of coal and iron, for instance at nearby Coalpit Heath, Iron Acton, Engine Common; and its cultural self-expression, in Salem Chapel (founded by John Wesley himself in 1787) and Ebenezer Chapel, founded in 1868 - and the single public house, the Mason's Arms, built between the two World Wars.

In the earlier part of this century Winterbourne continued its slow process of expansion, chiefly along the High Street and the other arms of the cross-roads. In the 1950s and 1960s, however, completely new roads were laid and new streets built. This had the effect of "filling in" the gap that had previously existed between the two poles of the ecclesiastical parish: the High Street and Watleys End. It is still possible for someone in Watleys End to say they are going "up" (an elevation of a metre or two, in a mile, is noticeable on foot) "to Winterbourne", for instance to collect their pension from the post office. Yet "Winterbourne" now generally means, therefore, the whole of this community, including both "poles". This third meaning is contiguous with the ecclesiastical parish of seven thousand people, which is the subject of this report.

The fourth main reference of "Winterbourne" is to the civil parish. This continues to include Winterbourn Down and Frenchay, to the south, although they became separate ecclesiastical parishes in 1858 and 1834, respectively. However, only those who are involved in the Parish Council's affairs would realise, unprompted, that the name might be used in this way. Similarly, only those directly involved would realise that "Winterbourne" was also the name given to the Reception and Re-settlement Centre, now closed (one of twenty-two in the country, for the forty years following the Second World War). The name is also used to refer to the telephone exchange which serves both the ecclesiastical parish and community of Winterbourne, plus Winterbourn Down to the south (but not Frenchay), and Frampton Cotterell and Coalpit Heath to the north; and to the postal sorting office for Bristol 17 district.

Winterbourne, then, is a recognised expression, although with various meanings according to context. Some are defined, administratively or legally; others are fluid, and depend more upon internal identification than external deposition. However, such meanings are by no means under the absolute control of those thus identified. A new state, such as the partitioned India of 1947, may decide to call itself Bharat, but the decision may soon be forgotten: identity must be bestowed, as well as adopted. A newly professed religious (in the technical sense), can likewise only usefully adopt a new name, with the peer-group's agreement. Indeed, the extension of the very concept of "*religious*" in the technical sense, to the *religions*, as in the concept of "popular [sic] religion", exemplifies the same process.

5.2.2   A relaxed sense of identity

The identifiable entity of Winterbourne, the ecclesiastical parish, has its own sense of identity. From time to time, for instance, new arrivals are asked, "How do you like Winterbourne?" Likewise, comments are passed on the "number of people who seem to be moving at the moment". In fact, it is probably only a third of the national average; but here, the "For Sale" notices and the removal vans are noted, and regretted - and the speaker believes the hearer will share a similar concern. A third sign of the sense of identity is to be found in the awareness that "it is changing", or, "has changed so much". Thus, an elderly bellringer, who decided that it would be wiser in future to walk down the length of the High Street to a different pub, than to cross the road to his accustomed one, observed: "You can tell how the place has changed, because the people you pass, who don't know you, don't speak to you now". Both the continuity and the change are real, as well as relative.

A fourth indication of this sense of identity is the repeated effort, on the part of a variety of bodies, to record various aspects of the parish. These range from periodic "guides", produced by the Church Council, to the statutory and voluntary organisations and the way to contact them, to invitations to their officers to portray their attractions in *converaziones* in the church or church hall or rectory garden; from a street-map produced by the scouts in 1971 and still selling in the 1980s, to a "parish diary", kept in the public library, in which organisations can enter their planned events and so try to avoid clashes of date; and from histories, reminiscences, local history talks and groups, and exhibitions of old photographs, to - this study itself.

Admittedly, it is not unknown for protestations of identity to exceed the reality. A new immigrant may try doubly hard to be "all-American", or a new convert may be "more Catholic than the Pope". This, however, does not seem to be the case here. The question, "How do you like Winterbourne?", has real meaning; but its importance is limited. The newcomer is not asked it daily; nor is there any suggestion that the future standing, at least of a private individual, or the *amour-propre* of the enquirer, depends upon the answer, as has been known elsewhere. It is not so much a test question, as a concern for the other's welfare. The modesty of the enquiry suggests a sincerity that is unhysterical. Even the references to "the village", which were still heard in the 1970s, arose from familiarity, as much as nostalgia. It was necessary for the hearer to up-date his understanding of "village" - as the planners of new towns were doing.

As a parish worker, with considerable experience of other communities in this country and elsewhere, suggested: "Winterbourne is unusually normal". Life-long inhabitants may not have welcomed the newcomers in the 1960s, but they accepted them quietly, even gracefully. Newcomers simply said, "Winterbourne is a nice place to live"; or, even more revealing, said that, "People say that Winterbourne is a nice place to live". They conveyed the impression that, "I haven't thought about it very much, but now we're talking about it, yes, I would agree. I must say, I like it. It isn't particularly posh, or *exclusive*, or well-heeled; and it isn't exactly what you'd call *out in the country*, not real country. But you've got most things here, including good schools, and open space; it isn't like being stuck in the middle of a big city, or housing estate. It's friendly, and we like it. I know I wouldn't want to move, unless we had to, for work, of course."

5.2.3   Four threats to the community's identity

This relaxed but real identity has been threatened in several ways during the second half of the twentieth century: first, by the building of the new houses in the 1960s, and the consequent influx of newcomers; secondly, by the loss of old landmarks, particularly in the 1970s; thirdly, by incorporation into Avon, and the fear of resulting anonymity, in 1974; and fourthly by the expansion of Bristol and the fear of consequent suburbanisation, especially towards the end of the 1980s. The nature of these threats, and the reasons why the sense of identity survived, are further pointers to the reality of the community's sense of identity. For the threat of extinction, as Dr Johnson said, clarifies the mind; and, as Robert Bolt showed, in *A Man for All Seasons*, it reveals the nature of any identity that may exist, beneath or beyond that which is threatened.

The building of the new houses in the 1960s, then, was seen more in terms of change, however fundamental, than of ultimate threat. The reasons for this will be expanded when exploring the community's character. Meanwhile, it suggests that the community did not see its identity as being fundamentally constituted by its existing size or shape; or by denying the continuing process of historical development; or by identification with any of those individual properties, large or small, that were pulled down.

Mention, particularly of cottages that were pulled down, leads onto the second threat, which came to the fore in the 1970s: the gradual elimination of various landmarks. Examples include, for instance, two ponds (which were subsequently restored), near to the Church; the projection of gardens into the middle of Watleys End Road (already mentioned); the Victorian ponderosity of the Perry Almshouses (subsequently reprieved); the sale and demolition of three of the six relatively large and antique houses, for building plots; the demolition of an old stone barn, near the High Street (widely though reluctantly accepted as beyond repair); or the loss of the title "Donkey Terrace", for a part of the High Street where a donkey used to be tethered.

The immediate appeal of these "landmarks" lay initially in their age, and visual attractiveness, although these are hardly distinguishable in the general aesthetics. More profoundly, then, it lay in their un-planned, asymmetrical, oddity. They haply and happily stuck out from their systematised surroundings, like a thumb that was *not* sore.

Unremarked, and apparently unobserved, they yet became personal landmarks, with whose idiosyncracy individuals could identify. They were the warts and scars and blemishes that gave the parish a particular face, biography, and character. This isolated, and largely unconscious, process meant they could slip away, gradually and unnannounced, unnoticed and unprotested. Any public decision, on the other hand, drew attention, and enabled many to discover that the individual identification of each had been a common, albeit private, experience. They were then defended, not of course on the grounds of the individuals' identity, but on the grounds that they "made the place what it is". That is to say, they made this place different from all other places, giving its community a separate and distinctive identity.

Yet their significance was limited. People worked hard to save them, but (so far, in this community) will not die for them. Their oddity gives them a value for persons, who also have eccentricities; but they are isolated survivals from the past, rather than themselves symbols of personal history or alternative reality. Apart from the fact of their existence, they have little meaning. In this way they are more akin to superstitions, than to a religious system (albeit an implicit one). The creeping threat to the existence of such "untidinesses" was, however, sufficient to bring into being a watch-dog conservation group, simply (and significantly) called, The Winterbourne Society.

The Society speaks, then, for one aspect of many people's attitudes; yet it is only one. The public sense, if not of history, then of "time's ever-rolling stream", ensures that it is limited. For its founders mostly came to the parish (as is the way of such phenomena) with the first of the newcomers. Indeed, had they "had their way", before they came (so to speak), then they themselves might never have arrived. But other attitudes are present, even when driven underground.

Changes are not welcomed, at least publicly (certainly it is safer not to do so); but they are generally accepted, with a sort of fatalism. "That's progress, I suppose!", is sometimes said with deliberate irony; but usually with regret, yet resignation. "It's no good crying over spilt milk", or, "over milk that will be spilt, willy-nilly", is the attitude. It is a general statement, that faces up to (but avoids preaching) the need to "make the best of a bad job". It is like saying, "Yes, thanks, we had a nice holiday; no, it rained all the time actually, but we enjoyed it - it made a change"; implying, "If we expected the weather to be perfect, that was our fault, not its".

As already mentioned, the re-organisation of local government in 1974 produced a third threat to the identity of the community. This had nothing to do with the boundaries of the parish. In fact when all such boundaries were examined a decade later, in this case they were left unaltered, confirming again the reality of the community's identity. The fear was usually expressed as one of "going in with Bristol", but that was a misnomer. Bristol did indeed pose a "threat" (to be considered in a moment), but in this case the fear was not, strictly speaking, of being "swallowed up by Bristol", but of being swallowed up by "Avon".

The name of the new county is placed in inverted commas in order to express what was the contemporary attitude: "What is this new, unknown monster, of what must be an artificial bureaucracy, which will simultaneously include the two very different realities of Bristol and Bath, that have nothing in common and are not even adjacent, and therefore also lots of other communities like ours, of whose existences they cannot even know?" The fear was of anonymity.

The desire was not to stay with Gloucestershire, as such: those who had most contact with the seat of government in that far-off county-town said, "Avon couldn't be worse than Gloucester, anyway". The sudden burgeoning of "Gloucester" was as the symbol of a confederation of parish-based communities, alike in their individuality and uniqueness. Ultimately, the fear of "going in with Bristol" and becoming a part of this "new-fangled Avon", was the fear of becoming "another London, here in the West [Country]".

The same fear was vividly demonstrated in the debate regarding the Severn-side Study, a 1972 Government Report. The Study predicted that the population in three areas (one of which centred upon the adjacent parish of Frampton Cotterell), bordering upon the River Severn, would grow by six hundred thousand by the end of the century. So it recommended a planned, rather than a piecemeal, policy, which would provide for an increase of nine hundred thousand. Local opposition focussed upon the disadvantage of encouraging further industrial development at Avonmouth, and further residential development at (in particular) Frampton Cotterell, since the latter was down-wind of the former. As it happened, the unexpected decline in the national birth-rate soon gave reason to think the recommendation redundant (although its predictions are being fulfilled).

The debate was significant in the present context because it failed to distinguish between the Report's predictions and recommendations. There was a similar inability to recall that three areas had been specified; or indeed to concert opinion in the three areas.

Reaction dismissed the Report out of hand, not because it suggested and envisaged (ie prepared for) a fifty per cent greater increase in population, but simply because it suggested and envisaged (ie foresaw) any serious growth, however inevitable or gradual. The picture that was painted was not "unimagine-able"; but it was so overweening as to obliterate the differences between predictions of what will happen and prophecies of what should happen. The projected scenario being "apocalyptic", rather than non-sense, the response was one of "know-nothing", in the face of eschatology (the end of our world). While the practical consequences might be the same as those resulting from an attitude of fatalism, the phenomenological approach was not one of resignation ("what will be, will be"), but of denial, as in the early stages of bereavement. It combined a moral protest, "It must not happen here", with the more ontological faith, "It could not happen here".

A fourth strand was distinguished among those elements in the environment which are sensed as threatening to the community's identity. The first was the increase in housing and population that took place, within its own boundaries, mainly in the 1960s. The second was largely consequential upon this, yet physically and psychologically different: a "tidying-up" or rationalising process, which removed idiosyncratic, old landmarks. The third was the parish's incorporation, as an anonymous element, within the unknown quantity of Avon (a then fictitious entity, lacking all quality, history, focus, or symbol). Such an incorporation could be seen as the translation, into terms of external relations, of the process of internal "improvement", which removed the odd, the obsolete and the redundant. This fourth element may likewise be seen as an external manifestation of the first-named, as the obverse side of the coin to the parish's own "development" in the sixties: the fear of being "swallowed up" by an ever-expanding "Greater Bristol". Some further discrimination, however, is again required.

Visitors to the parish who have referred to this "leafy suburb" have tended to assume that its recent immigrants have been fleeing from Bristol. They have seen confirmation of this in the initial opposition to their being included in Avon. This interpretation was only encouraged by its frequent expression in terms, not of "Avon", but of "Bristol". (This opposition was shared with the people of Bath; which was a major reason for the choice of a new, albeit characterless, title.) The surprise that has been expressed when a family has "moved back into Bristol", lends support to this supposition.

The opposition is not, however, so much to Bristol, as such, but to becoming a suburb of Bristol; just as the fear of Avon was not so much of gigantism, or bureaucratisation, as of an unknown, and becoming an unknown. The perceived danger is less of Bristol-isation (or Avon-isation), than of suburban-isation, conceived (rightly or wrongly) as loss of communal identity.

Bristol itself is, after all, the place to which many of the inhabitants are glad to have come, from rural Somerset, from the south, or from the (then) industrial north, or from Scotland. Everyone knows that Bristol (meaning, the centre) is a "nice place": interesting, characterful, fairly clean, busy, varied, combining history and the arts with modernity and amenities. What is lacking is any visible boundaries to, or central features of, its outlying parts. For those who do not know them, it seems inconceivable that Downend, Fishponds, Eastville, Bishopston, Bedminster and the rest, can be communities: they seem to lack both frontier and symbol.

This fourth fear has surfaced on three particular occasions. The first was in 1973, when the (civil) Parish Council decided it should call a public meeting, before entering into an agreement with the education authority responsible for the comprehensive school, to build a swimming-pool, which would necessitate a significant and long-term increase in the local "rate" (tax). As it happened, work had also just begun on improving the old road from Bristol to Chipping Sodbury, which runs through all three of the ecclesiastical parishes into which the Civil Parish is divided. The annual parish asssembly, when the Council renders account of its stewardship, usually manages to muster hardly a dozen or a score of the general public. This extra-ordinary assembly, however, brought together six hundred and ten members of the public (five per cent of the total population, of all ages).

The meeting was overwhelmingly in favour both of proceeding with the swimming pool, and of *ceasing* the improvement of the main road. While discussion of the latter concentrated upon the danger to children, arising from a consequent further increase especially in commercial vehicles, allied to it was the less easily voiced fear that an arterial road would reduce the Civil Parish's three communities to linear neighbourhoods.

The second occasion occurred in 1980, when the County Structure Plan met with the widespread use of the slogan, "Keep the Green Belt Green". Despite the obvious susceptibility to the accusation that their primary concern was with the value of their own property, or with its scenic advantages, many of the parish's inhabitants probably were also motivated by the desire that the community should retain its own identity (and even, although sensitive to appearances of hypocrisy, that Bristol, too, should retain its frontiers and identity).

The third occasion when this desire has been publicly demonstrated, was when a builder repeatedly sought permission, at the end of the 1980's, to add fifty or a hundred per cent to the population of Winterbourne, through building, not on the fields between the High Street and the church, but on the other side of the parish, in the fields between Winterbourne and its neighbouring communities of Winterbourn Down, Frampton Cotterell and Coalpit Heath. The extent of local opposition attracted national comment. It concentrated upon both the loss of such natural amenities as flora and fauna, and the overloading of such social amenities as roads and drainage; but it also stressed the loss, through the infilling of agricultural land, of what might be called the spiritual amenities, such as the sense of identity and community.

5.2.4   Four factors fostering identity

It may be that identity, whether individual or corporate, can only be known either through direct apprehension ("inter-subjectivity") or through its "works" ("functions"), as was said both of the soul, and of divinity. So far in this account, the identity of the residential parish has been sketched, firstly, by showing what it means (that to which it is seen as referring); secondly, by suggesting that the sense of identity is greater (not less) than the articulation of it; and thirdly, by describing what has been seen as threatening to it. It remains to show in this section why and how this inevitably ineffable mystery is nevertheless not contradictory to what is already known of other phenomena (a sort of "natural theology", for what may ultimately only be intuited), by listing factors which foster this sense of identity.

Firstly, then, although circuitous, it is also true that the sense of identity has for a millenium been fostered by the parish's having a name (probably when it was less a community, than a fiscal unit and geographical expression), and by the general acceptance (in the Domesday Book of 1086, for instance) that it had a reference. Secondly, this double-sided process of identification (external distinction, internal participation) was "incarnated" (or "petri-fied") by the building of the parish church, of which more will be said later.

Thirdly, the threats to this identity over the millenium have been both internal and external, but, whether they have been warded off or acceded to, they have reinforced the sense of identity. Thus, internally, the centre of the community departed in the fourteenth century from Winterbourne Court and the parish church, to the cross-roads on the High Street: those institutions were never again to be dominant. In the seventeenth century the first two, of what were eventually to become half a dozen, large houses were also built; but none was ever pre-dominant, and all were ancillary to the community around the High Street. In the eighteenth century Watleys End was settled, technically within the parish, but with its own identity and symbol (in Salem Chapel), although at an individual and family level many of its inhabitants continued to use the parish church for "rites of passage".

Frenchay, which had also been developed, especially by Dissenters, following the Five Mile Act of 1662, would have been hard to hold in such living tension, due to the greater distance; and likewise, but due to its propinquity, Winterbourn Down. However, each of these was hived off ecclesiastically (as they were popularly), when ecclesiastical and civil parishes were distinguished, during the nineteenth century.

Thus the final internal development, the in-filling with houses of the land that used to separate Winterbourne's "heart" from its Watleys End rival, prepared the way for a relatively uniform understanding of the community's identity, when that appeared to be threatened, in some ways for the first time, from the outside, in the 1970s.

At this time also, the internal division between Church and Chapel, was, for various reasons, beyond the ministers themselves, converted into a mere distinction, largely of geography. It might have been succeeded by a similar division between the two Churches as such, and the population as a whole, following a pattern that had been developing, on both sides, in the 1960s. This was especially possible following the "establishment" of the Community Association in its own "Centre" in 1976, despite the fact that much of the membership and leadership were common to both. Clerical support, and the Association's leaders' appreciation of it, however, preserved the unified identity of the community, and retained the possibility of choosing between ecclesiastical and secular *priorities*, rather than excluding either.

Fourthly, in this period of external pressure, visible expression has been given to the identity of the community through two kinds of "iconography". Walking or jogging, cycling or horse-riding, in the fields that are left within the parish boundary, the built-up area can be seen, on its slight elevation, with some of the tangible coherence of a medieval town or village. Alternatively, all the adjacent parishes seem to hold up a (slightly idealised) reflection of this one: old and new houses together, in bounded communities. Thus its identity is discovered by, and consists in, its being simultaneously similar to, and yet distinct from, its neighbours and peers.

5.2.5   A community with an openness of character

No one doubted the existence of God, it has been said, until a series of Lectures was founded, about the turn of the seventeenth century, with the object (*inter alia*) of proving his existence. The comment is a witty and apposite instance of the sociology of knowledge, and the whole history of religious experience. It is referred to at this point, because it prompts a similar reflection regarding the appearance of sociology at a particular point in social development. Society only began to be studied, in a would-be systematic and objective way, when the coherent existence of independent societies could no longer be taken for granted. A small but significant indication of this double development was the eventual need to invent a new adjective, *societal*, by which to refer to the character of the whole *as a whole*; and also by the widespread inability of members of such societies to understand that meaning.

This in turn may serve as a model for the current use of the concept of "community". Concentration upon the concept increases (very naturally) with loss of the reality. So it tends to be used to refer either to a classification according to some common element, or else to a "consummation that is devoutly to be desired". Examples can be found in Northern Ireland (or Belgium, or the Lebanon, or India); in the use of expressions such as "the Protestant [or Roman Catholic] community", or "the Northern Ireland community".

A similar tendency, to refer to a number of human beings who just happen to live in an identifiable territory, may be suspected in this study. In the present context, however, it will be used more precisely: to refer specifically to that which binds them together, to their relatedness, rather than to what many may have, but hold separately. "Community concerns", not what is common, but what is in common.

The general consciousness of the parish, which has already been described as possessing a real, though relatively relaxed, sense of identity, will now be shown as indicative of a real, but relatively "open", sense of community.

The quality of "openness" or "closedness" is not a function of the size of a society: both families and nations can be either. Openness depends, rather, upon a communal and personal identity which bestows sufficient integrity to enable participation in variety, which may be experienced externally but is borne internally. To take a specific example, which may be more often sensed than said: sympathy and empathy require inner certitude. In this particular case, the quiet confidence of identity was accompanied by a matching awareness of variety *within* the whole.

Just as there were certain indications of, and reasons for, the existence of Winterbourne's identity, so there are signs and causes of its having a culture which enables its differences to be treated as opportunities for reflection and dialogue, rather than repression or anathema. They may be summarised in terms of three polarities: style of residence, "end" of the parish, and position in the social structure.

Following the increase in the population of the parish in the 1960s, from about three thousand to about seven thousand, the contrast between the "older" inhabitants and the "newcomers" was almost as pervasive in the general consciousness, as the universal distinctions of age and sex. Yet it never became an absolute division. This can be partly explained by various features of the ways in which the development took place. Above all, it was piecemeal. Thus, while returning parishioners spoke (somewhat exaggeratedly) of "new estates", none did or could speak of a single, new estate. The significance of the old and positively odd, is balanced by the importance of the new and un-uniform.

The new settlers, like the old, were relatively scattered about the parish: both groups were therefore inter-mingled. Nor were the older inhabitants fully aware of the extent of the new development. A dozen roads were extended, a couple of dozen *cul-de-sacs* were added, by a number of builders (liquidation was the fate of at least three of them). The sequence of events and the approach was in marked contrast with the repeated proposals of the later 1980s, to expand and even double the population. The contrasting tenor could be summarised in the phrases, "Permission was granted", and, "Planning application has been made".

The types of dwellings were also various. Three-bedroomed "semi's" predominated in the 1960s, but there were also four-bedroomed houses, detached and semi-detached (built mostly in the 1950s), and detached and semi-detached bungalows. There were also terraces of council houses and of council flats, again mostly built in the 1950s, and groups of elderly persons' bungalows, and (mainly in the 1970s and '80s) privately-owned flats and single-bedroomed flats. Each of these catered especially for that "rising generation" of single grandparents, who began to join their married offspring but could not always be accommodated in "extensions" over the garage.

Their detailed design was similarly variegated, with different roofing materials, wall-finishes, window-frames, fencing arrangements, and internal divisions, not only between but within the roads, matching the differences in starting-date and builder. Neither the older inhabitants nor the newer immigrants, therefore, could dismiss them as entirely "characterless", because (in view of what was suggested above, regarding the effects of "idiosyncracies") they were not uniform. There were differences within, as well as between, both old and new areas of settlement.

The second major local distinction has likewise already been indicated: that between the two "ends" of the parish. This was not only a serious division, but an antagonistic one, at least among the children at the Church elementary school before the Second World War. With the in-filling during the 1960s of the former gap between the two settlements, however, this division inevitably diminished.

Other factors included the founding of a secondary modern (later, comprehensive) school in 1954. While this was on the High Street, it catered not only for both "ends" of this parish, but also for the four neighbouring parishes, thus introducing into a wider context those age-groups that are most prone to the loyalties of an immediate group.

The founding in 1961 of a new (County) Primary School, in the vicinity of Watleys End, and its division into a Junior and an Infants School, when an adjacent school was opened in 1966, also gave Watleys End (what it saw as) its own school. Opposite the school was also a "parade" of half a dozen shops, providing a miniature "shopping centre". The widening of Watleys End Road, the improvement of the roads from Watleys End to Frampton Cotterell, the attraction of Frampton Cotterell Primary School to the inhabitants of that "end", and the enhanced value of their older properties, enabled comparisons between the two "ends" to be made with humour in the 1970s, as well as candour, and in the 1980s rendered them all but historical.

The third and last of the main local divisions, at the social rather than the biological level, is class. To some extent it lay behind the two that have just been considered: between the old and the new inhabitants, and the two "ends". It also played its part in the ecclesiastical history of the parish: in the building of first one, and then another, Methodist chapel, and then in the establishment of an Anglican presence in their midst, in the shape of a Curate's house and a Mission hut, finally abandoned between the two World Wars.

However, the contrast between "them" and "us" was never simply an economic

contrast between the High Street and Watleys End. Certainly, the High Street
end of the parish contained, geographically, and above all socially, all the half-
dozen or so "big houses". Thus, the Reverend Austen Leigh (a relation of
the novelist, Jane Austen, and of the Leigh banking family) and his wife and
five children, employed a full-time staff of eight, while others came in part-
time, when he was Rector, 1875–90. Yet the Winterbourne "end" therefore
also contained far greater economic disparities than Watleys End. Indeed,
there were probably far more forerunners of a "property-owning" democracy in
Watleys End than at the High Street end of the parish, in view of the traditional
way of building one's house and settling there. At least two of the "big houses"
on the other hand, although they may have "tempted ambition" to occupy and
maintain, probably also taxed the owners' ability, since they kept changing
hands every generation.

Nor, on the other hand, was the contrast primarily social, unless that be
narrowly defined in ways that are less than truly social. Thus the Rectory
employed three full-time gardeners, as late as 1939, "and sometimes a fourth,
because there was a lot of unemployment in those days, you know". With its
vegetable garden, and orchard, and seven-acre field for grazing its twelve cows,
the property ran to fourteen acres. Yet there is little sense in the reminiscences,
of fear or servility (or compensatory truculence). When the much-loved Canon
Burrough (universally known as Canon Burroughs) took his holiday on the
continent in the 1920s, the men-servants took the opportunity of giving their
girl-friends a ride in his car. During the rest of the summer, when they were
in residence, the son who played cricket for Gloucestershire, practised on the
front lawn with some of those who were unemployed. The Rectory garden is
remembered as the finest, if only because it was the most often open to the
public. They may have "cocked a snook" at the incumbent when he was on
holiday; but every visiting tradesman was also given a drink of home-made
cider.

So the impression is gained that it would be an anachronism to see their phenomenological relationship primarily in terms of either economic inequality or
of conflict. It smacks more of an inter-personal meeting, which included inter-
subjective communication. It would be doctrinaire to presume that a class
struggle based on economics, however successfully masked by false consciousness and bourgeois ideology, was a more profound interpretation of human
reality, for individuals who lived in relationship for years, than (say) a sense of
a common identity, based on their shared humanity and inter-dependence.

In this context, the rites of passage had more to say to, and were a better
"fit" with, their own experience, than *impersonal* analysis and "objective" concept. The shared recognition of birth, marriage, death, and such intermediate
experiences as puberty, sickness and bereavement, provided the limiting (and
ipso facto religious) parameters, for the lesser (and secular) "accident" (in the

philosophical, not scientific or moral sense) of what they did not both have - and yet, as social beings, could have, if only vicariously and partially, *in common*. Difference does not necessarily entail distance, between those who are growing up, or growing old, together.

Thus the two "ends" were each relatively cohesive in themselves. Insofar as they related to each other, the "order" of the day consisted in the "feuding" of a feudal society, rather than the class struggle of an industrial society. It was geographically based, traditionally inspired, familially determined, community-oriented, and concerned with the nuances of personality-types. It was, therefore, ultimately cultural, psychological, and subjective.

However, the primary reason why the parish retained and maintained a single identity, which yet allowed dialogue to develop, was not the moderate character of any one of those divisions: longevity of residence, geographical distribution, or cultural difference. It was not so much the absence of their absolute polarisation, singly or otherwise; as the non-equivalence of the poles themselves. The incomplete polarisation was matched and reinforced above all by a matching lack of (to use the Netherlands term) pillarisation.

The development was piecemeal, in every way. Now, the contrast between *gemeinschaft* and *gesellschaft* remains, but without its former importance.

Rivalling this factor in importance, however, is one other. This was the deliberate desire on the part of many to retain, maintain and achieve, community. Such willed determination cannot simply determine the foregoing causes, or even signs. It may be itself largely determined by such factors, and others like them; but it can be, was, and is, determinative of the outcome. If identity needs to be accepted as well as bestowed (or, in the case of new nations and individuals, accepted by others as well as asserted), so community must be willed, as well as inherited or imposed.

5.3   Intensive Concerns, with Extensive Effects

5.3.1   Children, its wilful divinities

At the beginning of the period of observation, one who had been much concerned with organising events in the community, advised: "You want to have something for the children - then the parents have to come". In the context of arranging yet another community event, the recommendation was given as a piece of social engineering, based upon years of experience. This observable and predictable behaviour, however, arises from a phenomenon whose extensive effects reflect its intensive character. The term chosen to pin-point the phenomenon, in the present context, is, therefore, simply, children.

As it happens, this focus first suggested itself to the present observer when he saw a nine-day old infant who had just arrived home from the maternity hospital, placed in her carry-cot in the middle of the floor of a large sitting-room, in which a score or more of mothers and grandmothers had been holding a meeting. They rose, as one, from their easy chairs and dashed to see what they could of the baby. Due to a plethora of swaddling clothes, it was virtually nothing. Yet their wondering, chorussed "Oh!", was so remarkable as to fetch their colleagues at the run from the kitchen where they were making tea, two rooms away. The child's near-invisibility, due to its smallness, did nothing to diminish its drawing power (E I Bailey, 1992).

The incident is recorded here, not because it is unique, but because it is illustrative. It happened to be the occasion when this particular observer began to reflect upon the significance of this phenomenon. The phenomenon, however, is so profound, and so widespread, as to seem all but universal. Indeed, until, first "baby-battering", in the mid-1970s, and then child-abuse, in the later 1980s, came into the domain of public knowledge, any hint of such behaviour, or even the mere absence of wonder, evoked confessions of incredulity and incomprehension.

As will be seen, the phenomenon is described in terms of children, both on their own account, and as a type-case. A parallel may be drawn with the "matter" of a sacrament, which is not only sacred itself, in Christian doctrine, but represents a sacredness that is implicit in other instances within its category. Reflection is, however, most profitably concentrated upon the type-case itself, as the "purest" instance, not in any superior sense, but as the "extreme" example, the most revealing demonstration of the experience. In which case, children may be described as the *wilful divinities* of the parish's implicit religion.

The sacred is, by common consent, ineffable. It is, however, by common observation, apparently unable to resist the temptation to try and find its appropriate expression (verbal and non-verbal, religious and secular). It therefore becomes possible to draw the kind of distinction between the various experi-

ences of sacredness, that have been drawn within the classical religious traditions by the use of such diverse expressions as *reverence, veneration,* and
worship. Thus, neither children, nor a particular child, can be adequately described as sacramental, or even as sacraments, for they are too individual. They
could indeed, and often are, described as sacred; but it is possible to be more
precise in describing the character of the experience. In view of their blatant
alterity, they could be described as holy, but (typically) they lack the power
to help themselves. Their description as "wilful divinities", however, suggests
identifiable centres of consciousness and independent sources of action, without either absolute power or absolute virtue. Each is known as an (ultimately)
unpredictable combination of the apparently divine and the possibly diabolical.

Parallels may be seen in other traditions, which are known as religions. They
may be called *jinn,* or Englished as sprites (signifiying, approximately, spirits
with wills of their own, and possibly humorous intent or effects). They may
be sacralised as a (or the) *Bambino,* or *holy child.* Inversely, a parallel may
be found in the position of the Kabaka among the Baganda: he who was most
obviously their absolute and autocratic ruler, was at one and the same time
their capricious "child". Similar contrasts can be seen in a motherly attitude to
a conscientious queen, in a constitutional monarchy: "I wouldn't want her job
for anything, poor dear".

The typological role of the child can be gleaned from the tendency, both
within the parish and in the use of the English language generally, firstly to
restrict the meaning of "children" to young children (as though adults are not
themselves also children), and secondly to extend its meaning from one's own
children to all young people. This child-like aspect of human relationships,
which serves as an integrating focus for commitments that are as wide as they
are deep, can be divided into "seven ages" or stages.

The first age, as already indicated, is infancy: the baby is a source of blessing.
Its influence is apparent before its birth. From the first news of conception,
the response is one of joy and shared (Durkheimian) excitement. Any linger-
ing doubt that the grandparents entertained regarding the suitability of the
parents' match fall away. So significant is the news (albeit virtually full-term
distant) that the sequence of those to whom it is announced calls for care
and caution, comparable to the eventual announcement of the baby's "arrival".
The accustomed response of "Congratulations", verbally or by special card, is
a public expletive, akin to the more traditional "Alleluiah".

The power of the appeal of the child-like is in inverse proportion to its size,
and to its strength "according to this world" (as "this world" seems to imagine
itself). Hence the typological significance of the first and last stages of childish-
ness and childlikeness. This characteristic is now daily apparent in the reaction
to child abuse, and abuse of the elderly. It is also apparent, however, in the
universal tendency, especially on the part of women, to refer to every new born

baby as a "little" boy or girl (even when emphasising how large it was, in the following sentence). The adjective describes, not the "object", but the speaker: it expresses her endearment, affection, approval, admiration, wonder, at the repeated instance of the miracle of the creation of human be-ing. Taken in the context of the importance that is attached to knowing whether it was "a little boy, or a little girl?", again especially on the part of women, it indicates that this reaction is not generalised (in the manner of this description), but highly individual. A personal event, for mother and child, is being responded to, in a personal way, as a person to a person.

Should the very young child bestow a smile upon his or her admirer, then the "Oh!", of distanced contemplation, is climaxed by the "Oh!" of triumphant blessing. Onlookers may insist upon the physical causation of the baby's expression of contentment; or, entirely earth-bound, insist that it has no meta-physical meaning whatsoever, being simply due to "wind". But the putative recipient of the smile persists in hoping, and tentatively believing, that the fleeting self-expression represents a dawning ability to enter into a relationship. Certainly, the pleasure that is given, even by such a possibility, shows that the child's own well-being by no means exhausts his or her significance for others. Its admirers also look to it for their own sakes.

Whether as deliberate, inter-personal communications, or as prophecies, given all but involuntarily, the baby's overtures are received as conveying a meaning. That meaning may be summarised as: be-ing is benevolent; persons are the purpose of existence; "friendly" is the "name of the game"; the "groaning" of creation is redeemed by the divinity of self-hood.

It could be that this is the type-case of the raw material of all meaning, all sacrifice, and all religion, in this society, as communion with the ancestors is sometimes said to be in more traditional societies.

If the blessing bestowed by a smile from the "muling and puking infant" is a type-case, its presence in the other six "ages of man" also requires sketching.

The child begins to exercise an integrating influence from conception. It continues to do so, when it moves out of the womb, and again when it moves out of the home as a toddler. Thus, the mother-and-toddler group, started in 1977, was intended to allow mothers to talk to each other, as well as toddlers to play, and in the 1980s frequently included almost every available candidate in the community. So the mother may find herself a member of a locality in a way she has never known since adolescence.

This first stage is probably the prime time for finding family resemblances. The parents' initial defensiveness, that "he is like himself", now gives way to the discovery of resemblances of face and mannerism. The search for them suggests a desire to discover, or at least an enjoyment of, the family's biological and spiritual continuity and coinherence. Like all living traditions, it converts what has otherwise merely "passed" (away), into their own (living) "past".

A period of geographical and social mobility has provided numerous methods, such as photography, conservation, collecting antiques and memorabilia,
compiling local histories and family trees, in addition to the "family likeness"
game (and the cult of longevity), in order to unify the instant and the lon-
glasting. The attempt might be compared with the underlying assumption of
reincarnation in Hinduism, especially if its less philosophical forms are more
concerned with empirical causes-and-effects, than with moral or mystical ones.
Nearer home, the comparison may be made with the traditional choice of a
guardian angel or a patron saint.

If the toddler is the source of a profound unity, the junior is a spur to more
practical sociability. What the "toddler" did for its mother, about the age of
Mothers-and-Toddlers (one to three years), of Playgroup (three to four), and
of Infant School (four to seven years), the "juniors", at least sometimes, do for
their fathers, at about the age of Junior School (seven to eleven) and Cubs
or Brownies, and of the pre-teen years at Secondary School, and Scouts or
Guides. It is at this stage that the parents begin to talk of being full-time
"chauffeurs" for their children's out-of-school activities. Their active assistance
is also needed, however, to maintain the bulk of their activities. So sociable and
activity-oriented children themselves produce socialised and activity-oriented
parents.

This second stage is the period of participation in the external world, rather
than of awareness of interior life; of meaning that is unconscious, and symbolism
that is unaware. Hence fathers, who up to about 1980 may not have believed
in either the existence or the desirability of the subjective dimension of life, can
enter into a communion of activity with their offspring. They may refer to this
age as "the best time of your life", and say it "keeps [them] young". Perhaps they
vicariously re-live their own stage of unselfconscious consciousness, of agility
without awkwardness, of faith without doubt, that initial maturity of an Eden
without self-transcendence. Whatever the processes involved, this above all is
the time when nothing is too good for the children. Hindu children may be
treated like kings until they are seven: Winterbourne children are like gods
until they are seven, and like kings until they are fourteen.

The adolescent child, on the other hand, is a source of suffering. This is
partly sympathetic suffering, for "all the problems they have to face today:
we didn't have their opportunities, but we didn't have their problems and
pressures either." And partly it is the suffering of the redundant, comparable
to the bereavement felt by the mother when the youngest child finally goes to
school. For the time has come when homework is too specialised for the parents
to keep up with (even by going to night-classes in the "modern mathematics");
when their own access to wheels (bicycle, bus, skate-board, lift, motor-bike,
"jallopy") makes chauffeuring unnecessary; when the companionship of parents
becomes an encumbrance. The changes may happen at neo-natal speed, but

they are less easily understood, less consistent, and less predictable. So, when relationships are strained, each generation can blame and wait upon the other.

The desire to serve the young gods has not diminished. While all sometimes feel distanced sympathy, social workers especially have frequently articulated a despair, or an anger, which may suggest a frustrated or disappointed worship.

By a polite convention, adolescence "ceases" at sixteen, the age of either entering the sixth form, or leaving school. It is hoped that this will be the beginning of an adult stage, inasmuch as the adolescent now has more serious disciplines imposed upon him or her by the demands of A Levels, or of *earning* a living; so they have to learn to think for themselves, establish their own guidelines, and become their own guru. But, by common consent, real adulthood begins with readiness for marriage; that is, for having children of one's own. Indeed, mothers in particular will advocate a pause before or after marriage, so the "young people can enjoy themselves", before they are embroiled with the time-consuming and energy-sapping responsibilities of parenting.

At this, the fifth stage, adult children become the source of judgement on their own parents. Mothers-in-law, and fathers-in-law, are not altogether powerless; yet the music-hall jokes have been taken to heart, so that parents-in-law and children-in-law frequently enjoy a relaxed companionable relationship. This is no doubt helped by the fact that they don't live too close to each other, and by grandparents' knowledge that mothercraft, work and so on, are not the same, practically or culturally, as they were in "their day".

Indeed, if the boot is anywhere, it is on the other foot. Give or take the inevitable vagaries of inheritance, circumstance, and free will, the younger people's lives, their material well-being, professional success, marital happiness, and own parenting, are the final verdict upon those whose own professional lives, like their family responsibilities, are drawing to a close. Thus, the younger generation's opinions, while not always accepted, are always heard, and will rarely be disputed.

As the grandchildren develop, the grandparents discover that they can and must live, and cannot avoid living, in and through their children and their children's children. Identity, which the adolescent individual had to fight for, and integrity, which the young adult had to safeguard, now take on their other dimensions: the adult who is grandparenting identifies with the second and third generations, and is integrated with them. The self is becoming a spirit.

In the last two stages, the elderly themselves fulfil the role of children. Much effort is put into visiting them, by family, friends, neighbours and organisations in the parish, particularly in the sixth stage, when they can become the source of tradition. During this stage, at the beginning of the period of observation, they tended to be lionised, and helped, like toddlers. But during the 1970s the national demographic trend was here accentuated by the arrival of widowed parents-in-law in the parish, and a distinction was drawn between the "(old age) pensioner", and those who were actually "elderly" or old.

Visibly portrayed by the odd "demonstration" in the capital, the OAPs asserted their identity, as the teenagers and the students had done in the previous decade. A "harvest auction" in the pub in Watleys End had raised £400 "for the Pensioners" in 1972. However, the tradition soon died, as it was discovered that they had so many parties arranged for them at Christmas (and so many outings, arranged by themselves, in the summer), that it was "a job" ever to "find them in" (their own homes). Old age, which at the beginning of the century began at retirement, and in 1970 may have begun at seventy, by 1980 seemed not to begin before eighty, or even later.

When the occasion presents itself, or is arranged, it is the juniors and the teenagers who strike up a special rapport with this "new generation", the really elderly. The younger age-groups are physically and mentally equipped for discovery, but their responsibility is limited to getting themselves about safely and being home in time. The older age-group have been relieved of all responsibility save looking after themselves, but still have the physical and mental powers to share and assist in the youngsters' discoveries. Ambition, and instrumentality, on behalf of their children and grand-children, tend to give way to a "sacramental" valuation, of the meaning and benefits, even of such practicalities as work prospects, exam successes, and home life.

A state of nature is replaced by a relationship of grace. They are "glad to be able to help", by looking after their grandchildren for instance; no longer needing to "keep one eye on the clock" ("watching the enemy" [sic]), they are available. Neither producing, nor reproducing, these two age-groups, with their shared subordinate relationship to the intermediate, parental generation, can relax, and listen to each other, as sub-species of the same childlike genus.

In this situation, they can again be the incarnation of a tradition, the witness to a viewpoint, the seer of insight, the mouthpiece of a wisdom, the prophet of divinities, a voice from an other world. If they and their young visitors watch black and white film of (say) the "Great War" or the "General Strike" or "Dunkirk", they can vouch for it, make it real (rather than a kind of reversed science-fiction), be revealed as living tradition.

In order to communicate their transcendence of the merely current, though, they must also be willing to participate in the contemporary (to be "with it").

So the relationship displays a balance between such observations as, "They're better off now, but I think we were just as happy; they've got more opportunities, but we had to make our own entertainment; we were more contented, life's full of problems now, but I wouldn't want to go back to the so-called good old days", on the one hand; and, on the other hand, tributes to their cheerfulness, friendliness, humour, interest in life, fortitude, will, hope, wisdom. Other societies may have credited the outstanding elderly with superior insight, or wisdom: this society credits those who demonstrate superior morale, or spiritual qualities.

In the seventh stage, the senile baby becomes a source of crisis. They are frequently compared with babies, on account of their limited functions, and the speed and upredictability of changes in their health and spirits. Their "foolishness" is again punctuated with *cries* about being neglected, but this is now again understood as pitiful rather than malevolent.

However, their "infantile" quality refers also to the kind of care and attitude they require. For this is simply not subject to order, at least in the case of many relatives. They therefore become a source of "crisis", not only in terms of the decisions that have to be made about going "into care" and so on, but also (in the original sense of the word), in terms of judgement. The daughter, etc, doesn't feel as loving as she feels she ought.

Their very existence is problematic; whereas that of the original baby had been an unquestioned blessing. The judgement is Johannine: "I came not to bring judgement, but life"; but the consequent judgement is Matthean: "Judge [yourselves] for yourselves". So power over others' consciences (the part that the powers of this world can hardly reach) returns to those who are impotent.

The ancestors have become the living dead, in a new sense. Once persons, but now reduced to shades of their former selves, in an impersonal *Sheol*, they arouse, at best, a negative wonder. They depress. The wheel has turned full circle. The pre-natal is cancelled by the pre-mortem, post-vitam.

5.3.2 Friendly, its revelatory ethic

"Friendly" introduces a categorial unevenness among the objects of intensive concern, discerned in the corporate life and general consciousness of the parish community. The other five integrating foci are all named substantively. The adjectival form is retained, because that is how this object of commitment is named in the evidence. Admittedly, not all of the five nouns that are used for the other five commitments are simple, direct and frequent quotations from the actors (in particular, "individualism"). Yet in this case, to have transposed the actual adjective used, into (presumably) an abstract noun, such as "friendliness" or "friendship", would have changed the tenor of the description.

In the United States, the French Enlightenment, or Hinduism, abstractions may be widely reified: but this is an unidealistic, ritual culture. If this particular quality is valued, it is not on ideological grounds. It may not even be on ethical grounds, despite the moralistic character of the society (and its formal religion). The valuation is of the inner attitude (including the effort made, if necessary, to show it): "it's the thought that counts", the "heart" is "the heart (*sic*) of the matter". The criterion is spiritual.

What is universally sought, should be universally practised. For it is personality, now, that is "hedged about" with divinity. "It's only my opinion", far from being a modest disclaimer of infallibility, is a solemn introduction to the expression of an opinion which is constitutive of identity. In the open community, as in the pluralist society, faith can speak (and may listen) to faith. "Speaking one's mind" may become a little less worrisome; its accompaniment by some fear, indicates that it is truly personal, rather than simply an "ego-trip".

This universal hope is nevertheless sought in particular places. In some cases, these are where it should be present; in other cases, were it to be discovered, its presence would be especially meaningful. They echo covenanted and uncovenanted mercies, God's right hand and left. Among the former are, of course, family and friends. Among the latter, because random, but pervasive, are neighbours, and such role-bearing contacts as shopworkers. Less frequent, but more symbolic of "the way things are", are contacts with professionals, such as the librarian, doctor, head teacher, or rector. If one of them goes a second mile to be "friendly", they bestow a blessing; if they are "stuck up", "up-tight", a "misery" or "wet blanket", and "put you in your place", they "give you the thumbs-down". They confirm that you are lost, communicate a curse, depress.

Groups are judged in this way, as well as individuals. Either they are "friendly" and "welcoming", or they are "unfriendly" and "cliquey" (pronounced "clicky"). The compliment echoes the proud boast, "You get all types in a pub"; the complaint echoes the interviewees' hatred of people "being categorised", "placed in pigeon-holes". It is this *liberalism* ("each one counts for one") that underlies the cultural meaning and valuation of both "equality" and "democracy" (understood as "equity" and "fair play").

The absolute character of this moral imperative is indicated, paradoxically but comprehensibly, by the inadequacy of the occasional attempt to justify it. "You never know when *you* might need a kind word", or "*I* might need help sometime", are not based upon any real belief in a providential super-plan. Neither the commitment nor the logic is convincing. The duty is accepted without question, as self-evident, un-reason-able.

However, the obligation that it entails is limited. Like the older term, benevolence, it must be spread thin, to spread well. Its symbol is a smile, rather than a Cross. Such a smile may be described as "cosmetic", so long as it is recalled that cosmetics reveal how a person would like to look, and to be perceived - and that they require application. Its practice will be commended in a similarly low-key manner, in some such popularly acceptable saying as, "You don't do anybody any good by going round looking miserable, do you? You only make matters worse for yourself."

Echoes, whether conscious or unconscious, may be heard of such Gospel sayings as, "When you fast, wash your face", or, "With what measure you measure to others, it will be measured to you". In this society, such parallelisms could be reached by independent reflection. More significant, perhaps, is the question whether this carefully unpretentious approach (echoing such sayings as, "Don't let your left hand know what your right hand is doing", and then, "It is finished", or, again, the joy of "filling out Christ's sufferings") owes more, unconsciously but historically, either to Christianity, or to Stoicism.

The limits of the obligation are imposed (or breached) semi-consciously. First, what is out of sight is soon out of mind, and almost as quickly out of obligation. Those whose work involves face-to-face contact (the current "eye-contact"), from commercial travellers to clergy, plan their visiting (and their substitute communications, by phone, letter, or deputy), on this principle. Second, although the immediate family imposes most obligation, even that is not unlimited. Self-sacrifice is valid, but as a means to an end, such as the self-development of the children, or the resurrection and salvation of the one self-sacrificed. Self-annihilation is suspect. To give one's body to be burned would hardly profit even one's proclaimed cause. Divorce is often preferable to murder, suicide – or self-sacrifice.

Thirdly, no commitment beyond the self is allowed to become total, or final. "Workaholism" may be tolerated, as a weakness; voluntary devotion to a cause or person will be admired, if the benefits redound to the devotee; but even the best end is diabolical, if it is destructive of the self. Even sincerity hardly suffices to salvage sectarianism.

A fourth limitation to the obligation is imposed by others: not all respond, even to the friendliest, most tactful, and patient, of overtures. The discovery that free will can be an immoveable object, as well as an irresistible force, sometimes surprises. It compels government departments, and charity trustees, to plead for claimants to come forward. It made the parish's streetwarden ("Neighbourlink") scheme disappear into the sand, as the offers of help always far outran the requests for assistance.

The deep and widespread character of this desire that all should be "friendly", was publicly demonstrated at the time of the Queen's Silver Jubilee, in 1977. Not only did most streets in the parish hold "street parties": most inhabitants participated in them. Indeed, some streets repeated the event, that Christmas and/or the following summer. But even more significant, from the present point of view, was the joy occasioned by their success. It was said to show, what all hope, but some doubt, that, really, everyone wants to be "friendly".

The universal, if limited, obligation to be friendly, of itself, may be depressing, for no individual can match up to that demand. Indeed, those whom "the world" sees as most able to conduct their lives with this éclat and élan may be the most willing to acknowledge their inadequacies in this respect. The primary emphasis of this concern, however, is not upon the moral duty felt by the individual. It is upon the prior appreciation by the individual of those occasions, when (s)he has been the recipient of such a friendly attitude.

Such an experience raises the sights, lifts up the heart, elevates the spirits, bestows new life, metes out faith and hope and charity. The smile, like the sunshine with which it is often compared, brings assurance that "all's well with the world; God's in his heaven".

5.3.3   Individualism, its profoundest solidarity

One key to understanding any body (individual or group), is to seek out their *ideals*. It can be especially helpful when we cannot even understand what they are *hoping* to achieve. Another, is to discover their *ideas* about the fundamental character of the reality presently experienced. This may be more difficult, but can help when we cannot see any logic in their behaviour: we do not know *their* logic. Yet the distinction between "ideas" and "ideals" may possess greater heuristic value, than phenomenological validity. What is desired, tends to be a revelation, albeit also purification, of what already is (otherwise it could hardly be envisaged); what *fundamentally* is felt to be the case, is usually what is felt to be desirable, although calling for increased recognition. Thus, applied to the Biblical literature, existence may be questionable, yet God *is*; but the One who is, promises to become *their* God. Indeed, the survival of identifiable companies who identified with this moral-ontological pair of beliefs may be in large part attributed to their faith in the desirability and reality of "their divinity" (the ambiguity is suggestive).

Applied to the general consciousness of the parish, a similar position must be accorded to the concept of the "self". What the interviews revealed of the consciousness of individuals, and the pub suggested regarding the principles of its clientèle, also makes sense *in* the parish - and makes sense *of* a great deal of its corporate life. As the single greatest underlying certainty, and simultaneously the single greatest integrating value, on empirical grounds it has as much right to an initial capital, as the divinity formally honoured in the Biblical religions. For the Self, like God, is not only a distinctive category (indeed, a distinctive kind of category), but doubles up as something of a proper name, given to the locus or focus of the whole, to enable it (or him or her) to be addressed. If the Self is not sacred or holy, divine or transcendent, ineffable and ultimate, in the life of the parish, then nothing is.

The history of religions, and of peoples, is familiar with the effect of journeys, from the Exodus to Dunkirk, upon viewpoint, view, and viewer. It can be seen in the life of the parish in the way in which people leave the world of work behind, with a twenty or thirty minute car journey, so effectively, that even their spouse may be ignorant of either the place or the nature of their work, or may know the formal description without having much idea of what it means. Indeed, a dispute at one of the major places of employment will be reported on local television news, and prompt the family to say they learned far more about it in that way, than from their own member who works there. The journey, whereby these two worlds are separated, has social signficance, in terms of the differences of role. There is also spoken evidence that it can have spiritual and "implicit-religious" significance, in terms of providing a time of meditation and solitude, within the car, through escape from role-play. It forms an important factor in, and model for, this and the following "concerns".

"You've got to look after yourself; if you don't, no one else will", may sound more "at home" in the world of work, but it is not unknown in the domestic world of the parish. Unspoken, it may not be without effect in the home itself. "You've got to look after yourself", in this culture is defined as a secular viewpoint, mainly because it omits mention of God, or of others. But it is a conventional, sincere, and ritual, saying, whose imperative may be seen as positively moral, as a piece of unofficial, but necessary, practical Christianity. Indeed, it is a piece of proverbial wisdom, that serves somewhat as a creed: a symbol, inviting the bearer to identify with it, and thus develop solidarity with the speaker. Like the mildly sniggering attitude towards buying a drink in a pub, or the pleasure in cocking a snook at mechanistic systems in science or society, it is not exactly anti-Christian, but it is, consciously, auxiliary to the official Church, a kind of do-it-yourself, essential gap-filler - which, it is assumed, God "will understand".

The gap between this concern, and the values enshrined in the High Culture, can hardly be seen more clearly than in the difficulty of finding a neutral word by which to describe this interest. Self-ish is the obvious term, but even its novel hyphenation is hardly sufficient to convey its innovative, non-judgemental use.

The contrast appears most vividly in the religious culture of the larger society. Thus when, in the 1970s, Dr Coggan, as Archbishop of Canterbury, invited a national debate to identify common objectives, he summarised their framework by saying that they should put "God first, neighbour second, and self last". So, when, in the 1980s, the ruling Party said that private interest should be given free rein and thus harnessed for public good, ecclesiastical pronouncements were generally hostile. Eighteenth century quotations from Adam Smith and Edmund Burke did not disguise its similarity to the popular philosophy which was known in the day of compulsory National Service as, "I'm all right, Jack". "Christianity" being largely understood in moral terms, among both active and inactive Churchmembers, "Jack" (as the attitude was often called) was seen as the antithesis of Christianity. Dr Coggan's prioritisation was seen as placing "self", not in modest third place, but in last place: its existence could not quite be annihilated, but it must become a means to the end, of serving God and neighbour.

Apart from an occasional avowed "secularist", popular morality, wearing its Sunday School hat, would not dispute this ideal, but would maintain that it was *only* an ideal, and only applicable in inter-personal relationships. It had long made Christ's Second Commandment ("and the Second is like unto it:

Thou shalt love thy neighbour as thyself") into the First Commandment of its "*Christianity's*" - and changed the order of its two halves. So when the Church, following psychology and led by Paul Tillich, "provocatively" stressed the love of self as positive and imperative, it was only catching up with popular psychology. Nowhere is the gulf between this understanding of morality, and the Church's understanding, more clearly demonstrated, than in the paucity of hymns based on the Second Commandment, particularly its second half: my "self" was almost diametrically opposed to "my soul".

From the point of view of this enquiry, such evaluations have only empirical significance. What matters is the very high degree of commitment to the self. That the High Culture, including the ecclesiastical culture, under-estimated both its strength and its valuation, was no doubt partly due to their dismissal of it as "sin". Thus they complained, "No one will commit themselves to anything these days"; meaning, typically, that parishioners would not promise to play the organ twice every Sunday, or sing in the choir fifty-two Sundays a year. Such analyses concentrated upon the lack of commitment to a single activity, and overlooked the multiplicity of their other commitments. Unwillingness to make promises to the ecclesiastical institutions was mistaken for the absence of any over-riding commitments. What logic suggests, observation in this community confirms.

When asked to undertake a continuing responsibility, the reaction, in this parish, typically, runs: "Well, tell me what it involves, first, and then I'll think it over. I don't like to say I'll do something, and then find I can't. If I say I'll do something, I like to do it properly. If I take it on, I may have to ask you to find someone else to do one of my other jobs. When do you want to know by?" Far from being arbitrary or impulsive, every strand of the response suggests a highly responsible approach, to a situation in which competing obligations and an ultimate commitment require that infinite covenants be reduced to limited contracts.

That ultimate commitment is the care of the Self. It has often been remarked (since M J Bayley, 1973) that more pastoral care is exercised by informal networks of family, friends, and neighbours, than could ever be exercised by formal agencies; but even more pastoral care of their own selves is exercised, in this community, by the individuals concerned. Similar actions may have different motives, which may include a simple "I want" to an aggressive "I'll show 'em". But among the range of motivations must be reckoned a charitable concern for the health and development of the Self.

This pastoral care is largely untutored; hence the appeal of soap-operas and "agony columns". Today it largely lacks even the prudential guidance formerly provided by proverbial wisdom. It is, therefore, wide open to *rationales* of the most elementary kind, whether homespun, exotic, or, even, traditional. So, *soul* and *supernatural* having been reintroduced into the vocabulary (in an empirical sense), in the 1970s, *culture* and *spirituality* were suddenly seen, in the 1980s, as inevitable dimensions of (group or individual) human being. The attention given by teenagers to the spiritual and moral nuances of romantic relationships, is paralleled by adults' awareness and judgement of political action. Such grass-roots self-care is often based upon rich experience, humble honesty, sophisticated sensitivity, acute analysis, deep devotion, and conscientious care. For the Self (like other divinities, in some lights) may be demanding, but it is also fragile; beyond control, it is subject to influence.

In the Anglican tradition, pastoral or spiritual conselling might possibly have been summarised in some simple threefold formula, such as the so-called Twofold (actually, tripartite) Commandment; or listening to, educating, and following, conscience; or public worship, private prayer, and scriptural study. Translated into a time-tabled Rule (*religio*) of Life, this last trio, for instance, became: Sunday service, daily prayers, quiet time with the Bible. It is, incidentally, remarkable how often even the most traditional exponents of such advice will tend to justify it in terms of the culture of the self or soul ("prayer does *you* good"; and so on). This justification makes most sense, not just from an *ad hominen* viewpoint, but from an *"ad Deum"* viewpoint as well: suddenly the tradition, and its divinity, become comprehensible, and human.

If a parallel formula were to be devised, to summarise the spiritual pastoralia of the indigenous tradition, it might be, Acknowledge your obligations, Avoid undue pressure, Accept finitude. Naturally, these too interlock and overlap. Translated into a visible life-style, they become: "Do unto others (as you would they do unto you)"; "Don't be afraid to say No"; and "Take each day as it comes". Some similarity may be found with the Christian trio of "theological virtues": charity, faith (in the ultimacy of the Self), and hope (for the morrow).

As already indicated, the care of the self is not just individual, personal and private. Experiential data are gathered publicly and vicariously. Indeed, the arts and human sciences render the subjective, objective, and the objective, subjective. Diagnoses and prognoses, prescriptions and proscriptions, are shared or exchanged, both commercially and freely. Indeed, such communication is the peak and test of personal communion, the simultaneously expressive and effective sacrament of friend-ship.

It is, however, integrative at a wider level than one-to-one. It is social, societal, and even corporate. Just as the conception of the self is, inevitably, a social and cultural (and religious) product, so is its protection, care and development. Solidarity arises from a reciprocal understanding of the one who says, *Ich kann nicht anders*. The "personal" story never fails in its appeal, because the individual, whether rejoicing or grieving, triumphing or protesting, focuses that which is sacred for all.

Three particular ways in which the self is protected, stand out. The first way has already been touched upon: the compartmentalisation of roles. Some of the roles, such as work and childbearing, may be customarily described as unwelcome; but few find them without meaning. "Successful" living, however, requires that none be allowed to become predominant, over all the others. That is the way of Self-annihilation.

The second way transposes that personal rule-of-life to the social level. It is apparent in the reaction to any one individual, group or institution, that arrogates too many roles to him, her, or its, self; or, having accepted or assumed them, complains of being over-burdened, and either pleads too plaintively for sympathy or gratitude, or hectors others too insistently for assistance. Indeed, intuitively this (which is not only "the moral basis of a *backward society*") is why leaders will only "*back* into the limelight" and come forward at the eleventh hour.

This *cynicism* (from the Greek, for *dogs*, who can only bark) is the ultimate basis of solidarity, within the open community. Only friends may say, but many will feel: "Not him/her/them again? It's all you ever hear of these days." "They don't have to do it, you know. They wouldn't do it if they didn't want to. Why can't they let someone else have a go for a change?" "Who do they think they are? They mean well, but can't they see I have other things to do? No one can do everything." In silent groans, expressing such apparently negative attitudes, the individual members of the community are as one and united.

The third particular way of protecting the Self builds upon the other two. The first found the Self in the freedom that comes at the interstices of the roles it has to play in the systems to which it belongs. As none of them are allowed to be meaning-full for the whole, then the true Self is the Self of the gaps. Forbidden activities may not be especially enjoyable or valuable in themselves, but successful rule-breaking, and discovering the chinks in the armour of systems, brings the Self to life. The second method of Self-defence was more aggressive. It positively cuts other Selves down to size, in order to leave room for its own Self, to be if not to grow. This third technique insists on keeping a part of life unstructured by role, unbidden even by obligation. It insists on its right to do nothing.

To speak of the "value" of being idle would, of course, be somewhat self-defeating. Perhaps this is why "meditation" or ritual "prayers", usually associated with Indian or Islamic religion, are more kindly tolerated than "prayer", seen as Christian and intercessory. But it does suggest that the justification of traditional religious practices in unashamed terms of the right of individuals to waste their time as *they* want, would make *common* sense. Only the Christian is expected to, or attempts to, justify them in terms of their benefit for others. Such an existentialist explanation ("because I enjoy it; I know not why - and why shouldn't I, anyway?"), would be in keeping with this third technique of Self-protection. Indeed, it is already often used, in less formal, domestic situations.

For this practice is based upon the significance of privacy, subjectivity, arbitrariness, unaccountability, the right to refuse to reach a decision, the need to *be* without "doing", the confirmation of individual peculiarity by simply opting out. If space allows, an allotment or garden shed, a workshop or study, a sewing-room or some other kind of "bolt-hole", will provide a place that "I can call my own, where I can leave my own mess lying about", an open space or wilderness where dreams can be dreamt and lived out, identity be proved. More often, though, it is expressed temporally. When the working-day is hourly, even minute-ly, determined, auto-determinism in the evening is to "sit and see what's on [the television]", fatalistically accepting, as given, even "rubbish". Here is "some time I can call my own".

The attitude could be expressed as: "It's so nice not to have to set the alarm or get up [or *know* when you are going to get up], but when we eventually do, we may visit grandma, or we may not; we don't have any engagements all day; but I could clean the car, and I may read the papers, although [ie because] they're a waste of time really; until the children go to bed, and that's a moveable feast anyway." Financially, the same attitude is recognisable in the husband's "pocket money", or the wife's desire for "pin-money", which (she says) she "covets for herself", because she wants to spend her money, and not her husband's, for instance on buying presents for him.

To the philosopher such existentialism may seem arbitrary; to the visionary it may be unproductive; to the moralist it may look inconsiderate; to the committed it may be feckless; to the spiritual counsellor it may smack of the tyranny of self-indulgence. But to the actor, it can be statement and proof of his intrinsic worth. In a highly-structured world, the sanctuary in which the individual takes refuge may lie in its intriguing midden. This, rather than ecstasy of any kind, may be the parish's answer to alienation. Polarity, without dichotomy, "rules", as the graffiti artists say, for the individual as for the community.

What looks like *anomie* may not always be simply a social malady. What seems like *accidie* may not always be a spiritual sickness. Apparent *apatheia* may not always be a psychological defect. They could be the *consequence of commitment*: a way of saying to the world, "No, I count, because I am - and I'll prove it, to myself at least, by doing nothing".

5.3.4 Buildings, its sacramental language

The significance of buildings in the life of the community can be demonstrated by the way in which it was possible to indicate both the thousand-year history and the contemporary culture of the parish by reference to two types of building: the parish church and the domestic houses. However, the building and buildings of the parish's schools will also serve to illustrate both the sequence of settlement and the social psychology of the community.

William Wilberforce, the noted anti-slave trade campaigner, who was Member of Parliament for Bristol, belonged to a group of (largely Evangelical) social reformers that met in one of the two public houses by the five-pointed cross-roads and began a "National" (ie Church of England) School in the parish in 1813. For two years the school met in the pub, until a building, which combined both schoolmaster's house and schoolrooms, was ready - at the point where the roads from the subsequent ecclesiastical parishes and communities of Winterbourn Down and Frenchay meet and enter Winterbourne (in the narrower sense).

In 1868 (when those two parishes had separated, and founded their own Schools) a new school was built. This time the headteacher's house was adjacent (distinct but joined on), so that only in the 1980s were the garden and plumbing arrangements finally separated. This building illustrated the centre of gravity of the changed catchment area. It was placed on the High Street, but on the Watleys End Road side of the five-armed cross-roads - and directly opposite the Rectory. Changes in the community, and in education, were accommodated by the addition of first stone, then brick, and finally "mobile" (temporary wooden) buildings.

In 1954 a "secondary modern" (for eleven to fifteen, then sixteen, year olds) school, in concrete and glass, was opened by the County. It was also on the High Street, because it catered both for Winterbourne and for most of the adjacent communities. No provision was made for housing the head, who bought his own house, within the parish.

In 1961 the County opened a Primary School, on the "Winterbourne" side of Watleys End (as already mentioned). Its placing matched that of the Church Primary School, which was on the Watleys End side of "Winterbourne" (in the late medieval, High Street, sense). In 1968, as mentioned, this new school was divided into adjacent Junior and Infant schools. In 1970 the Church School was also divided into Infant and Junior schools. In each case the latter enjoyed the new buildings. In 1980 the four schools were re-amalgamated into two Primaries, in the building used by the Junior half (with the plumbing appropriately amended for Infant use). At all these stages the heads saw to their own housing: none lived within the parish (although the head of the Church School wished to do so).

During the period 1945-1991 an independent school occupied one of the older of the half-dozen larger houses that were mentioned earlier. Founded in Bristol in 1903 by three Christian-minded sisters, for boarding and day girls, it gradually established more local contacts, bringing to six the number of schools within the community in the 1970s. Education was, therefore, the major industry and employer actually situated within the parish. The number and variety of other activities, for children or adults, with an educational dimension, substantiates the qualitative significance, as well as quantitative importance, of this interest. As Bede could write an *ecclesiastical* history of England, so Winterourne history could be told in *educational* terms, at least in the last two centuries.

The sequence, siting, structure and style of school buildings all suggest hypotheses, which prove to have validity. They demonstrate the psychological or spiritual dimension possessed by buildings, within the community, as symbols which communicate at both conscious and unconscious levels. In a general way, this is well appreciated by members of the public. On the one hand, "looking" at the imagined exterior, some of the Community Association's founders acknowledged (eg in 1971) that they wanted a building of their own "as a symbol", to prove the Association's reality, and demonstrate that it had "arrived", "on the scene". On the other hand, "looking" at the interior, the Scout leaders (eg in 1973) wanted their own premises, as somewhere they could leave their badges up, and belongings out, and so feel they had "a base" they could call their own.

This accent upon buildings, then, is the fourth of the integrating foci observed in the life of the parish. Its pheomenological dimension will be explored, first, in terms of the home (with which must be coupled the garden), where its meaning is most personal. Then it will be explored in terms of the parish church (with which will be coupled the churchyard), which forms the communal type-case of the value. The particular significances of other public places and spaces will then be considered. Finally, in this connection, the horror of vandalism will be suggested as (so-called "negative") evidence of the (implicit-religious) significance of this whole focus.

5.3.4.1 The home

House and family, the physical and the social, meet in the cultural concept of home. In a community largely composed of three-bedroomed, semi-detached houses, the three terms can become inter-changeable. A "fundamentalist" immediacy of pre-conscious meaning is also to be detected in the elision of the empirical and the ideal.

There are many signs of the power of this valuation. Its purchase involves sacrifice, for instance. Certainly, that sacrifice is given financial encouragement by the government, in the form of remission of taxes. Such rebates facilitate purchase, and so encourage prices to rise, thus increasing the need to "get into the housing market" as soon as possible. But they are not responsible for the original desire to own a home of one's own. Indeed, in terms of the (avowed) non-party policy of "encouraging saving", they serve, not to sweeten a bitter pill, but as icing on the cake. Financial incentives are unnecessary, when such emotional, or indeed spiritual, issues as individual and corporate identity are so clearly dominant. To "have a home" (ie of one's own) is to be a family, and become an individual in one's own right (not as a member of someone else's family, in their home). "Growing up" is completed upon "leaving home"; so that "not to have left home" suggests continuing dependence.

Particular phenomena evoke reactions that are consonant with this general valuation. The sight of other houses being built fascinates. Surprise is expressed that they are so small, so simple, so slipshod, and rise so quickly: the mechanics of a mystery are being made clear. What attracts, also repels. More continuous, however, is the sacrifice of time, effort and money to maintain and improve the majority of homes. Such an "investment" can only be accounted for in Marxian terms, of the power of labour to infuse matter with spirit.

Most homes in this community have a garden. Because the garden is left un-made by the builders, it has as much scope for the expression, creation and confirmation of identity, as has the house, even its interior. Almost all the gardens are carefully designed, and meticulously tended, in part, no doubt, because this is the "public face" of identity. Yet, more important than the scope for creativity or the demonstration of domestic devotion, may be the garden's function as providing space between houses, homes, families, and roads. Gardening the ground between them legitimates the desire for distance. If "the Engishman's home is his castle", the garden is its moat.

That it is primarily a respectable way of being anti-social is suggested by the readiness with which extra spurs have been added to the tarred or concreted drive, to provide parking space for the wife's car, upon her return to work as the children went to school in the 1970s, and then for the teenagers' (or grandparents') car in the 1980s, as they left school (or came to live in a "granny flat", added over the garage). That the air matters more than the soil, the gap than the ground, is finally confirmed by the desirability and price of totally detached houses, in preference to "semi's", even when the space between them is the minimum few feet allowed by the authorities. Indeed, in the majority of those gardens from which fences were omitted, in the "open-house" style of the 1960's, boundary walls have now been added. Too low to povide protection against trespass by humans, or any animal more mobile than a tortoise, or against weeds, they serve only to complete a subjective sense of privacy. It is an emblem, a (non-functioning) portcullis.

Modest though they be, the homes of the parish meet the myth, mainly for first generation owner-occupiers, of the advertisers' aptly-titled "dream", of a house-and-garden. It is not surprising, therefore, that discerning visitors from France, whose individualists largely live in flats, have been filled with admiration or envy, of the way the majority of parishioners here, each have "un petit château" of their own.

The house (with its garden), then, provides the setting and medium for the life of the family (and individual). Its economic and cultural importance can be gauged from the amount of attention given to even minor variations in mortgage rates and council charges, and from the size of the nearby "Do-It-Yourself" emporia. Indeed, without the various aspects of "D-I-Y" (including the maintenance of cars), and television, and holidays, it is difficult to know what occupations would have engaged the time, devotion and money of the semi-affluent. As it is, life is like the proverbial re-painting of the Forth Bridge. (The way that such a recent phenomenon has so quickly become proverbial testifies to its comprehensibility and typicality.) Yet its emotional and spiritual significance is even more profound and pervasive: it provides the reason and energy for all this.

So reflection has gradually suggested that the home plays a similar part in the life of the parish, to that apparently played by land in agrarian societies and animals in pastoral societies. In each case, they are the chief focus of attention. Survival and identity, for which they are essential, may be oriented towards the family or the tribe, and towards food or fulfilment; but in each case the biological basis of life is recognised as sacred through the symbolism based upon it. Indeed, further reflection suggests that this parallelism, and in this particular form, might have been hypothesised in advance of their observation. That they were not, may be credited to the determination (already mentioned) not to look in these studies merely for parallels to phenomena that had been observed elsewhere and labelled as "religious".

In each case, land for food, and housing for shelter, demand concentrated attention. In each case, though, the devotion offered outstrips the needful, even according to their own rationalities. Both are biologically necessary, yet spiritually significant. Each operates according to laws of their own, in response to the general rhythms of the seasons and to particular characteristics of the immediate locality. But both provoke, invite, or inspire, reactions, activities, or efforts, which go beyond the instrumentalities of investment. They are felt to be, in some way, worthwhile, for their own sake. Perhaps in some degree personalised, it is felt that they will respond in a more-then-merely-mechanical manner, to efforts or oblations that are more-than-merely-minimal. They have a spiritual dimension. They do not have a will of their own, yet works of supererogation (i.e. bless sacrifices) will carry their own reward.

Insofar as a rational justification for such attitudes can be discovered, it may be found, not only in the needs of dependents, but also in a sense of mystery: that seeds consigned to the soil turn into plants, or that the human seed can come forth, and learn to relate. Growth, and the passage of time, resonate with reciprocal mystery. If the one is the abode of the ancestral spirits, who learned and taught the vital agri-culture, the other is the abode of the wilful divinities of the future, who must also be taught and learn a (social) culture. For the sake of, and in the eyes of, each type of spirit, the physical medium of their life is sacred.

5.3.4.2 The parish church

This church does not greet visitors with a notice describing it as "God's house", as many used to do. That they did so, agrees with what has been said about buildings acting as a sacramental language, and the primary source of meaning being the triumvirate of house, home and family. The type-case, or, perhaps better, caricature, however, is the parish church, rather than the family house. For the church has a distance, an objectivity, a designated, official, corporate, ancient, and proven, sanctity, which no family house can claim, certainly in this parish. As it happens, some of its canonical traditions support this. Thus, "the pillars of the Church" (Galatians 2:9) must have been based on architectural analogy; while the "household of God" (Galatians 6:10, Ephesians 2:19, and the Collect for Trinity XXII in the Book of Common Prayer) is, on the other hand, probably re-interpreted by most hearers, now (being unfamiliar with house-*holds*), as referring to the building, instead of the people. The message, repeated by clergy for two generations, that "church" means people not buildings, is hardly necessary now. Church and church, with and without the capital, are not so much equated, or confused, but closely associated, and so are loosely inter-changeable; precisely as are Home and house.

The intention at this point is to concentrate on the significance of the church building; the Chruch community will be considered later in this chapter. Naturally, some of the points to be made about this parish church will be common to many of the other eight thousand medieval churches in England, or sixteen thousand parish churches in all. Others, because they are observations regarding this parish's church, will be more idiosyncratic.

Firstly, then, as already indicated, the church lies half a mile to the west of the High Street (which, even today, is not entirely built-up, on that side of the road), while most of "the parish" (in the modern sense, of its people, rather than its acres) lies to the east of the High Street. With the conversion of some farm buildings, the number of homes by the church has recently doubled - to double figures, almost.

The Rector is frequently asked why "the church is so far away" (by today's motoring standards; not by the pedestrians' measure of distance, which was still prevalent here in 1945) "from the village". That is to say, it is both surprising, and somehow contradictory. The surprise originates in the dominance of the myth that the church was always in the centre of the ancient community, geographically as well as socially. It seems likely that this, a Saxon pattern, has rendered invisible an even older, Celtic geography of religion, which (in Cornwall, for instance), placed the holy building, like the holy man, and the holy well, outside the community. The "contradiction" is probably of an assumption, not simply that the church should be central in order to sanctify or represent or lead the community, as that it should be central in order to be easily accessible and so serve the community.

Secondly, the church stands in the middle of a churchyard. Although its gravestones only go back a couple of centuries, it is, no doubt, as old as the church building itself. Its use will subsequently be examined in more detail. Here it may be noted that it provides a "natural" bridge from the fields surrounding the church, to the building itself. This quality is enhanced by the fact that almost all the monuments set in the grass around the church are of local stone.

Thirdly, the church combines a tower, of unforbidding height, with a relatively tall spire. This compensates for its being in a slight hollow, and makes the church visible to traffic on the nearby London-South Wales motorway, and south-west to north-east railway. This feature, and the slight jumble of roofs over the nave and north aisle, the chancel and the organ chamber, the manor room and vestry, result in combining the small-scale with the complex, the homespun with the impressive. The rough-hewn appearance of the crumbling, local red sandstone enhances this antique yet homely air.

The interior of the building has similar significance. Most of it, even the altar, is visible immediately upon entering. It is therefore unfrightening, unmysterious. It will seat two hundred and fifty adults in comfort, and has been known to hold almost twice as many people of varying sizes, standing and sitting in every available space. Yet it retains the attraction of smallness, on account of its openness, of the division of the pews into blocs of two, four, seven or eleven, and of the contrast with the somewhat imposing spire above.

Secondly, it is asymetrical. It has a north aisle but no south aisle. So the room under the tower projects on the south side, as though to form the right arm of a cruciform plan, yet without a balancing left arm. The windows vary in height, number of lights, style and glass. Above all, each side of the chancel arch leans outwards - but to a differing degree.

Consequently, the overriding impression is of antiquity. With this, two further characteristics are almost indivisibly associated: beauty, and genuineness. "Historical" is the portmanteau term for this trinity of virtues. A pair of other characteristics, however, completes this account of its attraction and significance: it is relatively bare - and hence available for diverse "personalisation".

Eight centuries of occupation have left only a handful of "souvenirs". There are effigies of two Crusaders and their spouses, of another knight (incongruously placed, during the nineteenth century, within a putative Easter sepulchre), and of another medieval female. Half a dozen brasses, now all placed on the walls, range from an unknown lady of *circa* 1380 (to judge by the style of her dress and under-clothing), to the donor of the electric lighting in 1935. A Puritan family memorial is succeeded by a handful of marble inscriptions from the eighteenth century. The flags of half a dozen uniformed organisations (the Royal British Legion and the United Nations Association, the Scouts and

Guides of various ages, and, in the 1970s amd '80s, the Red Cross) relieve the bare verticality of the rear walls between the stained glass windows, while the mechanism of the eighteenth-century clock has been re-assembled in the museum-like far corner. But predominantly the church stands empty, awaiting its chief furnishing: people. So each successive gathering fills it with its own life and character. It has a certain presence of its own, yet above all provides a setting for others to use.

Individuals find memories made in this setting: "I was Christened in that Font", "I sang in the Choir in the Chancel", "I was Confirmed at the Chancel Step, by the Bishop of Bristol/Malmesbury", "I Served at the Altar", "we were Married in your Church", "my parents are Buried in the Churchyard", "all my children were Christened there", "we always used to go to St Michael's".

The group's memories are more legendary than historical. The effigy placed within the Easter sepulchre on the north wall when the church was re-pewed in 1877 "is" (popular opinion says) that of a knight who made a pact with the Devil, and so was buried (sic) half in and half out of the church. The eighteenth-century "folly", in what was part of the garden of Winterbourne Court and is now (since 1946) the New Churchyard, is called The Monks' Walk, "because the monks used to walk up and down" its elevated path, between the raised sides, "reading their prayer books". Underground passages are said to stretch the three miles from it to (Iron) Acton Court, with the daughter of whose owner the knight in the Easter sepulchre eloped, thus inspiring the local ballad, "O who will o'er the Downs so free". And so on.

The disappointment shown when the Rector, as "keeper" of the local traditions, doubts their historicity, indicates both their function as myth, and their need for veracity. In this culture, myth does not ignore factuality: it requires it, and insists upon having it. Yet the inappropriate adhesion of an oak shield, to the end of a pine pew, arising out of a conflict between the Rector and the owners of the pew that was being removed in 1877, has been forgotten, even by the descendants of the family concerned; while the obvious incompleteness of the lists of names, on some of the marble monuments in the chancel, occasions no comment whatsoever.

So, by a mixture of good luck and good management, the parish church possesses sufficient corporate symbols to avoid "institutional" anonymity, and enough individual momentoes to make it personal without becoming any body's private shrine. Similarly, its structural simplicity combines systems which necessitate personal or financial participation (by playing the organ, or contributing to a tower fund, for instance), with an openness that calls for such "house-work" and home-like decoration as cleaning and flower arranging.

So the sermon is only one of a number of items which are offered publicly, following private preparation, and continually renewed, because always ephemeral. Indeed, the number of parishioners who, having their own keys, enter the locked church, which is "so far off the beaten track", throughout the week, would surprise even the most frequent worshippers, if they knew of all their comings and goings. In many cases, such a "labour of love" is enjoyed (and half-seen) as a form of meditation through activity, the *orans* of one who is *laborans*, akin to the spiritual painting of icons on Mount Athos - or the more modern forms of religious retreat. Such contributions "keep the whole show going". Such "house-work", like that in the family home, is vicarious - and is often seen as such, not least by those parishioners who always assume that someone else will do it for them.

The church building having been more conspicuous than the Church community, in recent centuries, it is natural to ask (as both the Early Christians, and their neighbours, asked of the Early Church itself), What does it imply, witness to, stand for? What are the characterstics of its deity or deities? For many, the building is deeply meaningful; but, as with all sacraments, those meanings may vary to the point of mutual contradiction, certainly as between individuals, if not also for individuals themselves.

The "household god" of the parish church, then, is, firstly, old. It is his ancient buildings, perhaps more than the occasional paintings or stained glass windows, that have suggested the putative popular stereotype of God, as not so much a Father, but rather as a bearded Great Grandfather. He is present, but always as one who is elderly. He is everlasting, but because he survives, preserved, rather than because he is eternal. Its longevity has to serve as analogy for his infinity; its "historical" character (meaning ancient, rather than important) is the springboard for his "transcendence" (or distance).

Secondly, this divinity pervades the building as such, rather than being localised in a particular item or function, such as the altar or its sacraments. Indeed, its *locus* would be in the Baptismal family around the Font, rather than in the congregating around the Altar of those Baptised into, and communicating through, the death and resurrection of Christ. Such a divinity inspires description and reflection, rather than prayer and adoration.

He is present, but as in a class-room, rather than a shrine. Other Christian societies, other religious cultures, have special corners in their living quarters for icons, and household gods: this one does not usually particularise its presence in that way, either in their houses or in His. He is most intimately present to the individual, when the church is empty: then the alone is with the Alone. If he is focused anywhere, it is within the on*look*er.

Thirdly, the god of this building is as one who is weak. His great days lie in the past. He is unable to speak for himself. He depends upon others' recognition. He is separate, but cannot initiate. He is therefore dependent, condemned to wait and hope, vulnerable. Antiquity, He certainly has; victory, is far less sure.

5.3.4.3   The use of the churchyard

If the "sum total" of the use of the churchyard be obtained through multiplying the amount it is used by the depth of the commitment expressed, then the churchyard is clearly an integrating focus in the parish, yet one that might be overlooked. The relationship between it and the parish church would appear to parallel that between the house and the garden. However, it could be that the dynamics are reversed, and that the energy or power or influence flows in the opposite direction, from the land to the building, rather than from the building to its surround.

The churchyard is used (personally, rather than vicariously) by at least as many people as use the church. Two fathers, whose seventeen-year old sons died on motor-bikes at different times, have been coming weekly, or more often, for approximately another seventeen years, each, now. Widows or daughters come as often and as continually. Some walk; many come by car, from the parish or from nearby communities.

Sometimes the male, driving the car, sits in it while his wife or mother visits the grave. Many visit alone, but probably more with a relation, and, especially on Sunday mornings, some with a family of mixed ages. On Mothering Sunday or on Easter Day, a glance into the "new churchyard", where some three hundred graves have been dug since 1946, shows half of them have been given fresh daffodils or other flowers. If they have been placed there by (on average) two visitors each, then the "aggregation", using the churchyard, equals or exceeds the "congregation" using the church. More parishioners keep family and even ecclesiastical festivals in this, their own way, than corporately.

Here, then, is a self-perpetuating religious practice, which is even, in some degree, ritual and objective, public and active, and voluntarily identified with Christianity and the Church. Although this churchyard is attractively situated, with trees, among fields, and within reach of various populations, there is, moreover, no reason to think that its use differs from that of more urban churchyards, or indeed of "secular" (if that descripion be allowed), municipal cemeteries. The aesthetics are a bonus, not the motive for coming. Strangely, the practice has been almost totally ignored, if not spurned, by the ordained leadership of the Church, and to some extent by academic students of religion; perhaps because the recent generation of students had little direct or indirect experience of bereavement, and regarded mourning as a hang-over from the past. The dead may be left to bury their dead; but, like the poor, will always be with us.

If the expression, "the use of the churchyard", is reminiscent of the technical term for describing the various liturgical "uses" that were prevalent before the first national Prayer Book of 1549, then the echo is apt. For the visit to the churchyard is a ritual, although conducted without "benefit of clergy". It exhibits variations upon a core theme.

The practitioners of this ritual come and go at times to suit themselves at any daylight hours throughout the week. They may, therefore, coincide more often with the volunteers (usually active churchpeople) who cut the long grass, than they do with each other. Despite the profundity of the experience they confessedly have in common, they express only a polite *camaraderie*. Should their paths happen to cross, while using the tap, or walking down the narrow path in the old churchyard, on the way to the new one, for instance, so that propinquity demands eye-contact and calls for verbal acknowledgement, the Victorian "English reserve" dictates a greeting that distances. It expresses what has already been described as the solidarity of individualism, in the parish, or, in the pub, the sociality of everyman's being allowed to (prove that he can) keep himself to himself.

The churchyard inspires too thin a fellowship to warrant that name (E I Bailey, 1994). Its commonality is rarely allowed to issue in inter-personal relationship. Although a churchyard festival in 1985 was sufficiently valued, six years later, for a repetition to be suggested for 1992, at the time it seemed to do little more than introduce school children to the craft of the monumental masons who demonstrated their skills, and to the historical interest of the epitaphs on the stones. The "powers" dominating the culture prevented the religiosity inherent in such a human experience from achieving social expression. It has, however, been asked for, yet again, for the octocentennial festival in 1998.

The "corporateness" of the churchyard is between the individual mourner, or at most their close friend or relation, with the departed, rather than any wider biological or theological sense of incorporation. Unconsciously, or semi-consciously, the churchyard may demonstrate the simultaneous incorporation of the human with the natural, and (by means of what the church "stands *for*") with the divine; but consciously the frame of reference is limited to the concern of the actor with the one buried.

Usually the visitor arrives with cut flowers. (Occasionally he, or a younger she, will come with seedlings, to be planted along the length of the grave, for since 1971 only headstones have been allowed.) Knowing their procedure, and its accustomed needs, they may also bring a gardening tool, and borrow one of the containers which they fill with water from the tap at the gate. Glancing at the "state" (of upkeep) of the churchyard, they make their way to "their" grave. Although the visitor will often be its other occupant in due course, it is called "their grave" because they tend, and so use, it, now.

Upon arrival at the site, the grave is usually surveyed overall, from its "foot". Ostensibly, this is an inspection, "to see what needs doing", but additionally, or even actually, it serves as a moment of preparation. Time is required for subjective recognition of its substantial significance, before taking tools to alter the accidents of its appearance. Then, whatever is necessary in order to "tidy" it, is done. This is a rational, practical, proceeding, after the manner of housework or gardening, but may be conducted with particular zeal and care: "for" the occupant mainly, but also for the visitor's satisfaction, and especially for the sake of the expression of pleasure in the relationship. This work will encompass all the immediate surround, but is not usually allowed to include any action to neighbouring graves.

The flowers are now placed in position. Further means of improvement are sought, but when (so to speak) the work is finished, all is done, and duty completed (indicating the discovery of additional sources of titivation), the whole is again surveyed, reflected upon, and pronounced satisfactory. The inscription on the monument is re-read, and a moment of (what can only be described as) communion is enjoyed.

Enquiry has shown that, both during the practical preparation, but especially during the inactive meditation which, if nerve allows, is the summation of the exercise, worries may be shared, guidance sought, memories enjoyed, the past re-lived, gratitude felt, thanks and apologies expressed.

The motivation involved in this, as (perhaps by definition) in all *human* activities, is complex, variable, and inchoate. Just as the validity of side-effects, such as fresh air, healthy exercise, and the aesthetic advantages of the setting, must be acknowledged, weighed, and distinguished from purposes (conscious or unconscious), so must the validity of the actors' own explanations be acknowledged, weighed, and, if necessary, distinguished. What they will reveal is, not what the authors think their hearers want to hear, but rather the frame of reference for understanding their selves which they possess, and feel able to share with their listener. Their description of their experience, including their motivation, communicates their understanding of it (within the parameters, sometimes, of their intuition, regarding their audience's capacity to comprehend them).

When they say they "are going to tidy the grave, because [they] always (like to) do so at Christmas", they are speaking the truth, and nothing but the truth, but not necessarily the whole truth, about what they are going to do, and why they are doing it, and about what they know, and what they think will be understood. The usual frame of reference, therefore, is active, pragmatic, conventional, and hedonistic. Whatever the sacrifice, whenever justification is necessary, the explanation that "works" in this culture will be one that avoids moral pretention, even to the point of dissimulation. Typically, it will disclaim both responsibility and altruism, "blaming" (say) habits instilled by up-bringing, and the "selfish" desire (as the interviews said) for an easy conscience. So, neither accepting nor rejecting the actors' own explanations uncritically, the observer may legitimately be allowed additional frames of reference.

Overall, then, the motive of the rite is an act of remembrance. Self-respect and public esteem are indeed involved in the desire to "tidy the grave" (along with the giving of respect and esteem to the departed himself - as it usually is, for women outlive men by at least seven years on average). But the tidying of the grave is itself only a means to an end, anticipated in part during that preparation and consummated following its completion. That end is achieved through the conscious, deliberate, and many-sided concentration of the person upon the similarly focused memory, memorial, and memorialisation, of the other.

The consequence is not auto-suggestion, in the sense of make-believe, to make true. Rather, it is re-present-ing; meaning, making present to the self, in the present, that which *is*, always, part of the self's own past, but cannot always be enjoyed consciously, directly, and uninterruptedly. If memory is the mental mechanism of this human capability, then the named stone, often marking the very place where the "remains" lie, stands midway in facilitating that process, between the particularity of the photograph on the one hand, and the generality of the home (or eucharistic bread and wine), on the other.

Perhaps because the rite of the Eucharist is particularly developed, the similarity becomes suggestive. Formally divided into two parts, the Service of the Word is a relatively practical sharing in the tradition, in accordance with the norms of the community, while the Service of the Sacrament facilitates a more direct, inter-personal communication through the medium of the sacramental "matter". Less words are used at the grave, but its "tidying" is mutually comprehensible, and sufficiently routine to allow the mind to meditate, while the flowers become the "matter" of this rite. It is, however, in the meaninglessness of the second half without its first half, or in the prefatory "invocation", and in the pause between the act of communion and the actual departure, that the spiritual realities involved show the clearest (and most significant) similarity.

So, it may be suggested, the consignment of the body (or the ashes) to the ground is less the end of a matter, than the beginning of another - indeed, a resurrection of the former life. Ultimately, the empirical fate or the spiritual legacy of the deceased may be as indistinct, if unquenchable, as the fate of his bodily remains. Within a short-range historical time, however, his spirit not merely exists, but lives again, every time he is "remembered". Indeed, it has been the recognised custom in some traditional cultures to pray for the departed, whenever their life has been recalled by the mention of their name.

The burial, then, begins to take on the significance of (the founding of) the "institution" - of a new rite of remembrance. The funeral becomes the consecration of a new space, for the conduct of this rite. The grave-stone becomes the reredos of a family shrine. The soil becomes sacred, because it houses that which is sacred (for the "dead" are no more *devoid* of existence, than the "departed" are, spiritually speaking, *absent*.) So the church may owe as much of its sanctity, to that which surrounds it, as the churchyard gains in sanctity, from the church building's propinquity. Indeed, the occasional eighteenth-century "table tomb", in the old churchyard, in which bodies could have been laid, becomes reminiscent of the Early Christian altar-tombs. The initially esoteric medieval custom of placing sacred relics in every altar, becomes startlingly homely.

Church of England clergy were very upset by the establishment of municipal cemeteries in 1854. This may therefore have been due in part to an intuition, based upon their experience, that the memory of the dead, representing both our past and our future, is, inevitably, one of the most "elementary" forms of all human and religious life. They may reasonably have suspected that the institution of non-ecclesiastical burials represented the formalisation of a secular religiosity that would be far more significant than the separation of civil registration of births and marriages, in 1836.

5.3.4.4   Other public places

If buildings are languages for communicating as well as machines for living; and if the family house, and the parish church, are the structural and historical type-cases of this symbolic system; then it may be asked what the meaning is of other buildings in the parish which, whatever their legal ownership, are public to the culture. While the art historian and social theorist concentrate on what the buildings "intend" to communicate, the present interest is in what in fact is conveyed by them. This account of this concern in the parish's life will then conclude by looking at the way in which this incarnate, petrified language can function *in negativo*. But first it is necessary to discuss the particular function of the parish church building in the Church community's parish.

The meaning of the parish church is not exhausted even by such double categorisation as an "historical monument", which also serves as a "denominational worship centre". "They also serve, who only stand and wait", points better to its unique role. Passivity, not activity, is its main function.

This was vividly demonstrated at a large public meeting in 1987 to discuss the route of the Winterbourne by-pass. Three of the nine suggested routes lay across the fields between the High Street and the church. Church Lane would therefore have been bifurcated, into a pair of *cul-de-sacs*, terminating either side of the new road. However, the meeting would not hear of such a scheme. Indeed, the planners themselves admitted that they had expected that response. They explained that they had only made this, the most obvious, suggestion, to avoid criticism for omitting consideration of it.

Only a hundred may worship there on each Sunday, and another three hundred go during the year. Only a hundred may attend each of the dozen weddings that are held there on Saturdays in the year, and another hundred, on average, each of the twenty funerals that are held on week-days. Two hundred may see to graves regularly, and another two hundred occasionally. Statistically, at such a meeting, this total was divisible into those who were too few to be worth counting, but were obviously committed; and those who went too little to be able to be counted, and were therefore apparently not committed. Yet the general complaint of the meeting was that, "It would cut the church off from the parish". Indeed, it precisely fulfilled the observations made, without any anticipation of such a test-case, in earlier reports of this study.

The church *stands for* (among other things) the parish. It is by far the oldest public building, and more than twice as old as the oldest, visible, privately-owned building. (A dove-cote, belonging to the adjacent Winterbourne Court, could be a century older than the church, but even its existence is little known.) Domesday shows that the church does not pre-date the parish, in the sense of an administrative unit, but it was here before there was sufficient population to comprise any real community. The actual history, however, is largely immaterial: it serves primarily mythologically, that is, as a vivid model of existential meanings. In the present tense, therefore, as well as historically, it can be said that the parish church gives the community its particular, distinctive and cohesive identity, and is one of the items that give it its character, making it what it is.

A second pointer to its peculiar status occurred in 1989, this time in the context of the Parochial Church Council. Told that the tower needed urgent, costly repairs (the cost of which falls on the Church within the parish, in England), and remembering that most parishioners cannot see even the spire of the church, enquiries were made as to the consequences if the local Church community ignored the need to repair it: what body owned it? The answer seemed to be that, while the Church's officers were responsible, any or all could resign their office; and that, while every resident of the parish had a right to burial in the churchyard, for instance, no body owned the building. It was probably the equivalent of truly common land. Whether or not this describes the legal position accurately, it certainly describes the existential facts. The congregation "keeps it going", but on behalf of the entire population of the parish, to whom it "belongs".

So the parish church is a curiously demanding yardstick against which briefly to measure the other churches in the parish, the schools, the common land, the public houses, and the "Community (Association's) Centre".

The minister of Salem, when the Rector first came to the parish, said he regarded the parish church as "his", in the sense of feeling a loyalty towards it. Conversely, the Rector has always admired the simple, classical lines of Salem chapel, and its association with John Wesley himself, who preached in Watleys End and then returned in 1787 to lay the foundation stone. However, a plain building probably needs pointed ("Gothic") windows, to qualify as a *real* church in England; and the Wesley connection does not seem to occasion very much rejoicing, even among the chapel's members. Neither its precise age, nor its founder (even had it been Jesus himself), seem to matter greatly.

While the Methodists care for their building devotedly, and there is some general awareness of its existence, there is little feeling in the parish at large that it is "ours". This is a reflection, not of its age, since any period previous to (approximately) grandparents, comes within the "olden days", and is relatively indistinguishable, and so akin to Eliade's *in illo tempore*. Rather, the attitude reflects the chapel's origins in a bounded Society, and its use by a "denomination". It is for "the people called Methodists"; while the parish church is for the parish.

At one end of Factory Road is Salem: at the other end is Ebenezer. A "Primitive" Methodist chapel, built of wood in 1868, it was officially closed for worship in 1970, although a devotee was allowed to conduct Sunday School there for another twenty years. With seating for the presbyters behind the holy table, it can claim unusual conformity to the canons of liturgical archaeology. However, as a more Evangelical off-shoot of Salem, its hold on the general consciousness of the parish must always have been slight.

Half-way between Salem and Ebenezer, on the one hand, and the parish church, on the other, at the junction of Watleys End Road and the High Street, is St Michael's Room. Initiated by the then Rector in 1887, to mark Queen Victoria's golden jubilee, it was intended, as he explained in the monthly church magazine, "to look (and feel) in part like a church", for the holding of some services on Sundays, in order to assist "the folk at Watleys End", as they had a mile or more to walk to church. It was also intended, however, for use as a church hall, for social events.

The desire to ease matters for people at Watleys End was no doubt due to the (then duplicate) Methodist presence there. (Subsequently, it led to the placing of a curate, with a mission hut at the bottom of his garden, *between* the two chapels.) The desire for a social venue no doubt reflected the growing sense of the Church as an identifiable community, both nationally and locally - and to widespread reluctance to revive the social use of the church in the medieval manner. Both wishes reflect the influence of the Oxford Movement, originating in 1833 and already spreading out to parishes by the middle of the century. So the parish exemplifies the micro-history of religion as precisely as the geography of the Church School (and the head's accommodation) exemplified its anticipated catchment area (and the head's role in relation to the school and community).

St Michael's Room, so far as is known, aroused no opposition within the parish. It was intended as an "ante-room", rather than alternative, to the parish church. The same cannot be said of the conversion of the eighteenth-century tithe barn, on the edge of the Rectory garden, into a "chapel-of-ease" by an incoming Rector in 1955. This was intended to take the worship services from St Michael's Rooms (by now it had kitchen and toilets); to ease access (before cars were ubiquitous); and to facilitate the introduction of a Parish Communion service, with a more "Catholic" style of worship, while avoiding any disturbance to the existing pattern at the parish church.

The *original* cause of the disagreement (assuming that it was a procedural lack of democracy, not a simple personality clash) would seem to have been that it "split the parish", in establishing two (Church of England) buildings, intended purely for worship. The continuum of opinion ran from faith in the Rector's intentions for worship, to incomprehension that the then Rector of all people should initiate a rival to the parish church.

Only one of the school buildings has inspired the kind of loyalty inspired by church buildings. This is the old Church School, in its second purpose-built form, on the High Street. Old-fashioned, it had not attracted parents in the 1960s and '70s; but, built of stone, and old, with fashions changing, its coming closure inspired widespread nostalgia in 1980. However, such expression was facilitated by the knowledge that a decision had already been taken. Moreover, the main fear was of an empty and vandalised building, in the centre of the community.

The Church School's playing field marches alongside the parish's Recreation Field, but without a dividing fence, so the whole is popularly known as "The Rec". It is used mainly by the parish's cricket and soccer teams, and of course by the school. Though well-used, it is perhaps even more highly valued. Its ten acres (four hectares), in the very centre of the community, though somewhat monotonously flat and bare when unpopulated, are a statement that sheer space is a good; that recreation, as well as production, is valuable; that land is not only for building on; and that the public can corporately discriminate, sacrifice profits, and make prohibitions.

The other "open spaces" in the parish are either school playing fields, or else roadside verges (of varying size). The former have all been fenced, during the period of observation, and so are now, if not "private", then very obviously "theirs", not "ours". The latter are a visual amenity, and assist drivers' vision, but are mainly used as car parking and/or cannine conveniences.

In varying degrees all of the five public houses have imported "traditional" *bric-a-brac* in order to fulfil the myth of the "local", especially for those from farther afield. More important than building or decoration, though, is the life inside them. From the present point of view, they share certain characteristics with "The Rec". They affirm the value of existence as well as action, of talking as well as doing, of passing time as well as pastimes. They witness in a catholic way to the sacredness inherent in simply being. But, while obviously more public than a private home, they are public not corporate; open to all, but on condition of a purchase, and of behaving in accordance with their ways. Despite their "human face", in the *persona* of the landlord, they are, indeed, public "houses", not homes.

The Community Association's founders acknowledged, at their Annual General Meeting on 6 January 1971, that they wanted a Centre, less for the sake of rooms for meetings, than "as a symbol". This was confirmed, negatively, by their almost complete ignorance, after ten years' fundraising in 1973, of the extent or character of the need for meeting rooms, and, positively, by their repeated refusal to receive brewery money and become a "club". The resulting Centre is the result of that determination. It is the most conspicuous example, perhaps, of the faith that brings into existence that which used not to exist, in the parish within recent years. Curiously, the majority of its capital eventually came from statutory grants, but it was the considerable sums, raised between 1963 and 1976, that attracted them.

The Association itself resembles the local Church community in many ways. Each has constitutent organisations, giving varying degrees of reality to their affiliation. Each has a monthly magazine, paid for by approaching a thousand or more of the two thousand homes in the parish. (Many homes receive both; some seem to mistake the Community Association's magazine for the Church's – perhaps because of its rather frequent, exhortatory moral character.) Each is led by a handful of enthusiasts, or better, hard workers, "supported" by a large majority of "well-wishers". But, asked what it stands for, the Community Association is silent. Perhaps the answer was, a "church hall" that is not a *Church* hall.

In which case the Rector reflected its basis, as well as the Church's, when in 1971 he urged support for it, in order to demonstrate that citizenship in the parish was not dependent upon Baptized membership of the Church. His interest in, and even support for, the Association, have both occasioned surprise, and been very warmly welcomed, indicating possibly a sense of its receiving the Church's blessing.

5.3.4.5   The horror of vandalism

Customers in British banks used to speak in hushed tones, if at all. Sometimes the observer wondered whether this reflected a respect for those doing mental arithmetic (in those days), or intimidation by the size of the institution, or reverence in the face of the personal significance of money, or awe in the presence of the "mystery" of finance as a system of global communication and power. During the 1970s the banks appeared deliberately to change that atmosphere, by their use (and choice) of background music: no doubt the older culture was inhibiting entry on the part of new social groups.

The significance of silence was early appreciated in the course of these studies. Composing the interview schedule constantly raised questions as to what might prove possible, or impossible, to discuss. Topics that might be broached, in view of the context and purpose, such as "embarrassing experiences", might nevertheless be answered with a defensive nonchalance, or lightheartedness. The public house illustrated the influence of the degree of acquaintance, of the number of hearers, and indeed of alcohol, upon the readiness to talk "personally". It seemed that a hierarchy of sacreds could be sketched; the top, or the base, of the pyramid would be composed of those topics that were unmentionable, because too revealing. Yet they might not be mentionable in any report, either; would their mention be (or, considered to be) revelatory simply of the author's own mind?

Participation in the life of the residential parish, with the continuity of its *Gemeinschaft* neighbourliness, highlighted the issue. An old observation, however, was also brought to mind: that swearing was positive evidence of that which was only improperly or imperfectly mentionable. Indeed, it revealed the marginal in two ways: by the form it used, and by the matter that occasioned it. Thus it had long been noticed, with some interest, that clergy, at least of the Church of England, swore, but usually "theologically". They invoked such concepts as "good Lord", or "heavens above", relatively freely; they referred to "God" or "hell" less often, especially than those to whom such references might be assumed to be less meaningful. With the exception of certain clergy since the 1970s, on the other hand, they never alluded to sexual (or scatalogical) concepts. The ritual character of swearing, however, suggested that this distinction owed less to the kind of religious prohibitions that made the naming of God taboo in the Old Testament, than to the dictates of social convention.

Experience in the Royal Air Force and elsewhere, on the other hand, showed that the "man in the street" swore both theologically and sexually with equal abandon, suggesting that, at least by convention, even the former method contained enough meaning to validate swearing by it. So swearing, like religion generally, could not be understood as *human* behaviour, if its meaning in each context was left out of account. The subjective dimension might require a different approach, and increased the range of the task, but it was not necessarily more complex, and, in any case, was essential. *Understanding* necessitated the exploration, and correlation, of both subjective and objective dimensions.

Slightly more straightforward, and more certainly revealing, however, were the matters that occasioned such swearing. The type-case, beloved of the music-hall, were incidents such as hitting one's thumb with a hammer, or slipping on a banana-skin, dropped by one's colleague. Such momentary reactions seemed to contain little implicit-religious content.

Yet other incidents aroused responses that had serious, on-going import. Sometimes the reaction included swearing, but basically the response was one of silence. Even the swearing, when it occurred, was intended to express a void: bafflement. Indeed, the silence was punctuated by statements such as, "I can't understand it ... how can they do such a thing? ... why? ... what makes them do it? ... what is the matter with people? ... I don't know what to think ... I'm at a loss for words ... It leaves me speechless." Repeated affirmations of speech*less*ness, such as this, alert the observer both by their quality of nonplussed "swearing", *and* by the reduction to dumbfounded silence.

The two commonest occasions of such reactions were child abuse (in the 1980s) and vandalism (property abuse) in the 1970s. The latter was frequently reported in the parish, at least in part because it is largely an age-related behaviour, and the secondary school on the High Street peaked at 1990 pupils aged 11-18 in those years (half of them coming from this parish). The vandalism in question mainly took the form of setting fire to their own school, or breaking into the primary schools, and certain shops; damaging public benches, and younger children's playground equipment; breaking into the church, damaging grave-stones; and throwing their refuse into gardens. An older age-group "vandalises" more audibly, by shouting as they emerge from pubs, "revving-up" bikes, or playing music loudly; and an older group still, by a desire to "get their hands on the fools" - but this attitude is relatively infrequent in this community.

The repeated response of "speechlesssness" suggested that a sacredness had been violated. In a property-owning democracy such as this, private or public *property* may plausibly be suggested as the vehicle of that sacred quality. However, it is doubtful whether that hypothesis will hold water, in this context. Certainly, the material was not written off as simply covered by insurance, and meaningless. But there is at least as much puzzlement, as anger. The reaction is not hysterical or populist. For the irreligious experience of this community is as "normal" as its religious experience, explicit or implicit.

The offence of vandalism lies in its being counter-productive, as well as meaningless. It is abhorrent, because it has something to say, but its manner of communication is self-defeating. The damage it causes is wasteful, and upsets people, but that is an additional, utilitarian, merely moral, issue. Its *profanity* lies in its being will-full, but "point-less". Shock, horror, and sadness are the reactions to this ritual use of the community's sacramental language to express, not so much nihilism, or fun, as irresponsibility.

5.3.5   Church, its major symbol

The possibility that the Church was the major symbol in the general consciousness of the parish came as a surprise to the observer. His own, inevitable, response was to suspect bias in the evidence that was presented to him, or (unconscious) prejudice in his own weighing of its significance. Three reflections, however, suggested reasons why the hypothesis could be comprehensible.

Firstly, sometimes the depth of the commitment to the Church could not be gainsaid, either when the *confession* (for such it was) was offered verbally (usually by a man), or when practical assistance was given (usually by a woman). Secondly, the Church functioned as the major symbol of the community's *cor-*

porate consciousness, whereas other symbols within the general consciousness, such as schools and political parties, voluntary associations and public houses, had sectional appeal. Thirdly, there was no other candidate.

On the one hand, the Community Association aspired to fulfilling this role, in suggesting, before it had its own Centre, that every resident automatically belonged to it, and afterwards that all should actively assist in maintaining it. But the former smacked of the "imperialism" shown by the Church of England under Queen Elizabeth I, which anticipated an *eschaton*, by hoping for a coterminous Commonwealth and Church through accident of settlement, without human choice; while the latter was moralistic to the point of hectoring. Lacking other symbolic resources, therefore, in practice it looked like either another small club (the band of enthusiasts who "ran" it), or else another would-be universal society (the marginal commitment of the members of the public who paid a subscription). On the other hand, single issue campaigns such as those against the Severnside proposal in the 1970s or the Frome Valley development in the 1980s, were limited in their life and aim, and indeed owed much of their success to that "secular" characteristic.

In the 1990s, therefore, presumably as in the 1190s, the Church (the ideal of community, whose symbol was the church building), was the major symbol of the parish, insofar as the members functioned as a *community*. The division of the civil parish into three ecclesiastical parishes in the nineteenth century had both reflected and furthered those self-same local identities. By contrast, the retention of the wider boundary for the civil parish, and the absence of any visual symbol for either the wider parish or its council (in the form of offices, such as a *mairie*), until 1995, precluded its stepping into this role.

Analysis suggests four main ways in which the Church, as an ideal with a social basis in reality, functions as a symbol. It is understood as being *expressed* in worship, as (say) eleven players going out onto the field demonstrate the particular purpose of a football club and all its supporting activities. It is understood as being *intended* for outreach, along the lines of Archbishop William Temple's oft-quoted description of the church as an unusual club, in that it exists for the benefit of those who are not members. It is understood as being *composed* by community, in the sense that it is neither the building (the preacher's accustomed *bête-noire*), nor even the people (the preacher's preferred meaning), but the attitudes evinced by participants (the Spirit, in Pauline terms). It is understood, lastly, as the *source* of identity, both communal and personal: hence the antipathy to sectional or dysfunctional behaviour of any kind (including evangelism), that cannot be seen to be a merely temporary means towards the end of a wider healing.

For a totally general Divinity is only consonant with holism; any differentiation, that is not vicarious, is an offense. Indeed, although any particular Church's success or failure, in any one of these four ways, will be fairly readily recognised, perspective is soon restored, by an implicit insistence that they are only dimensions of a life that is many-sided but single.

5.3.5.1   Expressed in worship

"Everybody always used to go to church", is an extraordinarily tenacious myth. Presumably it arises from the Church's historical dominance of the High Culture, up to the beginning of this century, and from childhood memories of those occasions when the church was full. These fail to take account of the far more numerous occasions when it was not (which less people therefore experienced), and of the statistical gap between even the largest congregations, and the total population of the parish.

The myth has three results. It exaggerates the extent, novelty and permanence, of this century's decline in churchgoing. It depresses those who worship, and the larger number who, while seldom if ever doing so themselves, wish that more people did so. It encourages those who do not do so, to regard those who do, as doing so, in some sense, on their behalf.

So, by the accident of coincidence, whereas "the Church" once instantly meant "the Vicar" (that is, the *deputy* of, for instance, a religious Order), "the Church" has now most immediately come to mean a group that vicar-iously "keep it going", by worshipping and undertaking responsibility for its life. Indeed, counted as they can be in mere dozens, both the Anglican and Methodist Churches of the parish, as so often elsewhere, may aptly be compared with the medieval Orders. The inter-changeability of "regularly" and "religiously", in such expressions as "reading the papers religiously", is an unconscious acknowledgement of the comparability of such behaviour with its type-case in Western European High Culture.

By the 1990s the population of the parish had been a fairly stable seven thousand for twenty years, and seemed likely to remain so for another twenty years. In 1858, following the establishment of Winterbourn (as it is spelt in the Act of Parliament) Down and the establishment of Frenchay (in 1834), as separate ecclesiastical parishes, the population was probably about two thousand. It is doubtful whether the number of worshippers has increased or decreased to any comparable extent. What has come (and largely gone, in the case of the Anglican Church) is Sunday School; and, in the case of the Methodist Church, Ebenezer Chapel.

In the mid-1990s, then, the number of worshippers in St Michael's and Salem (including those children attending Sunday School) on any single ordinary Sunday, totals two hundred at most. The number should, however, be approximately doubled, to allow for the regular participants who are absent on any particular Sunday on account of other commitments, ranging from the Confirmation of a godchild elsewhere, to a holiday abroad. Four hundred is, indeed, the approximate number of names on the Rolls of the two Churches, or would be if children were included.

At five or so per cent of the population, even this figure represents hardly half the proportion which, all national surveys seem to show, are in some church on a Sunday. While the absence of churches of other denominations from the community necessitates more parishioners than usual going out of this parish to worship, it is difficult to imagine that their number equals those who stay, or come in from other communities.

To these "regulars" should be added a second category: those who may come just as regularly, as it happens, but far less often. Typically, they come (or used to come, because increased travel abroad, on holiday, is having a marked effect) "every year", at (for instance) Harvest (in the Methodist case, especially), Remembrance, Christmas, or Easter; for services in which their children are involved; or at a sequence of such occasions. Over the course of the year, they must amount to a further four hundred people. They could be called the "occasionals", because they come infrequently (the modern meaning of "occasional"), and at special times (the older meaning of "occasional").

Church bodies often speak of them as "fringe" members. Because of the semi-Gemeinschaft character of this community, the "regulars" in this parish are less inclined to feel that such "occasionals" are visiting birds-of-passage; but they have difficulty integrating them into responsibility for the Church's worship and life. Often already well integrated in other circles, familial or communal, the "occasionals" keep such invitations at arm's length.

A third category uses the church to mark occasions in the life of their family and friends. They come at their invitation. Due to the demographic structure of the parish, and as part of the general, national decline in requests for children to be Baptized, the number of Baptisms has changed over the last twenty-five years from forty infants, and a couple of teenagers (at Confirmation), to a dozen or less, plus a couple of teenagers or adults (at Confirmation). To this may be added one a year at the Methodist Church. As each Baptism party averages about a dozen people, this brings another hundred people to a public service in the course of a year. The annual Confirmation averages ten candidates, with fifty guests, outside the regular congregation. Twenty weddings, including three at Salem, with a hundred guests, bring two thousand more people, to a more "private" service. Twenty funerals may bring two thousand more people to church during the working week. There is little overlap between these groups, except within the group of mourners. Actual parishioners, however, form a minority, except at funerals.

So the four thousand or so participants in these occasions may simply double the number of members of this community who appear in its two churches each year, making it two thousand instead of one. This means, however, that of those who have lived here (say) ten years, the majority will have been inside its worship buildings at least once. They will also have a little experience of several other churches elsewhere.

The existential meaning of worship is only just beginning to be explored, in ecclesiastical as in academic or education circles. Discussion with the individual "regulars", and with the Church Council or with the separate congregations as a whole, focussing upon possible changes in worship, can however be supplemented by evaluations offered by the "occasionals" and by former worshippers. The character of the experience does not differ greatly; which explains why individuals, here as elsewhere, can so easily drop into, and out of, Church life.

The overall impression is less of a one-to-one inter-personal relationship with the Holy, than of a common celebration of sacreds, which may suggest a transcendent dimension.

The regulars value, first, the opportunity for solidarity with fellow-Christians. Again, they gain support, in what they experience as a lonely path, not so much from personal fellowship, as from the reassurance of finding others are in the same boat. Secondly, they value worship because the atmosphere is "different", because it is quiet and reverent: it is an experience of another side of life in this world, rather than an experience of life in another world. Thirdly, or more particularly with reference to that value, they have spoken of the beauty of its language, and the other ways in which it conveys truths about God and about Christ, and about the value of the opportunity to meditate, leading to communion with God. They have described attendance as a duty, imposed by conscience, but also owed as a witness to their neighbours.

Some of those who come regularly but occasionally, or who come for family events, used to come regularly, usually as children. To call them "lapsed" may be simplistic, since the early Church's *lapsi* had actually denied the faith, often in the face of persecution. They may more accurately be called the "formers", or "erstwhiles", from the point of view of worship, since they neither deny the validity of the faith, nor, probably, have they been overtly persecuted. As pluralistic dialogue succeeds guilt-induced taciturnity, in the wider culture, so the views they volunteer become even more valuable and less suspect.

Like the regulars, they value the sight of others who are on "the side of the angels"; like the "occasionals", they value the presence of a crowd, proving that what they believe in is not yet dead. But this group in particular will quite often say how much they "enjoyed" a service they have attended, and add that they "must come more often", and "don't understand why [they] don't", and even ask the listener to tell them. Usually, their own opinion is that "other things" crowded in, something "broke the habit", and then they "just got too busy"; "not that that's any excuse really: you can always find time if you want to," they usually add.

As they share their memories of their experience of worship when they were younger, they convey the impression of finding, through it, their place in the universe: humbled, rather than humiliated, transcendence had given self-*respect*. It had been instructive, helpful and self-authentically "right". The split (E D Starbuck, 1899), in this case between the internal moral law and external natural law, had been healed.

The great majority of those who worship think they do so for themselves. Yet when they speak phenomenologically of the experience of worship, they begin to describe a sense of integration: communal, social and moral, personal and cosmic. Most in this community are well aware of the reality referred to by such technical terms as "vicarious" and "coinherence", but very few, even in the Church, have any concepts to describe such experience. Those outside the worshipping community may therefore have a clearer appreciation of this.

In practical terms they may "take [Church] for granted". If necessary, in practice they would no doubt soon adjust to its disappearance. Nevertheless, if the issue were raised, then (as with the possibility of increased severance from the building by the by-pass), an adamant conviction would emerge from the unconscious. It would not be the first time that "scribes" failed to appreciate the many-sidedness of mysteries of which they were stewards. Semitic theists apart, classical Brahmanism speaks for many in feeling that the gods and the cosmos depend on our sacrifices.

5.3.5.2   Intended for outreach

Worship is understood as the primary activity of the Church, in the sense of being its *sine qua non*. But outreach is felt to be primary, in the sense of being its *raison d'être*. Worship is prior, but worship that does not lead to outreach is considered invalid and pointless. That such outreach should take place in the parish, and should be concerned with all, without distinction of colour, class or creed; that it should show "the Christian spirit", of compassion, and especially to those in particular need of it, is agreed by all. That is exactly what is meant by a pastoral, parochial Church, at its best.

That such outreach should also concern itself with those outside the parish, that it may require more attention to be devoted to some at the expense of others, that it should recognise the particular needs or potential of those with power or of those without power, that it should find a peculiar affinity with fellow-believers or a peculiar longing for non-believers; that it might challenge as well as comfort, question as well as accept, initiate as well as respond, organise as well as pray, argue as well as affirm, politicise as well as sympathise - such forms of outreach find differing, more limited constitutencies. The myriad groups of those with such specialist interests, receive little support from the parish as a whole.

The archetypal means of outreach is the home visit. A widespread and influential myth says the clergy used to visit all their parishioners regularly.

Indeed, they spent most of their time doing this; their only other form of work was the preparation of sermons, and of course the conduct of worship on Sundays. Following the "Evangelical" and "Oxford" movements, and the establishment of "theological colleges", such house-to-house visiting did indeed become part of their professional ideology. In some well-organised parishes, with a large team of assistants, it was indeed practised, between the middle of the last century and the middle of this century.

It is by no means so clear, however, that all lone incumbents freed themselves from their social and family round sufficiently in the last century; or that they penetrated beyond the door, or offered more than bread and coal. Nor is it clear that in this century they freed themselves sufficiently from ecclesiastical meetings or clerical associations; or that they could have kept pace with a doubling of the population, while their own numbers halved, and halved again. A converse myth is, therefore, now appearing: that "the clergy have stopped visiting (entirely)".

The mythological and statistical situation in this parish is similar to that in the country at large. From the present point of view, history, in the sense of what actually happened, only matters when it is mythology: is believed *in*, because it impinges on some concern. Phenomenologically, the only purpose served by recorded history is to confirm and simplify current myths, or else to widen the choice among available scenarios.

So, traditionally (that is to say, in the last hundred years), the first antic-ipated means of outreach has been the home visit by the incumbent. There is some expectation today that he has come for a specific purpose. Regular worshippers especially will teasingly ask what he wants them to do. But an older, and still prevalent view, assumes that he has come to meet them, find out "who they are", and take an interest in them, as they are, holistically. The unconscious assumption is that he does this, because God is like this.

Indeed, as an increasing number of people, have a decreasing sense of shame about not worshipping, he is less and less likely to have to carry their projected guilt. Often the person knows he has come, for instance, to discuss the meaning of Baptism and then arrange a date for it, or on account of bereavement. Often they may not: he comes because they have appeared in church and he did not know them, or to invite a teenager whom he Baptized to consider Confirmation. Yet virtually never, in twenty-six years of his experience, and in a further twenty years' experience on the part of assistant ministers, has entry been refused. The churchgoer may well ask, Why have you come?; the non-churchgoer will wonder, Why hasn't he come before?

However, the "Church", of whom outreach is expected, is no longer equated with and restricted to the clergy. All who publicly identify with its empirical re-ality, either by accepting office within it (eg through membership of the Church Council), or by attending worship, become vehicles of its symbolic significance.

So home visiting on their part is likewise accepted, albeit with slightly less width of concern or depth of meaning, as part of the Church's outreach. Thus, part cause and part consequence, between one and two dozen people in 1972 visited six hundred homes that had had some link with St Michael's in the previous seven years, to seek their further involvement. In 1974, every home that did not receive the Churches' Newsletter was invited to do so. In 1977 almost every home was visited simply "in the name of the Church". In 1979 and 1981 (in two stages), and again in 1984, the two hundred households on the Church Roll were asked to consider their "stewardship" of "time, talents, and money". In 1988 several hundred houses were again visited "in the name of the Church". In 1990 and 1992 every house was, first, invited to contribute financially to the repair of the building, and, then, thanked for the Appeal's success.

The overwhelming response to all those visits, made simply "in the name of the Church", has been a polite but clear, "No, there is nothing I want to know, about times of Services and so on – I know where the Church is, if I want it", coupled with a sincere and emphatic, "but *thank you very much for coming*". (The specific request for money for repairs to the building, of course, evoked a more varied response.) However slight the quantitative gain, the attitude discovered in the course of such repeated and widespread visiting cannot be denied, and must be taken on board in any account of the parish.

Such face-to-face visiting, by the Rector or active Churchmembers, is much more likely to achieve a positive response, for instance, to any request for assistance. As well as showing "the human face" of the institution, such visiting contains a sacrificial element. What may never be translated into action for the sake of a principle, may well be done for the sake of another person (as the Interviewees said). Beneath the quantifiable results of such communication, however, is the qualitative dimension of communion, which is considered to be of the essence of Church. The "coming" itself "shows the Church cares".

Another means of outreach, expected of and used by the Church, in the parish, is the written word. For a hundred years most parish Churches have had a monthly magazine, with a circulation anywhere on the spectrum between the congregation and every household. Here, in typed and duplicated form, it was resumed bi-monthly in 1970, and monthly in 1979. Over half the households were prepared to receive (and pay for) it, when asked in 1974, although this number (despite visiting new arrivals) has gradually fallen to one-third. However, every household has been given some other form of written communication, approximately once a year.

This has taken a wide variety of forms. For instance, in 1970, following the incumbent's arrival, and in 1976 and 1979, following changes of assistant, and in 1982, and most years since, it took the form of a Christmas card (individually signed, in 1970, by the Rector and his wife). In 1971, 1972 and 1973, it took the form of an invitation to join in a conference, in the parish, on the respective themes of industry, education, and the Church. In 1973 and 1974, in conjunction with the Parish Council and the nascent Community Association, a brochure of events within a Parish Festival was sold, and the notice was given regarding a Streetwarden Scheme. In 1977, 1978 and 1979, invitations were given, respectively, to a flower festival to mark the Silver Jubilee of Queen Elizabeth II's accession (along with notice of the forthcoming "harvest visiting"), to a "festival of the family", and to an "education festival". In 1981, 1982 and 1983 invitations were given to contribute to the re-decoration of the church interior, to join in a thanksgiving service upon its completion, and to enjoy another flower festival, in that setting, to mark the re-hanging of the bells in the church tower. In 1975, in 1987, and in 1994, a portmanteau invitation was given to share in any of a variety of events, from entry into the European Union, to considering Confirmation. In 1990 and 1992 informative literature was delivered in the course of the visiting in connection with the major Appeal.

Such literature is not merely a time-saving but otherwise poor substitute for house-to-house visiting. Like the traditional printed magazine, it also fulfils a different function. It allows parishioners to observe and weigh the signs and the life it describes. It leaves them free to make up their own mind, without personal pressure. It enables him or her to become the spectator, as of a television programme. Indeed, the appeal is reminiscent of the traditional gossip, or *voyeur* of life, elsewhere.

Certainly the regular Newsletter is read attentively by many whose behaviour gives no outward evidence of it whatsoever. Such careful attention runs the whole gamut, from the reader who would not like it to be amalgamated with the Community Association's magazine, because "it's special - I keep it by my bedside", to those who say, "I'm not a Christian, but I always read it, because I like to know what's going on, what you're doing".

Both visiting and literature are, then, being watched, in order to read between the lines. "Outreach", assumed to be the purpose of the Church in the parish, is not simply a matter of certain activities. Neither is it a matter of certain aims, such as recruiting new members. Both of these are recognised as legitimate; but what is meant by this expectation is an attitude, even a spirit. The question and test is relatively conscious: is this a Church, which therefore exists for others, or is it simply a club? By its members' concern for other individuals (where they actually are, at home for instance), and by its readiness to talk about what it is doing and to submit it to others' judgement, it will openly and publicly reveal the quality of its own life, as a community.

5.3.5.3 Composed by community

Outreach is recognised as a purpose and criterion of the Church, without its being the only purpose or the single criterion. Outreach, whether evangelistic or humanitarian in aim, specific or general in character, is expected to be the inevitable by-product which flows naturally from a strong and *healthy* community life. The relationship of its variegated forms and that prior core may be compared to a Catherine wheel which, as it spins round upon its anchoring pin, disperses sparks of colour and light all around itself.

This central spirit is expected to be equally present in the *minutiae* of interpersonal relationships, and in the manifestations of institutions. To attempt formal worship at all, legitimates this hope. For, insofar as the general consciousness of the parish has reached the point of "splitting" (E Durkheim, 1915, E D Starbuck, 1899) at all, the split is less a medieval division between the natural and supernatural, or a hellenic division between the material and mental, or a Marxist "them" and "us", than the semi-Pauline distinction between the letter or law (of structures) and spirit or Spirit (of subjectivity). Services (of worship) and the organisations of the local Church (such as its Council), are two particular spheres in which the life of the community may be expected to be manifest.

Worship is not seen as having direct and immediate "practical" consequences, in the same manner as some of the rituals featuring in Malinowski's *Magic, Science, and Religion*. Yet it falls within Weber's dictum that "most religion is secular". For it is simultaneously seen as entirely symbolic, and yet quite utilitarian. Even those males whose minds were formed before the 1960s, increasingly recognise that (in their terms) emotion is as real as reason. So, "Church [-going] is all right for them as likes it", is now a much more positive verdict than it used to be. It recognises that such unrelievedly symbolic activity may only "make sense" to a minority, without thereby suggesting that it is of marginal significance to them, or to the community, or indeed in itself.

It is almost always assumed that the motive for participating in worship, therefore, is "What you get out of it". A few extraneous clergy, and the occasional parishioner, may wish to introduce the concept of God, and his deserts, into the reasoning. Alternatively, a median point may be cited: "I know you get out what you put in". Yet the attitude is not necessarily simply calculating, individualistic and selfish. A spiritual blessing, that is beneficial for the inner life of the individual and hence of benefit to others, is the desired reward. Should such "peace" not "materialise", then this kind of sacrifice would not seem to be the sort required by the Divinity of this particular person. They would be seen as called to a different kind of Service (usually, ethical rather than liturgical).

Whether "worship is", or "is not", "for me", is, in practice, therefore, of slight moment. Few even of that small minority who worship regularly, *long* for others to join in it. Worshipping parents are disappointed when their children cease to come, but acknowledge that "you can't force them"; ultimately, indeed, that, if worship is not willing, it cannot be worship ("in spirit"). Spouses may accommodate themselves to an arrangement which allows for a certain division of labour, and also of company. "Everyone must decide for themselves" is the key saying. It combines a moral ideal (that it is wrong to try to impose one's view upon others), with a recognition of the empirical situation (that there is no way of compelling participation). Such moral-empirical elision, however, obscures the associated possibilites: that all ought to "make up their own mind", but few do in fact consciously decide for themselves.

Regardless of the individual's position on this scale, the expectation is that such (Self-seeking) worshippers should be (what is usually described as) "friendly". This consists in being friendly towards each other, in the first place; to visitors, and to total strangers, in the second place; and, in a sense, to themselves and to Divinity, in the third place. Indices of such attainments are the extent and content of conversation; a smiling helpfulness, and willingness to give money *away* (to other causes); happiness, reverence, and whole-hearted participation, especially in the singing (vocal music still being the most popular ritual medium). The unquestioned assumptions give grounds for anticipating an aggregate of individuals, but the criteria of the Church as a worshipping community demand that the Christian congregation should exhibit at least some of the marks of a fellowship.

Apart from the worshipping congregation, the main locus in which the community life of the Church is sought is in its affiliated organisations. Chief among these is the Mothers' Union, accompanied by those groups concerned with current social issues, or with such projects as raising funds to repair the church or hall, or happenings connected with events, such as elections and jubilees, in the world at large. Most significant, because presumably most typical or characteristic, however, is the life of the Parochial Church Council, that organisation within the local Church which is intended both to facilitate personal inter-action (as the congregation's worship is intended to facilitate interaction with the Almighty), and to be representative.

It consists of about twenty-five people at any one time, and combines continuity of membership with change. So, in the course of twenty-six years, it has been composed of some two hundred individuals, ranging from the utterly regular to less frequent churchgoers. It therefore has statistical, as well as institutional and symbolic, representative significance.

Procedurally, the Council begins its monthly meeting at half past seven and concludes just after ten, having paused for coffee, accompanied by much interpersonal talk, for a quarter of an hour before nine o'clock. Probably no other body within the community, therefore, meets so regularly, for such a length of time, to discuss matters of such human interest, to decide such a variety of questions, in such an atmosphere of free speech, with so many members. However, interest in it in this context centres less upon its specific decisions, or its place within the Church and the community, than upon the manner in which it conducts its debates.

Analysis of its work and working may model itself upon its title, for its perceived agenda is aptly described by the (separate) terms Parochial and Church, while its process is indeed Conciliar.

Throughout the earlier part of this century, "parochial" like "provincial", had a pejorative air, in the minds of *déraciné* metropolitanites, who established their own would-be cosmopolitanism as the public norm. The image of the "parish pump" became the cliché with which to excommunicate the possibility of intelligent consideration. Recently, the pendulum has swung, as journalists have realised that individuals know best where the shoe pinches, as politicians have recognised that local Churches are more in touch with "ordinary people" than they themselves are, as the social services have learnt that they can only supplement, not replace, the voluntary sector; and as management of all kinds (business, educational, and ecclesiastical, for instance) has embraced "subsidiarity". Indeed, an equally narrow-minded identification of the "real" with the "local", *without remainder*, might become, for some, a substitute dogma.

The former attitude played a significant part in the disproportionate decline of the national Church, for, even following the religious, theological, administrative, and organisational revolutions of the last century, associated with Simeon, Newman, Blomfield and Samuel Wilberforce, the Church of England remained, both financially and attitudinally, fundamentally a confederation: each parish was an independent corporation. The revised attitude, reacting to the democratisation and "diocesanisation" of the 1970s, appeals to a preference for pietism on the part of centralist politicians, to a romanticisation of the rural on the part of week-enders, and to nostalgia for a marginalised culture on the part of displaced groups and their supporters.

Those who opt for membership of the Parochial Church Council share, with those who actively identify with the local Church, the distinction of being typical of neither extreme, but of the majority of the population. They sense or suspect (rather than self-consciously know or believe) that "even" a parish pump is of both practical and social importance to those who, whether by choice or out of necessity, draw their water from it. The main difference between them and the majority of the population is neither ideological nor devotional, but simply that they are, at this point in time, actively involved in the institution. The limited nature of this difference, coupled with the general consciousness of the parish as a whole, means that the Council sees even its congregational business in the context of the larger community, while at the same time still tending to some extent to rule out matters of wider concern, both religious and secular.

The second word in the Parochial Church Council's name is as apt as the first. Just as "Parochial" refers to the local community rather than to the specific congregation, but ignores all that is focussed in the diocese or in the state, so "Church" legitimates the discussion of such group concerns as property and finance, worship and outreach, but still tends to exclude personal testimony and life-style. Individualistic assumptions regarding worship (and preaching) are balanced by corporate assumptions regarding the business of the Church Council.

The substantive, "Council", is equally apt. Indeed, the word could be regarded as a verbal noun, focussing upon the on-going conciliar *process*, rather than the members composing the body. If they knew of the Ecumenical Councils, some of them might claim to follow, albeit in parochial fashion, in that tradition, in that the task is to explore the humdrum, yet ever-new, inter-face between the Gospel and (this minute portion of) the world.

Ecclesiastical or scriptural precedents are seldom referred to, but God is bracketed *in* (as in algebra) rather than bracketed *out* (as in phenomenology), by the prayers with which meetings open and close.

The lack of explicit reference to Him, or to particular means of revelation, arises partly from diffidence, and lack of specific information; but it also speaks of a confidence, that the members follow Him, in leaving room for all to express their individual insights, as part of a communal quest for Wisdom. In this way the very individualism of members' motives, facilitates the development of *communitas*, as with the general "solidarity of individualism".

5.3.5.4   Source of identity

In the 1950s and '60s, when the Church of England began to be more "practical", in a (so-called) *business*-like sense, some of its leaders followed a then current fashion, in assuming that those who did not enter church buildings had no use for them. However, the difficulties encountered in the democratic course of closing some of them, showed that they had even more significant functions for those who did not observably use them, than for those who did. The earlier sketch of the general consciousness of the parish of this particular study suggested that the specific function its church building performed lay in the realm of identity. The attention, and in particular the chronological primacy, given to similar buildings on the Russian Steppes, in the Nevada Desert, and in Hindu India for instance, suggests this phenomenon is widespread.

In the nature of the case (as with other divinities), this is more easily specified in negative terms than positively, because it is a "taken-for-granted", a bedrock, a *sine qua non*. So the part it plays in the life of the parish is demonstrated by comparison with a "control situation", through imagining its elimination.

The probability is, that if it no longer existed, the community would lose an important contributor to its sense of commonality, biography, and peculiarity.

To say that the church building "makes" the community may appear exaggerated, in the light of the tangible evidence, for those within the system. To say that the parish church makes the *parish* may appear tautologous. Yet it can be described as making the place what it is, in the sense of separate and distinct, different and unique, idiosyncratic and individual. The building helps make the parish, in some degree, communal and personal. Its history, as by far the oldest public building, and its legal status, as the most public building, functions as myth, because it acts as both model and "explanation" of this empirical, existential, almost ineffable, substratum within consciousness.

The Church as community becomes a source of this identity, in part by keeping this tradition alive. Rarely if ever has this (or the other eight thousand, medieval, English) church buildings been so carefully maintained, or its history been so jealously sought. There have probably been times when it has been less populated: there has probably never been a time when it has been (in ordinary language) so "religiously" tended, by those who use it physically and/or spiritually. It is, however, the services of various kinds that take place there, that prohibit its restriction to the simple status of relic or archive. Indeed, those who wish to relegate religion to the past (to history as obsolete) have often tried (and sometimes failed) to convert such buildings into "museums", or categorised their rituals as "cults". Their retention as "worship centres" may be compared with the societal functions performed by the Catholic Mass and Orthodox Liturgy in the Communist and Ottoman empires.

The building and its known use (to focus a life which is expressed in worship, intended for outreach, and constituted by community), are, then, primary means by which the Church becomes a source of identity. Although integrally related, two other particular means may, however, be usefully mentioned at this point. For the "rites of passage" and the ordained "ministry", perform similar functions, both latent and manifest.

Rites of passage, from one "world" to another, are socially recognised rituals through which that which has hitherto been beyond, other, and transcendent, to those undergoing the passage, is made immanent. Rites such as weddings and funerals, that mark natural transitions, tend, equally naturally, to be performed, by both leaders and participants, in an approximately appropriate spirit of sincerity. More problematic are the celebrations of such ecclesiastical transitions as Baptism and Confirmation.

With the renewed distinction between the Supernatural and the mundane, following the Evangelical and Oxford movements, these rituals were seen less as commemorations of the natural processes of birth and puberty, and increasingly as signs of Divine initiative, requiring a human response.

The initial perplexity (again, in the 1950s and '60s) caused by the day-to-day application of this expectation, was seen in a common clerical misunderstanding of the traditional description of such rituals as "occasional offices". While "office" in the sense of "work" seemed simply archaic, "occasional" was sometimes thought, in the modern way, to mean "infrequent", rather than "important", forgetting that a "sense of *occasion*" meant, not "casual", but quite the opposite: "significant". Such misunderstanding illustrates, from the particular point of view of one profession, a tendency to concentrate upon the quantifiable, such as church attendance, at the expense of the qualitative, such as identity. For it is with questions of identity that the rites of passage are concerned.

The clearest evidence that this is indeed the case lies in the number of parishioners who will tell the Rector that they were "christened", "confirmed" (and, often, "sang in the choir", or "served at the altar"), and married, "at" (or, "in") "your church". Indeed, they can often say who the minister of the ceremony was. The contrast between the significance they apparently attach to that event, and their current absence from the building, only highlights the importance of the former, as a component of their biography, and constituent of their identity. What was, to the observer, apparently merely momentary, may nevertheless, to the actor, be momentous. While the clergy were tending to minimise expectations, emphasising that Confirmation was "only" a ceremony in which nothing would happen "magically", teenagers were asking to be Confirmed in the parish church, instead of the neighbouring non-Anglican church they attended, because "it doesn't feel like a Confirmation there", "it isn't sufficiently important", "it doesn't seem to make a real difference". When the official Divine is seen as the polar opposite to the Self, the appointed guardians of the sacred may least understand either its dynamics, or those connected with the Self.

The other main way in which the Church bestows identity, upon individuals and the community (in addition to the building and the services performed there) is through its Rector. Ecclesiastical authorities are fully conversant with the depth and ubiquity of the feelings aroused in smaller parishes, when they indicate that the next incumbent will be non-resident. Every incumbent is aware of the offense taken when he has to confess he has forgotten the names of individuals. It is as though he had eliminated them from the community, excluded them from his prayers, obliterated their very existence. *They* know *him*, so of course he "must" know them. The attitude expressed by two children in 1971, lingers long, below the level of logic. "Of course you know us: you came to our School" - for a Christmas Service attended by five hundred parents and children.

The minister, then, is the "human face" of the Church as a whole. More mobile than any building, more local-ised than any community, more questionable than any institution, more ordinary than any spirit, he is expected to bestow identity with the same ease with which (wearing a clerical collar) he is identified. However, this is more than a question simply of names and appearances. Because of what he stands for, his comments are likely to be repeated, his intentions analysed, and his chance encounters remembered. The hope, and sometimes the assumption, is that he will give the same care to every person he meets. Even those who kindly volunteer, "You don't remember me", indicate that they are working within the same parameters of possibility. It is not only at Baptism that the Church and the priest, by using the individual's name(s), bestows a new (or renewed sense of) identity.

5.3.6 "Christianity", its professed faith

5.3.6.1 The perceived experience of Christianity

Less people today than twenty years ago can say (as so many then did), "We used to have to go to church each Sunday", or, "twice every Sunday", or even (including Sunday School), "three times", "when I was young". Said with resignation or satisfaction or resentment, it indicates the primary form in which Christianity is perceived to have been experienced. The observer may sometimes wonder whether all the churches in the land could have accommodated all those who "had" to attend them; no doubt the explanation lies in the memorability of attendance and the failure of absence to make a similar impression.

The significance of attendance at services has already been sketched. Adults who experienced Sunday School as children, however, scarcely distinguish it from Church, in the sense of worship. This again stands in marked contrast to recent clergy, in particular those who have emphatically differentiated between worship and fellowship, religion and ethics, Church and society, the holy and the human. Seeing little point in "learning *about* Jesus", the decline in Sunday School was assisted by their prophecies of its demise. To the youngsters, however, both types of activity largely consisted of sitting still, on hard chairs or pews, listening to one adult, talking mainly from a large book called the Bible, interspersed with occasionally standing to sing, or kneeling to pray. Each was interpreted primarily in terms of lengthy exposition upon the theme, "Be good, and don't do what you'd like to do".

The influence of the Sunday School upon the ethos of "Victorian" England (which itself has lingered on throughout the following century) may only be comparable with that of the "public" (i.e., independent) schools. They formed a curious pair. Whereas the religion and culture of the latter was dominated by Stoicism and the classics, the former taught a "gentle Jesus, meek and mild" that was almost feminine - and was without appeal for adolescents or adults of either sex, except at such moments of unavoidable femininity as child-bearing and (in many, but not all, groups, even within this parish) mourning. The decline in the distinctive life of especially the "boarding" schools, and in the numbers attending Sunday School, has been both a significant effect of social change, and a significant cause of cultural change, even during the period of this study.

Other ways of experiencing (what is commonly perceived as) Christianity have, however, developed *pari passu*. First among these is the Christianity of the media (meaning television, rather than radio, for all but the elderly house-bound, many of whom continue to worship, with the help of the Daily Service). This allows an Archbishop Anthony Bloom or a Cardinal Hume to become a "domestic chaplain", to more houses in the parish than the Rector can ever hope to visit. However, if the parish's own minister speaks on local radio, he simultaneously receives some of the charisma bestowed by the glare of public spotlights, and becomes a guest of honour in his own parish.

A second way of experiencing Christianity which has come much more to the fore in this period, is through the development of specialised institutions and activities. In the last century, the original source of identity was not neglected: major work upon the church building was undertaken in 1828, 1856, and 1887, for instance. At the same time, the Church (community) that was thus identified, further expressed itself in the building (and re-building) of the Church School, in 1815 (and 1868); of the Perry Almshouses, in 1851; and of St Michael's Rooms, in 1887. So, in this period, since 1970, there has been an abundance of (social, organised) "good works", in the community as in the society generally, ranging from children's festivals to visiting the elderly. While few are seen as part of the "Church", unless the Rector is involved in some way, almost all would be seen as expressions of Christianity.

A third, non-ecclesiastical, way in which Christianity is perceived, continues to be in and through the schools. Their relationship with the Church is, in-evitably, as significant as the story of their building. Thus the existence of a "Church" primary primary school poses no problems. Indeed, for much of the period of observation the County primary school seemed more overtly religious than the Church school. This religiosity, moreover, was expected to consist both of general aims and atmosphere, and of special periods of instruction and assembly. For Christianity (as has already been said, when speaking of the Church) is perceived as being holistic in intent, and non-challenging; while re-ligion was assumed to be exemplary and exhortatory, in a moral rather than theological sense.

Equally significant, however, is the *assumption* that the Secondary School is not Church-related; and that religious instruction and assemblies continue to avoid the specifically religious questions, and should gradually be replaced by avowedly humane or secular education. The immediately practical has now be-come too "serious" for the pupils' life-chances to be jeopardised by the "merely" enjoyable, provocative, important, profound, or fundamental.

Christianity is experienced in the parish, then, through Church, the media, the organisation of good works, and the schools; it is also encountered through confession of faith in it. This can take the implicit form, of "helping a little old lady across the road" (which has become the contemporary type-case of the Good Samaritan). Or it can take the explicit form of an avowed creed, usually expressed in the form, "I believe in Christianity". Each form is costly, in a society that spurns hypocrisy above most vices.

For a fundamentally ethical type of religion, practical helping serves as a kind of ritual. Indeed, as R.R. Marett said, "Some men's religion is danced" (cp Ecclesiasticus 38:24-34; and 1 Timothy 1:15.)

For a religion that suspects all words, and especially those expressing commitment to ideals, a public, verbal confession of faith is possible only for those who are "plain ignorant", "like a bull in a china-shop". However, this is not the first religion whose adherents' hesitation to name their gods reveals, not their absence, but the deeply personal nature of their faith in them. It is the meaning of such avowals that we must now explore.

5.3.6.2 The content of this faith

If the apparent "creed" of the parish were to be set out, as in the previous sections of this essay, somewhat after the manner of the Islamic creed, it might run:

> I believe in Christianity;
> I insist on the right of everyone to make up their own mind;
> and I affirm the value of values.

The creed has been most often expressed to the observer by the thousand or more parents who, over twenty-six years, have given it as their ultimate reason for wanting their child to be Baptized. In that context, the second clause refers in particular to Confirmation, as a time of choice (akin to marriage), and the third, to the impossibility of value-free nurture or living. Both, however, are seen as particular applications or consequences of the first clause – which is by no means confined to that pre-Baptismal context (E I Bailey, 1986, 1989, 1990).

Those who are familiar with particular words may too easily assume that all use them with the same meaning. It is therefore all too easy to overlook what is said so often as to be commonplace. It is easy to fail to be interested in what appears so general. It is possible to doubt the validity of what is either too slight, or too subtle, to measure. Yet a cliché may be the only acceptable (or known) way of verbalising what is a confession of faith (despite sin). When weighed, as well as counted, the proper question can no longer be *whether* it is meant, but *what* it means. What does it affirm - and deny, or ignore?

"I believe in Christianity", then, does not mean exactly the same as, "I believe in Christ". The difference is not simply a circumlocution, due to reticence. The intention is different. Belief in Christ is not being denied. Indeed, he plays an important part in the "Christianity" that is believed in. He is the most admired human. Those who come in his name enjoy a better image than any other body in this society (the monarchy, the police, any of the professions, or the most reputable of public liability companies). So the verbal similarity is more than merely accidental or historical. Yet this faith is not simply inter-personal, as that of the New Testament is sometimes thought to have been.

Neither, on the other hand, does this creed mean quite the same as, "I believe in God". Again, he plays a part in the "Christianity" that is being confessed. Indeed, to some (including some who have little or nothing to do with the Church community), he is real, his presence is near, and his care is certain. But, for most, he is only one part of that "Christianity" in which they believe. Like the stage, or back-cloth, or *proscenium* arch, in the traditional theatre, he is a permanent part of the world-view, an essential piece of the furniture; but he is not the hero of the drama, the centre of attention, the primary object of the belief. This also is a living faith, but it is not that of the Old Testament; at least, not at its most characteristic.

Nor is it, thirdly, a belief in the Church. As it happens, the Church also plays an important part in "Christianity". Sometimes it is specifically said to be "believed *in*". But the belief in it is a derivative belief, dependent upon the prior and primary belief in "Christianity". "Christianity" is the god in whom hope is placed, from whom salvation might come. Christ, God and the Church are no more, though no less, than three of its most important elements, expressions, facets, forms, faces, or *personae*.

However, "Christianity" does not hold quite the place in this popular (and largely implicit) kind of Christianity, that the LORD holds in the Biblical religions, for instance. This is not just a parallel form of trinitarian personalism. For the "Christianity" of this creed is less the object of a faith, than the theme of the believing. Thus, to believe (in almost anything) is to partake in "Christianity". Indeed, "if only everyone believed", then all would be well. It is this valuation of the idea as ideal, that makes it ultimately religious, rather than philosophical or moral. It is an object of devotion, including sacrifice – even of the Self.

Chapter 6

THE IMPLICIT RELIGION OF CONTEMPORARY SOCIETY

6.1 Reprise

Even as recently as the late 1960s, when these studies were first instigated, it was customary to report the choice of topic and approach, the data discovered, and the conclusions reached, with apparent impersonality. In part, this reflected the recently-acquired prestige of the natural sciences as "science" *par excellence*. In part, it was inspired by the ideal of a global rationality that would, not so much unite or combine, as transcend, all particular traditions, temperaments, experiences and insights.

By the early 1980s, a participant but part-time observer of the culture of *academe* could conclude that such impersonality was no longer considered either possible or desirable. Whatever may be the case in the study of (the sub-human) "natural world", so far as "*human* nature" was concerned, the personality of the observer, analyst, and commentator, was an inevitable and essential aspect of the whole methodology. Data without subjectivity would in fact have lacked both humanity *and* objectivity. Tacitly, and then openly, it was increasingly acknowledged that the questions and methods and conclusions had actually been *chosen*, albeit within parameters of necessity. To describe, rather than deny, the personal element was seen to be more empirically accurate, methodologically mature, and intellectually constructive.

This change in the academic culture can be seen as reflecting a growing recognition of the social and psychological *Sitzimleben* of all rationalisation, and hence of the contextuality of all its conceptual tools. In addition to the obvious intellectual ancestry of such ideas, their flourishing since the 1980s may be seen as reflecting a growing feminisation and democratisation, within an *academe* that had once been explicitly hierarchical, and indeed monastic.

Whatever the causes of the change, one of the consequences is that there is no longer any need to "pretend" (in the old-fashioned, non-judgemental sense, of "claim") that the student's concern with these issues was of intellectual inspiration only, or that the concepts owed their validity simply to their bibilographical pedigree. The conventions no longer require us covertly to attribute some *ex nihilo* origin to our concerns, or bestow an impermeable character upon our concepts, or to dignify our conclusions with an *ex cathedra* authority. Just as primogeniture is seen as one among many possible ways of transferring mundane benefits, and tactile Apostolic Succession as one of many ways of conveying charisma, so verbal rationalisation, in accordance with the rules of western logic, is only one of many ways of communicating inter-subjectively. So, for instance, the anecdotal, although as susceptible as statistics to tedium, irrelevance, and downright exploitation, can nevertheless claim to find an insight through an incident, at the same time as recognising that (as ever) both event and interpretation are individual, spasmodic and piecemeal.

At this point in public time, therefore (and at this stage in this essay), the contribution of the fortuitous may readily be confessed. Inevitably, this involves returning to the beginning of the studies reported here - and selectively working backwards, from that point.

Autobiographically, then, three years as an assistant chaplain in a large, Anglican, independent boarding-school, included, in addition to clerical duties, responsibility first for religious education throughout the school, and then for the teaching of "current affairs". These ecclesiastical, educational, and (in the widest sense) political interests, led to a concern for what was initially called "secular religion".

The way was prepared, at the very beginning of the three years, by a meeting of staff-members to discuss the school's policy regarding daily and weekly worship, which had always been compulsory for virtually all pupils. Observing the impassioned discussion, it soon transpired that even a relatively precise, and self-confessed, label, such as "Evangelical", was totally unreliable, as an indicator of actual preference in a matter of practical choice; for one such, an official Reader of the Diocese, could argue that any means, that was not itself immoral, was justified, if it led to one person hearing the Gospel; while the other Evangelical Reader argued that, as "compulsory worship" was a spiritual self-contradiction, then the attempt to enforce it was itself immoral. Such a conflict of opinion might have been understood in terms of a Lutheran-Pauline contrast between a religion of law and a religion of grace.

As the meeting progressed, however, two other attitudes, originating in positions of far greater contrast, were revealed, not only as leading (perhaps surprisingly) to the conservative position (albeit by different routes), but also (and most importantly, from the present point of view) as issuing from a solidity of commitment that was comparable to that of any Anglican Reader or Christian cleric. For, on the one hand, an occasional worshipper supported keeping compulsory attendance, as in his time as a boy in the school, because "it had helped him during the War"; while, on the other hand, the self-confessed humanist, with his intimate knowledge of both Graeco-Roman and European classical lierature, also thought it should be retained, as introducing pupils to "part of our culture's Christian heritage". Ninian Smart's expression, "a dialogue [or should it be, a *symposium*?] of religions", seemed the only way of describing the human situations revealed in *praxis* by such a nodal point.

Just as Christian externals were an inadequate guide to (self-perceived) Christian faith, so Christian faith, although itself a portmanteau term, was only a single type of faith, even in such a traditionally Christian setting. So the *sine qua non* of understanding the other, as both other and real, was the recognition that, even if (as the new Church of England liturgy expresses it) "their faith was known to God alone", they must be assumed (pending proof to the contrary) to possess commitment(s) comparable to that (or those) of the most ardent and articulate, self-conscious and deliberate, self-defined "believer". Or, to put it differently, doctrinal agnosticism and religious inertia can be as conscientious and firm (or, as obstinate and immoveable) as any other, more overt, bigotry and fanaticism.

Soon afterwards, when re-visiting the parish church of which I had been assistant curate, I could not help noticing, on the other hand, how little the liturgy (for which this church had long been noted) seemed to speak to (or for), especially the younger members of the congregation, despite the fact that they were all present of their own accord, of course - and many had to make considerable effort in order to be there.

Living and ministering, not least within a largely adolescent community, also brought home lessons that were less commonly discussed in the 1960s than they are, thirty years later. Chief among these, from the present point of view, was the way in which words, and the concepts they formulated, and the commitments they expressed, were like the tip of an ice-berg: to some, but only some, they were the most easily visible (or, audible) part of the human person. Less apparent (to those who had been trained to observe sense-data), however, was the more fundamental part of the person, which may be more tellingly expressed in bodily posture, for instance.

These "hidden" (or inarticulate, or unconscious, or implicit) depths of the human person (or of the human community) may find their expression in and through explicit religion (as in the case of the Evangelical Lay Readers). They may, on the other hand, be relatively detached from that portion of personality which is above the water-line, as with the conforming Chapelgoer - and yet be subject to its influence, under the conflicting pressures of wind and tide. Again, they may consciously (and conscientiously) make use of the tradition, as the humanist suggested. Or they may be out of kilter with (apathetic about) that which was officially representative, as in the case of the would-be worshippers in the parish; or, alienated, they may be in the process of detaching themselves, with varying degrees of explicitness.

The readiness with which arguments could be produced, and then changed, on the one hand, and yet their real and continuing quality of sincerity, on the other hand, illustrated Newman's point, that, by themselves, reasons convert no one. The limitations of a "fundamentalist" approach (tending to equate the vehicle with the meaning), however, should not obscure doctrine's symbolic significance. In the process of argument, particular doctrines (religious or otherwise) could be used like cudgels, to browbeat an opponent, or like offerings, to gain support. The realisation that creeds and commandments (beliefs and morals) could be seen as sacramental, phenomenologically if not ontologically, nurtured an interest in religion, as being wider than theology.

The same development was encouraged by another aspect of life and ministry in such a community. For one aspect of Harvey Cox's description of the vocation of the Church in *The Secular City*, seemed so out of keeping with (what often was taken to be) the general tenor of his essay. His emphasis upon exorcism, reflecting his Biblical and Baptist background, although eccentric, even ecclesiastically in the 1960s, made sense of an important aspect of both corporate and individual life. Just as a friendly greeting, whoever it was (ad)ministered by (cleric or pupil, baby or cat), could lift the spirits of an individual (facing another round of duties, on Monday morning, say), so could sunshine, or an unexpected half-day holiday, or the approach of the end of term, change the communal atmosphere. Because such exorcisms, being directly concerned with the spirit, were more obviously miraculous, they were no less everyday occurrences.

Rationalisation, like law, usually (rightly and inevitably) lags behind experience and practice. However, it is difficult to act *against* reason. (If the disjunction is recognised, it is thereby neutralised.) In this case, the "circle was squared" by the semi-fortuitous reading of a pair of short articles by David Martin in the (now-defunct) lay Christian journal, *Frontier*. As a sociologist, he warned that the secularization thesis, which had recently become popular with the theologically-minded, was only a hypothesis; in particular, there was no proof that such a process was, or would become, either inevitable or irreversible, let alone universal.

This inter-disciplinary comment removed the intellectual blockage to the experientially-based interpretation of much of non-ecclesiastical life, as containing within itself strands that were nevertheless religious in character (cp

E I Bailey, 1995). The utility and potential of *religion* as an interpretative concept had been nurtured by the preceding two years as a curate in a city-centre parish. They served as an *introduction*, as it happens, to the life of a *local* Church (in contrast with such specialised spheres as the armed services or educational institutions). During them, without intending to weigh motives or form judgements, the usual processes of observation and reflection led to two, associated, tentative conclusions.

The first was that, regardless of any particular observer's personal evaluation of the Christian faith, no account of the behaviour or motivation of many of those who worshippped regularly could be considered empirically satisfactory if it ignored the part which that tradition played in their lives. The second conclusion was that the influence of that tradition, imbibed in large part through recurrent participation in, and identification with, the liturgical year, was far deeper than the members themselves realised. Thus, while they were unconscious of any such link, there was a comprehensible logic that led, from worship through sacraments, to a certain regard for the body and its apparel, or, from a repeated listening to spiritual teaching, to the ability to place those opinions in critical perspective.

Following two years' discovery of the power of a lived religion in the life of "ordinary" people, therefore, the concept was available (unfashionably, at that time), as a phenomenological reality and a hermeneutical tool for the understanding of human beings. Used neutrally (like race, or sex, or class), but typologically, to refer to *commitment*, of whatever form or intensity, it was applicable far beyond the bounds of organised religion. The initial concept of "secular religion" (changed after two years to "implicit religion", in 1969), labelled the apprehension, in order that the hypothesis could be tested. Whether the similarity was metaphorical, or ontological (or, indeed, which way the metaphor flowed: E I Bailey, 1997), could, and should, be left in abeyance for the time being.

The part played by the fortuitous does not, of course, end with the initial apprehension, or with its articulation and comprehension, by a rational concept or a paradoxical expression. Enquiry of a noted Department of Religious Studies, as to the possibility of a course in "secular religion", having led nowhere, in 1967, the following year the opportunity of attending a function at the University of Bristol was taken, to make a similar enquiry, and hence meeting possibly the one person (F B Welbourn) in this country, who, at that time, truly grasped the drift of what was intended. As, "No, nothing has been written on the subject, so you'd better come and do some research under me", was the result.

Looking back, it is, not surprisingly, possible to see three moments (incidents, of moment) from student days, that were thus combined, fulfilled, and rescued from oblivion. First in time, in this backwards direction, was the priest who said he wondered what other people did, each morning, which filled a similar role to his reading of his prayer book - and who subsequently spent a month without any religious activities at all, "to see what it felt like". Second was the intuition, when scanning the nation's daily newspapers in the students' Common Room, that systematic comparison of their comment and content, their style and lay-out, would reveal a set of coherent (even if incomplete, or internally inconsistent), contrasting world-views and value-systems, which, despite their self-conscious sales techniques, would nevertheless themselves be based upon essential basic assumptions. Third was the long-standing conviction that, if "change and decay" be synonymous, then any God there may be, must be dead - united with the suspicion of the historian that, while forms change constantly, "uniqueness" (religious, or secular) demands meticulous empirical proof.

The reasons for diverting time and effort to such a quest as that for implicit religion have hardly grown in sophistication. Fundamental is the desire to understand people (among other ways), *as they see themselves.* (To put the same point negatively, and hence more dramatically, it was, and is, despair and disapproval regarding the ill thought-out dismissal of others as "fools", *tout simple.*) The results of such understanding may include sympathy (and learning), and dialogue (and disagreement): a more catholic identification, and yet a more specific identity. This dual process may have consequences for personal spirituality and inter-personal (or corporate) evangelism, for party platform and propaganda, for production and sales techniques; for philosophy and objectives, on the part of the explicit religions, of politics, and of the entrepreneurial and service industries. Inevitably, such understanding is simultaneously capable of use and abuse.

The primary purpose of the quest, however, remains the discovery of "what makes people tick?" At the close of a person's life we may well reflect what they stood for. Both human survival, and the good life, could profit by asking what they live for (and might die for), while they are still alive.

6.2   Three Implicit Religions or One?

All three of the studies that were carried out, using the concept of implicit religion, tried to be meticulously empirical. They attempted to record discrete data. In interpreting the meaning of those data for their human actors they were willing, where necessary, to include possibilities that were of religious studies origin, as well as understandings suggested by the other human sciences. They carefully avoided, however, either the assumption that the data must have an implicit-religious significance, or that in aggregate they must add up to any single, implicit religion. For, just as sociologists have lately learned to recognise the loss of "great narratives", so historians, and most of those concerned with "real" (or ordinary) life, at least in this country, have long been suspicious of "grand designs". The experience of the 1649-1660 interregnum has made even *laissez-aller* or utilitarianism or welfarism seem dangerously ideological, utopian and messianic.

The passage of time, however, and the objectivisation consequent upon conceptualisation, make possible a degree of generalisation, which ought to be attempted. For, among all the numerous particular lessons that have been learnt from the studies, certain threads continually emerge as significant.

First, then, is that apprehension on the part of the interviewees that was described in the report as the sacredness of the Self. "I matter - therefore I must be" (whatever "I" am), would express the core of the intuition. From this, all else flowed: ethics, ontology, epistemology. Given the chance ("encouragement" might suggest pressure), they affirm a bi-focal conviction in the reality of a certainty which is simultaneously a mystery. Indeed, anything less double-sided would have been either mere knowledge, or else game (belief, or superstition). This, then (the Self, and the apprehension of the Self), is the hierophany of the Interviews, the location of sacredness, the locus of the Sacred, that experience of ultimacy which suggests an echo of infinity.

The life of the public house, it was suggested, centred upon the right of everyman to be himself. (The gendered language, it was explained, was, empirically speaking, not anachronistic.) This was, however, by no means a license for libertarianism. On the contrary, behaviour was strictly controlled. Thus, the state could, on the one hand, "license" the pub to sell alcohol, while its customers could so govern its consumption that it virtually never led to anti-social behaviour, even when that was defined with the utmost strictness. For, while everyman had the right to enter the pub, and purchase a drink, each had the simultaneous duty of allowing others to be themselves, wihout the imposition even of inconsequential conversation. The unwonted had to be assumed to be unwanted.

The residential parish was described as possessing a conscious, and common (in the sense of frequent, more than corporate) belief in "Christianity". Analysis of the assumptions contained within that symbol suggested that they owed much of their appeal to their similarity with Christ's Second Commandment ("Love your neighbour, as yourself"), to the appeal of his ministry (he "went about, doing good"), and to the self-denying (or perhaps better, self-effacing) aspects of his death. The consequences of such a belief (of a belief in such an ethic) were to be seen in the predilection for individual acts of kindness, and against the assumption of roles that might suggest any sort of moral superiority.

The three avenues of study were chosen, in large part, because they were seen as complementary to each other, as has been said. They have been pursued, recorded, analysed, summarised, interpreted, and drawn upon, almost entirely without inter-connection, at any conscious level. However, if only to satisfy the original concern with the implicit religion of contemporary society, it must eventually (now) be asked, how they compare with each other.

First, it may be observed that the reports, even in summary form, show little overlap. The Self as sacred, the right of everyman to be himself, and the belief in a "Christianity" of "helping a little old lady across the road", utilise different vocabularies. Their dissimilarity might suggest both the accuracy with which they reflect their material, on the one hand, and, on the other, the disjunction between the contexts within which (even the same) members of contemporary society operate. For societies which do not divide their members' lives within ghetto-like wholes of race, religion, culture, language, family, class, profession, and so on, seem to divide the life of the individual by those very role-categories, according to colour, denomination, life-style, accent, orientation, income, occupation, etc. So the description of three separate examples of (what may aspire to be called) implicit religion, could be satisfactorily seen as the end of the matter. Contemporary society may be seen as possessing a certain consensus (or level of conflict) regarding means (the rules of the game) but lacking in any civil religion, other than in the most aetiolated sense of either of those terms.

However, the members themselves assume that they do possess a certain continuing identity: that it is the same "one man" that "in his time plays many parts". Not only do they experience an "I" that often enjoys changing roles: legally, they acknowledge a diachronic responsibility for them. So it is possible, then, that behind or beneath or beyond the language-games, there is a common core?

Despite the variation in the manner of the expression, the matter of the intentionality in each of the three studies transpires to be remarkably similar. The socio-cultural context inevitably dictates the form of communication, if it is to be true to its environment; but such substantive heterogeneity witnesses to an essential homogeneity. Curiously, and (at the conscious level) entirely coincidentally, as has been said, the forms taken by the putative implicit religion in the three contexts exactly reflect the three definitions of the concept that were posited at the very beginning of any of them.

For the Self, that was found in the Interviews to be so sacred, is the self-same Self that in the pub is engaged in a relatively relaxed game of role-play with other Selves, all of whom must obey the same rule, that Selves are sacred. Indeed, the public-house represents a mid-point on a continuum between total self-absorption in "my" self-expression, and total absorption in others' expression and non-absorption in one's own. Midway between alcoholic self-isolation and "groupie" self-abnegation, it demonstrates licensed subversion, socialised ecstasy, civil-ised libertarianism. The commitment to the Self (one's own and others') finds integrating foci (with others and for one's self).

Likewise, the salvation that is looked for in "Christianity", consists of the self-fulfillment of every Self. Superficially, it has difficulty in accounting for self-denial, and self-sacrifice. Its symbol is a smile, rather than a (or the) cross. Thus on the one hand, it finds the cross an everyday experience; and on the other hand, it is suspicious of any claim to self-sacrifice. "They wouldn't do it, if they didn't want to"; "I couldn't live with myself, if I did it/didn't". It suspects all do-gooding as tainted, but looks for a silver lining to every cloud: sacrifice is never perfect, in either sense. (Christologically, it might suggest that, "It is finished", was a cry of triumph, even within the anguish.) "Christianity", then, is that intensive concern, with extensive effects, that allows the in-gathering of all that is meant to be, in the Self and its relationships (which may, therefore, in this context extend beyond the human).

If the continuity of such an implicit creed be allowed, can such a way of life be described as an implicit religion? In the following and concluding section, it will be suggested that the "implicitness" of its religiosity is no more a bar to its being a way of life, than is its holism; if anything, indeed, quite the contrary. Similarly, the existence of a "rule" is no more a diminution of its religiosity, than is the ineffability of its core conviction; again, if anything, quite the opposite. So, it is suggested, the way of life to be found within contemporary, "secular" society may, indeed, be accurately and helpfully characterised as being, not only implicitly religious, but also, because rather than despite that reason, as being nothing less than simply religious itself.

As a system, its implicit religion can be described as involving the sacredness of the Self, as its highest common factor; the sacredness of other Selves, as its lowest common multiple; and the sacredness of relationships with other Selves, as its infinite extrapolation. It is, however, better demonstrated, than described, by its willingness to pursue, and indulge in, self-sacrifice, for the sake of Self itself.

6.3   This Implicit Religion, and Religion

Societies have been typologically distinguished as small-scale, historical, or contemporary. Students of the phenomenology of religions have unconsciously tended to distinguish between a sense of the sacred, and the encounter with the holy. Thus the *sacred* has been used as the more appropriate description for the "object" of that experience which has been considered to be religious, by students especially of small-scale societies; while the *holy* has been used as the more appropriate description for the "object" of that experience which has been considered to be religious, by students especially of historical societies.

As it happens, when this difference in terminology was observed, it was discovered that the choice of terms accurately reflected the distinction that had been drawn by the interviewees (cp Chapter 3.2.6) five years earlier, when they had been asked, for quite different reasons, to define each term: *holy* was, in a nutshell, more "God-ly", and more directly and specifically "religious", while "sacred" was "special" and set-apart, but more general.

The differences in the descriptions of religious experience in the two types of society would seem to match the different ways of being "personal" in them. Just as the dawn mist, all-encompassing yet settling on certain surfaces, gathers with the warmth of the sun into stark white clouds, set against the blue sky of infinity, so human beings become increasingly distinct from their natural environment, from the remainder of "the animal kingdom", from each other - and from a divinity that has become similarly differentiated, focussed, self-willed, and (in the new sense) personal.

There are straightforward exceptions to this generalised contrast. Nevertheless, an overall distinction exists, between anthropologists and historians of religion, reflecting the context of the object of their studies. More important, however (it may be suggested), than the contrast between the character of the object of the experience as a *sacred* or as the *holy*, is the one that has here been introduced (not, of course, *ab initio*), in the character of the experiencing itself: between *a sense* and *the encounter*. (The shift between the indefinite and definite article represents a third way of trying to convey the actors' reports.)

Turning from the study, around the world, of what (mainly western-oriented) scholars have called religion, to what religion has come to mean in western societies, another set of observations may be suggested. English, as it is generally spoken, cannot be alone among western European languages in using *religious* to refer to practices, and hence beliefs, that are simultaneously repeated yet meant, public yet sincere, promised yet spontaneous, outward yet inward, predictable yet voluntary. Typical are such expressions as, "I read the newspapers religiously"; that is, every day, yet with care. That this is a considered usage can be seen by such comments as, "She goes to Church every Sunday, but her real religion is her family".

This use of the word would seem more akin to its use in medieval than in classical Latin. In view of the extraordinarily wide spread and deep penetration of western Europe, first by the Order of St Benedict (the "religious" *par excellence*) and then by the other "religious" Orders (G G Hardy, 1990), the kinship of meaning would seem to be genetic as well as generic. The core meaning of *religious* in English, therefore, would appear to be a holistic way of life (as in a small-scale society) which is being followed voluntarily (according to a *Regula*, Rule). (The meaning of *regular* and *habitual* no doubt reflect the same historical process.)

Thus, the suggestion that ordinary (what might momentarily appear to be "secular") life in contemporary society, might be implicitly religious, was to suggest that such life might contain a sense of the sacred (akin to that found in small-scale societies). Such experience could be seen as prior to its institution-alisation, differentiation, specialisation, and professionalisation, in practices, buildings, writings, and personnel dedicated to the purpose and to that alone. However (by hindsight), it can also be seen as having suggested that within this (*religiously* unselfconscious) way of life may be found those who (like the Benedictine *familiae*) were deliberately dedicated, not so much to *religio* in general, as to the practice of a holistic way of life according to their particular Rule. Indeed, just as the obvious etymology of *religion* in classical Latin, may obscure the continuity of its Benedictine usage, so, the ease with which religion in general is discussed by the *déraciné*, may obscure its conscientious popular practice.

Juxtaposing these two sets of observations, the question arises, what is the (implicit) religion of contemporary society, or at least of those corners of it that have been touched upon by these exploratory studies? In other words, what is the character and content of that experience, comparable to a sense of the sacred in small-scale society, and with the encounter with the holy in historical society, which students of contemporary society might similarly describe as "religious"? The suggesion is: a commitment to the human.

The particular choice of expression arises especially from some of the responses in the Interviews. It was, however, seen to be either near the surface of, or at least compatible with, much of the data in all three of the studies. Furthermore, none of the data has been considered contradictory.

Initially, the *human* was adopted as the most appropriate general description of the data with a certain misgiving, as it seemed categorially inappropriate, alongside the *sacred* and the *holy*. The expression was reluctantly used, however, as being accurate, even if it did raise difficult questions about the comparability of this implicit religion, with religious as traditionally understood. However, at its most difficult, the question must, if necesssary, be faced, whether something new, in kind, has arisen? To which the answer must be, that, if there is ever anything new under the sun, it must start somewhere, at some time.

Less controversially, however, it can be suggested, on the one hand, that the *sacred* (if not the holy) has usually been quite mundane; and, on the other hand, that its *human* is both transcendent and avowedly ineffable - and hence is in character with what is customarily called religious experience, especially of the *holy* kind. Further, the same emphasis upon the phenomenological character of the *commitment*, in preference to the attempted descriptions of its object or content, is intended in this case as in the others: in its case, the change is entirely comprehensible, as one merely of form.

However, an "evolutionist" suspicion remained. If this was a third stage in a procession of religious types (and even if the possibility of further stages were allowed), did this not somehow suggest the superiority of the contemporary over earlier stages? Even if such possibilities had to be faced, it was essential to ensure that they were not assumed. For their very acceptability to some, would guarantee their unacceptability to others.

Several, partial, mollifications of this uncomfortable position suggested themselves. Firstly, small-scale, historical and contemporary types of society should no more be seen as inevitable progress, than as inevitable regress (or as a process of rise and then fall). Secondly, as types, they were not necessarily stages, succeeding each other, and eliminating their predecessor. They were, indeed, coexistent. Within the three studies themselves, were numerous reflections of the three, co-existing, different types of experience.

Thirdly, each individual (assuming he or she participates in contemporary society, to some degree) has passed through all three types of experience. Starting with the small-scale society of mother's knee and nuclear family (and known personally by expletives such as "Darling"), we have "progressed" (chronologically, differentially, and in terms of the degree of individuation) to the "historical" society of the primary school, for instance (where we were probably known personally by our forename or family name); and subsequently, in adolescence, we moved on to the "big, wide world" of secondary school and college, and the "concrete jungle" of work and leisure, where we enjoyed and/or endured anonymity, and had to identify ourselves by both names and numbers, or even by photograph and card (E I Bailey, 1985).

This, however, still left those of us who have experienced all three types of experience at "the top of the pile". So, fourthly, it was necessary to add that, just as societies do not leave their previous stages behind them, so, neither, do individuals. Just as societies contain nuclear families and face-to-face associations, as well as supermarkets, so do individuals move between family-like contexts and personal-name work groups, as well as airport lounges. Or, rather (so it would seem), should do; for psychic health would seem to require that, if we have entered the third realm at all, then we shall be correspondingly disadvantaged if we lose our reciprocal contact with the first and second.

Likewise, then, if completeness of humanity requires that, possessing three legs to our experiential tripod, we should use all three; so maturity of religion (and of religious expectation) would seem to demand that we anticipate, and cater for, all three types of religious experience. A dimensional religion that was once a world-view but is now localised, and a relational religion focussing upon a personalised deity, are needed to balance, and need to be balanced by, a universalising religion that values the humane. Divinity, in other words, must be as pluriform as humanity.

REFERENCES

ABRAMS Mark, GERARD David & TIMMS Noel (eds), *Values and Social Change in Britain: studies in the contemporary values of modern society*, London: MacMillan, 1985

ACKERMANN Robert John, *Civil Religion in the United States*; in *Religion as Critique*, University of Massachusetts Press, Amherst MA, 1985

ACLAND Richard, *We Teach Them Wrong*, London: Gollancz, 1963

ADORNO Theodor Wiesengrund & Others, *The Authoritarian Personality*, New York: Harper and Row, 1950

ALBERT Ethel Mary, "The Classification of Values: a method and illustration"; in *American Anthropologist*, LVIII, 1956, Menesha, Wisconsin: American Anthropological Assoc., 1956

ALEXANDER Christopher, ISHIKAWA Sara, SILVERSTEIN Murray, *et al*, *A Pattern Language*, New York: Oxford University Press, 1977

ALLCOCK John, *Kosovo: the heavenly and the earthly crown*, Paper presented at XIV Denton Conference, 1991

AMES Edward Scribner, *The Psychology of Religious Experience*, London: Constable, 1910

APPELBAUM David, *Everyday Spirits*, Albany: State University of New York Press, 1993

ASTLEY Jeff & DAY David (eds), *The Contours of Christian Education*, Great Wavering, Essex: McCrimmons, 1992

AVON COUNTY COUNCIL'S STANDING ADVISORY COUNCIL ON RELIGIOUS EDUCATION (SACRE), *Mystery and Meaning: the Agreed Syllabus for Religious Education in Avon*, Avon County Council Publicity and Advertising, 1993

AYO Nicholas, *The Creed as Symbol*, Notre Dame, Indiana: University of Notre Dame, 1989

AYER Alfred Jules, *The Humanist Outlook*, London: Pemberton, 1968

AYROOKUZHIEL Abraham, "An Enquiry into the Idea of God and Pattern of Worship in a South Indian Village"; in *Religion and Society*, XXII, 4, Bangalore, S India: Christian Institute for the Study of Religion and Society, December 1975

BADHAM Paul (ed), *Religion, State and Society in Modern Britain*, Lampeter: Edwin Mellen Press, 1989

BADONE Ellen (ed), *Religious Orthodoxy & Popular Faith in European Society*, Princeton: Princeton University Press, 1990

BAËTA Christian Goncalves (ed), *Christianity in Tropical Africa*, Studies presented and discussed at the Seventh International African Seminar, at the University of Ghana, 1965, London: Oxford University Press, 1968

BAILEY Edward Ian, *The Religion of a "Secular" Society*, MA Thesis, Bristol University Library, 1969

—— *Belief*, London & Sydney: Batsford, 1974

—— *Emergent Mandalas: the implicit religion of contemporary society*, PhD Thesis, Bristol University Library (catalogued as The Religion of a Secular Society), 1976

—— "The Implicit Religion of Contemporary Society: an orientation and plea for its study"; in *Religion: Journal of Religion and Religions*, 1983, XIII, London: Academic Press, 1983

—— "Civil religion"; "Common religion"; "Folk religion"; in J M Sutcliffe (ed), London: SCM, 1984

—— "Identity as the Sacred/Holy of Contemporary Society"; in *Religion Today: a Journal of Contemporary Religions*, II, 1, London: Ethnographica Publishers, 1985

—— "The British Form of the "Civil Religion" Debate"; in *Zivilreligion: Gesellschaftlicher Konsens in mythischer und ritualler Form*, Heinz Kleger & Alois Müller-Herold, München: Kaiser-Verlag, 1986(a): 104–120

—— "The sacred faith of the people"; in Tony Moss (ed), London: Firethorne, 1986(b): 178–188

—— "The folk religion of the English people"; in Paul Badham (ed), Lampeter: Edwin Mellen Press, 1989: 145–158

—— "The "Implicit Religion" Concept as a Tool for Ministry"; in *Sociological Focus*, XXIII, 3, Dept. of Sociology, Bowling Golden State University, Ohio 43403, August 1990(a): 203–217

—— "The implicit religion of contemporary society: some studies and reflections"; and, "Implicit religion: a bibliographical introduction"; in *Social Compass*, XXXVII, 4, London: Sage, December 1990(b): 483–498, and 499–509

—— "Human communion and Christian communication"; in Jeff Astley and David Day (eds), Great Wavering, Essex: McCrimmons, 1992: 153–161

—— "Why "Implicit Religion"?"; in *The Notion of "Religion" in Comparative Research*, Selected Proceedings of the XVI IAHR Congress, 1994; in Ugo Bianchi (ed), Rome: L'Erma di Bretschneider, 1994(a): 863–872

—— "A form of belonging"; in *Country Way*, 7, Arthur Rank Centre, Stoneleigh Park, Warwickshire: Rural Publications, Autumn 1994(b)

—— "Implicit Religion: a follow-up to David Martin"; in *Crucible: Journal of the Church of England General Synod's Board of Social Responsibility*, London: Church Information Office, 1995(a): 19–25

—— "Implicit Religion"; in John Hinnells (ed), Harmondsworth & Oxford: Penguin & Blackwell's, 1995(b): 234–5

—— "Religion and Implicit Religion: Which is the analogy?" in *Modern Believing: Journal of the Modern Churchpeople's Union*, 1997

—— "Belief in Self and in "Christianity": the Ultimate Reality and Meaning of the "Implicit Religion" of an English suburb"; in *Ultimate Reality and Meaning: inter-disciplinary studies in the philosophy of understanding*, XIX, 2, Toronto: University of Toronto Press, June 1996: 132–9

BAILLIE John, *The Interpretation of Religion: an introductory study of theological principle*, Edinburgh: T & T Clark, 1929

BAIRD Robert D, *Category Formation and the History of Religions*, The Hague: Mouton, 1971

BAKER Noel, *Eastington, a Living Theodicy?*, Thesis presented to Trinity College, Bristol for Advanced Diploma in Theological Studies (Implicit Religion), 1990

BALLARD Martin, *Who Am I? A book of world religions*, London: Hutchinson, 1975

BANTON Michael (ed), *Anthropological Approaches to the Study of Religion*, London: Tavistock, 1966

BARKER Ernest, *National Character and the Factors in its Formation* (3 Volumes), London: Methuen, 1927

BARNES Michael H, *In the Presence of Mystery: an introduction to the story of human religiousness*, Mystic, CT: Twenty-Third Publications, 1985

BAROJA Caro Julio, *The World of the Witches*, trans by N Glendenning, London: Wiedenfeld & Nicholson, 1961

BARON Sala Wittmayer, *Modern Nationalism and Religion*, New York: Harper & Bros, 1947

BATESON Gregory & MEAD Margaret, *Balinese Character: a photographic analysis*, New York: Academy of Science's Special Publications, 7 Dec 1942

BATSON C Daniel & VENTIS W Larry, *The Religious Experience: a social-psychological perspective*, Oxford: Oxford University Press, 1982

BAYLEY Michael J, *Mental Handicap and Community Care: a sudy of mentally handicapped people in Cambridge*, London: Routledge & Kegan Paul, 1973

BEARDSWORTH Timothy, *A Sense of Presence: the phenomenology of certain kinds of visionary and ecstatic experience, based on a thousand contemporary first-hand accounts*, Oxford: Religious Experience Research Unit, 1977

BECHER Jeanne (ed), *Women, Religion and Sexuality: studies of the impact of religious teachings on women*, Geneva: World Council of Churches, 1990

BECKER Howard Saul, *Through Values to Social Interpretation: essays on social contexts, action, types and prospects (1950)*, New York: Greenwood, 1968

—— "Current Sacred-Secular Theory and Its Development"; in H Becker and A Boskoff (eds), New York: Rinehart and Winston, 1966

BECKER Howard and BOSKOFF Alvin (eds), *Modern Sociological Theory in Continuity and Change*, New York: Reinhart & Winston, 1966

BELL Colin & NEWBY Howard, *Community Studies: an introduction to the sociology of the local community*, London: Allen & Unwin, 1971

BELL Michael Mayerfield, *Childerley: nature and morality in a country village*, Chicago: University of Chicago Press, 1994

BELLAH Robert Neelly, *Tokugawa Religion: the values of pre-industrial Japan*, Glencoe: Free Press, 1957

—— "Religious Evolution"; in *American Sociological Review*, XXIX, 1964; reprinted in W A Lessa & E Z Vogt (eds), 1965; and in R Robertson (ed), 1969

—— *Religion and Progress in Modern Asia*, Glencoe: Free Press, 1965

—— *Civil Religion in America*; in *Daedalus, Journal of the American Academy of Arts and Sciences*, XCVI (1), Winter 1967

—— *Beyond Belief: essays on religion in a post-industrial world*, New York: Harper & Row, 1970

BELLAH Robert Neelly & HAMMOND Phillip Everett, *Varieties of Civil Religion*, San Francisco: Harper & Row, 1980

BELLAH Robert N, MADSEN Richard, SULLIVAN William, SWIDLER Ann & TIPTON Steven, *Habits of the Heart: individualism & commitment in American Life*, New York: Harper & Row, 1985

BENDIX Reinhard, *Max Weber: an intellectual portrait*, London: Methuen, 1960

BENNION Francis Alan Roscoe, *Professional Ethics: the consultant professions and their code*, London: Charles Knight, 1969

BENZ Ernst, "On Understanding Non-Christian Religions"; in *History of Religions*, M Eliade & J M Kitagawa (eds), Chicago: Chicago University Press, 1952

BERGER Peter L, *The Noise of Solemn Assemblies*, Garden City, NY: Doubleday, 1961

—— "Towards a Sociological Understanding of Psychoanalysis"; in *Social Research: an international quarterly of political and social science*, XXXII. 1, New School for Social Research, NY: Graduate Faculty of Political & Social Science, Spring 1965

—— "Foreword" to *The Culture of Unbelief*, Caporale R & Grumelli A (eds), Berkeley: University of California Press, 1971(a)

—— *A Rumour of Angels: modern society and the rediscovery of the supernatural*, Harmondsworth: Penguin, 1971(b)

BERGER Peter L & LUCKMANN Thomas, "Sociology of Religion and Sociology of Knowledge"; in *Sociology and Social Research: an international journal*, XLVII, 4, July 1963

—— *The Social Construction of Reality: a treatise in the sociology of knowledge*, London: Allen Lane, 1967

BERNBAUM Edwin, *Sacred Mountains of the World*, San Francisco: Sierra Club Books, 1992

BIANCHI Eugene C, *The Religious Experience of Revolutionaries*, New York: Doubleday, 1972

BIANCHI Ugo, *The History of Religion*, Leiden: Brill, 1975

BIANCHI Ugo (ed), *The notion of "religion" in comparative research: selected proceedings of the XVI Congress of the International Association for the History of Religions*, Rome: L'Erma di Bretschneider, 1994

BIANCHI Ugo et al (eds), *Problems and Methods of the History of Religions*, Leiden: Brill, 1972

BIBBY Reginald W, *Fragmented Gods: the poverty and potential of religion in Canada*, Toronto: Irwin Publishing, 1987

—— *Unknown Gods: the ongoing story of religion in Canada*, Toronto: Stoddart Publishing, 1993

BLEEKER Claas Jouco, "The Contribution of the Phenomenology of Religion to the Study of the History of Religions"; in *Problems and Methods of the History of Religions*, Numen, Supplement XIX, U Bianchi, C J Bleeker & A Bausani (eds), Leiden: Brill, 1972

BLUM Fred, *The Ethics of Industrial Man: an empirical study of religious awareness and the experience of society*, London: Routledge & Kegan Paul, 1970

BOCOCK Robert, *Ritual in Industrial Society: a sociological analysis of ritualism in modern England*, London: Allen & Unwin, 1974

BOLEN Jean Shinoda, *Gods in Everyman: a new psychology of men's lives and loves*, New York: Harper & Row, 1989

BOOTH Charles, *Life and Labour of the People in London*, London: MacMillan, 1903

BORG Meerten ter, "Charisma today", Paper presented at XII Denton Conference on Implicit Religion, 1989

—— *Een Uitgewaaide Eeuwigheid: het menselijk tekort in de modern cultuur*, The Hague: Harm Meijer, 1991

BOUQUET Alan Coates, *Comparative Religion: a short outline*, Harmondsworth: Penguin, 1954

BOWKER John W, *The Sense of God*, London: Oxford University Press, 1973

BRECHER Michael, *Nehru: a political biography*, London: Oxford University Press, 1959

BROTHERS Joan (ed), *Readings in the Sociology of Religion*, Oxford: Pergamon, 1967

BROWN Peter, "Sorcery, Demons and the Rise of Christianity from Late Antiquity into the Middle Ages", in M Douglas (ed), London: Tavistock, 1970

BROWN Stuart C, *Do Religious Claims Make Sense?*, London: SCM, 1969

BUBER Martin, *I and Thou (1923)*, trans R G Smith, Edinburgh: T & T Clarke, 1958

BULL Norman John, *Moral Education*, London: Routledge & Kegan Paul, 1969

BURY John Bagnell, *A History of Freedom of Thought*, London: Butterworth, 1913

—— *The Idea of Progress: an inquiry into its origin and growth*, London: MacMillan, 1928

BUTCHER John Beverley, *The Tao of Jesus: a book of days for the natural year*, San Francisco: Harper, 1994

BUTLER Cuthbert, *Western Mysticism: the teaching of SS Augustine, Gregory and Bernard on Contemplation and the Contemplative Life, with afterthoughts*, London: Arrow, 1960

CAILLOIS Roger, *Man and the Sacred*, trans M Barash, Glencoe: Free Press, 1959

CAMPBELL Colin, *Toward a Sociology of Irreligion*, London: MacMillan, 1971

—— "The Other Protestant Ethic", *Paper presented at IX Denton Conference on Implicit Religion*, 1986

CAMPBELL Joseph, *The Hero with a Thousand Faces*, Princeton, NJ: Princeton University Press, 1972

—— *The Masks of God*, Harmondsworth: Penguin, 1976

CAMPBELL Joseph (ed), *The Complete Works of C G Jung*, London: Routledge & Kegan Paul, 1953f

CAPORALE Rocco & GRUMELLI Antonio (eds), *The Culture of Unbelief: studies and proceedings from the First International Symposium on Belief*, Rome, 1969, Los Angeles: University of California, 1971

CARMEN John B & STRENG Frederick J (eds), *Spoken and Unspoken Thanks: some comparative soundings*, Harvard University: Center for the Study of World Religions, 1989

CARSTAIRS G Morris, *The Twice-born: a study of a community of high-caste Hindus*, London: Hogarth, 1968

CARTER Stephen L, *The Culture of Disbelief: how American law and politics trivialize religious devotion*, New York: Anchor Doubleday, 1993

CHADWICK Owen, *The Secularization of the European Mind in the Nineteenth Century*, Cambridge: Cambridge University Press, 1977

CHERNUS Ira, *Dr Strangegod: on the symbolic meaning of nuclear weapons*, Columbia, SC: University of South Carolina Press, 1986

CHATTERJEE Margaret, *The Concept of Spirituality*, New Delhi: Allied Publishers, 1989

CHRISTIAN William A, Jr, *Local Religion in Sixteenth-Century Spain*, Princeton: University Press, 1981

CHURCH OF ENGLAND DOCTRINE COMMISSION, *Christian Believing*, London: SPCK, 1976

CLARK G Kitson, *The Making of Victorian England*, London: Methuen, 1965

CLEMENTS Frederic Edward, *Primitive Concepts of Disease*, University of California: Publications in American Archaeology and Ethnology, XXXII, 2, 1932

CLOUSER Roy A, *The Myth of Religious Neutrality*, Notre Dame, IN: University of Notre Dame, 1991

CLYNES Bill, *A Sense of the Divine: the implicit and explicit expression of religious consciousness in an "urban priority area"*, Thesis presented to Trinity College, Bristol for Advanced Diploma in Theological Studies (Implicit Religion), 1990

COLE G D H & POSTGATE Raymond, *The Common People, 1746-1946*, London: Methuen, 1964

COLE Guy S, "War, Remembrance and the Cult of the Dead", *Paper presented at XXIII Winterbourne Study Day*, 7 February 1991

COLERIDGE Samuel Taylor, *On the Constitution of the Church and State*, Kathleen Coburn (ed) London: Nelson, 1930 (1830)

COMSTOCK Gary L, *Religious Autobiographies*, Belmont, CA: Wadsworth, 1995

COOK Stanley Arthur, "Religion"; in *Encyclopaedia of Religion and Ethics*, Vol X, James Hastings (ed), Edinburgh: T & T Clark, 1918

COX Harvey, *The Secular City: secularization and urbanization in theological perspective*, London: SCM, 1965

CRAGG Kenneth, *Counsels in Contemporary Islam*, London: European Universities Press, 1965

—— *Christianity in World Perspective*, London: Lutterworth, 1968

CSIKSZENTMIKALYI Mihaly & ROCKBERG-HALTON Eugene, *The Meaning of Things: domestic symbols and the self*, Cambridge: Cambridge University Press, 1989

CUMPSTY John S, *Religion as Belonging: a general theory of religion*, London: University Press of America, 1991

CUTLER Donald R (ed), *The World Year Book of Religion: the religious situation*, Vol I, London: Evans, 1969

DAMON William, *The Moral Child: nurturing children's natural moral growth*, London: Collier MacMillan, 1990

DAVIDSON Robert, *The Courage to Doubt*, London: SCM, 1993

DAVIES John Gordon, *Every Day God: encountering the holy in world and worship*, London: SCM, 1973

DAVIS-FLOYD Robbie E, *Birth as an American Rite of Passage*, Oxford: University of California Press, 1992

DESPLAND Michael & VALLÉE Gerard (eds), *Religion in History: the word, the idea, and the reality*, Editions SR, XIII, Wilfred Laurier University Press, 1992

DEVANANDAN Paul David (ed), *The Gospel and Village Religion in South India*, Bangalore: Christian Institute for the Study of Religion and Society, 1961

DIEL Paul, *The God-Symbol: its history and its significance*, trans Nelly Marans, New York: Harper & Row, 1986

DILLISTONE Frederick William, *Traditional Symbols and the Contemporary World*, London: Epworth, 1973

DOEL David C, *Out of Clouds and Darkness*, London: Lindsey Press, 1992

DOUGLAS Jack D, *Understanding Everyday Life*, London: Routledge & Kegan Paul, 1971

DOUGLAS Mary, *Purity and Danger: an analysis of concepts of purity and taboo*, Harmondsworth: Penguin, 1970

DOUGLAS Mary (ed), *Witchcraft, Confessions and Accusations*, London: Tavistock, 1970

—— *Rules and Meanings: the anthropology of everyday knowledge: selected readings*, Harmondsworth: Penguin, 1973

DRIVER Tom F, *The Magic of Ritual: our need for liberating rites that transform our lives and our communities*, San Francisco: Harper, 1991

DUBE Shyama Charau, *Indian Village*, London: Routledge & Kegan Paul, 1955

DUERLINGER James (Ed), *God, Ultimate Reality and Spiritual Discipline*, New York: Paragon, 1984

DUNHAM Barrows, *Man against Myth*, New York: Hill & Wang, 1962

DUPRÉ Wilhelm, *Patterns in Meaning: Reflections on meaning and truth in cultural reality, religious traditions, and dialogical encounters*, Kampen: Kok Pharos, 1994

DURKHEIM Emile, *The Elementary Forms of the Religious Life*, trans Joseph W Swain, Glencoe: Free Press, 1947 (1915)

—— *Professional Ethics and Civic Morals*, trans C Brookfield, London: Routledge & Kegan Paul, 1957

EDELSWARD L M, *Sauna as Symbol: society and culture in Finland*, New York: Peter Lang, 1991

EDWARDS David Lawrence, *Religion and Change*, London: Hodder & Stoughton, 1969

ELIADE Mircea, *The Myth of the Eternal Return*, New York: Pantheon, 1954

—— *Patterns in Comparative Religion*, trans R Sheed, London: Sheed & Ward, 1958

—— *The Quest: history and meaning in religion*, Chicago: University of Chicago Press, 1969

ELIOT Thomas Stearns, *Murder in the Cathedral*, London: Faber, 1935

ELLUL Jacques, *The New Demons*, trans C Edward Hopkin, New York: Seabury, 1975

EMBREE Ainslie T, *Utopias in Conflict: religion and nationalism in modern India*, Berkeley, CA: University of California Press, 1990

ERIKSON Eric H, *Childhood and Society*, New York: Norton, 1950

—— "Identity"; in D L Sills (ed), 1968

EVANS Kenneth G, *The Religion of Sociology*, MA Thesis, University of Bristol, 1974

EVANS R J, *The Victorian Age, 1815-1914*, London: Arnold, 1950

EVANS-PRITCHARD Edward Evan "Witchcraft (mangu) amongst the Azande"; in *Sudan Notes and Records*, XII, 1929; reprinted in M G Marwick (ed), Harmondsworth: Penguin, 1970

EVOLA Julius, *The Metaphysics of Sex*, New York: Inner Traditions International, 1983

FALLDING Harold, *The Sociology of Religion: an explanation of the unity and diversity in religion*, London: McGraw Hill, 1974

FEELEY-HARNIK Gillian, *The Lord's Table: the meaning of food in early Judaism and Christianity*, Washington: Smithsonian Institution, 1981

FEINSTEIN David & KRIPPNER Stanley, *Personal Mythology: the psychology of your evolving self*, Los Angeles: Jeremy P Tarcher, 1988

FENN Richard, *The Dream of the Perfect Act: an inquiry into the fate of religion in a secular world*, New York: Tavistock, 1987

FEUERSTEIN Georg, *Sacred Sexuality: living the vision of the erotic spirit*, Los Angeles: Jeremy P Tarcher, 1992

FIRTH Raymond, *The Work of the Gods in Tikopia: second edition with new introduction and epilogue*, London: Athlone, 1967(a)

—— *Tikopia Ritual and Belief*, London: Allen & Unwin, 1967(b)

FISH Michael "Doing Your Own Thing"; in A S C Ross (ed), London: Deutsch, 1969

FORDE Daryll (ed), *African Worlds: studies in the cosmological ideas and social values of African people*, London: Oxford University Press, 1954

FOWLER James W, *Stages of Faith: the psychology of human development and the quest for meaning*, San Francisco: Harper & Row, 1981

—— *Faith Development Manual: research with the Faith Development Interview*, Mimeograph, 1985

FOWLER James W & KEEN Sam, "Life Maps: conversations on the journey of faith"; in Jerome W Berryman (ed), Waco, Texas: Word Incorporated, 1988

FOX Matthew, *The Coming of the Cosmic Christ, the healing of mother earth, and the birth of a global renaissance*, New York: Harper & Row, 1988

FRANKENBERG Ronald, *Communities in Britain*, Harmondsworth: Penguin, 1966

FRANKFORT Henri et al, *Kingship and the Gods: a study of ancient Near Eastern religion as the integration of society and nature*, Chicago: University of Chicago Press, 1948

—— *Before Philosophy: the intellectual adventure of ancient man: an esay on speculative thought in the ancient Near East*, Harmondsworth: Penguin, 1949

FRIEDMAN Maurice, *The Human Way: a dialogic approach to religion and human experience*, Chambersburg, PA: Anima, 1982

FROMM Erich, *The Sane Society*, London: Routledge & Kegan Paul, 1956

GAGLIARDI Pasquale (ed), *Symbols and Artifacts: views of the corporate landscape*, New York: Aldine de Gruyter, 1990

GARDELLA Peter, *Innocent Ecstasy: how Christianity gave America an ethic of sexual pleasure*, New York: Oxford University Press, 1985

GARFINKEL Harold, *Studies in Ethnomethodology*, Englewood Cliffs: Prentice Hall, 1967

GEERTZ Clifford, *The Religion of Java*, London: Collier MacMillan, 1960

GEERTZ Clifford, "Religion as a Cultural System"; in *Anthropological Approaches to the Study of Religion*, Michael Banton (ed), London: Tavistock, 1966

—— "Islam Observed"; in *Religion and Society*, XVIII, 3, Bangalore, S India: Christian Institute for the Study of Religion and Society, September 1971

GEHRIG Gail, "American Civil Religion: an assessment"; in *Society for the Scientific Study of Religion*, Monograph Series, No 3, Storrs, CT: University of Connecticut, 1979

GERTH Hans Heinrich & MILLS C W, *From Max Weber: essays in sociology*, London: Routledge & Kegan Paul, 1947

—— *Character and Social Structure: the psychology of social institutions*, London: Routledge & Kegan Paul, 1954

GIBB Hamilton Alexander Roskeen, *Modern Trends in Islam*, Chicago: University of Chicago Press, 1947

GLOCK Charles Y & STARK R, *Religion and Society in Tension*, Chicago: Rand McNally, 1965

GOLDENBERG Naomi, *The Changing of the Gods: feminism and the end of traditional religions*, Boston: Beacon, 1979

GOODMAN Felicitas D, *Ecstasy, Ritual and Alternate Reality: religion in a pluralistic world*, Indianapolis: Indiana University Press, 1988

GOODY Jack & WATTS Ian, "The Consequences of Literacy"; in *Comparative Studies in Society and History: an international quarterly*, Vol V, 1962-63

GORER Geoffrey, *Exploring English Character*, London: Crescent, 1955

—— *Death, Grief and Mourning in Contemporary Britain*, London: Crescent, 1965

GORRINGE Timothy J, *Discerning Spirit: a theology of revelation*, London: SCM, 1990

GOUDZWAARD Bob, *Idols of our Time*, trans Mark Vander Vennen, Illinois: Inter-Varsity Press, 1984

GOVE Philip Babcock (ed), *Webster's Third New International Dictionary*, Chicago: Encyclopedia Britannica, 1971

GRAHN Judy, *Blood, Bread and Roses: how menstruation created the world*, Boston: Beacon, 1993

GRAY Robert Fred "Some Structural Aspects of Mbugwe Witchcraft"; in J Middleton and E H Winter (eds), London: Routledge & Kegan Paul, 1963

GRAZIANO Frank, *Divine Violence: Spectacle, Psychosexuality, and Radical Christianity in the Argentine "Dirty War"*, Boulder, Co: Westview, 1992

GREELEY Andrew Moran, *The Persistence of Religion*, London: SCM, 1973

GREGORIOS Paulos Mar, *A Light Too Bright —- the Enlightenment Today an assessment of the values of the European Enlightenment and a search for new foundations*, Albany: State University of New York, 1992

GRETTON John, "Denmark's Garden of Sex": in *New Society*, 30 October 1969

GUNNEMANN Jon P, *The Moral Meaning of Revolution*, New Haven, NJ: Yale University Press, 1979

HALBERTAL Moshe & MARGALIT Avishai, *Idolatry*, trans N Goldblum, Cambridge, MA: Harvard University Press, 1992

HALL Edward T, *The Hidden Dimension*, New York: Doubleday, 1969

—— *The Dance of Life: the other dimension of time*, Garden City, NY: Doubleday, 1984

HALL James A, *The Unconscious Christian: images of God in dreams*, (ed) Daniel J Meckel, New York: Paulist Press, 1993

HALMOS Paul, *The Faith of the Counsellors*, London: Constable, 1965

HAMMOND Phillip Everett, "The Sociology of American Civil Religion: a bibliographic essay"; in *Sociological Analysis*, XXXVII, 2, 1976

HAMMOND Phillip Everett (ed), *The Sacred in a Secular Age: toward revision in the scientific study of religion*, Berkeley, CA: University of California Press, 1985

HARDING Stephen & PHILLIPS David with FOGARTY Michael, *Contrasting Values in Western Europe: unity, diversity and change*, London: MacMillan, 1986

HARDY Gilbert G, O. Cist., *Monastic Quest and Interreligious Dialogue*, New York: Lang, 1990

HARNED David Baily, *Creed and Personal Identity: the meaning of the Apostles' Creed*, Edinburgh: Handsel, 1981

HARRISON Jane Ellen, *Prolegomena to the Study of Greek Religion*, Cambridge: Cambridge University Press, 1908

HARRISON Paul Mansfield. "The Character and Contribution of the Sociology of Religion"; in P Ramsey and J F Wilson (eds), Princeton: University Press, 1970

HARRISON Thomas Harnett, *Britain Re-visited*, London: Gollancz, 1961

HATCHETT Marion J, *Sanctifying Life, Time and Space: an introduction to liturgical study*, San Francisco: Harper & Row, 1976

HAULE John R, *Pilgrimage of the Heart: the path of romantic love*, London: Shambhala, 1992

HAVENS Joseph, "Religious Awareness and Small Groups: warmth versus enlightenment"; in *The Dialogue Between Theology and Psychology*, Peter Homans (ed), Chicago: University Press, 1968

HAY David, *Exploring Inner Space: scientists and religious experience*, Harmondsworth: Penguin, 1982

HAYES Carlton Joseph Huntly, *Nationalism: a religion*, New York: MacMillan, 1960

HEALD Gordon, "A Comparative Study of Value in Japan, the United States and Britain", *Paper presented at VI Denton Conference on Implicit Religion*, 1983

HEER Friedrich, *The Intellectual History of Europe*, trans J Steinberg, London: Wiedenfeld and Nicholson, 1966

HEIN Norvin J, "Hinduism"; in C J Adams (ed), Glencoe: Free Press, 1965

HELLER David, *The Children's God*, Chicago: University of Chicago Press, 1986

HEPBURN Ronald William and Others, *Religion and Humanism*, London: BBC, 1964

HERBERG Will, *Protestant-Catholic-Jew: an essay in American religious sociology*, New York: Anchor Doubleday (revised edition), 1960

—— "Religion in a Secularised Society"; in J Brothers (ed), Oxford: Pergamon, 1967

HESELTINE Janet Ewing, "Introduction"; in W G Smith, 1935

HEWITT W E (ed), *The Sociology of Religion: a Canadian focus*, Vancouver: Butterworth's, 1993

HEYWARD Carter, *Touching our Strength: the erotic as power and the love of God*, San Francisco: Harper Collins, 1989

HILDEBRAND Dietrich von, *Liturgy and Personality*, Baltimore: Helicon, 1960

HILL Michael (ed), *Sociological Year Book of Religion*, London: SCM, 1973

HINNELLS John (ed), *A New Dictionary of Religions* (2nd edition), Harmondsworth & Oxford: Penguin & Blackwell, 1995

HINSON E Glenn, *A Serious Call to a Contemplative Lifestyle*, Macon, GA: Smyth & Helwys, 1993

HOBSBAWM Eric John, *The Bandits*, London: Weidenfeld & Nicholson, 1969

HOFF Benjamin, *The Te of Piglet*, London: Dutton (Penguin), 1992

HOGGART Richard, *The Uses of Literacy: aspects of working-class life with special reference to publications and entertainment*, Harmondsworth: Penguin, 1958

—— "Higher Education and Personal Life: changing atitudes"; in W R Niblett (ed), London: Tavistock, 1969

HONIGSHEIM Paul, "Sociology of Religion: complementary analyses of religious institutions"; in H L Becker & A Boskoff (eds), New York: Holt, Rinehart & Winston, 1966

HOPKINSON T, *The Pub and the People*, London: Gollancz, 1945

HORTON Robin, "A Definition of Religion and its Uses"; in *Journal of Royal Anthropological Institute*, XC, 2 July-Dec 1960

—— "African Traditional Thought and Western Science"; in *Africa:Journal of International Africa Institute*, XXXVII, London: Oxford University Press, 1967

HOULT Thomas Ford, *The Sociology of Religion*, New York: Holt, Rinehart & Winston, 1958

HUME David, *Dialogues Concerning Natural Religion*, London: Fontana, 1963 (1779)

HUNGERFORD Thomas Arthur Gay (ed), *Australian Signpost: an anthology*, Melbourne: F W Cheshire, 1956

HUXLEY Julian, "The New Divinity"; in *Essays of a Humanist*, London: Chatto & Windus, 1964

HYDE Lawrence, *The Nameless Faith*, London: Rider, nd (c 1948)

IMBER-BLACK Evan & ROBERTS Janine, *Rituals for our Times: celebrating, healing, and changing our lives and our relationships*, New York: Harper-Collins, 1987

INGLIS Kenneth Stanley, *The Churches and the Working Classes in Victorian England*, London: Routledge & Kegan Paul, 1963

JAMES William, *The Varieties of Religious Experience: a study in human nature*, London: Collins, 1960 (1902)

JOHNSON William A, *The Search for Transcendence: a theological analysis of non-theological attempts to define transcendence*, New York: Harper, 1974

JONES Emrys, *Towns and Cities*, London: Oxford University Press, 1966

JUNG Carl Gustav, *Collected Works*, H Read, M Fordham & G Adler (eds), London: Routledge & Kegan Paul, 1953f

—— "The Spirit of Psychology"; in J Campbell (ed) London: Routledge & Kegan Paul, 1955

JUNG L Shannon, *Community and Identity: a sociological introduction to religion*, Atlanta, GA: John Knox Press, 1980

KALLEN Horace M, *Secularism Is the Will of God: an essay in the social philosophy of democracy and religion*, New York: Twayne, 1954

KATO Genchi, *A Study of Shinto: the religion of the Japanese nation*, London: Curzon, 1971 (1926)

KEHRER G & Bert H, "Sociological Approaches" (2); in F Whaling (ed), 1985

KELSEY Morton & Barbara, *Sacrament of Sexuality: the spirituality and psychology of sex*, Warwick: Amity House, 1986

KESSEL Neil & WALTON Henry, *Alcoholism*, Harmondsworth: Penguin, 1965

KEYES Dick, *Beyond Identity: finding your self in the image and character of God*, Ann Arbor, MI: Servant Books, 1983

KITAGAWA Joseph M, "Chaos, Order and Freedom in World Religions"; in *The Concept of Order*, P G Kuntz (ed), Seattle, WA: Washington University, 1968

KLAPP Orrin Edgar, *Collective Search for Identity*, New York: Holt, Rinehart & Winston, 1969

KLEGER Heinz & MULLER-HEROLD Alois (Eds), *Religion des Bürgers: Zivilreligion in Amerika und Europe*, München: Kaiser Verlag, 1986

KLINE George Louis, *Religious and Anti-religious Thought in Russia*, Chicago: University of Chicago Press, 1969

KLUCKHOHN Clyde, *Navaho Witchcraft*, Boston: Beacon, 1967

KNOWLES David, O. S. B., *The Monastic Order in England: a history of its development from the times of St Dunstan to the Fourth Lateran Council, 943-1216*, Cambridge: Cambridge University Press, 1949

—— *The Evolution of Medieval Thought*, Gateshead on Tyne: Northumberland Press, 1962

—— *The Religious Orders in England* (3 volumes), Cambridge: Cambridge University Press, 1979

KOENKER Ernest Benjamin, *Secular Salvations: the rites and symbols of political religions*, Philadelphia, PA: Fortress, 1965

KOLB William L, "Images of Man and the Sociology of Religion"; in *Journal for the Scientific Study of Religion*, II, Oct 1961

KOPP Sheldon B, *Guru: metaphors from a psychotherapist*, Palo Alto, CA: Science & Behaviour Books, 1971

KRAUSZ Ernest, *Sociology in Britain: a survey of research*, London: Batsford, 1969

KUNDA Gideon, *Engineering Culture: control and commitment in a high-tech corporation*, Philadelphia: Temple University Press, 1992

KUNTZ Paul G (ed), *The Concept of Order*, Seattle, WA: Washington University, 1968

LASKI Marghanita, *Ecstasy: a study of some secular and religious experiences*, London: Cresset, 1961

LEACH Edmund R (ed), *Dialectic in Practical Religion*, London: Cambridge University Press, 1968

LECKY William Edward Hartpole, *History of European Morals, from Augustus to Charlemagne*, London: Longmans Green, 1894 (1869)

LEEUW Gerardus van der, *Religion in Essence and Manifestation: a study in phenomenology*, New York: Harper, 1963

—— *Sacred and Profane Beauty: the holy in art*, trans. D E Green, London: Weidenfeld & Nicholson, 1964

LENSKI Gerhard, *The Religious Factor: a sociological study of religion's impact on politics, economics, and family life*, New York: Doubleday, 1955

LESSA William A & VOGT Eva Z (eds), *Reader in Comparative Religion: an anthropological approach*, New York: Harper & Row, 1965

LEUBA James Henry, *The Psychological Origin and Nature of Religion*, London: Constable, 1909

LEWIS Eve, *The Psychology of Family Religion*, London: Sheed & Ward, 1968

LIENHARDT Godfrey, *Divinity and Experience: the religion of the Dinka*, Oxford: Clarendon, 1961

LING Trevor Oswald, *A History of Religion East and West*, London: MacMillan, 1968

—— "Anthropology and International Understanding: the role of comparative religion", *Paper presented to the Indian Anthropological Society*, November 1971

LINTON Ralph, "Totemism and the AEF"; in *American Anthropologist*, XXVI, 1924 Re-printed in W A Lessa and E Z Vogt (eds), New York: Harper & Row, 1965

LIPPMANN Walter, *Essays in the Public Philosophy*, New York: Mentor, 1956

LIPPY Charles H, *Being Religious, American Style: a history of popular religiosity in the United States*, Westport, CT: Praeger, 1994

LOISY Alfred Firmin, *Y a-t-il deux sources de la religion et de la morale?* Paris, 1933

LOOMIS Charles Price, *Socio-economic Change and the Religious Factor in India*, New Delhi: Affiliated East-West Press, 1969

LOUDON Joe, "Religious Order and Mental Disorder: a study in a South Wales rural community"; in *Social Anthropology of Complex Societies*, M Banton (ed), London: Tavistock, 1966

LOUKES Harold, *Teenage Religion: an enquiry into attitudes and possibilities among British boys and girls in Secondary Modern Schools*, London: SCM, 1961

—— *New Ground in Christian Education*, London: SCM, 1965

LOVEJOY Arthur Oucken, *The Great Chain of Being: a study of the history of an idea*, Harvard: University Press, 1936

LUCKMANN Thomas, *The Invisible Religion: the problem of religion in modern society*, London: MacMillan, 1967

—— "Belief, Unbelief and Religion"; in R Caporale and A Grumelli (eds), Berkeley: University of California Press, 1971

LUKE P Y & CARMEN John B, *Village Christians and Hindu Culture: study of a rural church in Andhra Pradesh, S India*, London: Lutterworth, 1968

LYND Robert S & Helen M, *Middletown in Transition*, New York: Harcourt Brace, 1937

—— *On Shame and the Search for Identity*, London: Routledge & Kegan Paul, 1958

McGIN Bernard, *Antichrist: two thousand years of the human fascination with evil*, San Francisco: Harper, 1994

MaCINTYRE Alasdair, *Secularization and Moral Change*, London: Oxford University Press, 1967

McLEISH John, *Evangelical Religion and Popular Education: a modern interpretation*, London: Methuen, 1969

MADGE Charles Henry, *Society in the Mind*, London: Faber, 1964

MADGE John Hylton, *The Tools of Social Science*, London: Longmans, 1953

MADGE Violet, *Children in Search of Meaning*, London: SCM, 1965

MAÎTRE Jacques, "The Consumption of Astrology in Contemporary Society"; in *Diogenes*, LII, Spring, 1966

MALEFIJT Annemarie de Waal, *Religion and Culture: an introduction to anthropology of religion*, New York: MacMillan, 1968

MALINA Bruce J & ROHRBAUGH Richard L, *Social-Science Commentary on the Synoptic Gospels*, Minneapolis: Fortress Press, 1992

MALINOWSKI B, *Magic, Science and Religion, & Other Essays*, Garden City, NY: Doubleday Anchor, 1954 (1925)

MARSDEN Dennis, "The Working Man: "Rough" and "Respectable""; in A S C Ross (ed), London: Deutsch, 1969

MARTIN Charles G, *Must Men Worship? an introduction to the study of religion*, London: Longmans, 1968

MARTIN David, *A Sociology of English Religion*, London: Heinemann, 1967

—— *The Religious and the Secular*, London: Routledge & Kegan Paul, 1969

—— "The Secularization Question"; in *Theology*, LXXVI, London: SPCK, February 1973

—— *A General Theory of Secularization*, Oxford: Blackwell, 1978

MARTIN Emily, *The Woman in the Body: a cultural analysis of reproduction*, Milton Keynes: Open University Press, 1989

MARTIN Ernest Walter, *The Shearers and the Shorn: a study of life in a Devon community*, London: Routledge & Kegan Paul, 1965

MARTINEAU James, *A Study of Religion: its sources and contents*, Oxford: Clarendon, 1899

MARTINSON Paul Varo, *A Theology of World Religions: interpreting God, Self, and World, in Semitic, Indian and Chinese thought*, Minneapolis: Augsburg, 1987

MARTLAND Thomas R, *Religion as Art: an interpretation*, Albany: State University of New York Press, 1981

MARTY Martin E, *The New Shape of American Religion*, New York: Harper, 1958

—— "The Spirit's Holy Errand: the search for a spiritual style in secular America"; in *Daedalus*, Winter, 1967

MARWICK Max G (ed), *Witchcraft and Sorcery: selected readings*, Harmondsworth: Penguin, 1970

MAUSS Marcel, *The Gift: forms and functions of exchange in archaic societies*, trans I Cummison, London: Cohen & West, 1970

MAYER Philip (ed), *Socialization: an approach from social anthropology*, London: Tavistock, 1970

MAYOR Stephen Harold, "The Religion of the British People"; in *The Hibbert Journal*, LIX, Oct 1960

MEAD George H, *Mind, Self and Society from the standpoint of a social behaviorist*, C W Morris (ed), Chicago: University of Chicago Press, 1970 (1934)

MEADOW Mary Jo & KAHOE Richard D, *Psychology of Religion: religion in individual lives*, New York: Harper & Row, 1984

MERTON Robert K, FISKE M & KENDALL P L, *The Focussed Interview*, Glencoe: Free Press, 1956

MEYER Jeffrey F, *The Dragons of Tiananmen: Beijing as a sacred city*, Columbia: University of Carolina Press, 1991

MILLARD Key, *Responses to Suffering – in poetry, the media, and interviews*, Thesis for the Advanced Diploma in Theological Studies (Implicit Religion), Trinity College, Bristol, 1995

MILES Grahame, "Transcendental and Religious Experiences of Sixth Form Pupils: an analytic model", *Paper presented at IV Denton Conference on Implicit Religion*, May 1981

MILLER David L, *The New Polytheism: rebirth of the gods and goddesses*, Dallas: Spring Publications, 1981

MINER Horace, "Body Ritual among the Nacirema"; in W A Lessa & E Z Vogt (eds), New York: Harper & Row, 1965

MOL Hans, *Identity and the Sacred: a sketch for a new social-scientific theory of religion*, Oxford: Blackwell, 1976

MOLLENKOTT Virginia Ramey, *Sensuous Spirituality: out from fundamentalism*, New York: Crossroad, 1992

MONICK Eugene, *Phallos: sacred image of the masculine*, Toronto: Inner City, 1987

MOORE Sally F & MYERHOFF Barbara G (eds), *Secular Ritual*, Amsterdam: Van Gorcum, 1977

MOORE Thomas, *Care of the Soul: a guide for cultivating depth and sacredness in everyday life*, New York: Harper Collins, 1992

MORENO Antonio, *Jung, Gods and Modern Man*, London: Sheldon, 1974

MORSE Christopher, *Not Every Spirit: a dogmatics of Christian disbelief*, Valley Forge, PA: Trinity, 1994

MOSS Tony (ed), *In Search of Christianity*, London: Firethorn, 1986

MOUW Richard J, *Consulting the Faithful: what Christian intellectuals can learn from popular religion*, Grand Rapids, MI: Eerdmans, 1994

MURPHY Gardner & Lois B, *Asian Psychology*, New York: Basic Books, 1968

MURRAY Henry, "Prospects for Science"; in *Science*, 11 May 1962

MURRAY James Augustus Henry, *A New English Dictionary on historical principles*, Oxford: Clarendon, 1888

MURRAY Margaret Alice, *The Witch-Cult in Western Europe: a study in anthropology*, Oxford: Oxford University Press, 1921

NADEL S F, *Nupe Religion: traditional beliefs and the influence of Islam in a West African chiefdom*, London: Routledge & Kegan Paul, 1954

NASR Seyyed Hossein, *Knowledge and the Sacred*, Edinburgh: Edinburgh University Press, 1981

NELSON James B, *Body Theology*, Westminster: John Knox Press, 1992

NESTI Arnaldo, *Il Religioso Implicito*, Rome: Januar, 1985

NEVILLE Robert Cummings, *Behind the Masks of God: an essay toward comparative theology*, Albany, NY: State University Press of New York, 1991

NEWCOMB T M with CHARTERS W W, *Social Psychology*, New York: Dryden, 1950

NEWTON Denise, "Secularisation and organised astrology", *Paper presented at III Denton Conference on Implicit Religion*, 1980

——   "Implicit religion in organised astrology", *Paper presented at V Denton Conference on Implicit Religion*, 1982

NIEBUHR H Reinhold, *An Interpretation of Christian Ethics*, London: SCM, 1941

NIBLETT William Roy, *Higher Education: demand and response*, London: Tavistock, 1969

NICHOLLS David, *Deity and Domination: images of God and the State in the 19th & 20th centuries*, London: Routledge, 1994

NILSSON Nils Martin Persson, *A History of Greek Religion*, trans F J Fielden, Oxford: Clarendon, 1925

——   *Greek Piety*, trans. H J Rose, Oxford: Clarendon, 1948

O'BRIEN Justin, *Toward a Theory of Religious Consciousness in its Reliance upon Western Man's Understanding of Nature, Ultimacy and Theology*, Montrose, PA: Montrose Press, nd (c 1980)

ODEN Thomas C, *The Structure of Awareness*, Nashville, TN: Abingdon, 1969

OGILVIE Robert Maxwell, *The Romans and their Gods in the Age of Augustus*, London: Chatto & Windus, 1969

OLIVER Roland, *The Missionary Factor in East Africa*, London: Longmans, 1952

OMAN John, *The Natural and the Supernatural*, Cambridge: Cambridge University Press, 1931

OPIE Iona and Peter, *The Lore and Language of Schoolchildren*, London: Oxford University Press, 1959

—— *Children's Games in Street and Playground*, Oxford: Clarendon, 1969

OPPEN Dietrich von, *Die Personale Zeitalter*, Stuttgart: Krenz Verlag, 1960

ORIENTAL STUDIES, JOURNAL OF, XXVI, 1, Semiannual 1987, Feature: *Beyond the Dichotomy of Secularity and Religion*, Tokyo: Institute of Oriental Philosophy, 1987

OTTO Rudolph, *The Idea of the Holy*, trans J W Hardy, Harmondsworth: Penguin, 1959 (1917)

PACKARD Vance, *The Hidden Persuaders*, Harmondsworth: Penguin, 1950

PADEN William E, *Interpreting the Sacred: ways of viewing religion*, Boston: Beacon, 1992

PAFFARD Michael, *Inglorious Wordsworths: a study of some transcendental experiences in childhood and adolescence*, London: Hodder & Stoughton, 1973

PANIKKAR Raimundo, *Worship and Secular Man: an essay on the liturgical nature of man, considering Secularization as a major phenomenon of our times and worship as an apparent fact of all times: a study towards an integral anthropology*, London: Darton, Longman & Todd, 1973

—— "Time and Sacrifice: the sacrifice of time and the ritual of modernity"; in D Park, N Lawrence & J T Fraser (eds), New York: Springer-Verlag, 1978

PARETO Vilfredo, *The Mind and Society*, London: Cape, 1935

PARK D, LAWRENCE N & FRASER J T (eds), *The Study of Time III: Proceedings of the Third Conference of the International Society for the Study of Time*, New York: Springer-Verlag, 1978

PARRINDER Edward Geoffrey, *What World Religions Teach*, London: Harrap, 1968a

—— *Religion in Africa*, Harmondsworth: Penguin, 1968b

PARSONS Talcott, "Belief, Unbelief, and Disbelief"; in R Caporale & A Grumelli (eds), Berkeley: University of California Press, 1971

PARSONS Talcott & SHILS Edward A, *Toward a General Theory of Action*, Cambridge, MA: Harvard University Press, 1951

PARTRIDGE Eric Honeywood, *A Dictionary of Slang and Unconventional English*, (2 Vols), 1961 & 1967

PETTAZZONI Raffaele, *State Religion and Individual Religion in the Religious History of Italy*, (Vol XVIII in Essays on the History of Religion), Leiden: Brill, 1967

PIAGET Jean, *The Child's Conception of the World*, London: Routledge & Kegan Paul, 1929

PIETTE Albert, *Les Religiosités Séculières*, Paris: Presses Universitaires de France, 1993

PRADES Jose A, *Persistence et Métamorphose du Sacré*, Paris: Presses Universitaires de France, 1987

PRADO C G, *Illusions of Faith: a critique of non-credal religion*, Toronto: Kendall Hunt Publishing, 1980

PRATT Vernon, *Religion and Secularisation*, London: MacMillan, 1970

PYE Michael, "A Common Language of Minimal Religiosity", in *The Journal of Oriental Studies*, XXVI,1, Tokyo: Institute of Oriental Philosophy, 1987: 21–7

QUALLS-CORBETT Nancy, *The Sacred Prostitute: eternal aspect of the feminine*, Toronto: Inner City, 1988

RABUZZI Kathryn Allen, *The Sacred and the Feminine: toward a theology of housework*, New York: Seabury, 1982

—— *Mother with Child: transformations through childbirth*, Bloomington: Indiana University Press, 1994

RAGLAN Lord Fitz Roy Richard Somerset, *The Hero: a study in tradition, myth and drama*, London: Methuen, 1936

RAHNER Hugo, *Man at Play or, Did you ever practice eutrapelia?* trans. B Battershaw & E Quinn, London: Burns & Oates, 1964

RASCHKE Carl A , KIRK James A, TAYLOR Mark C, *Religion and the Human Image*, Englewood Cliffs: Prentice-Hall, 1977

RAVINDRA Ravi, *The Yoga of the Christ in the Gospel according to St John*, Shaftesbury, Dorset: Element Books, 1990

READER Ian & WALTER Tony (eds), *Pilgrimage in Popular Culture*, London: MacMillan, 1993

REAT N Ross & PERRY Edmund F, *A World Theology: the central spiritual reality of humankind*, Cambridge: University of Cambridge Press, 1991

REDFIELD Robert, *The Little Community: viewpoints for the study of a human whole*, Chicago: University Press, 1955

REED Bruce D, *The Dynamics of Religion: process and movement in Christian Churches*, London: Darton, Longman & Todd, 1978

REYNOLDS Vernon & TANNER Ralph, *The Social Ecology of Religion*, Oxford: Oxford University Press, 1995

REX John, *Key Problems of Sociological Theory*, London: Routledge & Kegan Paul, 1961

RICHARDS A I, "Socialization and Contemporary British Anthropology"; in P Mayer (ed), London: Tavistock, 1970

RICHARDSON Herbert W, *Nun, Witch, Playmate: the Americanization of sex*, New York: Edwin Mellen, 1981

RIESMAN David L, GLAZER N & DENNEY R, *The Lonely Crowd: a study of the changing American character*, Cambridge, MA: Yale University Press, 1950

—— *Faces in the Crowd: individual studies in character and politics*, (abridged edition), Yale: University Press, 1952

ROBERTSON Roland & CAMPBELL Colin, "Religion in Britain: the need for new religious strategies"; in *Social Compass*, XIX, 2, 1972

ROSS Alan Strode Campbell (ed), *What Are You?* London: Deutsch, 1969

ROUSSEAU Jean Jacques, *The Social Contract or, Principles of Political Right*, trans. H J Tozer, London: Sonnerschein, 1895

ROWE William L, *Religious Symbols and God: a philosophical study of Tillich's theology*, Chicago: Chicago University Press, 1968

ROWNTREE Seebohm B & LAVERS G R, *English Life and Leisure*, London: Longmans, 1951

RUSSELL Anthony, *The Clerical Profession*, London: SPCK, 1984

RUSSELL Bertrand, *History of Western Philosophy and its connection with political and social circumstances from the earliest times to the present day*, London: George Allen & Unwin, 1946

RUSSELL Dora, *The Religion of the Machine Age*, London: Routledge and Kegan Paul, 1983

SALIBA John A, *'Homo Religiosus' in Mircea Eliade: an anthropological evaluation*, Leiden: Brill, 1976

SAMPSON Anthony, *Anatomy of Britain Today*, London: Hodder & Stoughton, 1966

SAVAGE William W Jr, *The Cowboy Hero: his image in American history and culture*, Norman, Oklahoma: University of Oklahoma Press, 1979

SCHLEIERMACHER Friedrich D E, *Über die Religion: Reden an die Gebildeten unter ihren Verächtern*, Bonn: Marcus, 1874 (1799)

SCHNEIDER K J, *Horror and the Holy: wisdom-teachings of the Monster Tale*, Chicago: Open Court, 1993

SCHNEIDER Louis & DORNBUSCH S M, *Popular Religion: inspirational books in America*, Chicago: Chicago University Press, 1958

SCHOEPS Hans-Joachim, *An Intelligent Person's Guide to the Religions of Mankind*, trans R & C Winston, London: Gollancz, 1966

SCHOOLS COUNCIL, *Religious Education in Secondary Schools*: Schools Council Working Paper, No 36, London: Evans Bros & Methuen, 1971

SCHREITER Robert J, *Constructing Local Theologies*, London: SCM, 1985

SEABROOK Jeremy, *The Unprivileged*, London: Longmans Green, 1967

SEXSON Lynda, *Ordinarily Sacred*, London: University Press of Virginia, 1992

SEZNEC Jean, *The Survival of the Pagan Gods: the mythological tradition and its place in Renaissance humanism and art*, Princeton, NJ: Princeton University Press, 1972

SHARPE Eric J, *Comparative Religion: a history*, London: Duckworth, 1975

SHERRARD Philip, *The Sacred in Life and Art*, Ipswich: Golgonooza Press, 1990

SHILS Edward & YOUNG Michael, "The Meaning of the Coronation"; in *Sociological Review*, N S, I, 2, Dec 1953

SILLS, D L (ed), *International Encyclopedia of Social Sciences*, London: MacMillan, 1968

SINGH Herbert Jai (ed), *Inter-religious Dialogue*, Bangalore: Christian Institute for the Study of Religion and Society, 1967

SKELLEY Michael, *The Liturgy of the World: Karl Rahner's theology of worship*, Minnesota: Liturgical Press, 1991

SMART Ninian, *The Yogi and the Devotee: the interplay between the Upanishads and Catholic theology*, London: Allen & Unwin, 1968

—— *Sacred Nationalism*, Leeds: British Association for the Study of Religion, Occasional Paper, 1994

SMITH Alan, *Folklore in Industry*, "Discovering" series Tring, Herts: Shire, 1969

SMITH Huston, "Secularization and the Sacred: the contemporary scene"; in *The World Year Book of Religion: The Religious Situation*, Vol I, Donald R Cutler (ed), London: Evans Bros, 1969

SMITH John E, *Quasi-Religions: Humanism, Marxism and Nationalism*, New York: St Martin's, 1994

SMITH M Brewster, *Social Psychology and Human Values*, Chicago: Aldine, 1969

SMITH Wilfred Cantwell, *The Meaning and End of Religion*, New York: MacMillan, 1964

SMITH William George, *The Oxford Dictionary of English Proverbs*, Oxford: Clarendon, 1935

STAAL Frits, *Rules Without Meaning: ritual, mantras and the human sciences*, New York: Peter Lang, 1989

STANNER William Edward Hanley, "The Dreaming"; in T A G Hungerford (ed), 1956; and in W A Lessa & E Z Vogt (eds), 1965

—— "On Aboriginal Religion", *Oceanic Monographs*, XI, Sydney: Betts, 1963

STARBUCK Edwin Diller, *The Psychology of Religion: an empirical study of the growth of religious consciousness*, London: W Scott, 1899

STARK Werner, *The Sociology of Religion: a study of Christendom*, London: Routledge & Kegan Paul, 1960f

STREIKER Lowell D, *The Gospel of Irreligious Religion: insights for uprooted man from major world faiths*, New York: Sheed & Ward, 1969

STRENG Frederick J, *Understanding Religious Man*, Belmont, CA: Dickenson, 1969

STRENG Frederick J, LLOYD Charles L Jr & ALLEN Jay T, *Ways of Being Religious: readings for a new approach to religion*, Englewood Cliffs: Prentice Hall, 1973

SUNDKLER Bengt, *The Christian Ministry in Africa*, London: SCM, 1962

SUTCLIFFE John M (ed), *A Dictionary of Religious Education*, London: SCM, 1984

SZASZ Thomas, *The Theology of Medicine the political-philosophical foundation of medical ethics*, New York: Harper & Row, 1977

TAYLOR Alan J P, *English History 1914-1945*, Oxford: Clarendon, 1965

TAYLOR John Vernon, *The Growth of the Church in Buganda: an attempt at understanding*, London: SCM, 1958

—— *The Primal Vision: Christian presence amid African religion* London: SCM, 1963

TELLENBACH Gerd, *Church, State and Christian Society at the time of the Investiture Contest*, trans R F Bennett, Oxford: Blackwell, 1940

TEMPELS Placide, *Bantu Philosophy*, trans C King, Paris: Presence Africaine, 1959

THROWER James, *The Alternative Tradition: religion and the rejection of religion in the ancient world*, The Hague: Mouton, 1980

TIELE C P, *Elements of the Science of Religion*, Edinburgh: Blackwood, 1899

TILLICH Paul Johannes Oskar, *Theology of Culture*, R C Kimball (ed), New York: Oxford University Press, 1959

—— *Ultimate Concern: dialogues with students*, D M Brown (ed), London: SCM, 1965

TOCQUEVILLE Alexis de, *Democracy in America*, trans H Reeve, London: Longmans Green, 1890

TORRANCE Robert M, *The Spiritual Quest: transcendence in myth, religion and science*, Berkeley: University of California Press, 1994

TOWLER Robert, *Homo Religiosus: sociological problems in the study of religion*, London: Constable, 1974

—— "The Competing Ideologies called Christianity", *Paper presented at III Denton Conference on Implicit Religion*, May 1980

TOWLER Robert & CHAMBERLAIN Audrey, "Common Religion"; in M Hill (ed), London: SCM, 1973

TRACY David, *Blessed Rage for Order: the new pluralism in theology*, London: Harper & Row, 1988

TRAWEEK Sharon, *Beamtimes and Lifetimes: the world of high energy physicists*, Cambridge, MA: Harvard University Press, 1992

TREVELYAN George Macaulay, *Illustrated Social History*, London: Longmans, 1952

TURNER John Evan, *Essentials in the Development of Religion: a philosophic and psychological study*, London: Allen & Unwin, 1970 (1934)

TURNER Victor W, *The Ritual Process: structure and anti-structure*, Harmondsworth: Penguin, 1974

TYLER Stephen A (ed), *Cognitive Anthropology: readings*, New York: Holt, Rinehart & Winston, 1969

ULANOV Ann & Barry, *Primary Speech: a psychology of prayer*, London: SCM, 1985

ULLMAN Walter, *The Growth of Papal Government in the Middle Ages*, London: Methuen, 1953

VOGT Evon Z, *Modern Homesteaders: the life of a twentieth century frontier community*, Cambridge, MA: Harvard University Press, 1955

—— "Water Witching: An Interpretation of a Ritual Pattern in a Rural American Community"; in *Reader in Comparative Religion: an anthropological approach*, William A Lessa & Evon Z Vogt (eds), New York: Harper & Row, 1958

VOGT Evon Z & Human R, *Water Witching USA*, Chicago: Chicago University Press, 1959

VRIJHOF Pieter Hendrik & WAARDENBURG Jacques (eds), *Official and Popular Religion: analysis of a theme for religious studies*, The Hague: Mouton, 1979

WAARDENBURG Jacques, *Classical Approaches to the Study of Religion: aims, methods and theories of research*, The Hague: Mouton, 1973

—— "Muslim Notions of Religion as Manifested in Interreligious Discourse"; in Ugo Bianchi (ed), 1994

—— "In Search of an Open Concept of Religion"; in Michael Despland & Gerard Vallée (eds), 1992

WACH Joachim, *The Sociology of Religion*, Chicago: Chicago University Press, 1967

WALCOT Peter, *Greek Peasants, Ancient and Modern: a comparison of social and moral values*, Manchester: Manchester University Press, 1970

WARNER W Lloyd et al, *The Living and the Dead: a study of the symbolic life of Americans*, New Haven, NJ: Yale University Press, 1959

—— *The Family of God: a symbolic study of Christian life in America*, New Haven, NJ: Yale University Press, 1961

WARREN Max A C, *The Missionary Movement from Britain in Modern History*, London: SCM, 1965

WEBER Max, *The Protestant Ethic and the Spirit of Capitalism*, trans T Parsons, London: Unwin, 1930 (1904–5)

—— "The Social Psychology of World Religions"; in H H Gerth and C W Mills (eds), London: Routledge & Kegan Paul, 1947

—— *The Sociology of Religion*, trans T Parsons, London: Methuen, 1965

WEBSTER Hutton, *Taboo: a sociological study*, Stanford, CA: University Press, 1942

WELBOURN Frederick Burkewood, *Atoms and Ancestors*, Leeds: Arnold, 1958

—— "Towards a Definition of Religion"; in *Makerere Journal*, 4, 1960

—— *Religion and Politics in Uganda 1952-62*, Nairobi: East Africa Publishing House, 1965

—— "A Note on Types of Religious Society"; in C G Baëta, 1968, London: Oxford University Press, 1968

—— *The Development of Religion and Society in Buganda* (unpublished lectures), 1968-9

—— "Healing as a Psychosomatic Event", *Paper presented to the seminar on witchcraft and healing at the Centre for African Studies*, Edinburgh, 1969(a)

—— "Towards Eliminating the Concept of Religion", *Paper presented at the 2nd Lancaster Colloquium on the study of religion*, 1969(b)

WELBOURN F B & OGOT B A, *East African Christian*, London: Oxford University Press, 1952

WESTCOTT Brooke Foss, *The Gospel according to St John*, London: James Clarke, 1958

WHALING Frank (ed), *Contemporary Approaches to the Study of Religion*, Vol I, *The History of Religions*, 1984; Vol II, *The Social Sciences*, 1985. Berlin: Mouton, 1984-1985

WICKHAM Edward Ralph, *Church and People in an Industrial City*, London: Lutterworth, 1957

WIEBE Paul C, "Religious Change in South India: perspectives from a small town"; in *Religion and Society*, XXII, 4 Bangalore, S India: Christian Institute for the Study of Religion and Society, December 1975

WIEMAN Henry Nelson, *Man's Ultimate Commitment*, London: University Press of America, 1991

WILLIAMS Christopher, *The Implicit Religion of SLAB: a study of the symbolic and ritual elements in a youth club for the "unattached"*, Contemporary Religious Behaviour Project (unpublished), Bristol University Dept of Religious Studies, 1974

WILLIAMS J Paul, "The Nature of Religion"; in *Journal for the Scientific Study of Religion*, II, 1, Oct, 1962

WILLIAM Peter W, *Popular Religion in America: symbolic change and the modernization process in historical perspective*, Englewood Cliffs: Prentice-Hall, 1980

WILLIAMS Raymond, *Culture and Society 1780-1950*, Harmondsworth: Penguin, 1958

—— *The Long Revolution*, Harmondsworth: Penguin, 1961

—— *Communications* (revised edition), London: Chatto & Windus, 1966

—— "Literature and Sociology"; in *New Left Review*, LXXVII, 1971

WILLIMON William H, *Worship as Pastoral Care*, Nashville: Abingdon, 1979

WILSON Bryan, *Religion in Secular Society: a sociological comment*, Harmondsworth: Penguin, 1969

—— "Unbelief as an Object of Research"; in A Grumelli & R Caporale (eds), Berkeley, CA: University of California, 1971

WILSON B R (ed), *Rationality*, Oxford: Blackwell, 1970

WILSON Monica, *Religion and the Transformation of Society: a study in social change in Africa*, Cambridge: Cambridge University Press, 1971

WINK Walter, *Naming the Powers: the language of power in the New Testament*, Philadelphia: Fortress, 1984

—— *Unmasking the Powers: the invisible forces that determine human existence*, Philadelphia: Fortress, 1986

—— *Engaging the Powers: discernment and resistance in a world domination*, Minneapolis: Fortress, 1992

WRIGHT J Eugene, *Erikson: identity and religion*, New York: Seabury, 1982

WRIGHT Susan (ed), *Parish Church and People: local studies in lay religion, 1350-1750*, London: Hutchinson, 1988

WUTHNOW Robert, *Rediscovering the Sacred: perspectives on religion in contemporary society*, Michigan: Eerdmans, 1992

—— *Producing the Sacred: an essay on public religion*, Chicago: University of Illinois Press, 1994

YANG C K, *Religion in Chinese Society: a study of contemporary social functions of religion and some of their historical factors*, Berkeley, CA: University of California Press, 1967

YINGER J Milton, *Sociology Looks at Religion*, London: Collier-MacMillan, 1961

—— *Religion, Society and the Individual: an introduction to the sociology of religion*, New York: MacMillan, 1965

YOUNG Michael & WILMOTT Peter, *Family and Kinship in East London*, Harmondsworth: Penguin, 1962 (1957)

YOUNG William A, *The World's Religions: worldviews and contemporary issues*, Englewood Cliffs: Prentice Hall, 1995

YUNGBLUT John R, *Shaping a Personal Myth to Live By*, Rockport, MA: Element, 1992

ZAEHNER R C (ed), *The Concise Encyclopaedia of Living Faiths*, London: Hutchinson, 1959

ZEPP Ira G Jr, *The New Religious Image of Urban America: the shopping mall as ceremonial center*, Westminster: Christian Classics, 1986

ZIMBARDO P & EBBESEN E B with MASLACH C, *Influencing Attitudes and Changing Behaviour: a basic introduction to relevant methodology, theory and applications*, Reading, MA: Addison-Wesley, 1969

ZOCK Tanja Henriette, *A Psychology of Ultimate Concern*, Amsterdam: Rodopi, 1990

ZOJA Luigi, *Drugs, Addiction and Initiation: the modern search for ritual*, trans M E Romano & R Mercurio, Boston: Sigo Press, 1989